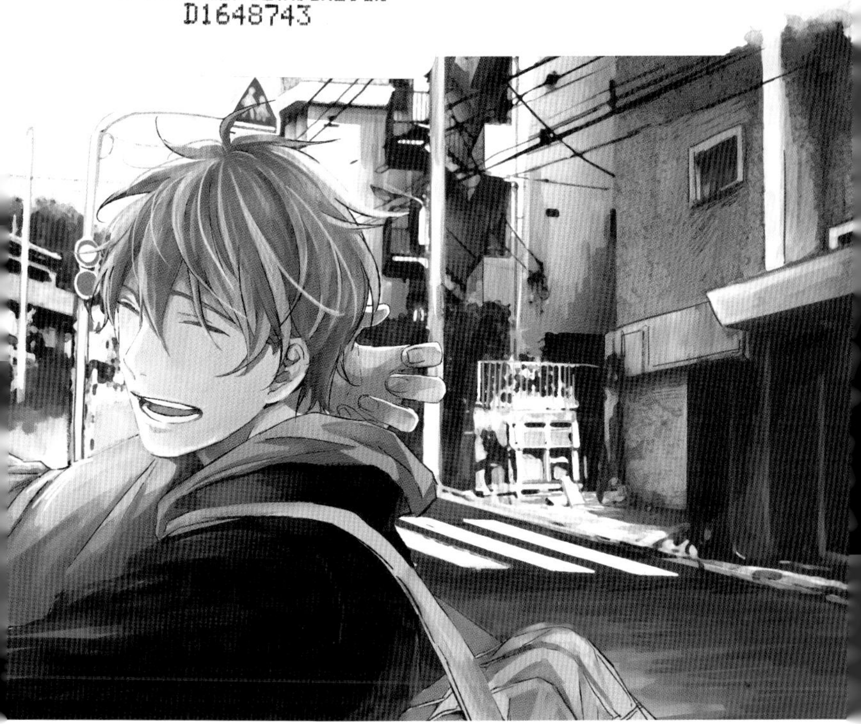

Given

Story and Art by **Natsuki Kizu**　　　　volume **1**

CONTENTS

SUBLIME

SuBLime Manga Edition

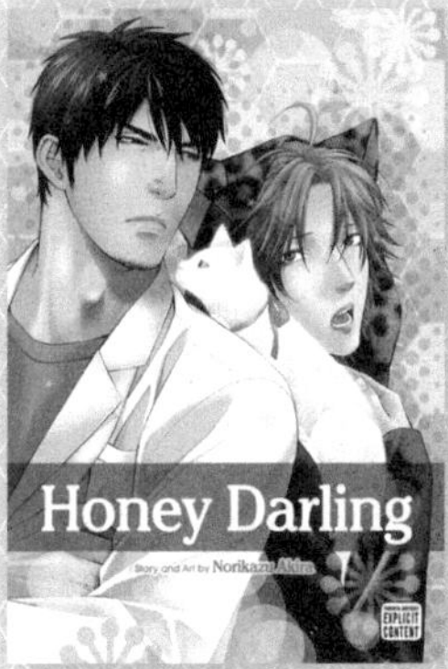
Honey Darling
Story and Art by Norikazu Akira
EXPLICIT CONTENT
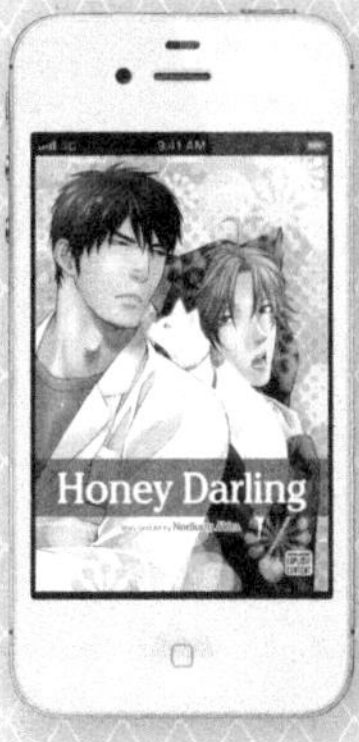
Honey Darling

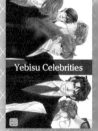

Given
Volume 1
SuBLime Manga Edition

Story and Art by **Natsuki Kizu**

Translation—**Junko Goda**
Touch-Up Art and Lettering—**Sabrina Heep**
Cover and Graphic Design—**Jimmy Presler**
Editor—**Leyla Aker**

© 2014 Natsuki KIZU
Originally published in Japan in 2014 by Shinshokan Co., Ltd.

Published by SuBLime Manga
P.O. Box 77010
San Francisco, CA 94107

10 9 8 7 6 5 4
First printing, February 2020
Fourth printing, March 2021

PARENTAL ADVISORY
GIVEN is rated T+ for Older Teen and is recommended for ages 16 and up. This volume contains suggestive themes.

www.SuBLimeManga.com

About the Author

Natsuki Kizu made her professional debut in 2013 with *Yukimura Sensei and Kei-kun*, followed by the short story collection *Links* and her breakout series, *Given*, which has been adapted into drama CDs and an animated TV series. To find out more about her works, you can follow her on Twitter at **@kizu_ntk**.

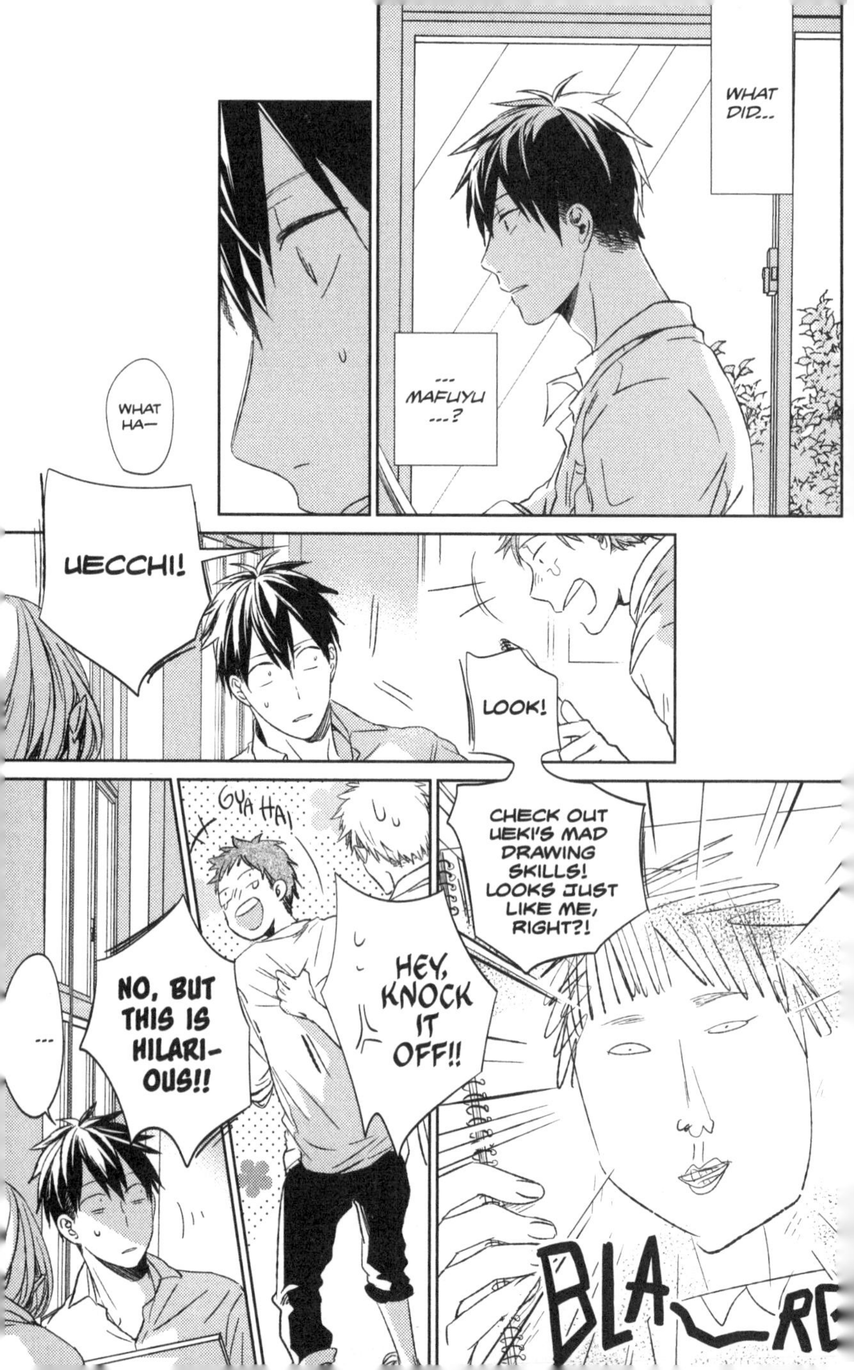
WHAT DID...
...MAFUYU...?
WHAT HA—
UECCHI!
LOOK!
CHECK OUT UEKI'S MAD DRAWING SKILLS! LOOKS JUST LIKE ME, RIGHT?!
GYA HA HA
HEY, KNOCK IT OFF!!
NO, BUT THIS IS HILARI-OUS!!
...
BLA—RE

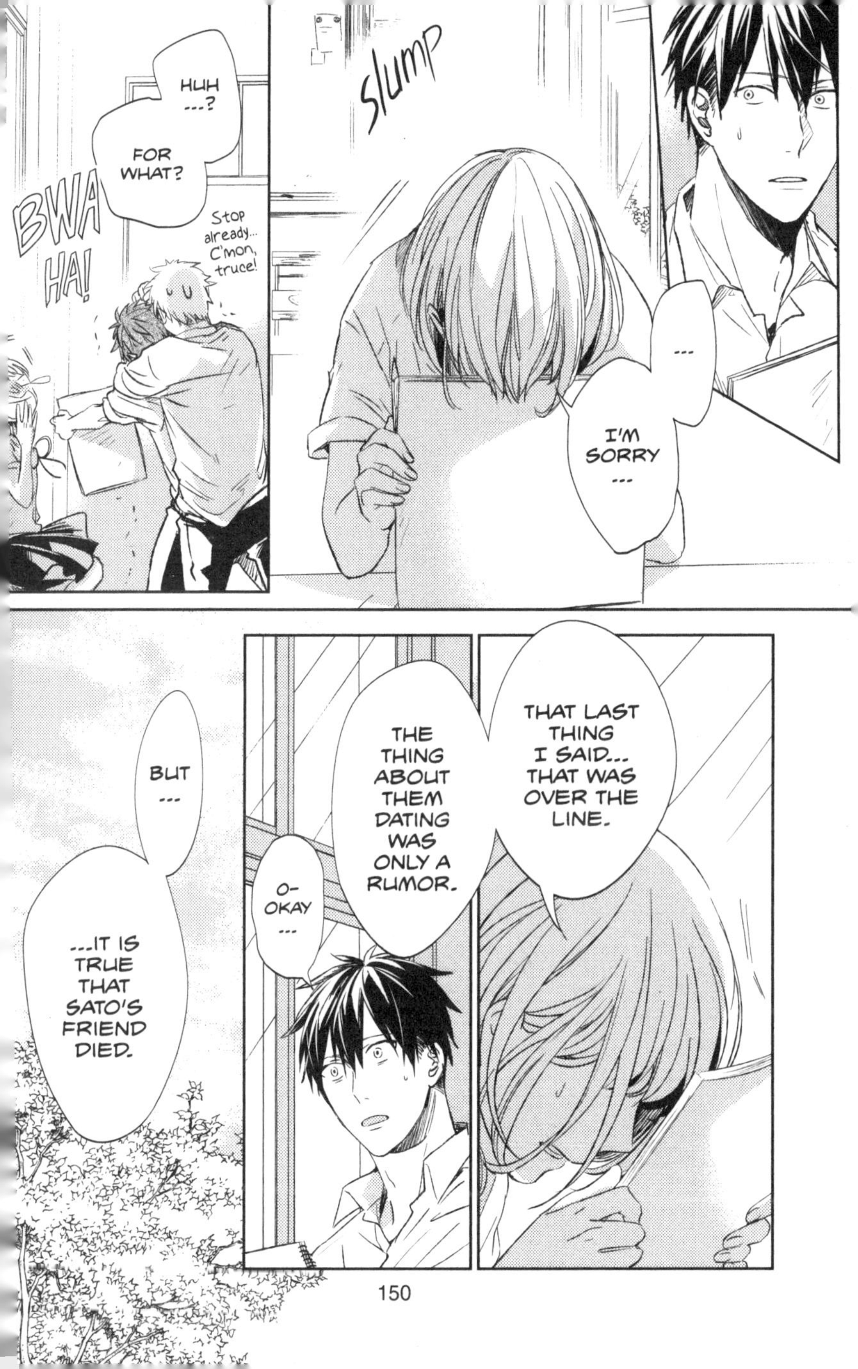
slump
...
I'M SORRY ...
HUH ...?
FOR WHAT?
BWA HA!
Stop already... C'mon, truce!
THAT LAST THING I SAID... THAT WAS OVER THE LINE.
THE THING ABOUT THEM DATING WAS ONLY A RUMOR.
O-OKAY ...
BUT ...
...IT IS TRUE THAT SATO'S FRIEND DIED.

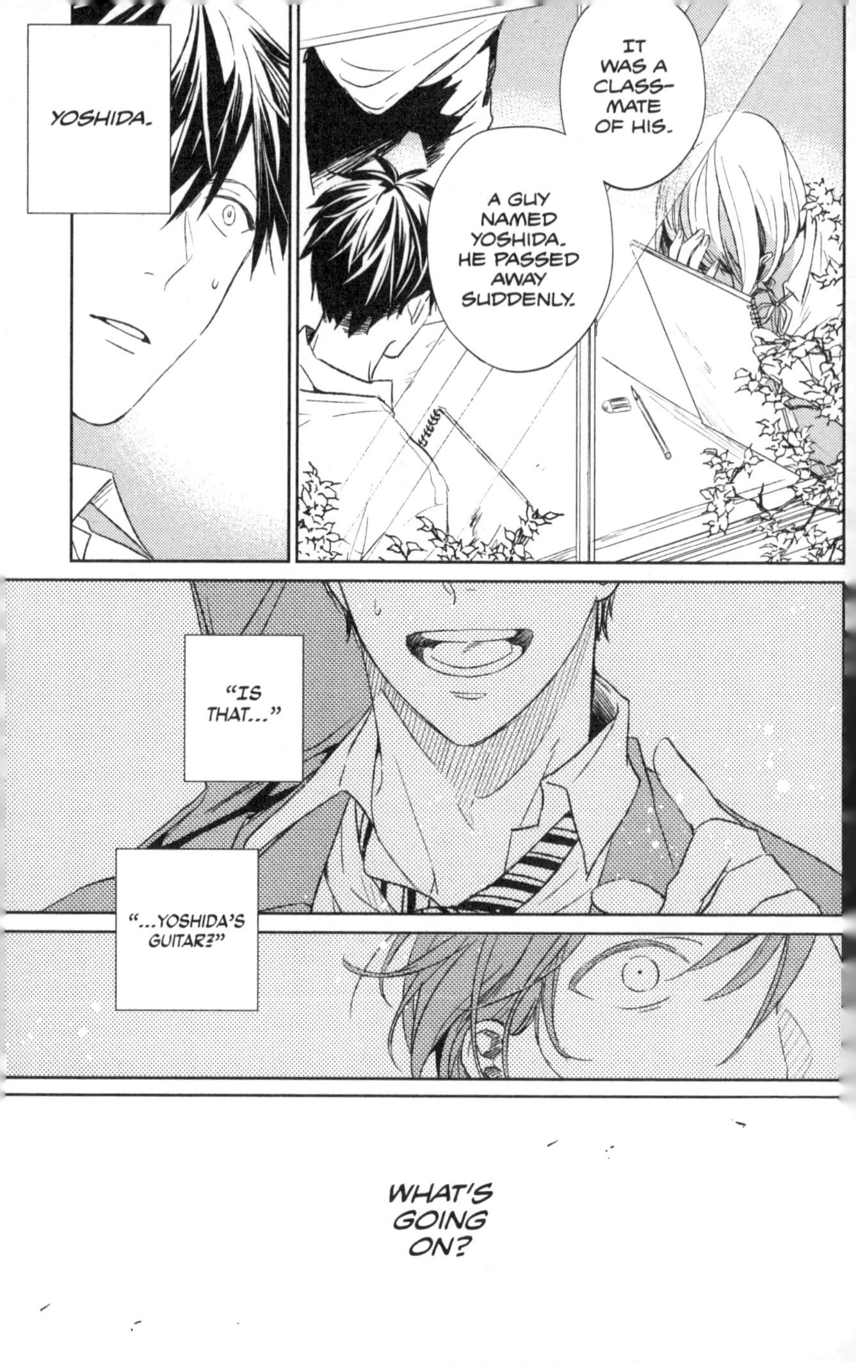
IT WAS A CLASSMATE OF HIS.
A GUY NAMED YOSHIDA. HE PASSED AWAY SUDDENLY.
YOSHIDA.
"IS THAT..."
"...YOSHIDA'S GUITAR?"
WHAT'S GOING ON?

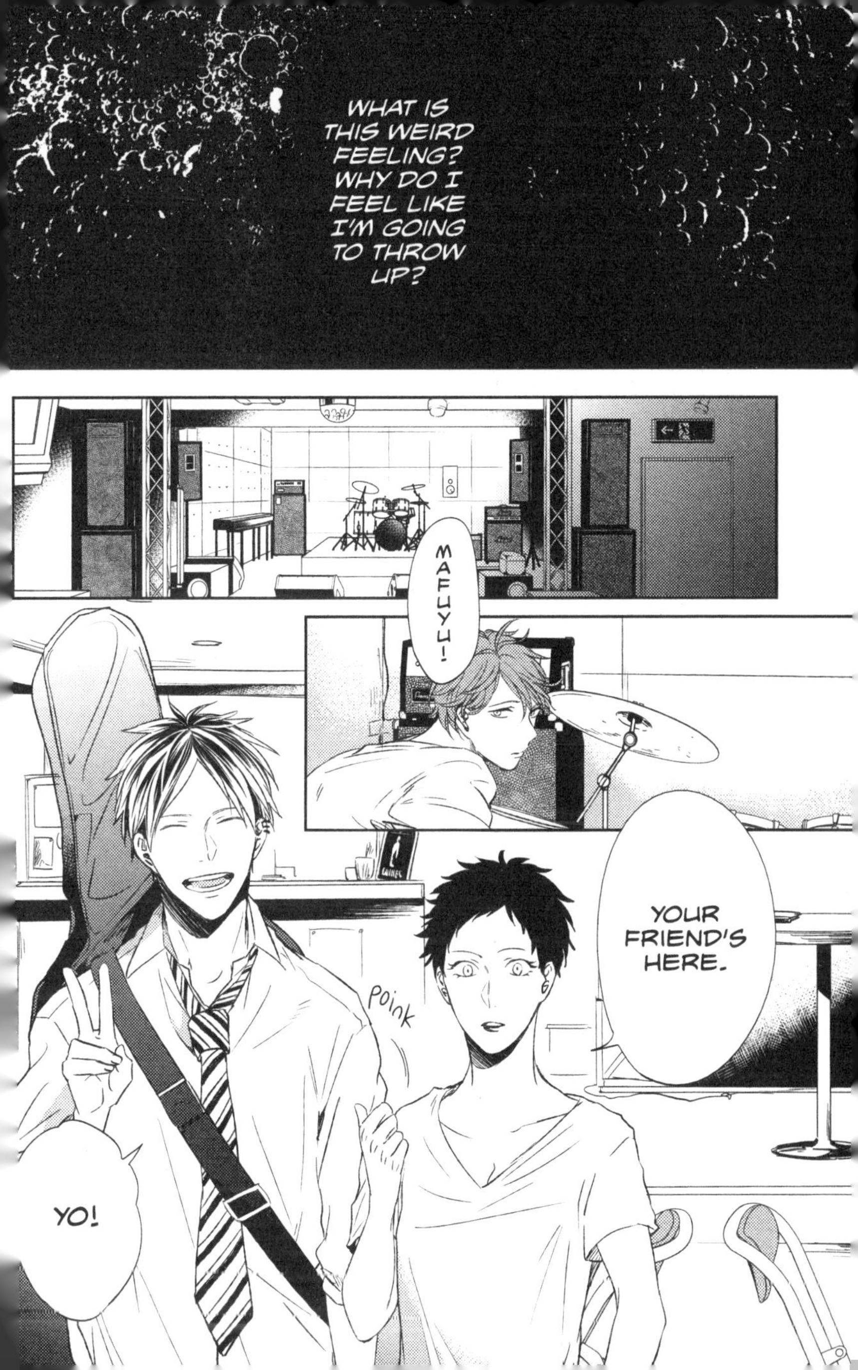
WHAT IS THIS WEIRD FEELING? WHY DO I FEEL LIKE I'M GOING TO THROW UP?
MAFUYU!
YOUR FRIEND'S HERE.
poink
YO!

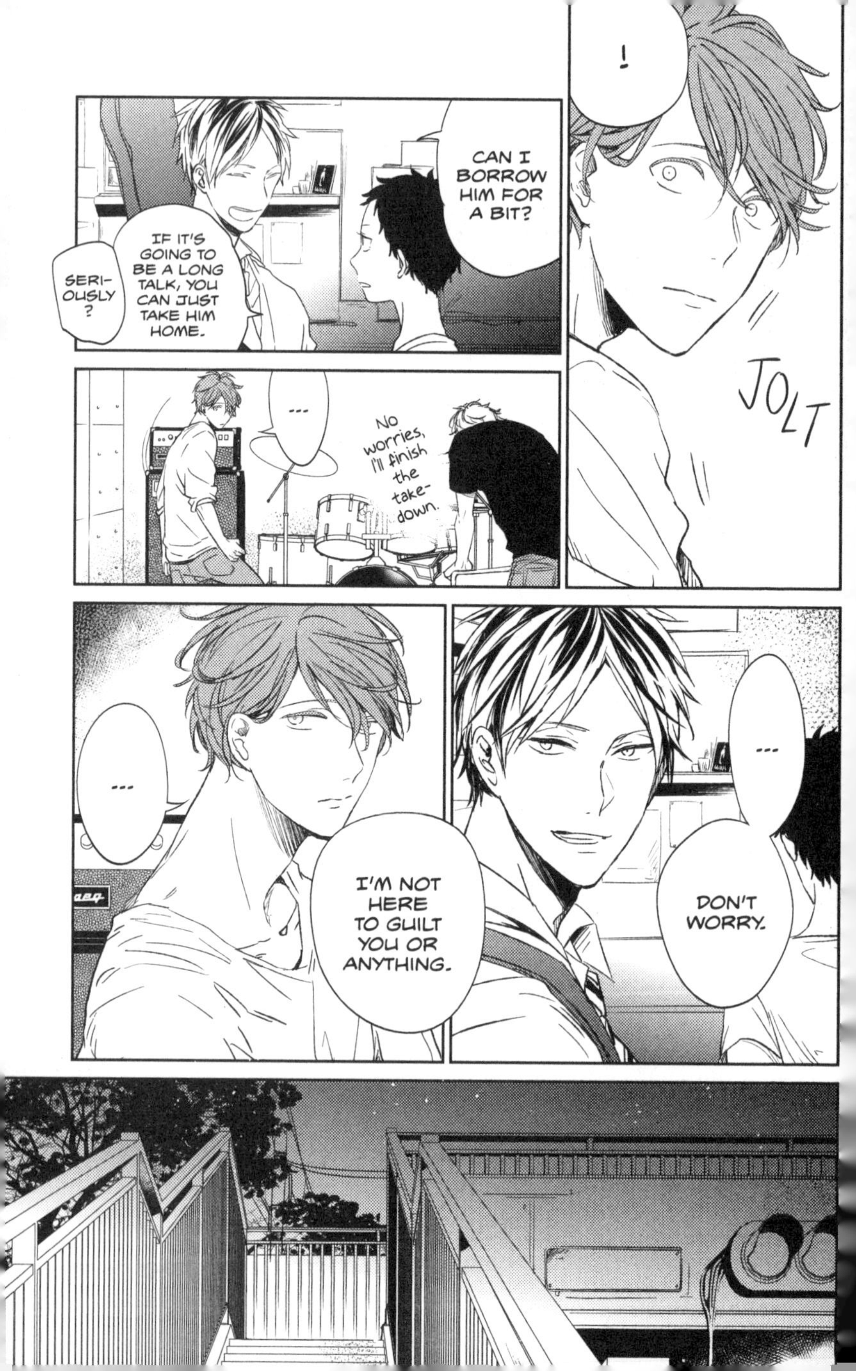
!
JOLT
CAN I BORROW HIM FOR A BIT?
IF IT'S GOING TO BE A LONG TALK, YOU CAN JUST TAKE HIM HOME.
SERI-OUSLY?
...
No worries, I'll finish the take-down.
...
DON'T WORRY.
I'M NOT HERE TO GUILT YOU OR ANYTHING.
...

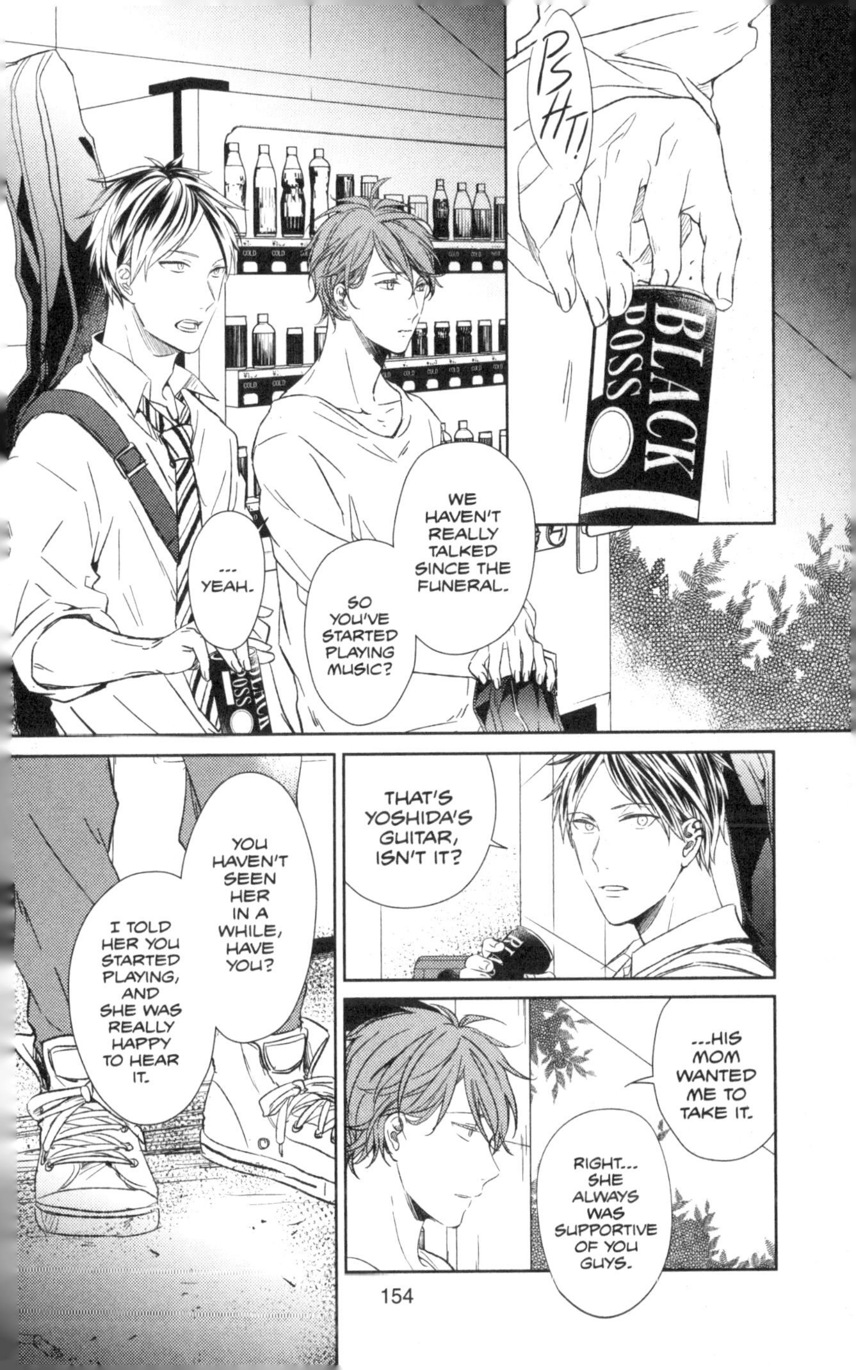
PSHT!
BLACK BOSS
WE HAVEN'T REALLY TALKED SINCE THE FUNERAL.
SO YOU'VE STARTED PLAYING MUSIC?
...YEAH.
THAT'S YOSHIDA'S GUITAR, ISN'T IT?
...HIS MOM WANTED ME TO TAKE IT.
RIGHT... SHE ALWAYS WAS SUPPORTIVE OF YOU GUYS.
YOU HAVEN'T SEEN HER IN A WHILE, HAVE YOU?
I TOLD HER YOU STARTED PLAYING, AND SHE WAS REALLY HAPPY TO HEAR IT.

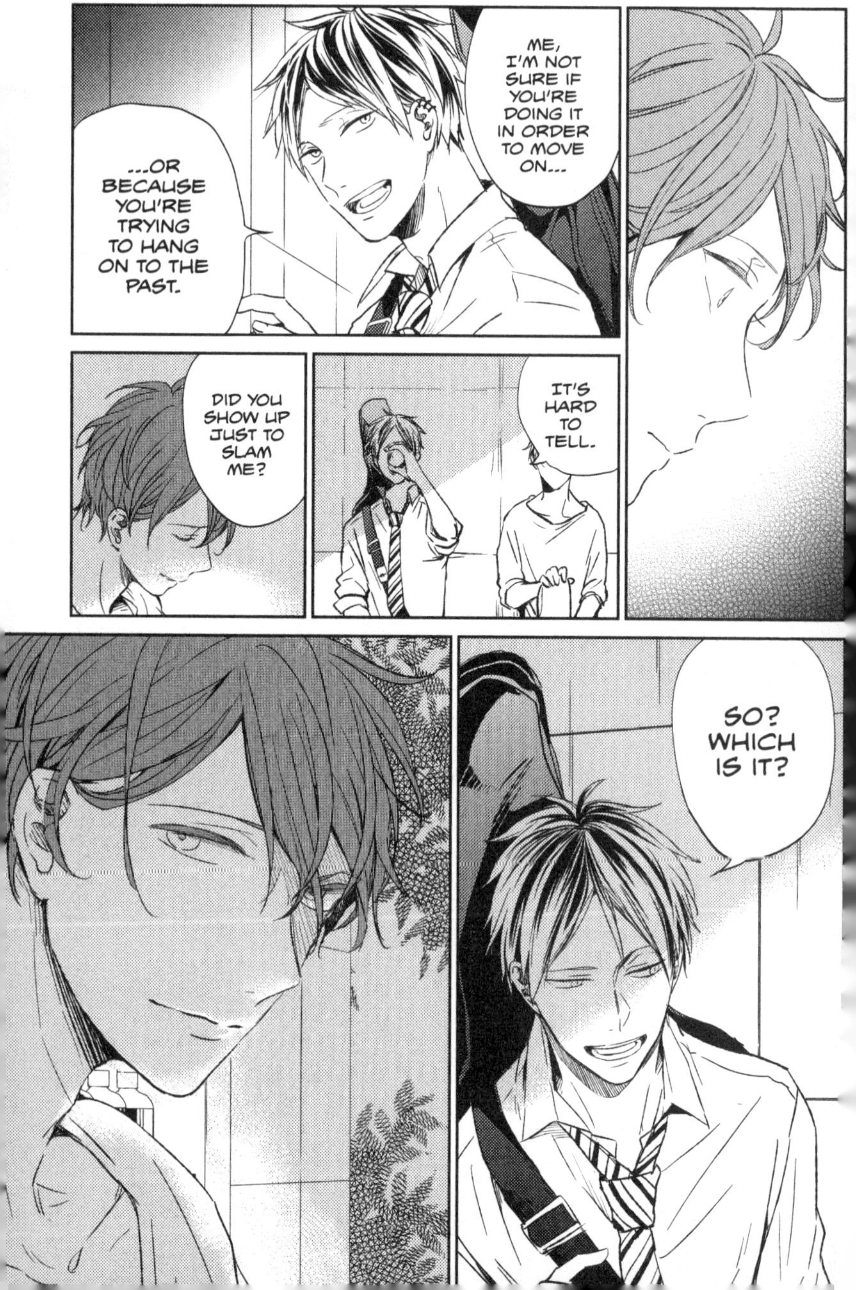
ME, I'M NOT SURE IF YOU'RE DOING IT IN ORDER TO MOVE ON...
...OR BECAUSE YOU'RE TRYING TO HANG ON TO THE PAST.
IT'S HARD TO TELL.
DID YOU SHOW UP JUST TO SLAM ME?
SO? WHICH IS IT?

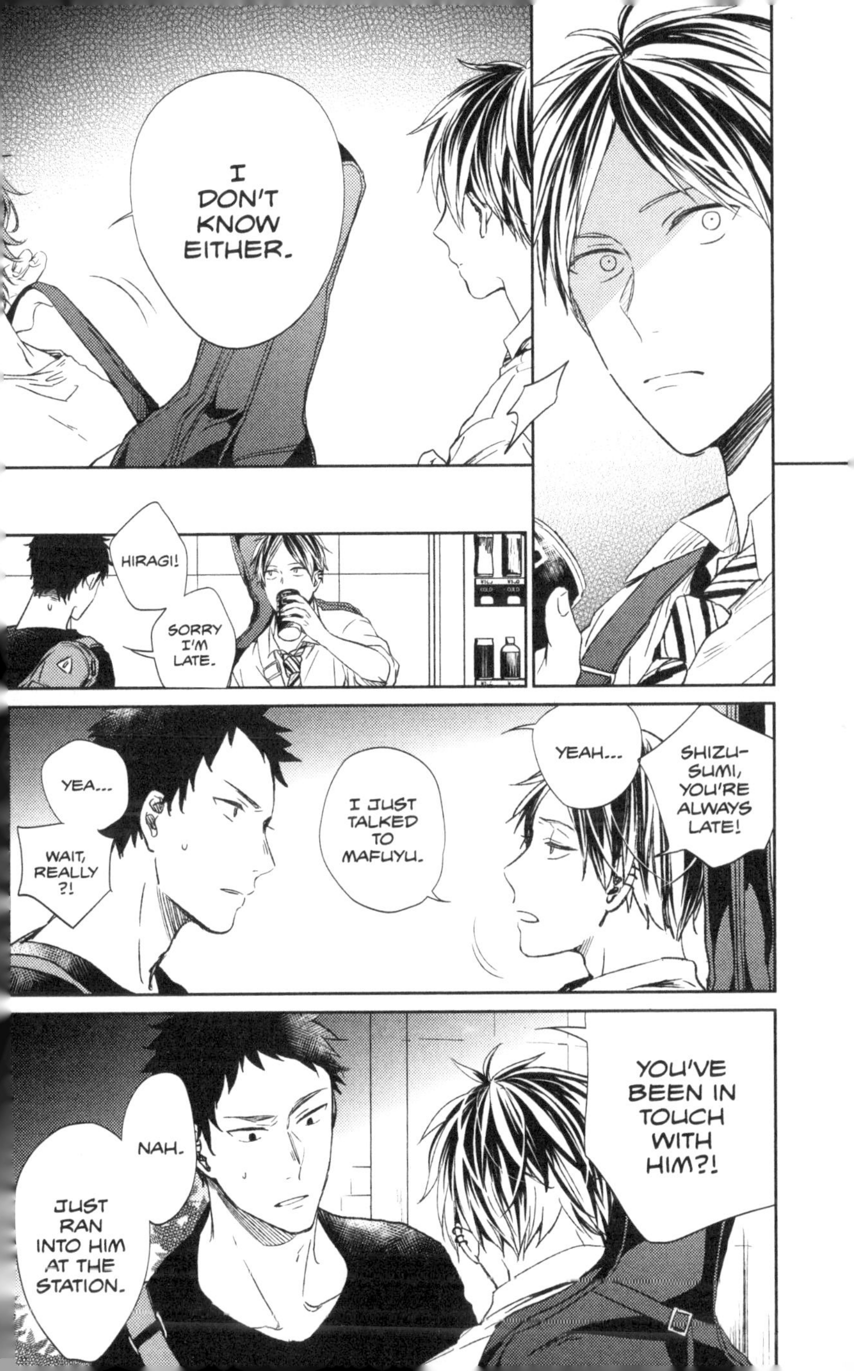
I DON'T KNOW EITHER.
HIRAGI!
SORRY I'M LATE.
SHIZU-SUMI, YOU'RE ALWAYS LATE!
YEAH...
I JUST TALKED TO MAFUYU.
YEA...
WAIT, REALLY?!
YOU'VE BEEN IN TOUCH WITH HIM?!
NAH.
JUST RAN INTO HIM AT THE STATION.

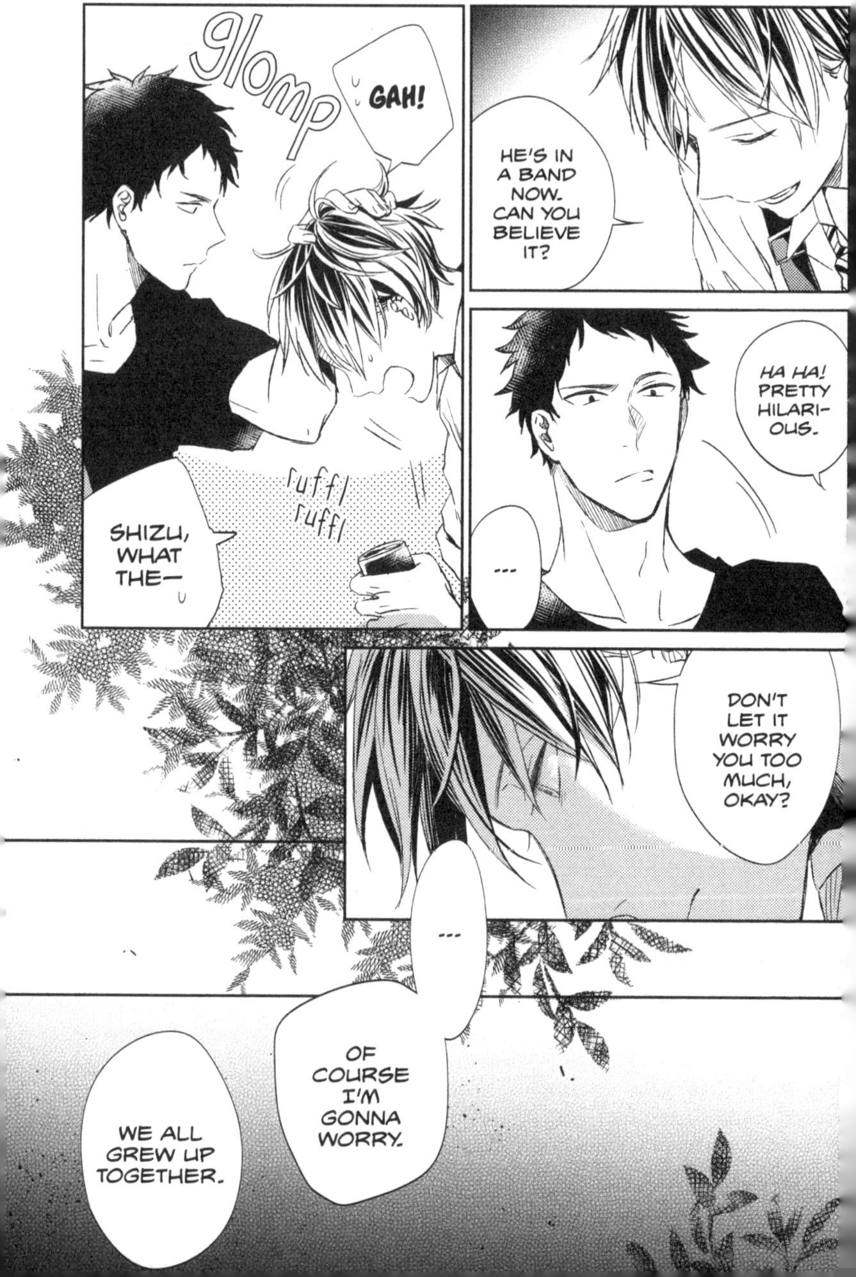
HE'S IN A BAND NOW. CAN YOU BELIEVE IT?
HA HA! PRETTY HILARI-OUS.
...
glomp
GAH!
ruffl ruffl
SHIZU, WHAT THE—
DON'T LET IT WORRY YOU TOO MUCH, OKAY?
...
OF COURSE I'M GONNA WORRY.
WE ALL GREW UP TOGETHER.

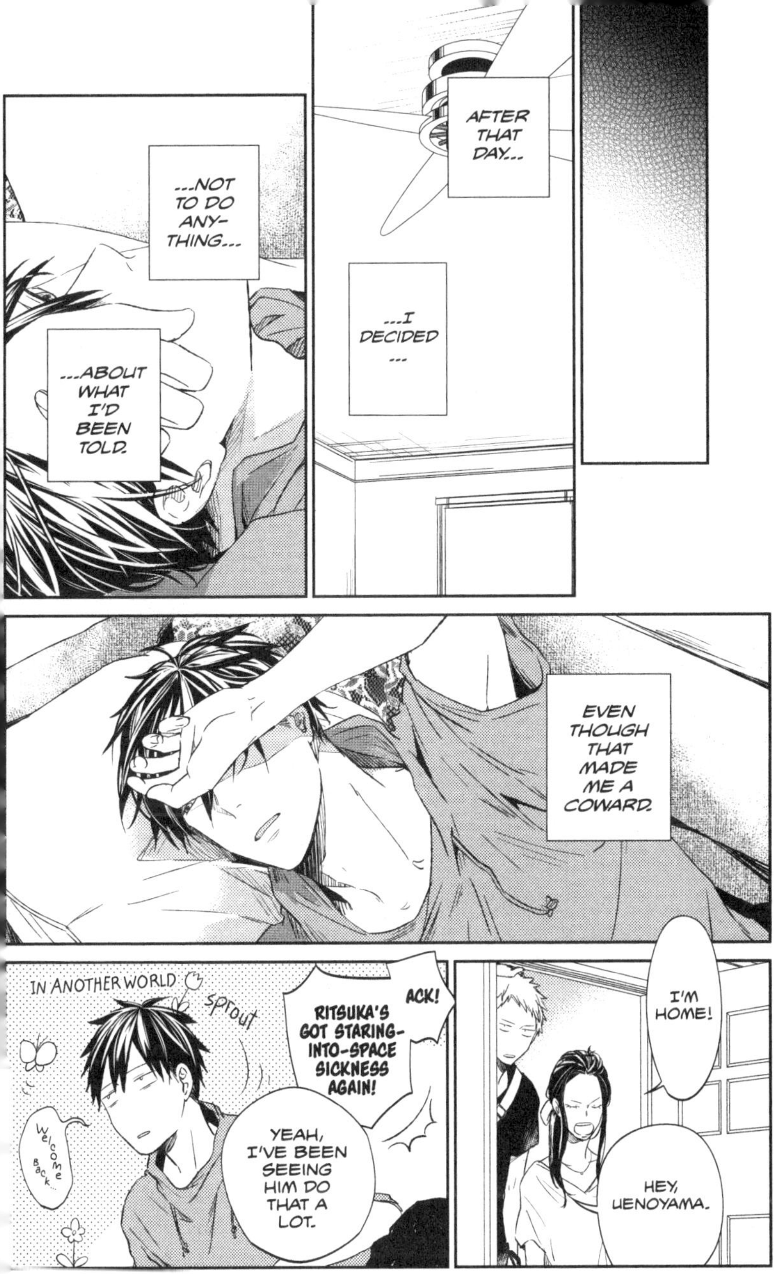
AFTER THAT DAY...
...I DECIDED ...
...NOT TO DO ANYTHING...
...ABOUT WHAT I'D BEEN TOLD.
EVEN THOUGH THAT MADE ME A COWARD.
I'M HOME!
HEY, UENOYAMA.
ACK!
RITSUKA'S GOT STARING-INTO-SPACE SICKNESS AGAIN!
YEAH, I'VE BEEN SEEING HIM DO THAT A LOT.
IN ANOTHER WORLD
sprout
Welcome back...

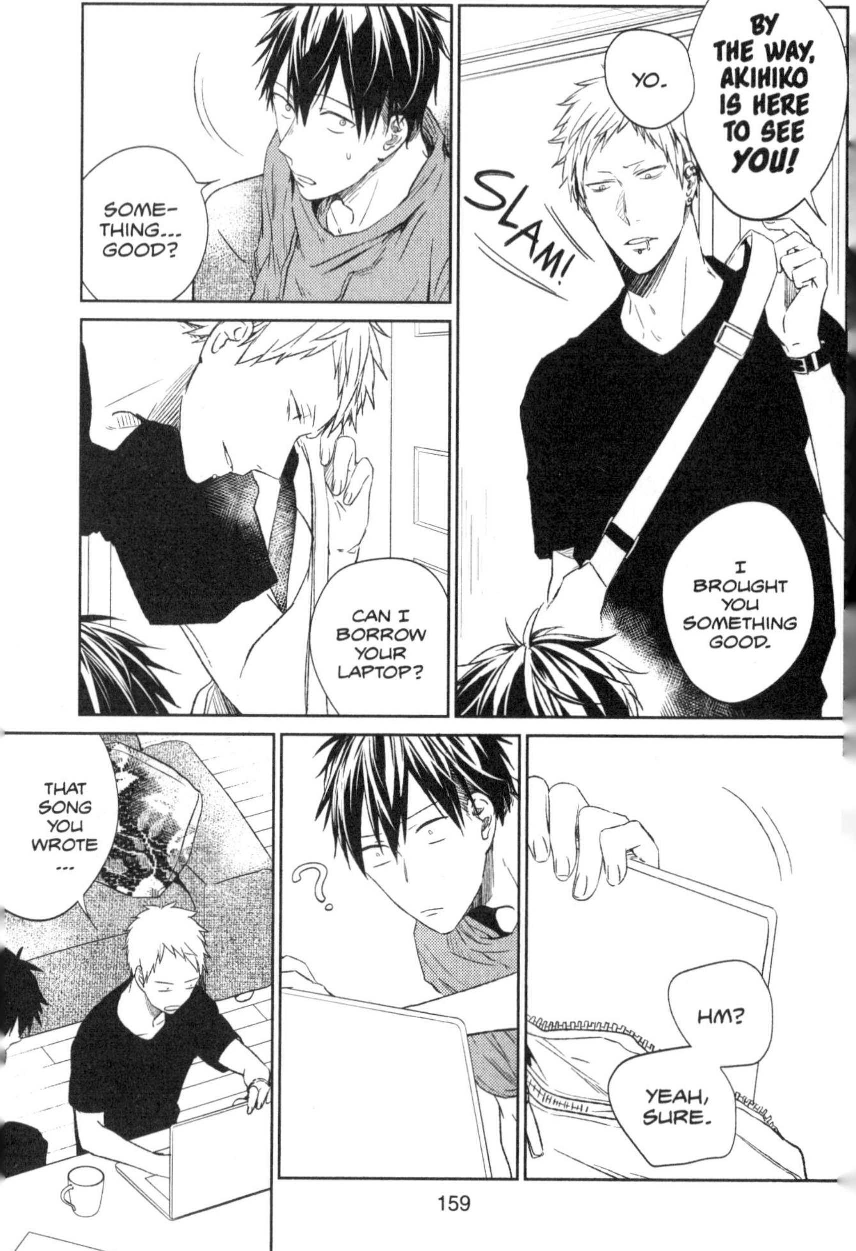

BY THE WAY, AKIHIKO IS HERE TO SEE YOU!
YO.
SLAM!
I BROUGHT YOU SOMETHING GOOD.
SOMETHING... GOOD?
CAN I BORROW YOUR LAPTOP?
HM?
YEAH, SURE.
?
THAT SONG YOU WROTE...

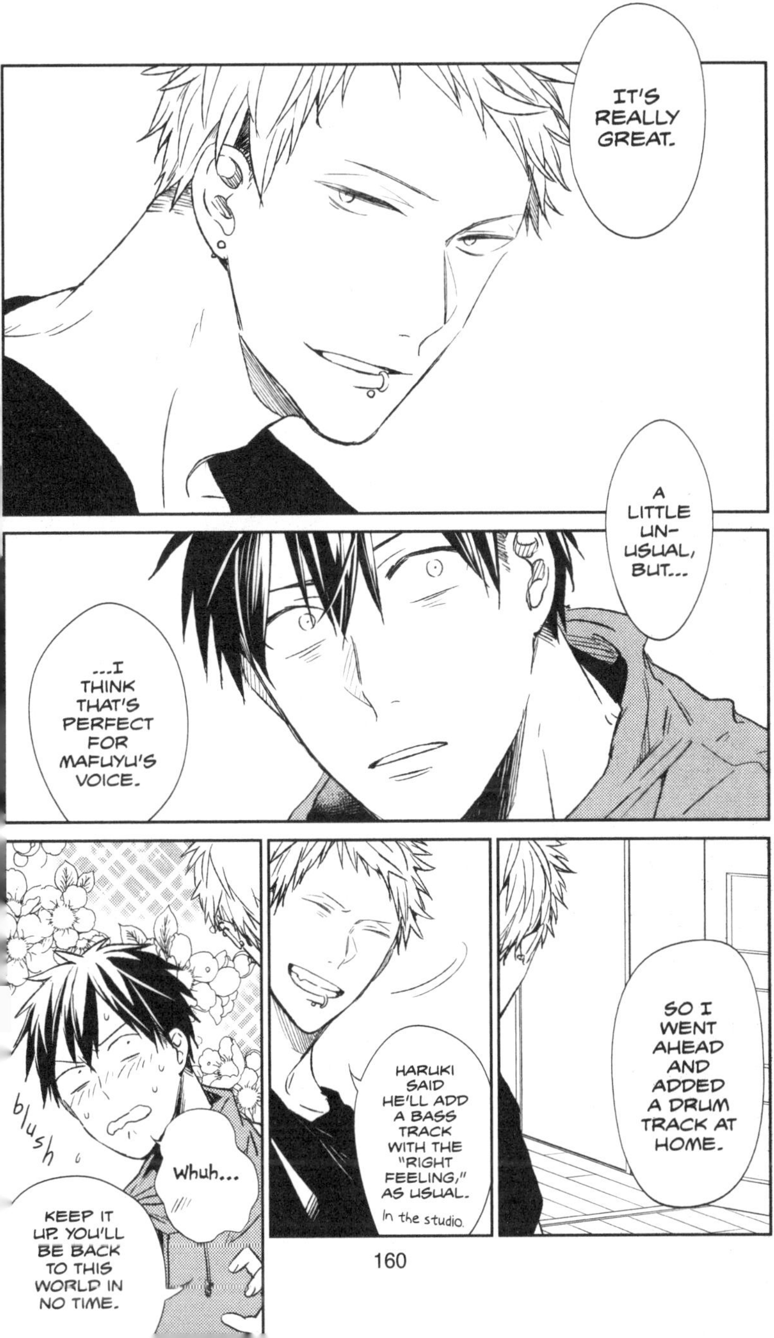
IT'S REALLY GREAT.
A LITTLE UN-USUAL, BUT...
...I THINK THAT'S PERFECT FOR MAFUYU'S VOICE.
SO I WENT AHEAD AND ADDED A DRUM TRACK AT HOME.
HARUKI SAID HE'LL ADD A BASS TRACK WITH THE "RIGHT FEELING," AS USUAL.
In the studio.
blush
Whuh...
KEEP IT UP. YOU'LL BE BACK TO THIS WORLD IN NO TIME.

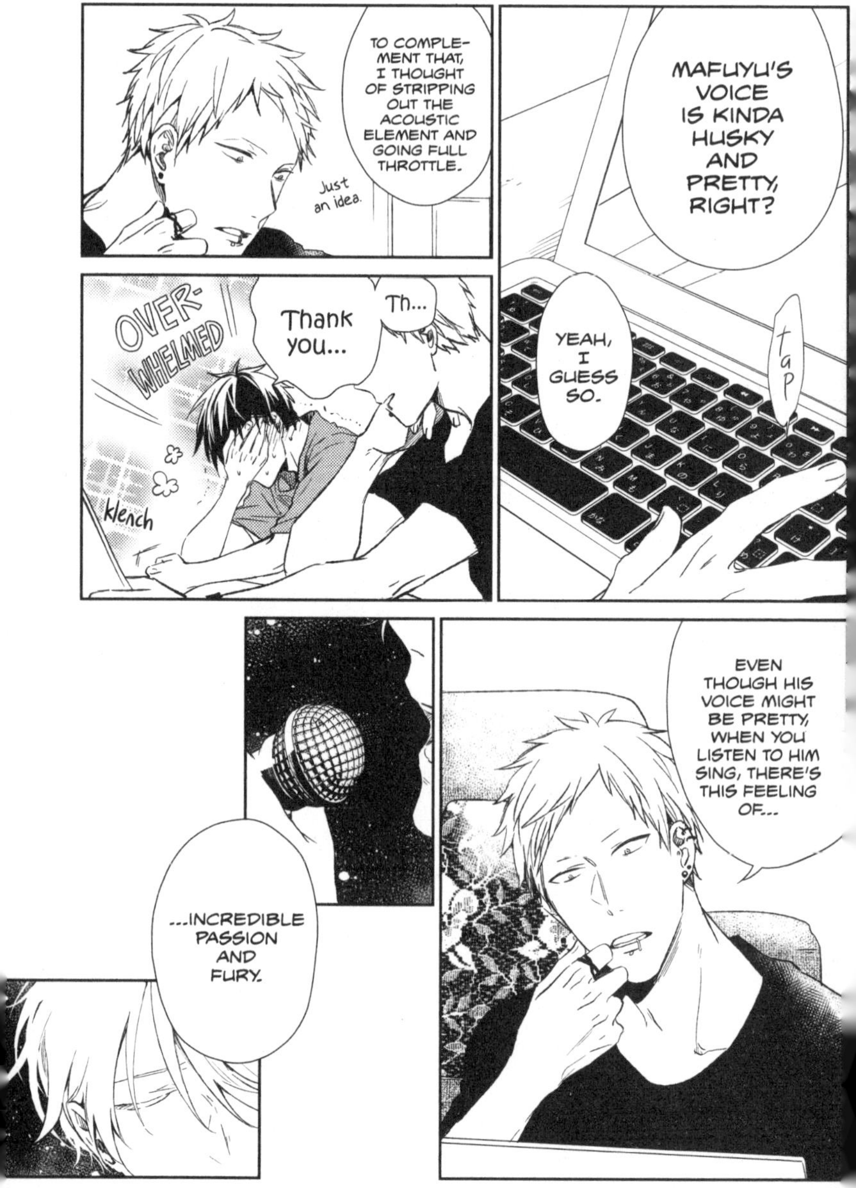
MAFUYU'S VOICE IS KINDA HUSKY AND PRETTY, RIGHT?
tap
YEAH, I GUESS SO.
TO COMPLEMENT THAT, I THOUGHT OF STRIPPING OUT THE ACOUSTIC ELEMENT AND GOING FULL THROTTLE.
Just an idea.
Th...
Thank you...
OVERWHELMED
klench
EVEN THOUGH HIS VOICE MIGHT BE PRETTY, WHEN YOU LISTEN TO HIM SING, THERE'S THIS FEELING OF...
...INCREDIBLE PASSION AND FURY.

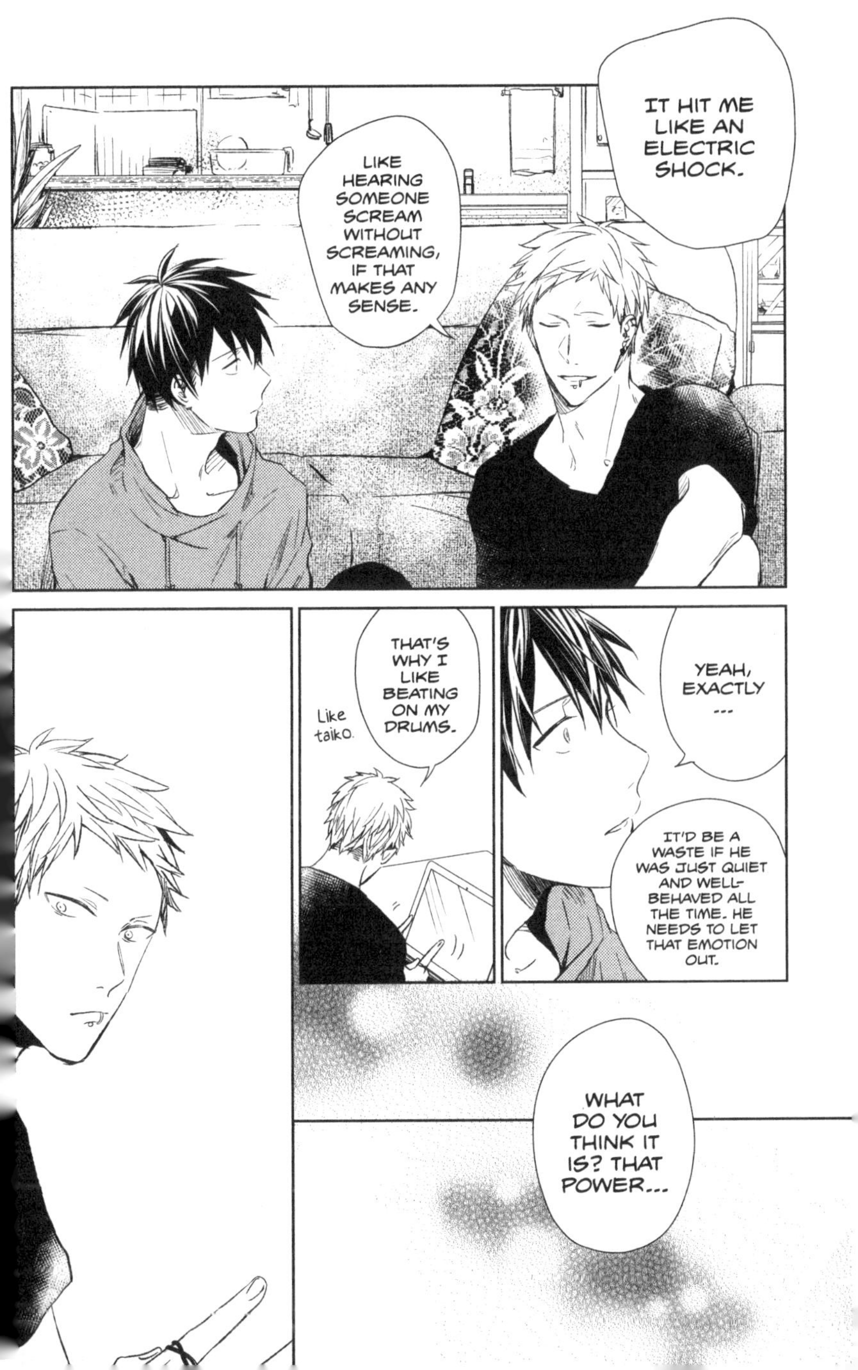
IT HIT ME LIKE AN ELECTRIC SHOCK.
LIKE HEARING SOMEONE SCREAM WITHOUT SCREAMING, IF THAT MAKES ANY SENSE.
YEAH, EXACTLY ...
IT'D BE A WASTE IF HE WAS JUST QUIET AND WELL-BEHAVED ALL THE TIME. HE NEEDS TO LET THAT EMOTION OUT.
THAT'S WHY I LIKE BEATING ON MY DRUMS.
Like taiko.
WHAT DO YOU THINK IT IS? THAT POWER...

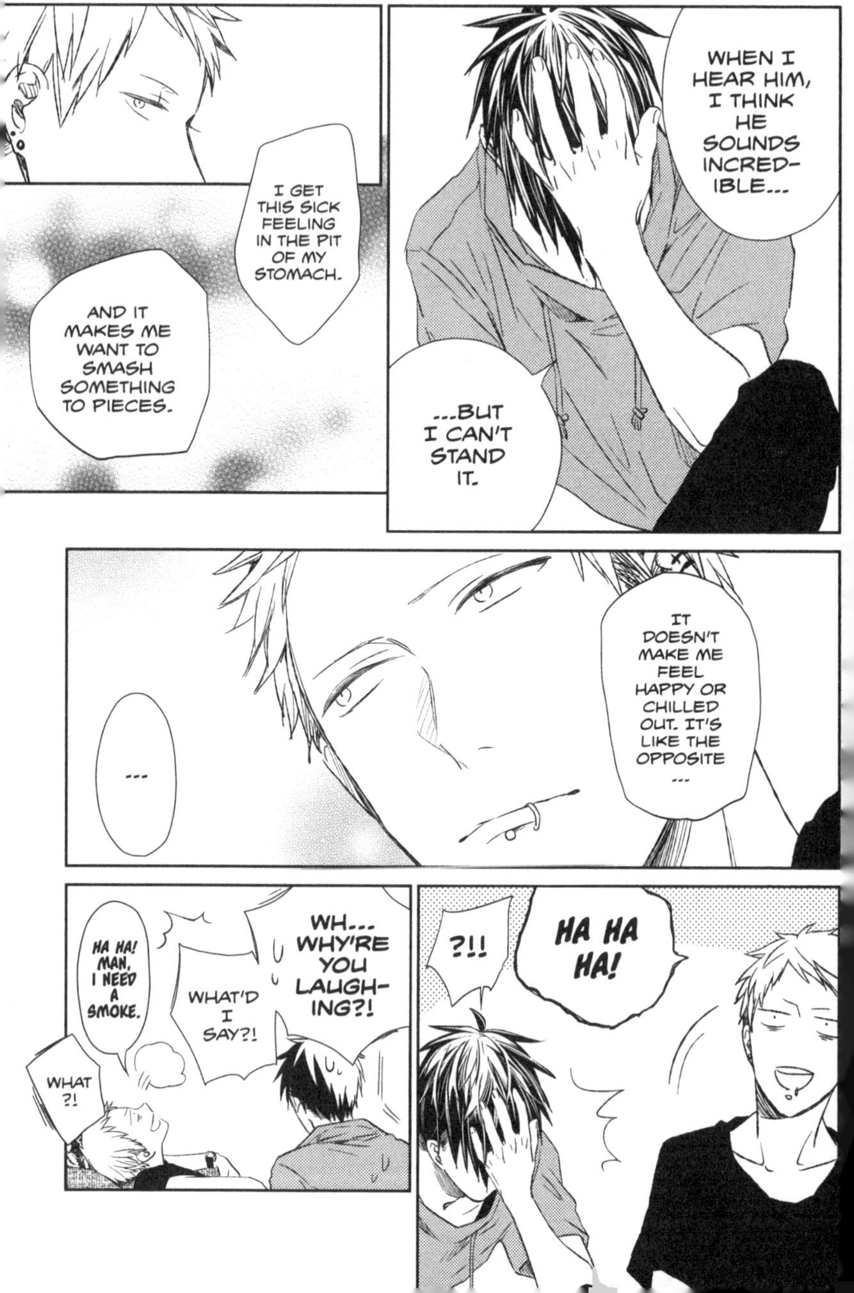
WHEN I HEAR HIM, I THINK HE SOUNDS INCREDIBLE...
...BUT I CAN'T STAND IT.
I GET THIS SICK FEELING IN THE PIT OF MY STOMACH.
AND IT MAKES ME WANT TO SMASH SOMETHING TO PIECES.
IT DOESN'T MAKE ME FEEL HAPPY OR CHILLED OUT. IT'S LIKE THE OPPOSITE...
...
HA HA HA!
?!!
WH... WHY'RE YOU LAUGHING?!
WHAT'D I SAY?!
HA HA! MAN, I NEED A SMOKE.
WHAT?!

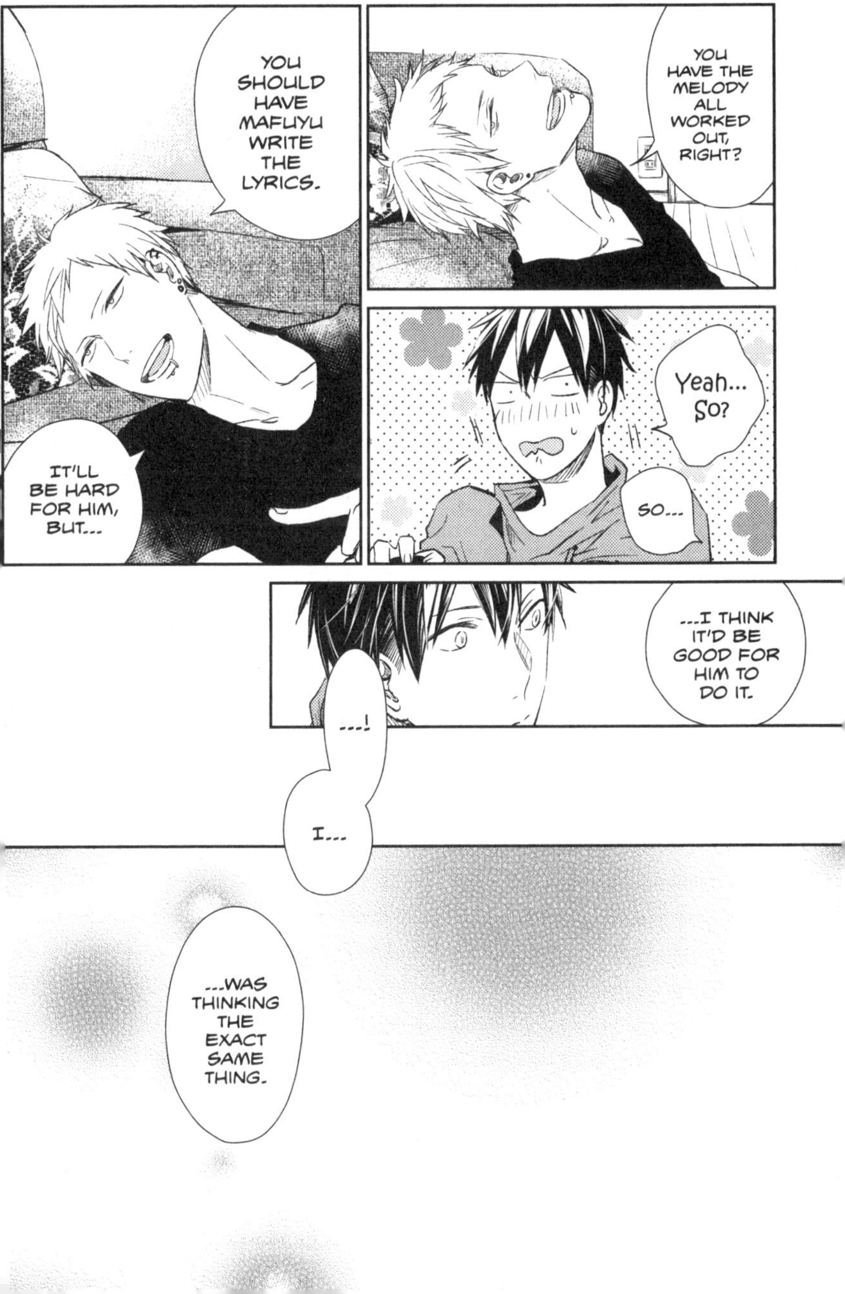
YOU HAVE THE MELODY ALL WORKED OUT, RIGHT?
Yeah... So?
SO...
YOU SHOULD HAVE MAFUYU WRITE THE LYRICS.
IT'LL BE HARD FOR HIM, BUT...
...I THINK IT'D BE GOOD FOR HIM TO DO IT.
...!
I...
...WAS THINKING THE EXACT SAME THING.

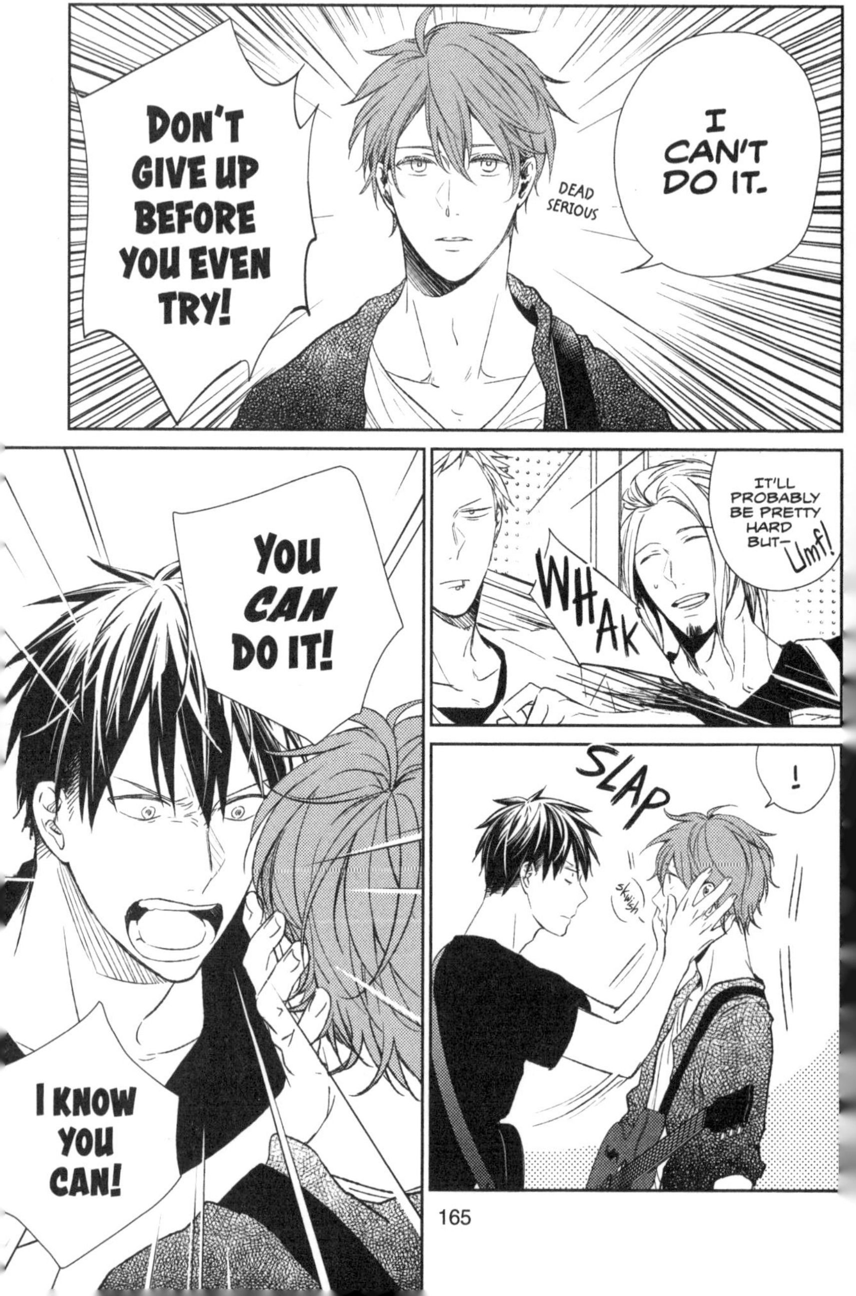
I CAN'T DO IT.
DEAD SERIOUS
DON'T GIVE UP BEFORE YOU EVEN TRY!
IT'LL PROBABLY BE PRETTY HARD BUT—
Umf!
WHAK
YOU CAN DO IT!
I KNOW YOU CAN!
!
SLAP
skwish

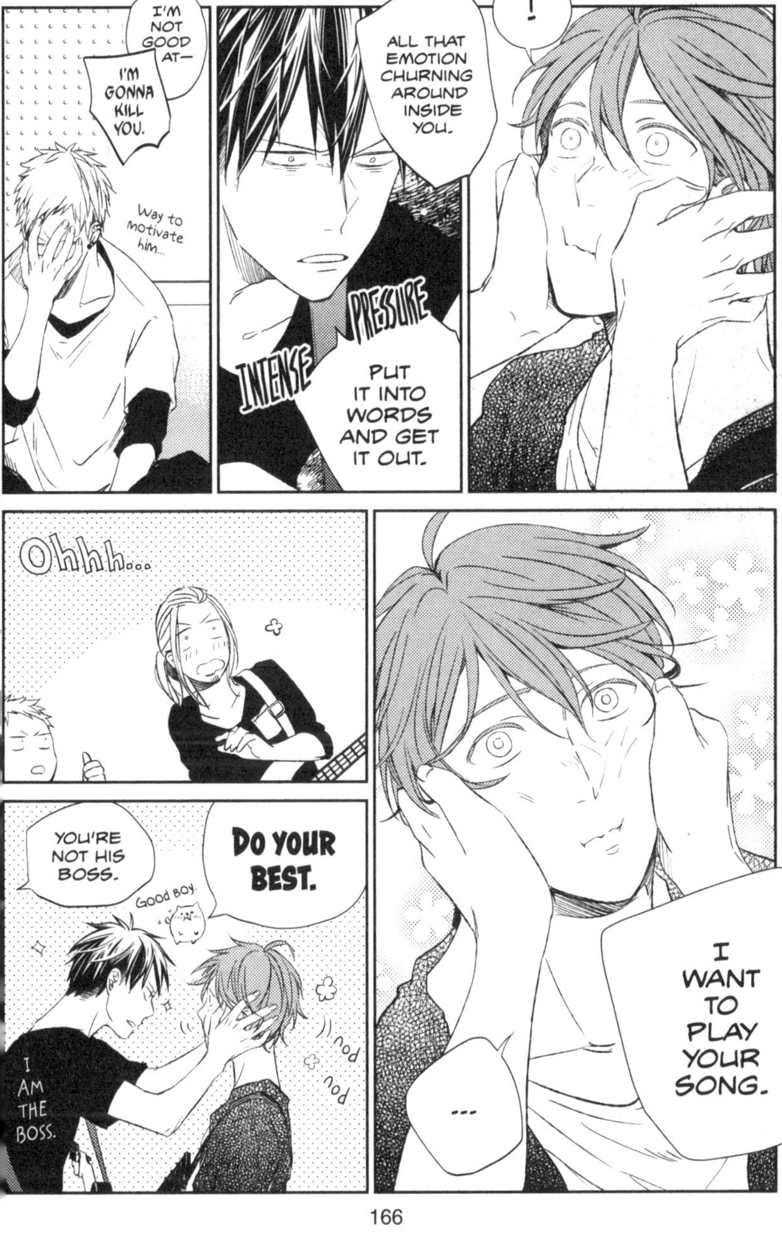
!
ALL THAT EMOTION CHURNING AROUND INSIDE YOU.
INTENSE
PRESSURE
PUT IT INTO WORDS AND GET IT OUT.
I'M NOT GOOD AT—
I'M GONNA KILL YOU.
Way to motivate him...
I WANT TO PLAY YOUR SONG.
...
Ohhh...
DO YOUR BEST.
YOU'RE NOT HIS BOSS.
Good boy.
I AM THE BOSS.
nod
nod

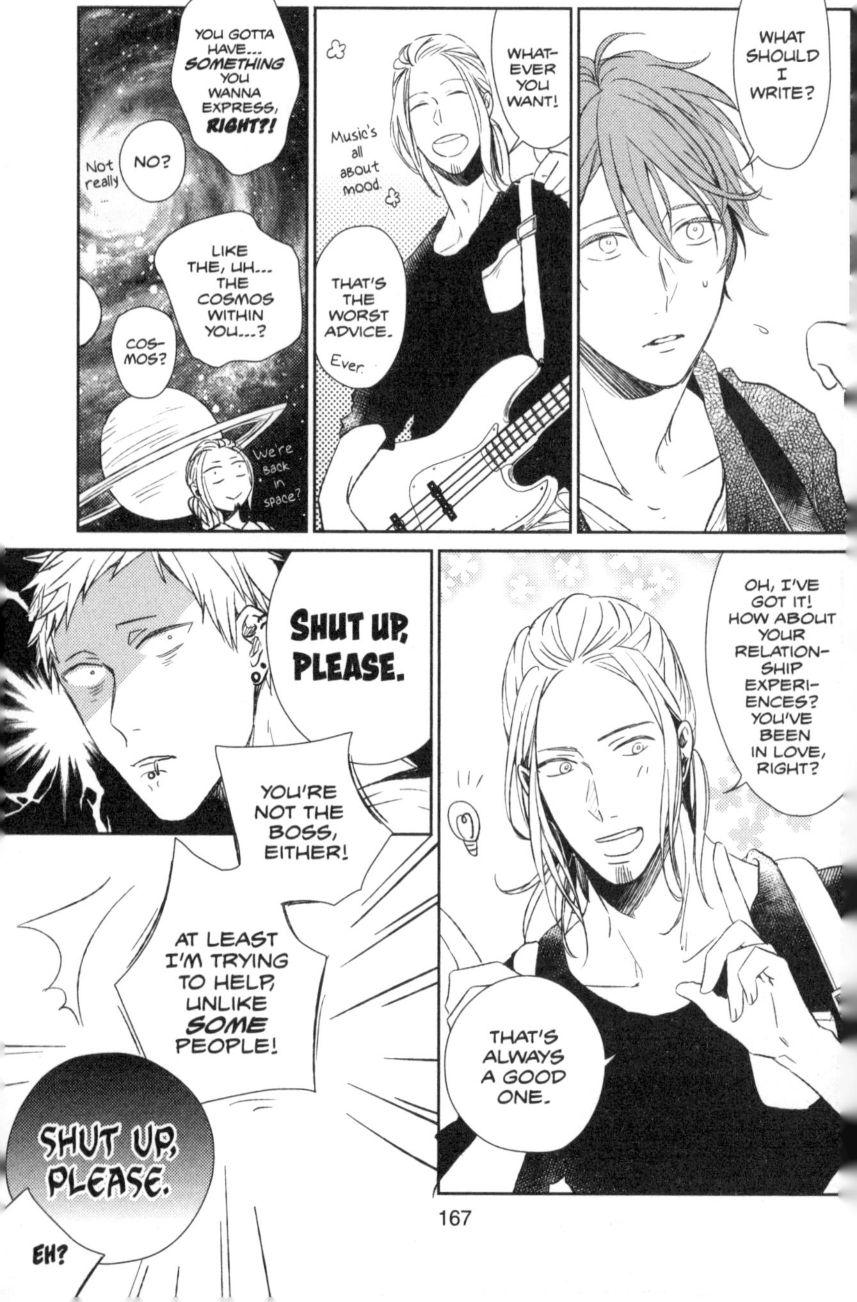
WHAT SHOULD I WRITE?
WHAT-EVER YOU WANT!
Music's all about mood.
THAT'S THE WORST ADVICE.
Ever.
YOU GOTTA HAVE... SOMETHING YOU WANNA EXPRESS, RIGHT?!
NO?
Not really...
LIKE THE, UH... THE COSMOS WITHIN YOU...?
COS-MOS?
We're back in space?
OH, I'VE GOT IT! HOW ABOUT YOUR RELATION-SHIP EXPERI-ENCES? YOU'VE BEEN IN LOVE, RIGHT?
THAT'S ALWAYS A GOOD ONE.
SHUT UP, PLEASE.
YOU'RE NOT THE BOSS, EITHER!
AT LEAST I'M TRYING TO HELP, UNLIKE SOME PEOPLE!
SHUT UP, PLEASE.
EH?

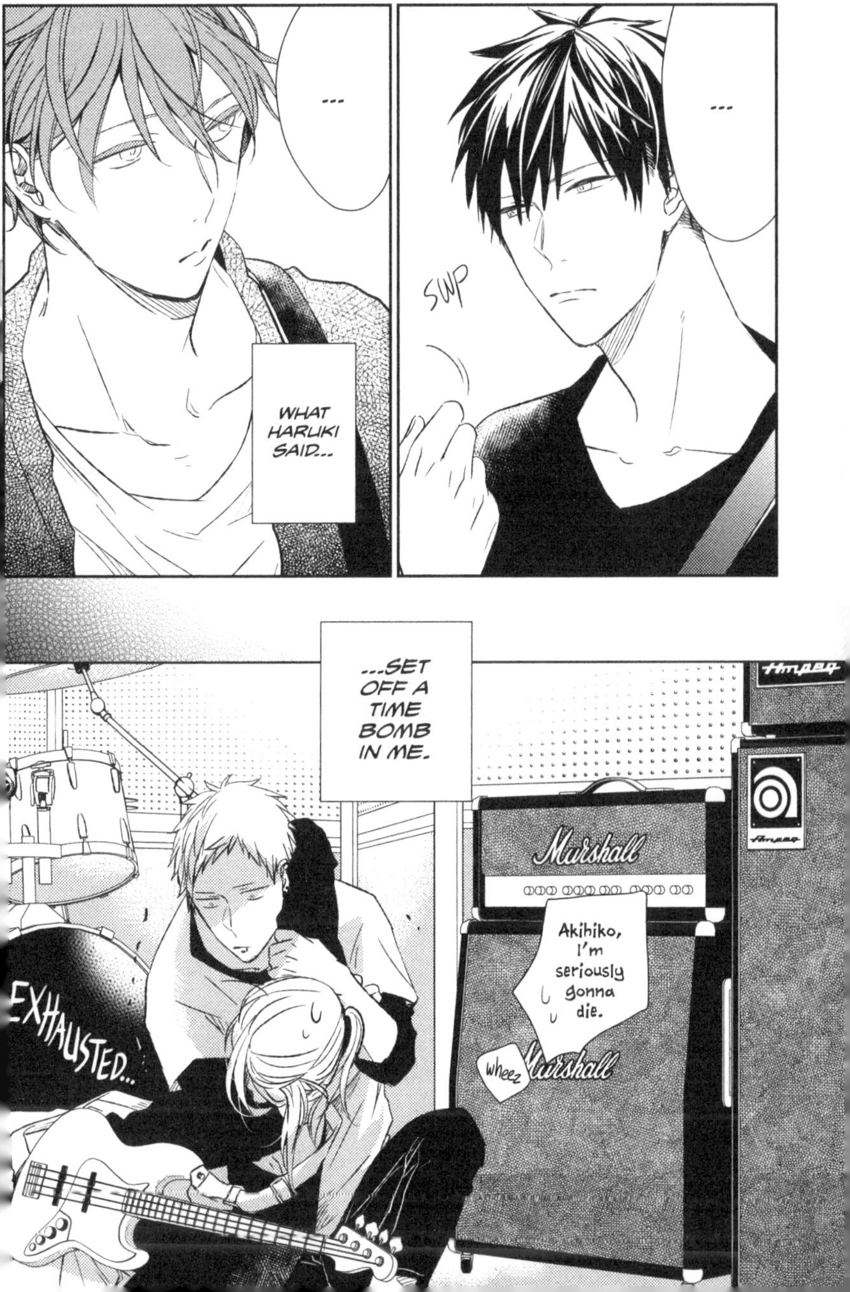
...
SWP
...
WHAT HARUKI SAID...
...SET OFF A TIME BOMB IN ME.
Akihiko, I'm seriously gonna die.
wheez
EXHAUSTED...
Marshall
Marshall
Ampeg

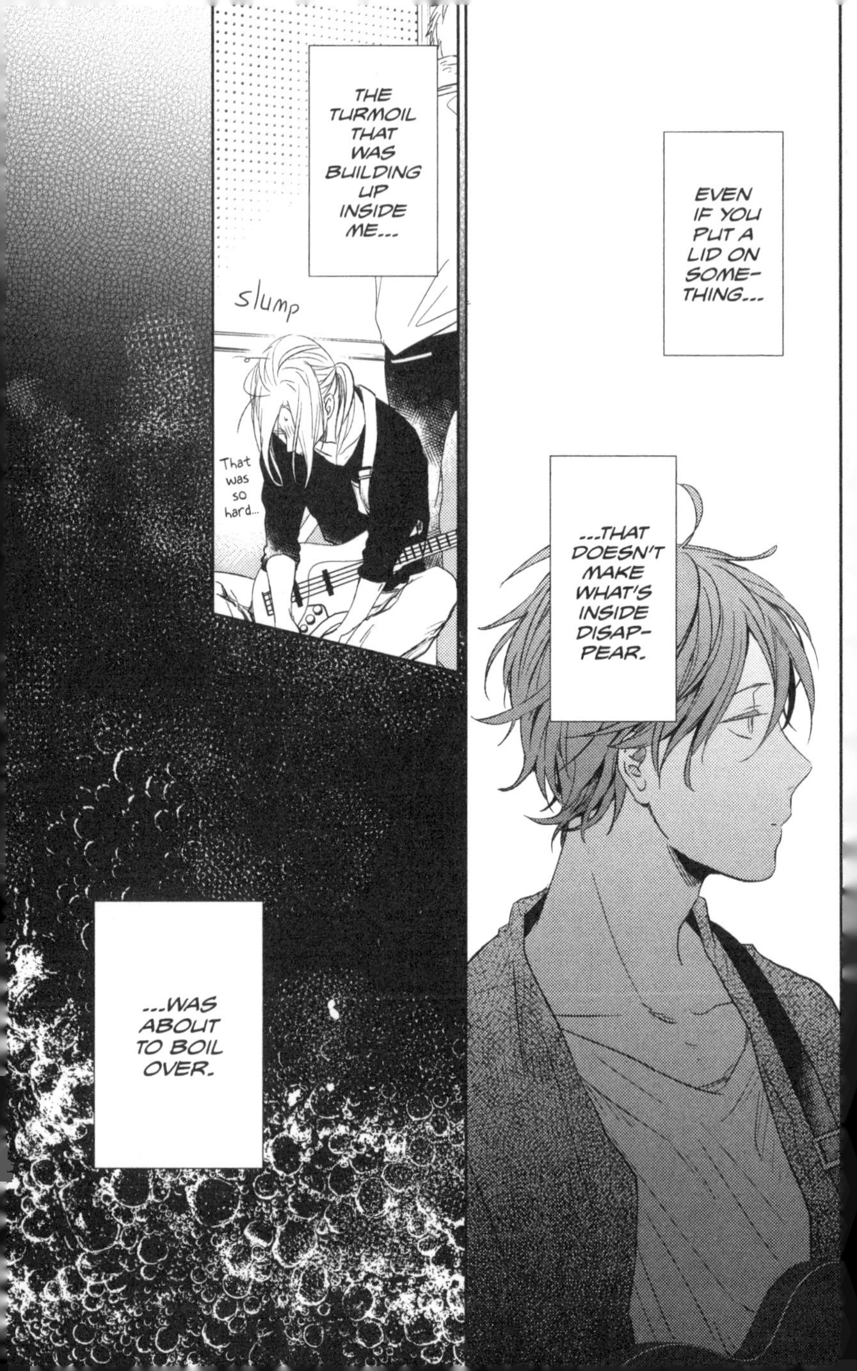
EVEN IF YOU PUT A LID ON SOMETHING...
...THAT DOESN'T MAKE WHAT'S INSIDE DISAPPEAR.
THE TURMOIL THAT WAS BUILDING UP INSIDE ME...
slump
That was so hard...
...WAS ABOUT TO BOIL OVER.

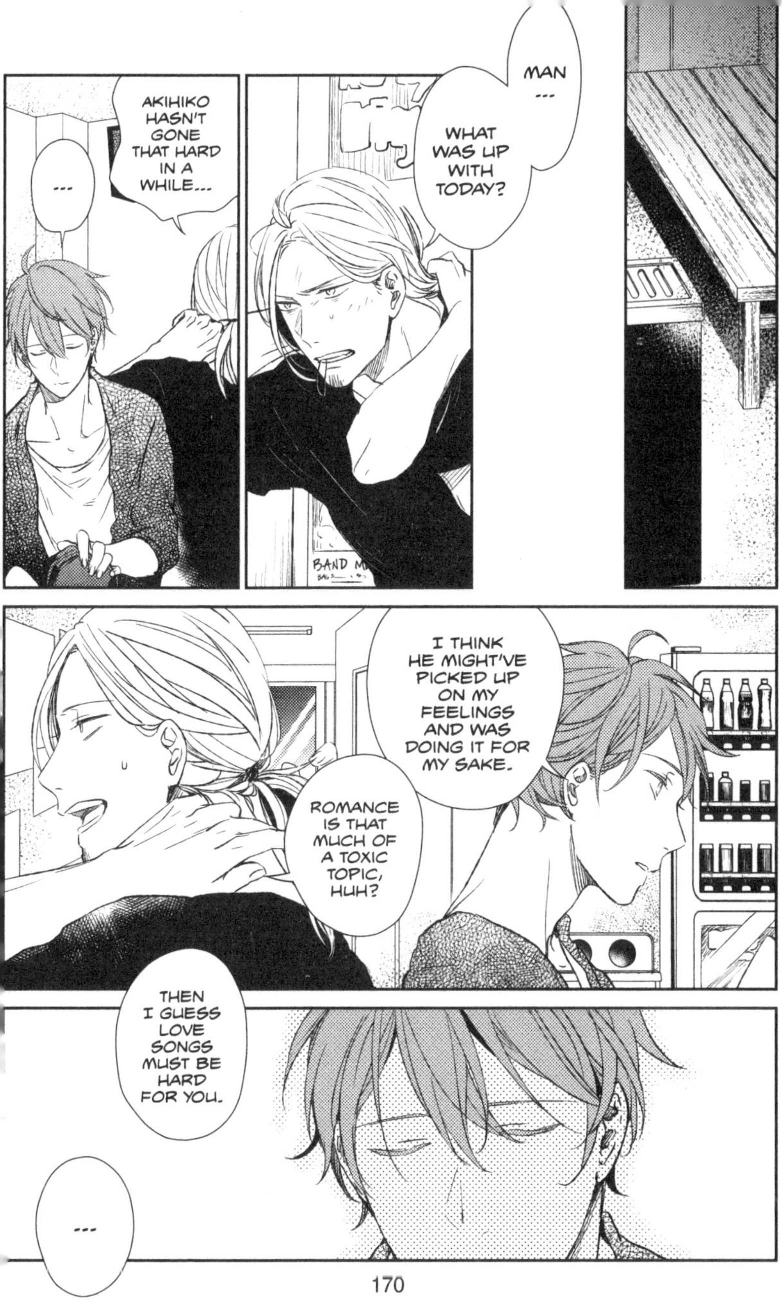
MAN ---
WHAT WAS UP WITH TODAY?
AKIHIKO HASN'T GONE THAT HARD IN A WHILE...

I THINK HE MIGHT'VE PICKED UP ON MY FEELINGS AND WAS DOING IT FOR MY SAKE.
ROMANCE IS THAT MUCH OF A TOXIC TOPIC, HUH?
THEN I GUESS LOVE SONGS MUST BE HARD FOR YOU.

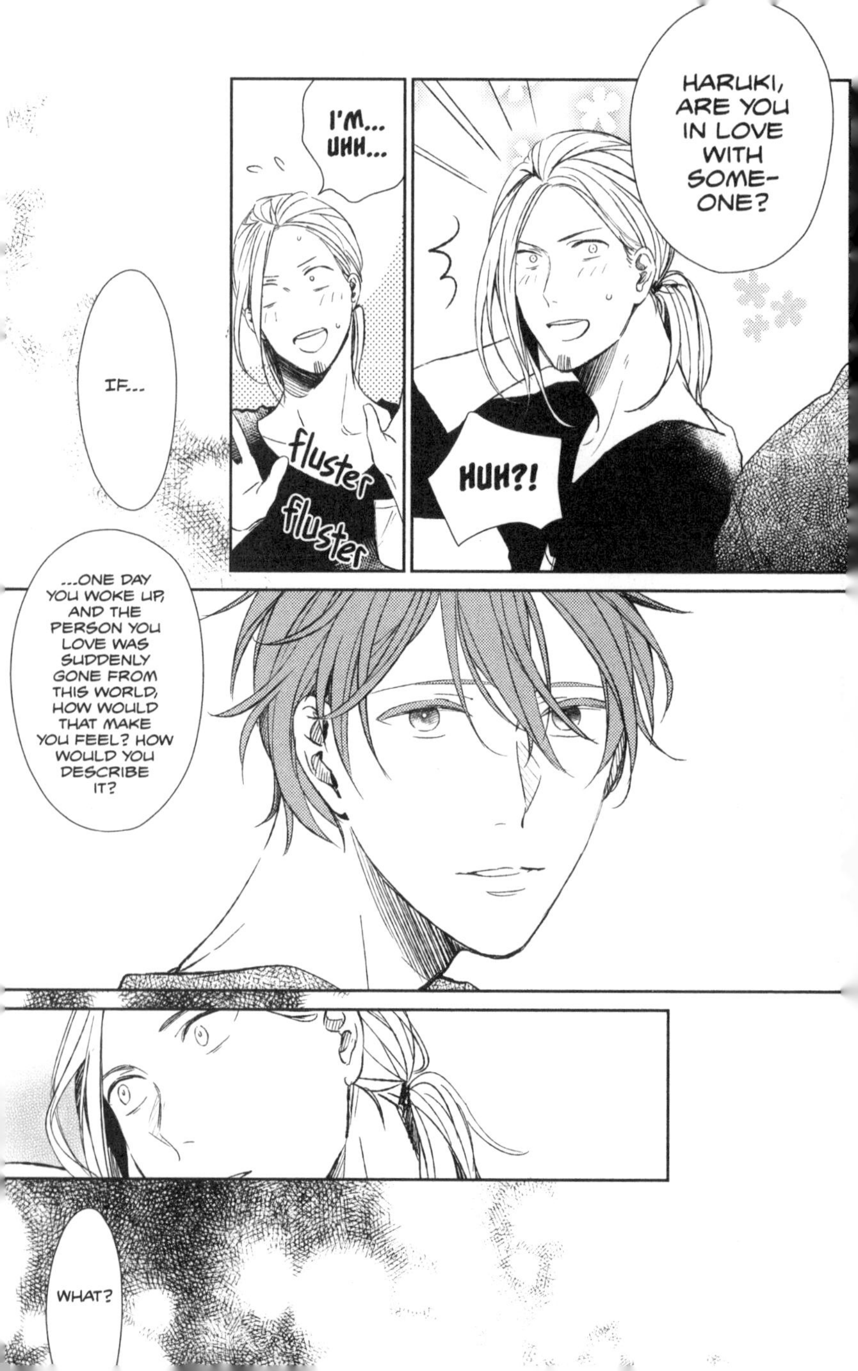
HARUKI, ARE YOU IN LOVE WITH SOMEONE?
HUH?!
I'M... UHH...
fluster fluster
IF...
...ONE DAY YOU WOKE UP, AND THE PERSON YOU LOVE WAS SUDDENLY GONE FROM THIS WORLD, HOW WOULD THAT MAKE YOU FEEL? HOW WOULD YOU DESCRIBE IT?
WHAT?

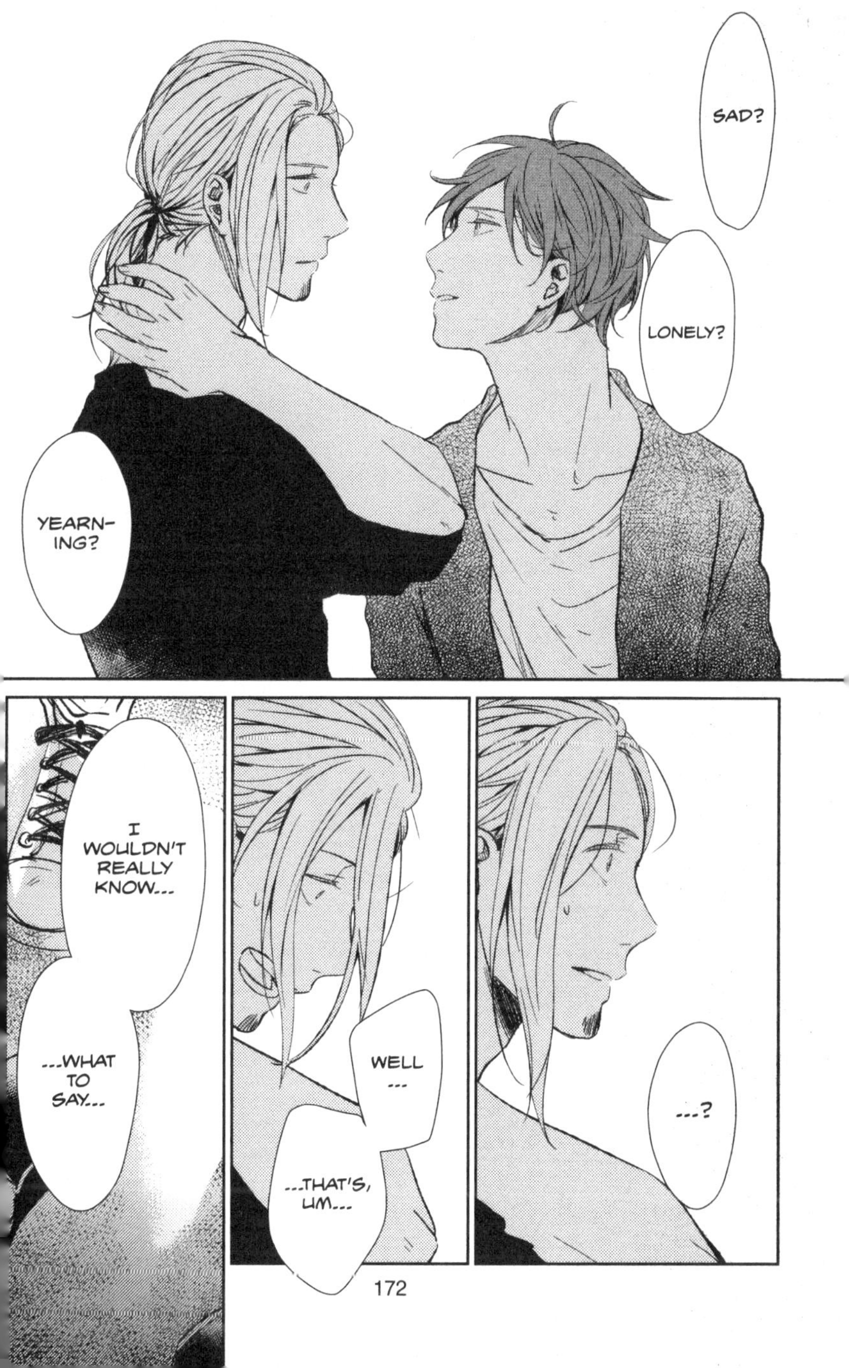
SAD?
LONELY?
YEARNING?
...?
WELL...
...THAT'S, UM...
I WOULDN'T REALLY KNOW...
...WHAT TO SAY...

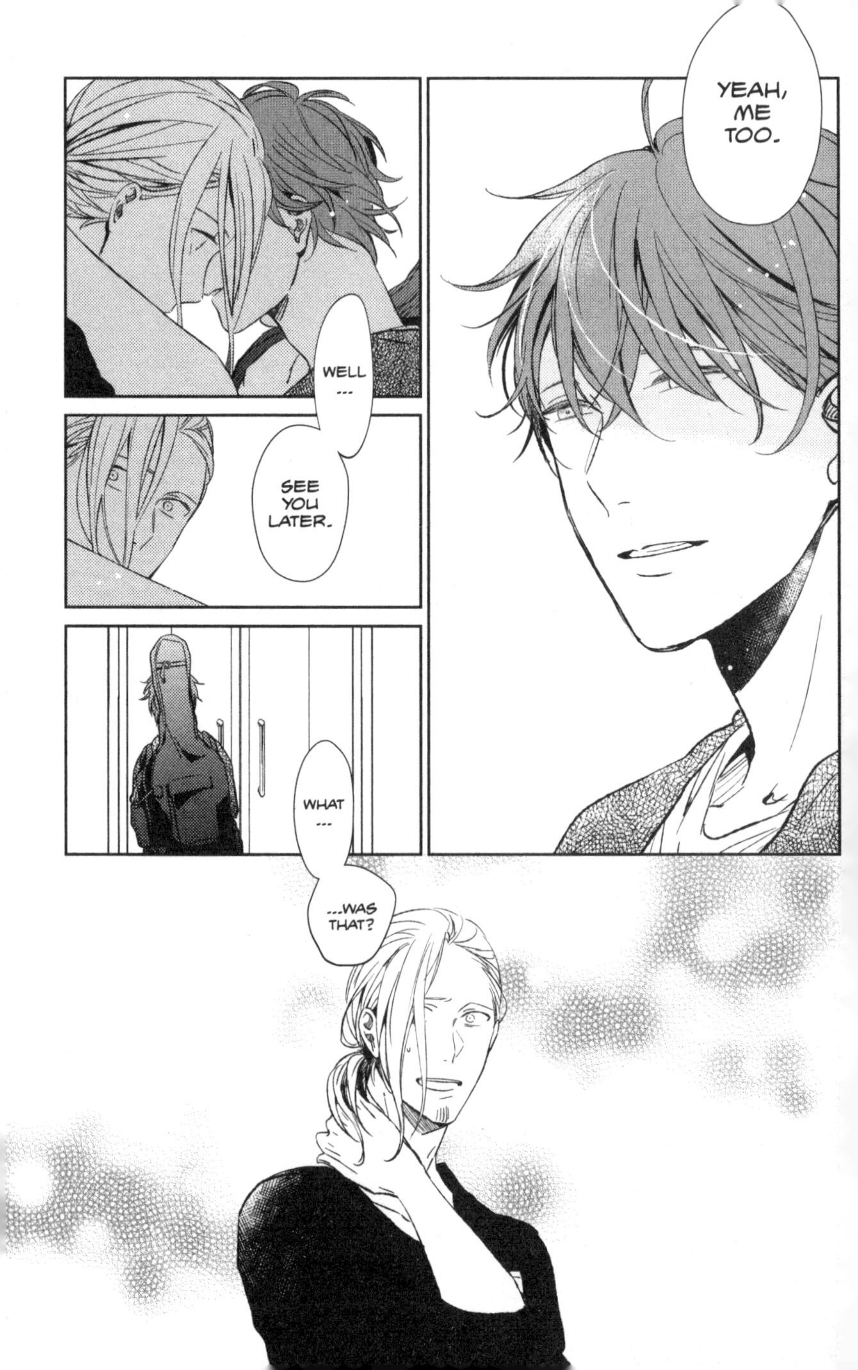
YEAH, ME TOO.
WELL...
SEE YOU LATER.
WHAT...
...WAS THAT?

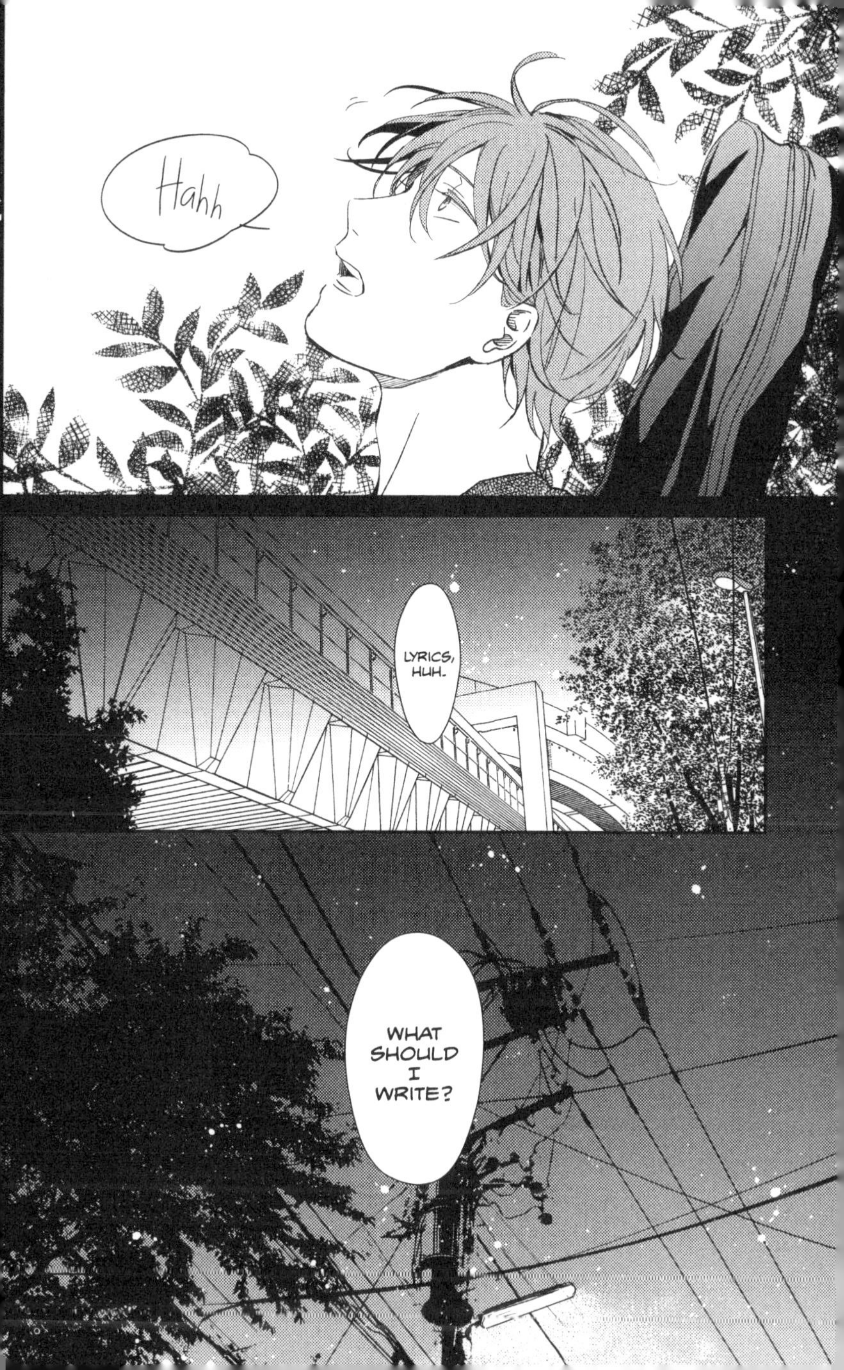
Hahh
LYRICS, HUH.
WHAT SHOULD I WRITE?

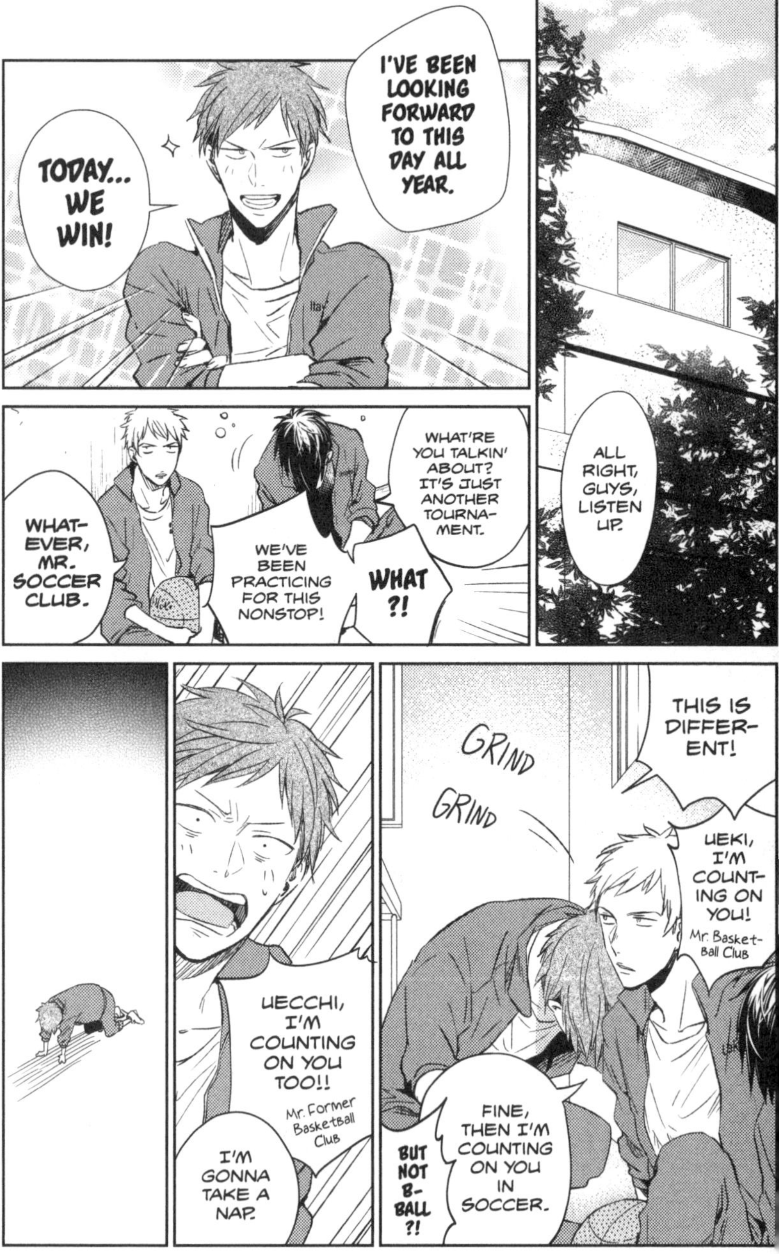
ALL RIGHT, GUYS, LISTEN UP.
I'VE BEEN LOOKING FORWARD TO THIS DAY ALL YEAR.
TODAY... WE WIN!
WHAT'RE YOU TALKIN' ABOUT? IT'S JUST ANOTHER TOURNAMENT.
WHAT ?!
WE'VE BEEN PRACTICING FOR THIS NONSTOP!
WHATEVER, MR. SOCCER CLUB.
THIS IS DIFFERENT!
GRIND
GRIND
UEKI, I'M COUNTING ON YOU!
Mr. Basketball Club
FINE, THEN I'M COUNTING ON YOU IN SOCCER.
BUT NOT B-BALL ?!
UECCHI, I'M COUNTING ON YOU TOO!!
Mr. Former Basketball Club
I'M GONNA TAKE A NAP.

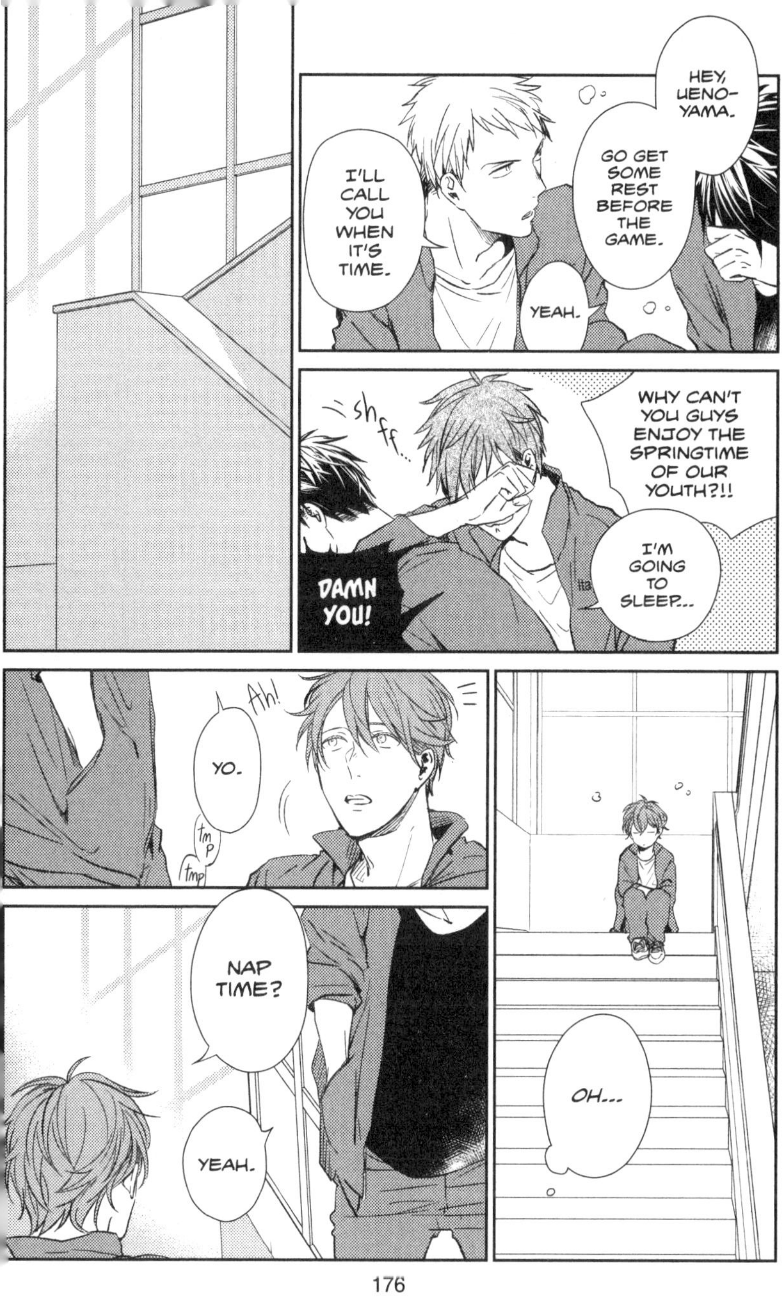
HEY, UENO-YAMA.
GO GET SOME REST BEFORE THE GAME.
I'LL CALL YOU WHEN IT'S TIME.
YEAH.
WHY CAN'T YOU GUYS ENJOY THE SPRINGTIME OF OUR YOUTH?!!
I'M GOING TO SLEEP...
shff...
DAMN YOU!
OH...
Ah!
YO.
tmp
tmp
NAP TIME?
YEAH.

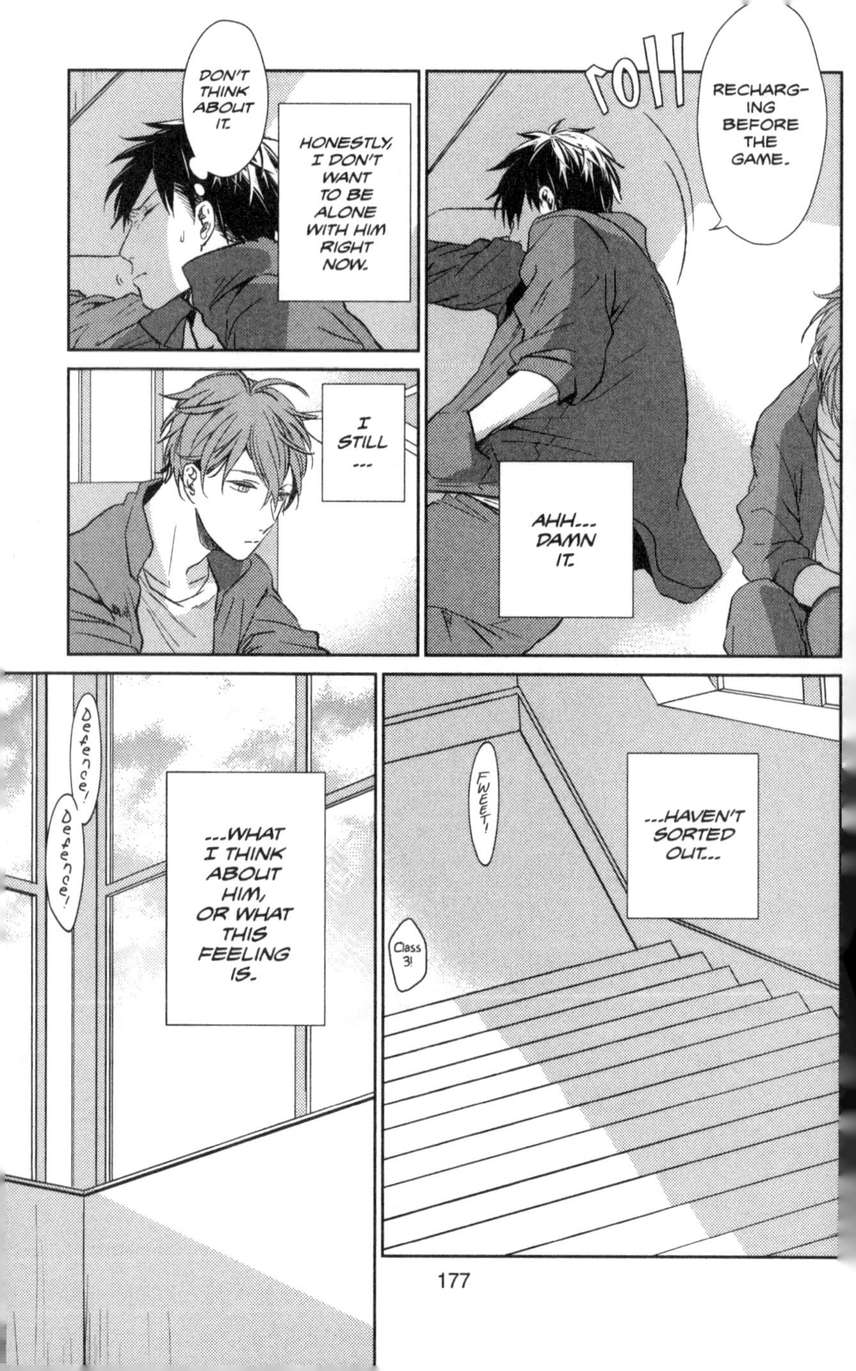
roll
RECHARGING BEFORE THE GAME.
AHH... DAMN IT.
DON'T THINK ABOUT IT.
HONESTLY, I DON'T WANT TO BE ALONE WITH HIM RIGHT NOW.
I STILL...
...HAVEN'T SORTED OUT...
FWEET!
Class 3!
...WHAT I THINK ABOUT HIM, OR WHAT THIS FEELING IS.
Defence!
Defence!

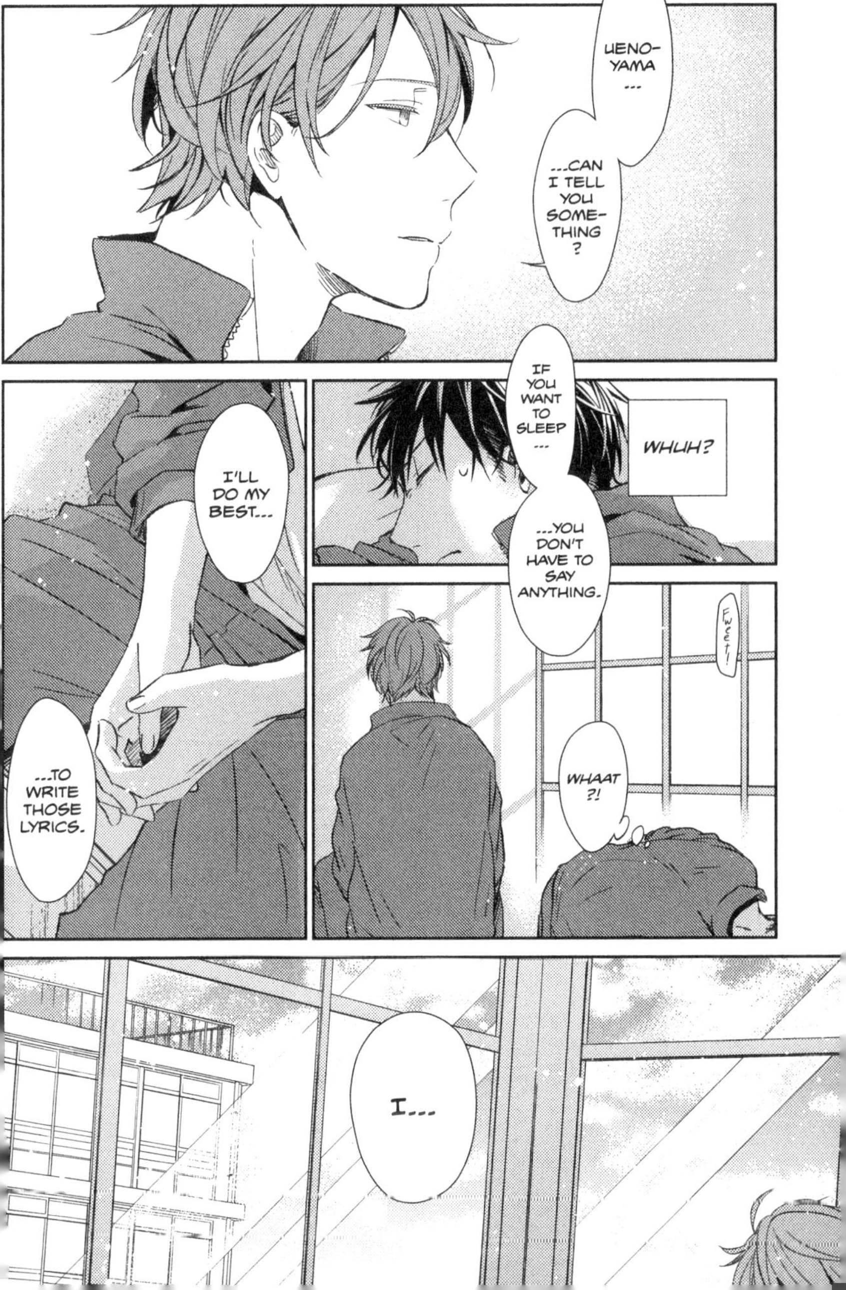
UENO-YAMA ...
...CAN I TELL YOU SOME-THING?
WHUH?
IF YOU WANT TO SLEEP...
...YOU DON'T HAVE TO SAY ANYTHING.
Fweet!
WHAAT?!
I'LL DO MY BEST...
...TO WRITE THOSE LYRICS.
I...

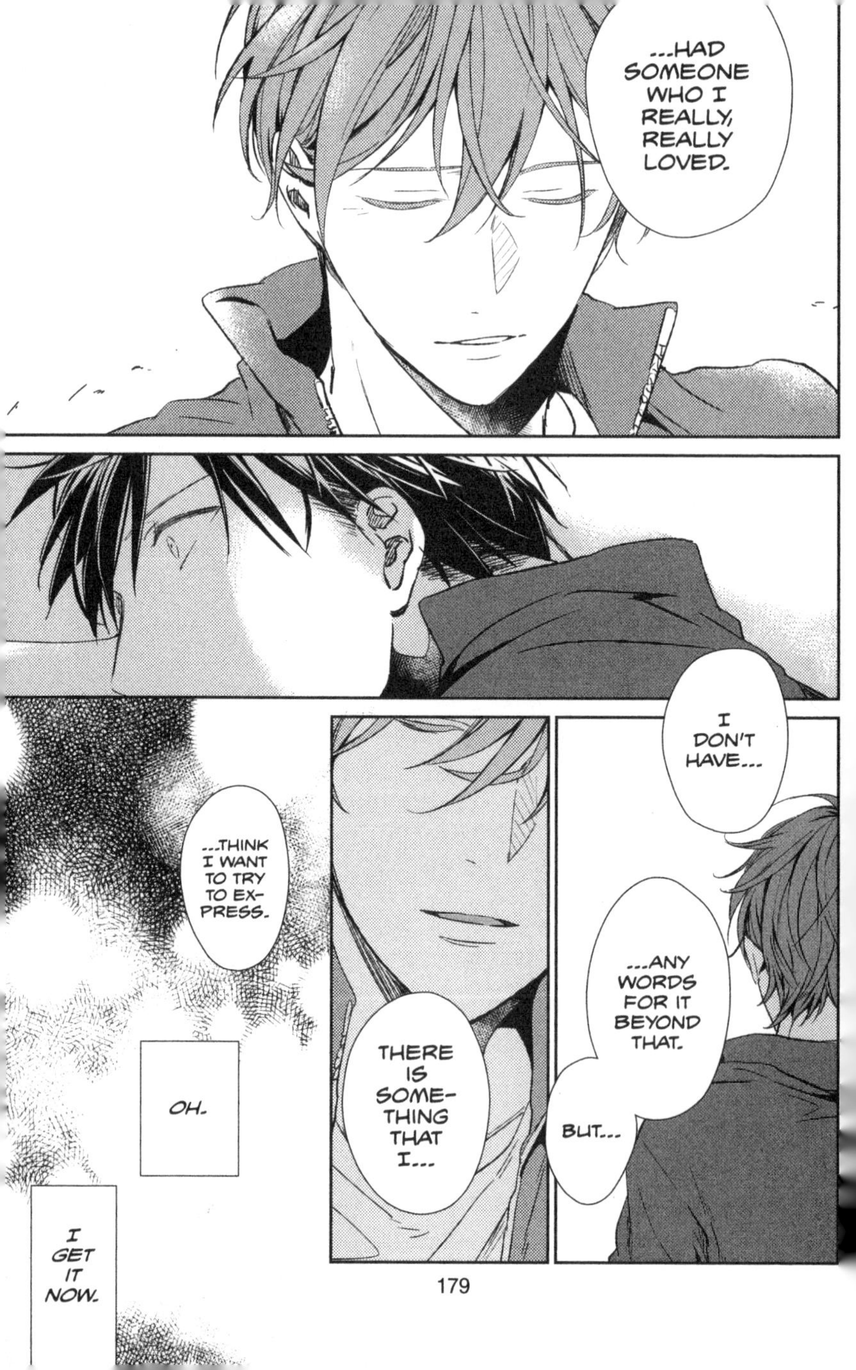
...HAD SOMEONE WHO I REALLY, REALLY LOVED.
I DON'T HAVE...
...ANY WORDS FOR IT BEYOND THAT.
BUT...
THERE IS SOME-THING THAT I...
...THINK I WANT TO TRY TO EX-PRESS.
OH.
I GET IT NOW.

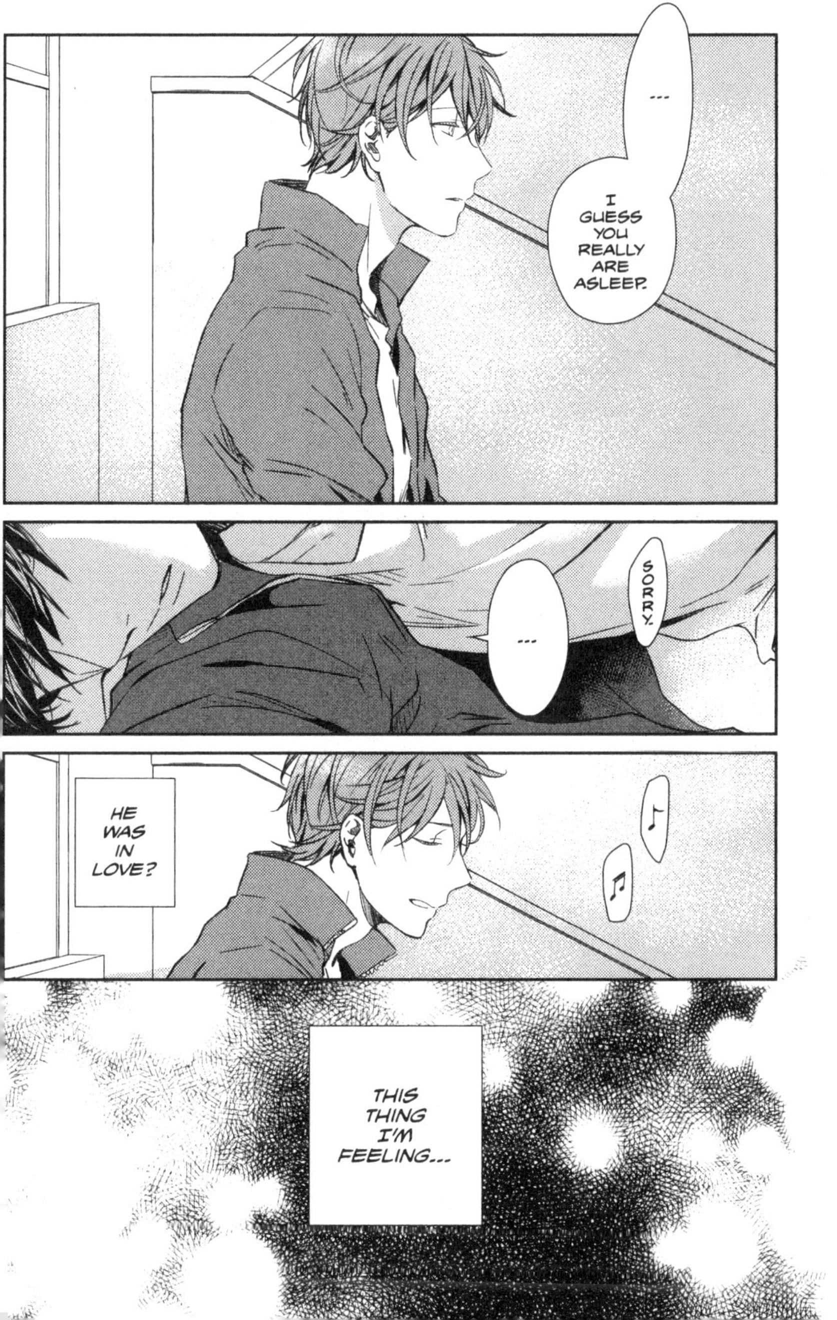
...
I GUESS YOU REALLY ARE ASLEEP.
SORRY.
...
♪
♫
HE WAS IN LOVE?
THIS THING I'M FEELING...

THIS IS
JEALOUSY.

To Be Continued...

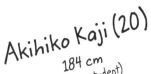

Akihiko Kaji (20)

184 cm
(College student)

Birthday: 10/21 Sign: Libra Blood Type: A

Drums → His current band isn't that tight, but he loves drumming hard regardless.
(His previous band was a pretty intense heavy metal group.)

Headphones are Beats, but earphones are Bose.

Favorite Music:
Heavy rock, metal, melodic hardcore, emo, screamo, alternative, trip hop, and similar genres
All the way up to:
All types of classical music, plus contemporary, ambient, experimental, and other instrumental genres

He's been practicing karate and violin since he was a kid.
He's majoring in music.

Family: Currently living with a roommate.
Father is in England.
Mother is living happily with her own family.

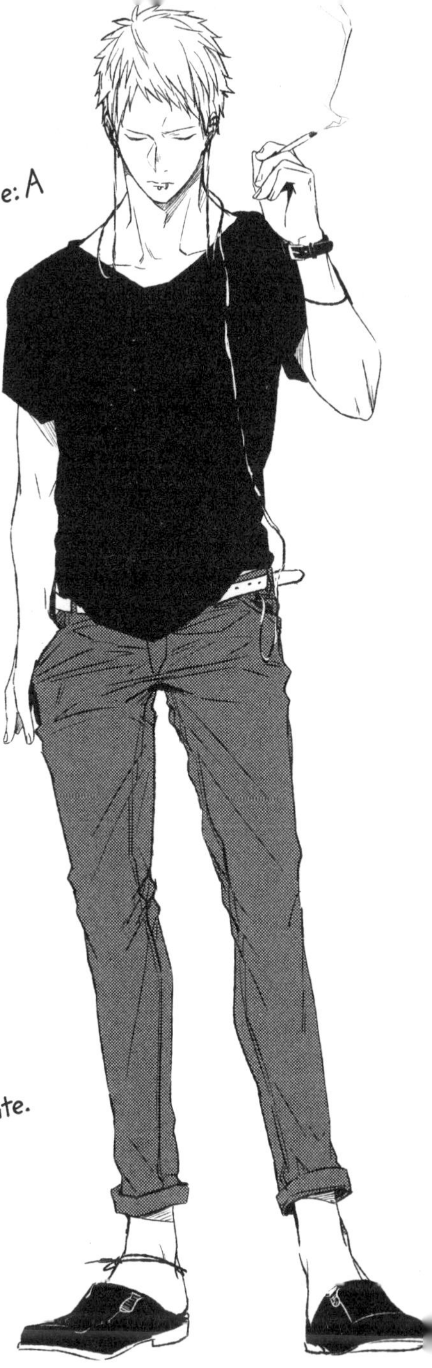

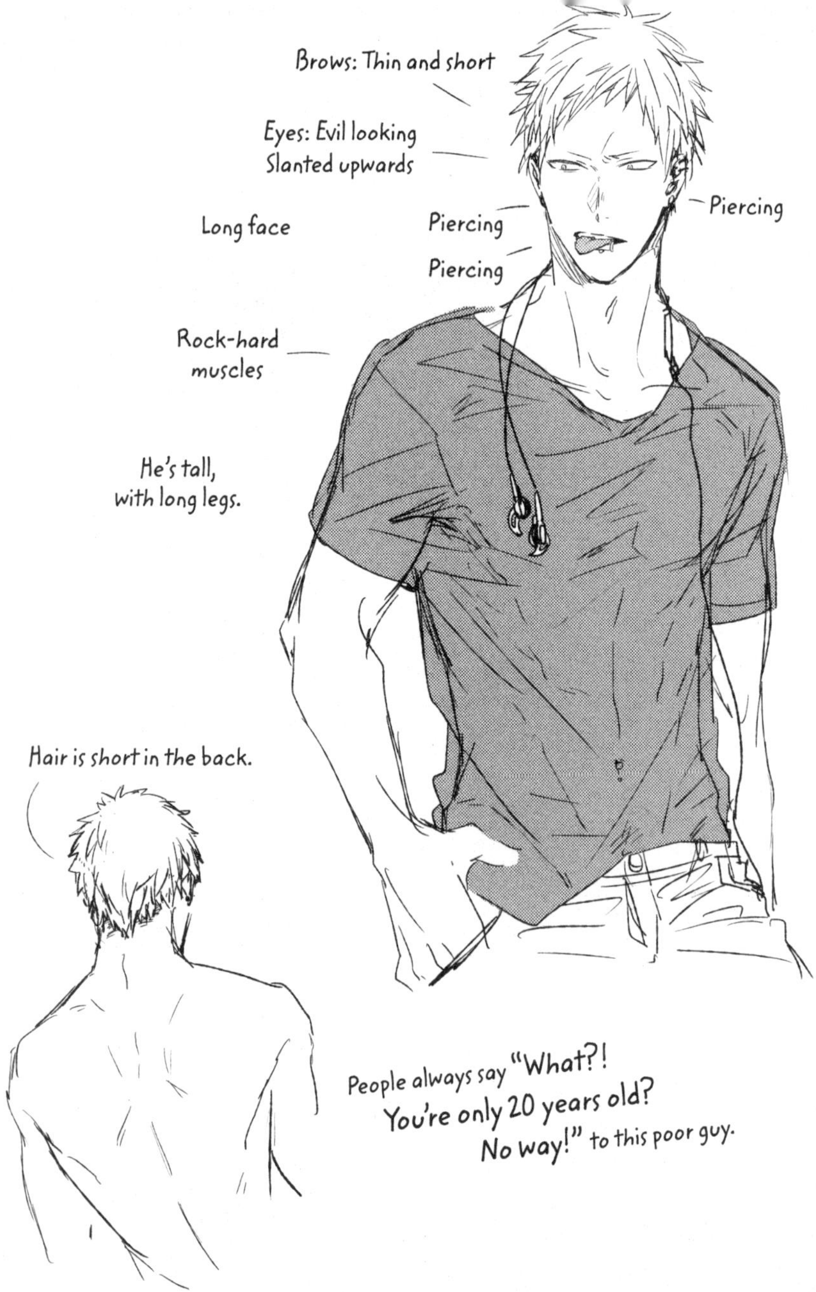
Brows: Thin and short
Eyes: Evil looking
Slanted upwards
Long face
Piercing
Piercing
Piercing
Rock-hard
muscles
He's tall,
with long legs.
Hair is short in the back.
People always say "What?!
You're only 20 years old?
No way!" to this poor guy.

given

by Natsuki Kizu

Part-time Job 1

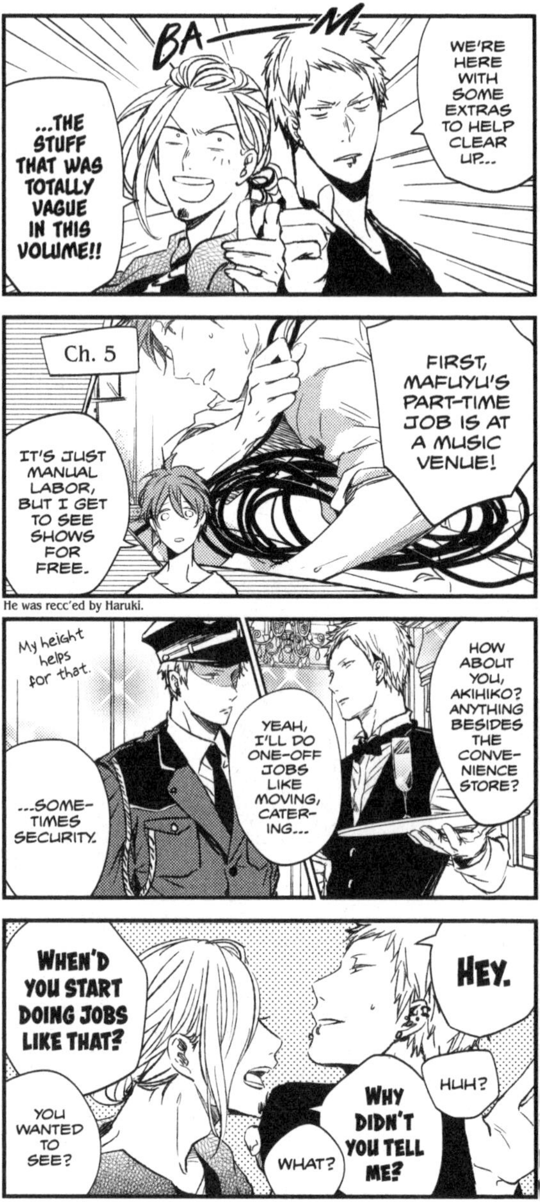
BA—M
WE'RE HERE WITH SOME EXTRAS TO HELP CLEAR UP...
...THE STUFF THAT WAS TOTALLY VAGUE IN THIS VOLUME!!
FIRST, MAFUYU'S PART-TIME JOB IS AT A MUSIC VENUE!
Ch. 5
IT'S JUST MANUAL LABOR, BUT I GET TO SEE SHOWS FOR FREE.
He was recc'ed by Haruki.
HOW ABOUT YOU, AKIHIKO? ANYTHING BESIDES THE CONVENIENCE STORE?
YEAH, I'LL DO ONE-OFF JOBS LIKE MOVING, CATERING...
...SOMETIMES SECURITY.
My height helps for that.
HEY.
WHEN'D YOU START DOING JOBS LIKE THAT?
HUH?
WHY DIDN'T YOU TELL ME?
WHAT?
YOU WANTED TO SEE?

(Would have given his life to see.)

Part-time Job 2

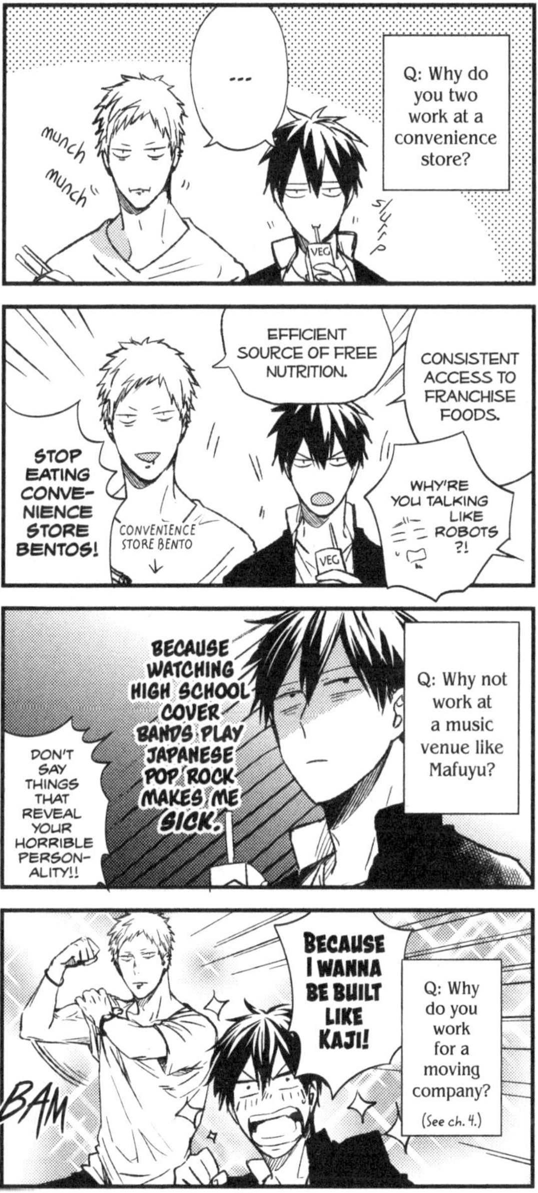

Q: Why do you two work at a convenience store?
...
munch munch
slurrp
VEG
CONSISTENT ACCESS TO FRANCHISE FOODS.
EFFICIENT SOURCE OF FREE NUTRITION.
WHY'RE YOU TALKING LIKE ROBOTS ?!
VEG
CONVENIENCE STORE BENTO
STOP EATING CONVE-NIENCE STORE BENTOS!
Q: Why not work at a music venue like Mafuyu?
BECAUSE WATCHING HIGH SCHOOL COVER BANDS PLAY JAPANESE POP ROCK MAKES ME SICK.
DON'T SAY THINGS THAT REVEAL YOUR HORRIBLE PERSON-ALITY!!
Q: Why do you work for a moving company?
(See ch. 4.)
BECAUSE I WANNA BE BUILT LIKE KAJI!
BAM

Haruki: "Uecchi, do you want rock-hard muscles too?"

Music and Friendship

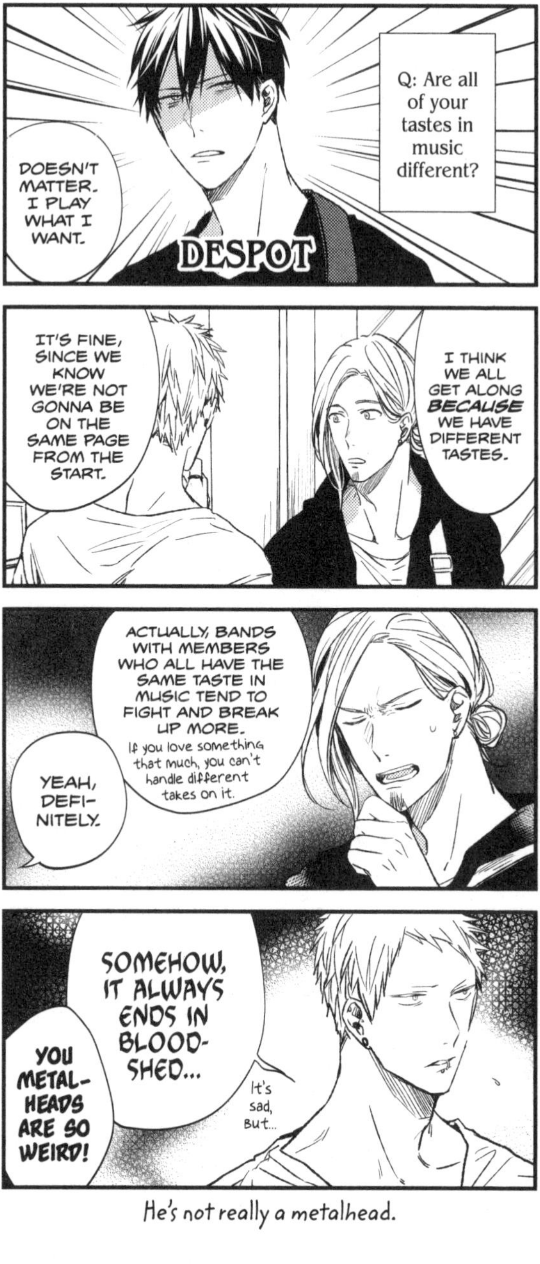
Q: Are all of your tastes in music different?
DOESN'T MATTER. I PLAY WHAT I WANT.
DESPOT
I THINK WE ALL GET ALONG *BECAUSE* WE HAVE DIFFERENT TASTES.
IT'S FINE, SINCE WE KNOW WE'RE NOT GONNA BE ON THE SAME PAGE FROM THE START.
ACTUALLY, BANDS WITH MEMBERS WHO ALL HAVE THE SAME TASTE IN MUSIC TEND TO FIGHT AND BREAK UP MORE.
If you love something that much, you can't handle different takes on it.
YEAH, DEFI-NITELY.
SOMEHOW, IT ALWAYS ENDS IN BLOOD-SHED...
It's sad, But...
YOU METAL-HEADS ARE SO WEIRD!

He's not really a metalhead.

Questions for the Band

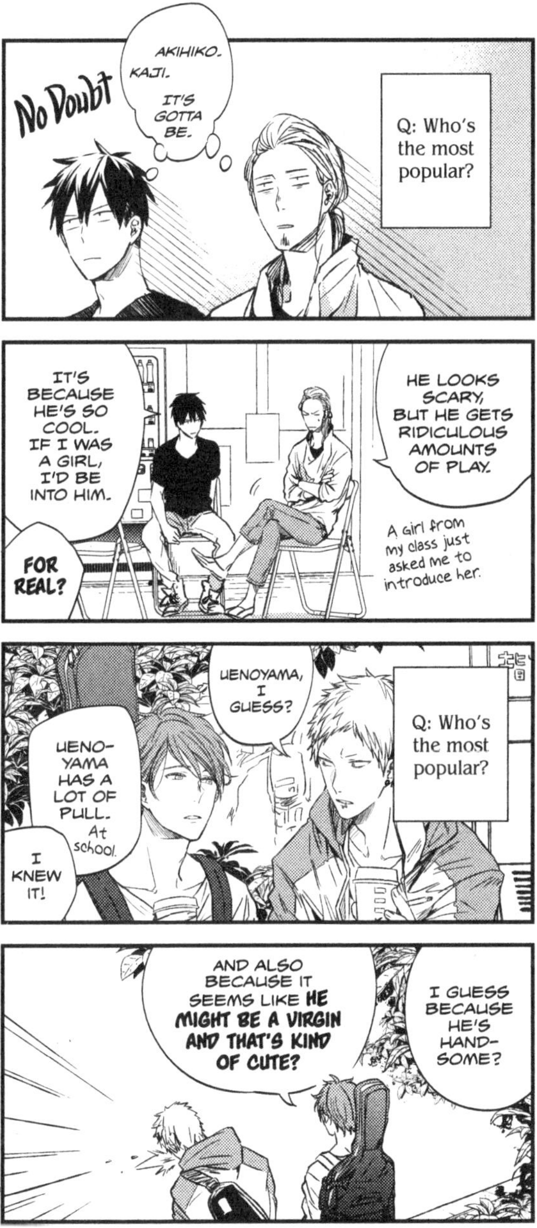

Q: Who's the most popular?
AKIHIKO. KAJI. IT'S GOTTA BE.
No Doubt
HE LOOKS SCARY, BUT HE GETS RIDICULOUS AMOUNTS OF PLAY.
A girl from my class just asked me to introduce her.
IT'S BECAUSE HE'S SO COOL. IF I WAS A GIRL, I'D BE INTO HIM.
FOR REAL?
Q: Who's the most popular?
UENOYAMA, I GUESS?
UENO-YAMA HAS A LOT OF PULL.
At school.
I KNEW IT!
I GUESS BECAUSE HE'S HAND-SOME?
AND ALSO BECAUSE IT SEEMS LIKE HE MIGHT BE A VIRGIN AND THAT'S KIND OF CUTE?

Immunity

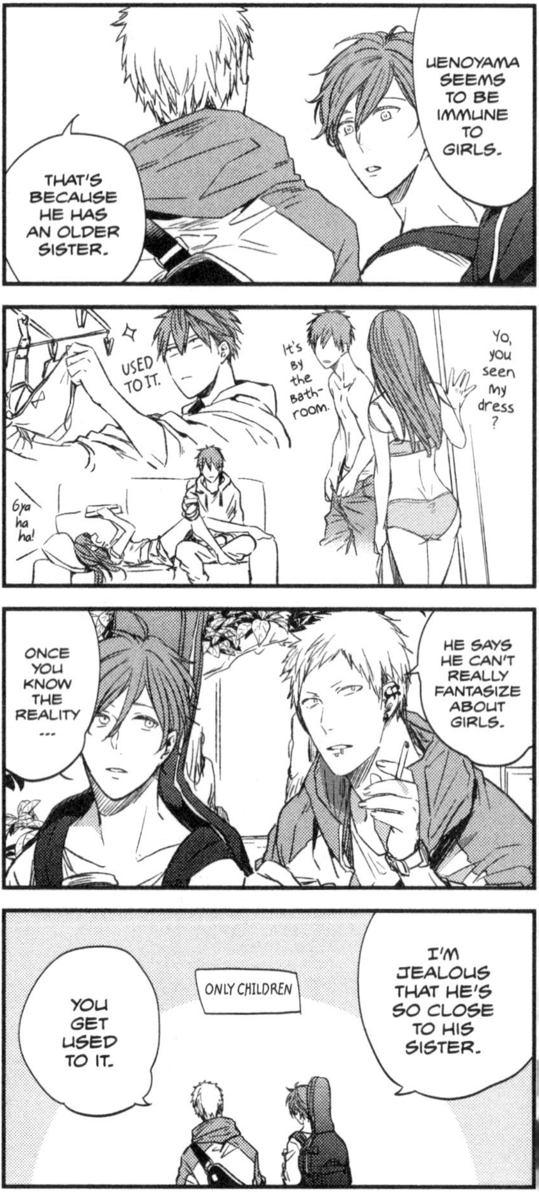
UENOYAMA SEEMS TO BE IMMUNE TO GIRLS.
THAT'S BECAUSE HE HAS AN OLDER SISTER.
Yo, you seen my dress?
It's by the bathroom.
USED TO IT.
Gya ha ha!
HE SAYS HE CAN'T REALLY FANTASIZE ABOUT GIRLS.
ONCE YOU KNOW THE REALITY...
I'M JEALOUS THAT HE'S SO CLOSE TO HIS SISTER.
ONLY CHILDREN
YOU GET USED TO IT.

"I want a little brother."

Little Brother Power

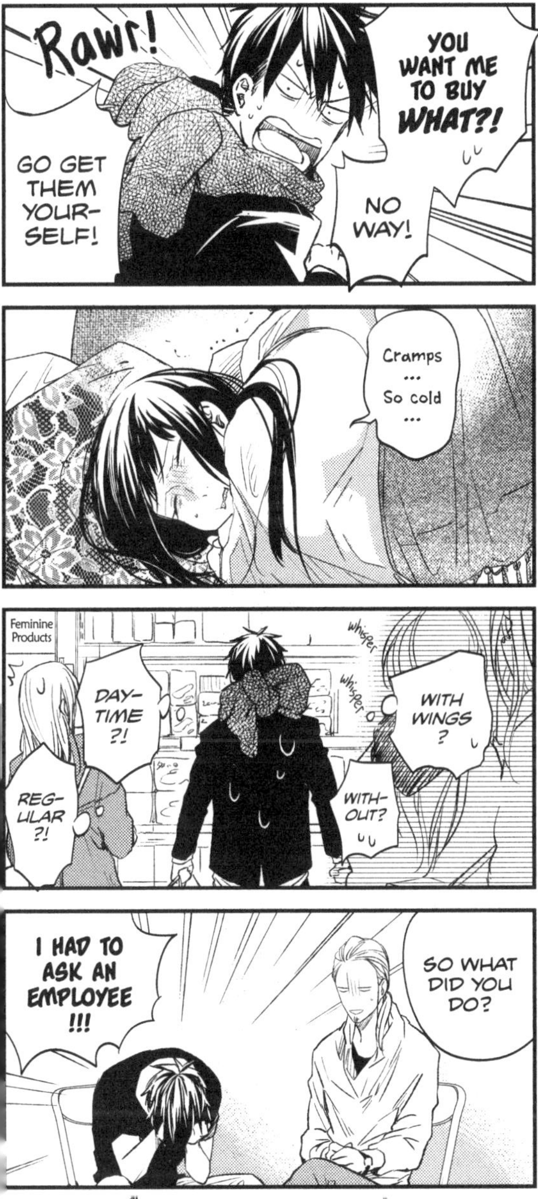

YOU WANT ME TO BUY WHAT?!
NO WAY!
Rawr!
GO GET THEM YOURSELF!
Cramps ... So cold ...
whisper
whisper
Feminine Products
WITH WINGS?
WITHOUT?
DAYTIME?!
REGULAR?!
SO WHAT DID YOU DO?
I HAD TO ASK AN EMPLOYEE!!!

Both have older sisters.

postscript

I was walking and thinking about all the things I've gained and all the things I've lost in order to finally get here. Thanks so much to all those involved.

2014

Supervising Editor & Assistance: Tamura-san (god), Daisuke (music advisor), H-kun (guitar advisor), Ayaka (research and support), the music venues (on-site research)

Special Thanks: Eiri Hayashi, Kitaura, Rin

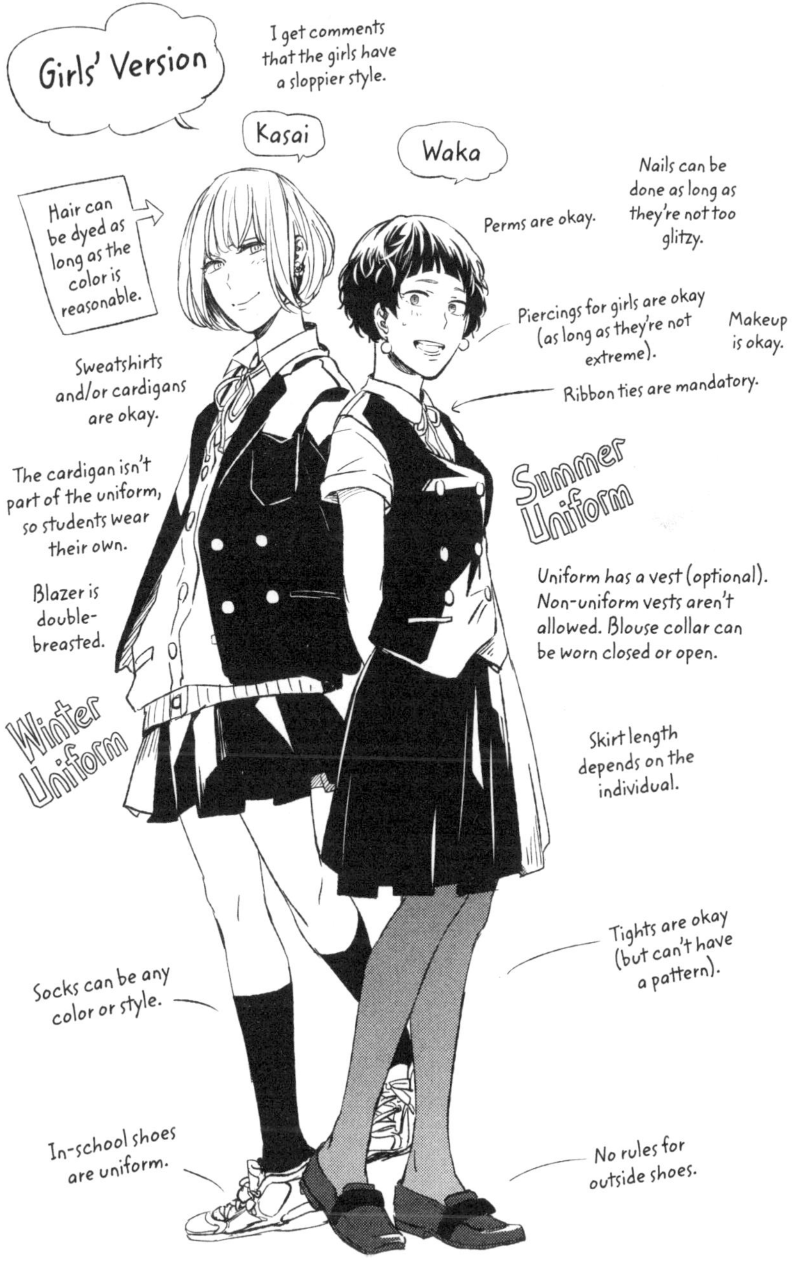
Girls' Version
I get comments that the girls have a sloppier style.
Kasai
Waka
Hair can be dyed as long as the color is reasonable.
Perms are okay.
Nails can be done as long as they're not too glitzy.
Piercings for girls are okay (as long as they're not extreme).
Makeup is okay.
Sweatshirts and/or cardigans are okay.
Ribbon ties are mandatory.
The cardigan isn't part of the uniform, so students wear their own.
Summer Uniform
Blazer is double-breasted.
Uniform has a vest (optional). Non-uniform vests aren't allowed. Blouse collar can be worn closed or open.
Winter Uniform
Skirt length depends on the individual.
Tights are okay (but can't have a pattern).
Socks can be any color or style.
In-school shoes are uniform.
No rules for outside shoes.

Extras

About Uenoyama and Mafuyu's High School

Boys' Version

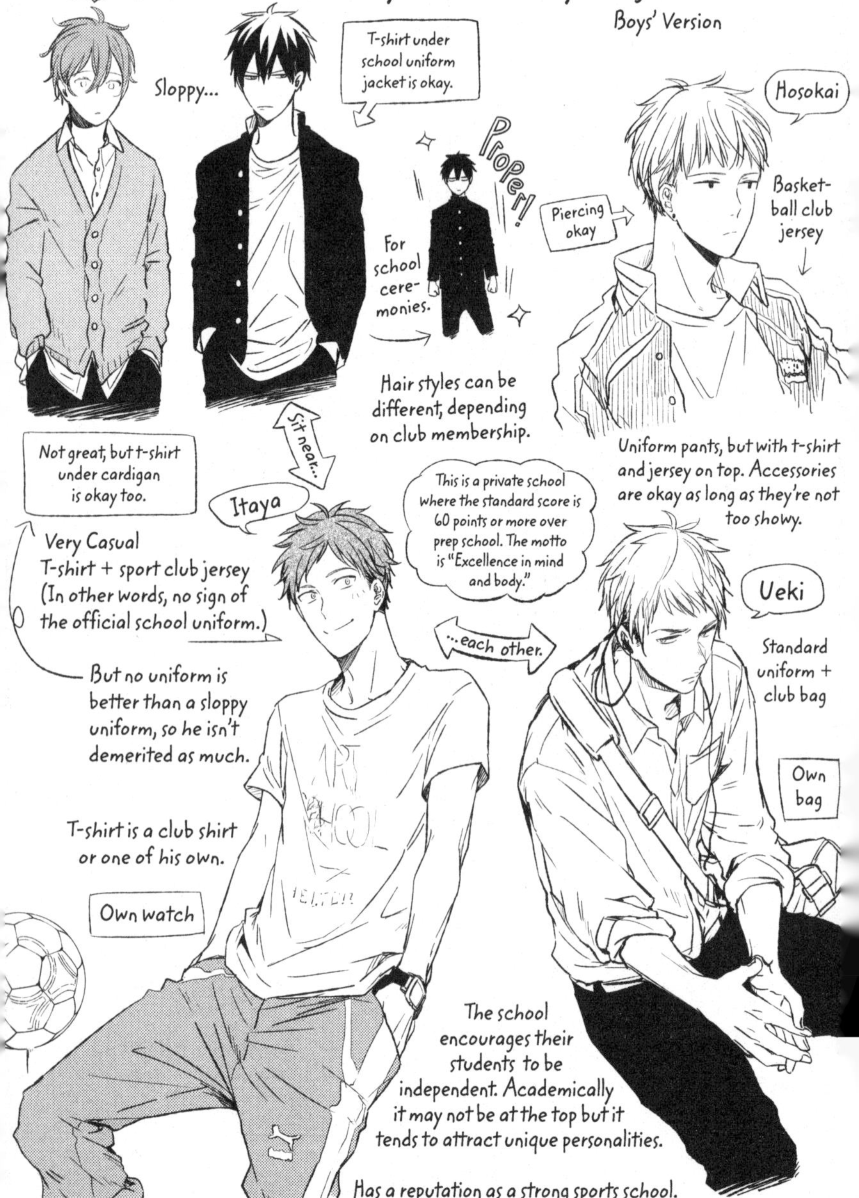
Sloppy...
T-shirt under school uniform jacket is okay.
Proper!
For school cere-monies.
Hosokai
Basket-ball club jersey
Piercing okay
Hair styles can be different, depending on club membership.
Sit near...
Not great, but t-shirt under cardigan is okay too.
Uniform pants, but with t-shirt and jersey on top. Accessories are okay as long as they're not too showy.
Itaya
This is a private school where the standard score is 60 points or more over prep school. The motto is "Excellence in mind and body."
Very Casual
T-shirt + sport club jersey
(In other words, no sign of the official school uniform.)
Ueki
...each other.
Standard uniform + club bag
But no uniform is better than a sloppy uniform, so he isn't demerited as much.
Own bag
T-shirt is a club shirt or one of his own.
Own watch
The school encourages their students to be independent. Academically it may not be at the top but it tends to attract unique personalities.
Has a reputation as a strong sports school. Some of the clubs are nationally ranked.

chapter 6

given

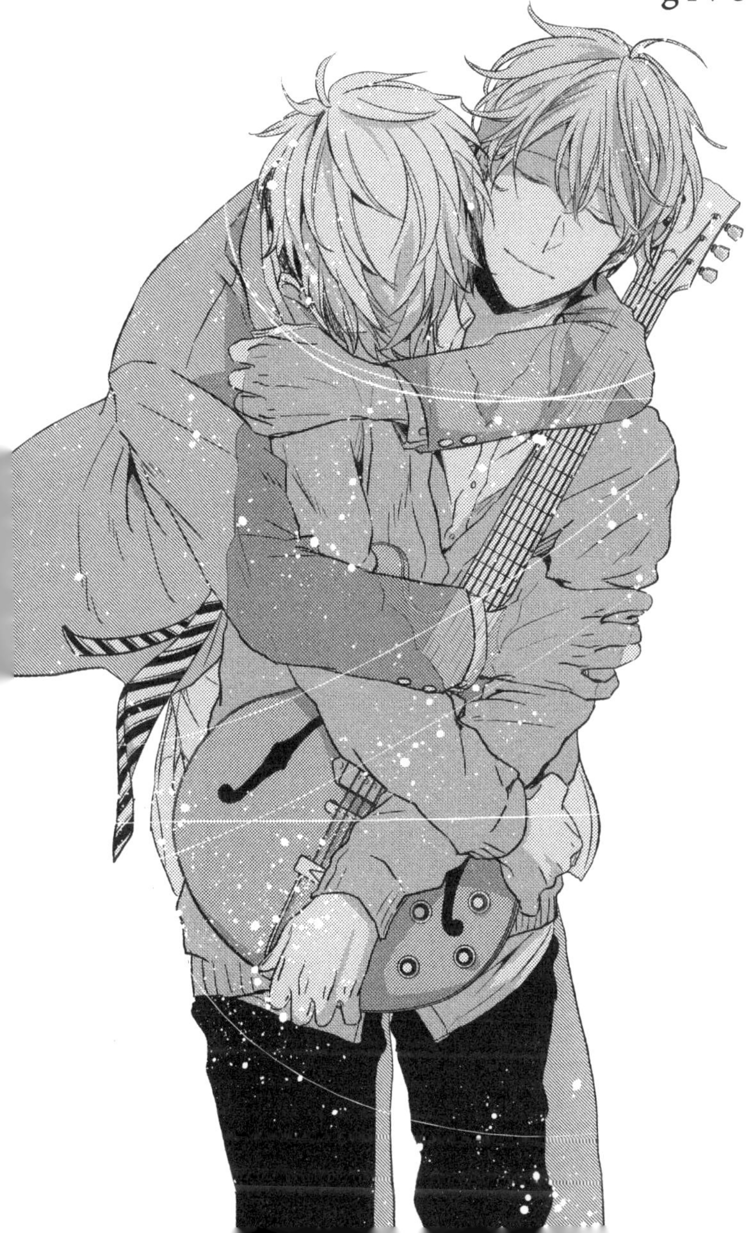

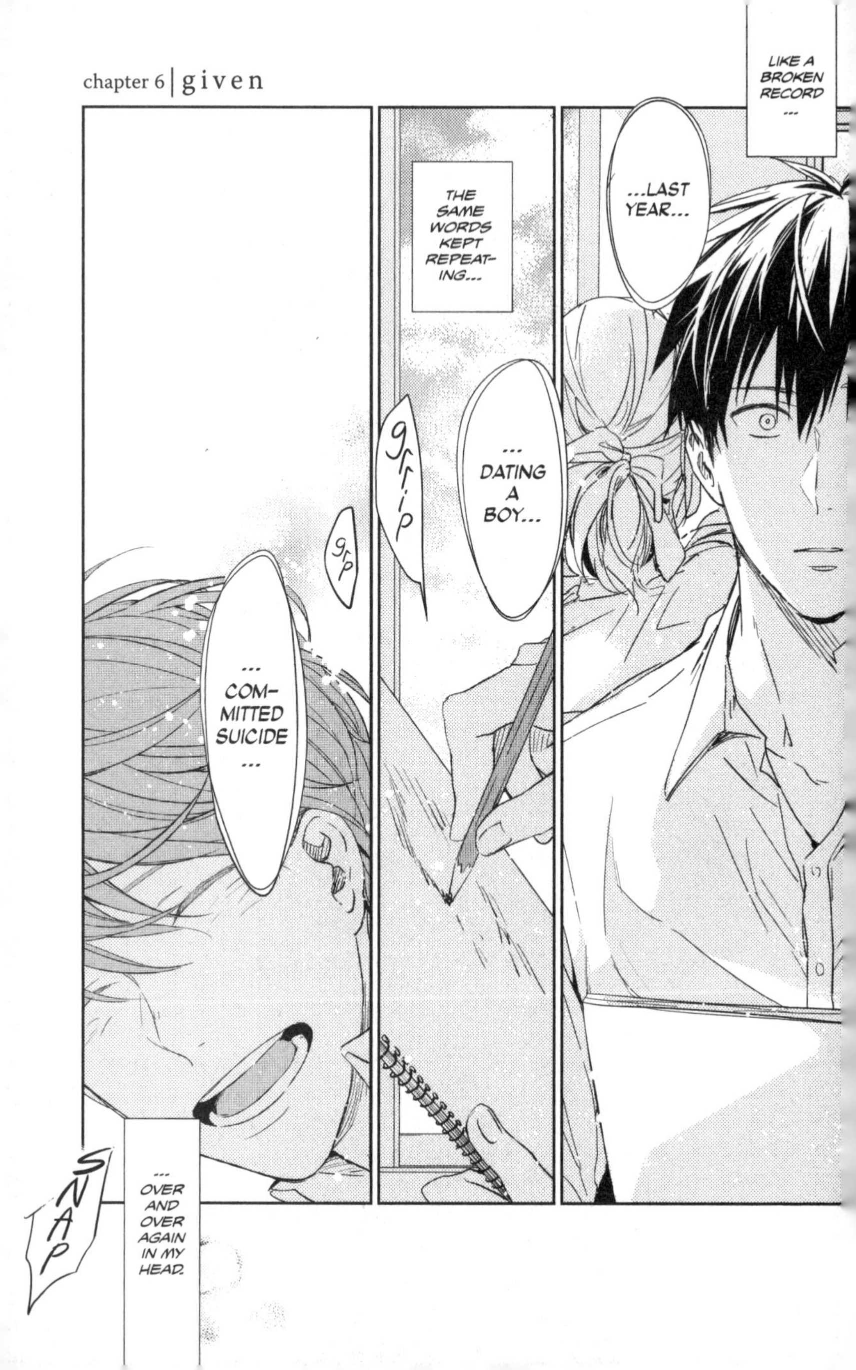
LIKE A BROKEN RECORD ...
...LAST YEAR...
THE SAME WORDS KEPT REPEAT-ING...
...DATING A BOY...
grrip
grp
...COM-MITTED SUICIDE...
SNAP
...OVER AND OVER AGAIN IN MY HEAD.

given

by Natsuki Kizu

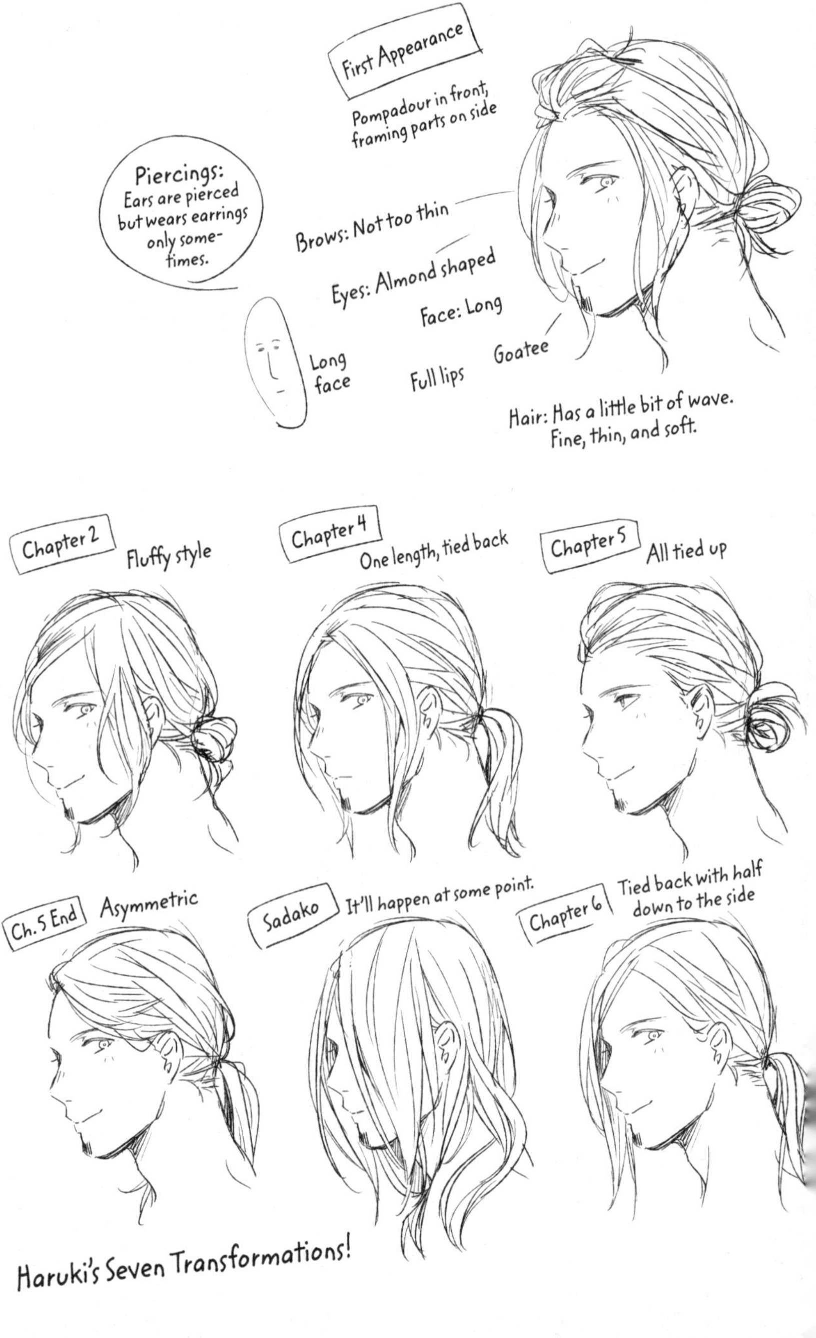
First Appearance
Pompadour in front, framing parts on side
Piercings: Ears are pierced but wears earrings only sometimes.
Brows: Not too thin
Eyes: Almond shaped
Face: Long
Long face
Full lips
Goatee
Hair: Has a little bit of wave. Fine, thin, and soft.
Chapter 2
Fluffy style
Chapter 4
One length, tied back
Chapter 5
All tied up
Ch. 5 End
Asymmetric
Sadako
It'll happen at some point.
Chapter 6
Tied back with half down to the side
Haruki's Seven Transformations!

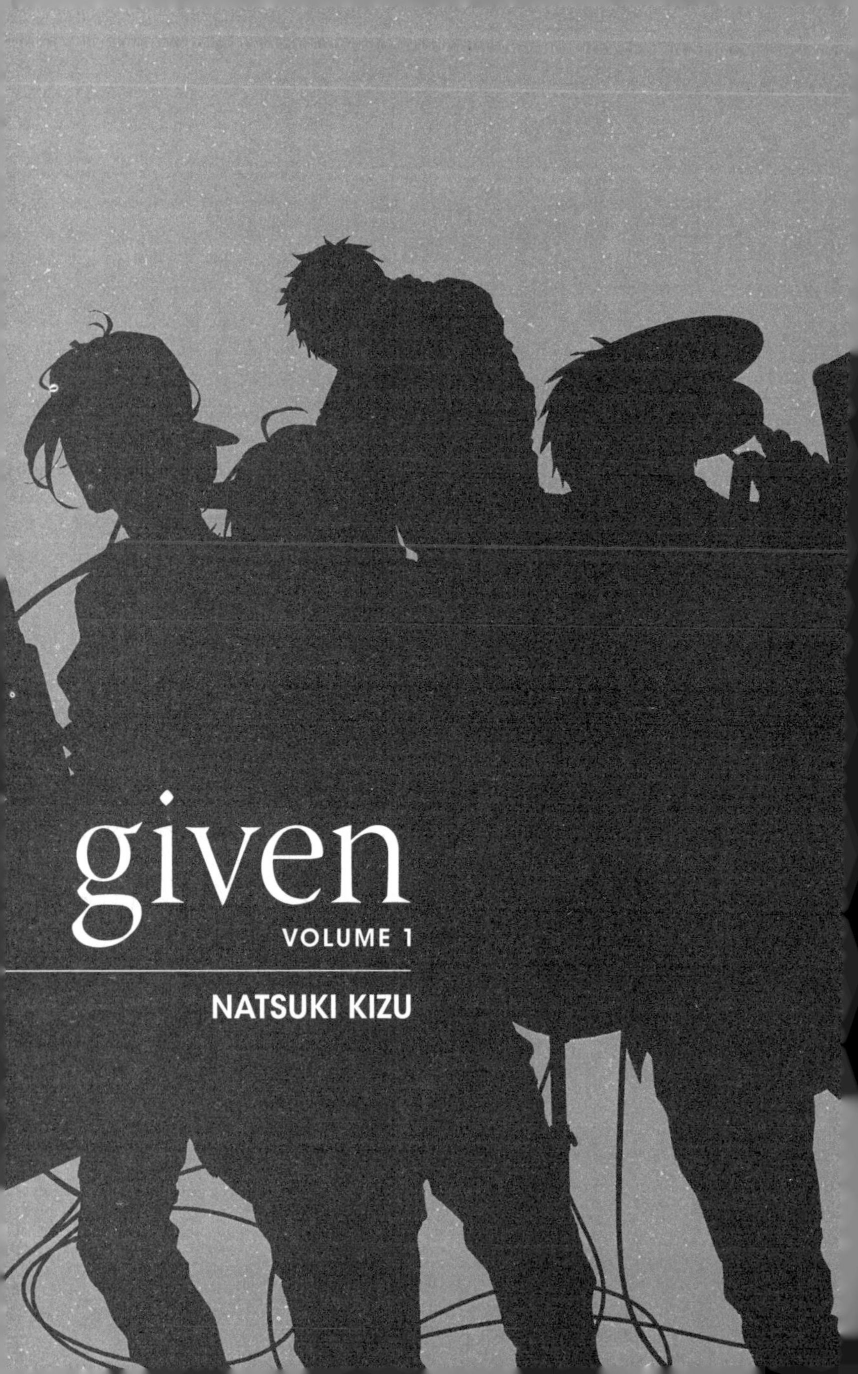
given
VOLUME 1
NATSUKI KIZU

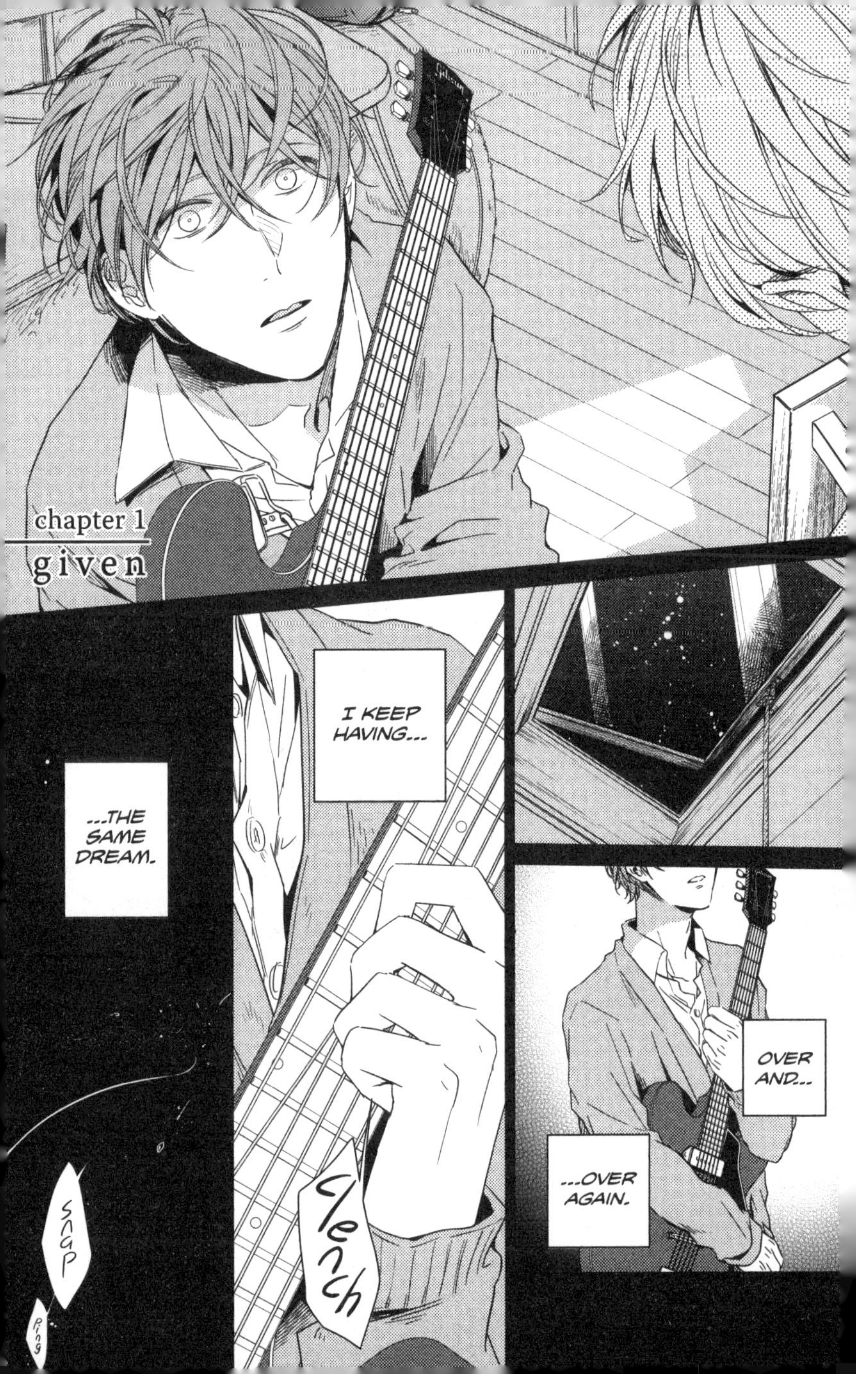
chapter 1
given
OVER AND...
...OVER AGAIN.
I KEEP HAVING...
Clench
...THE SAME DREAM.
SNAP
Ping

given

chapter 1

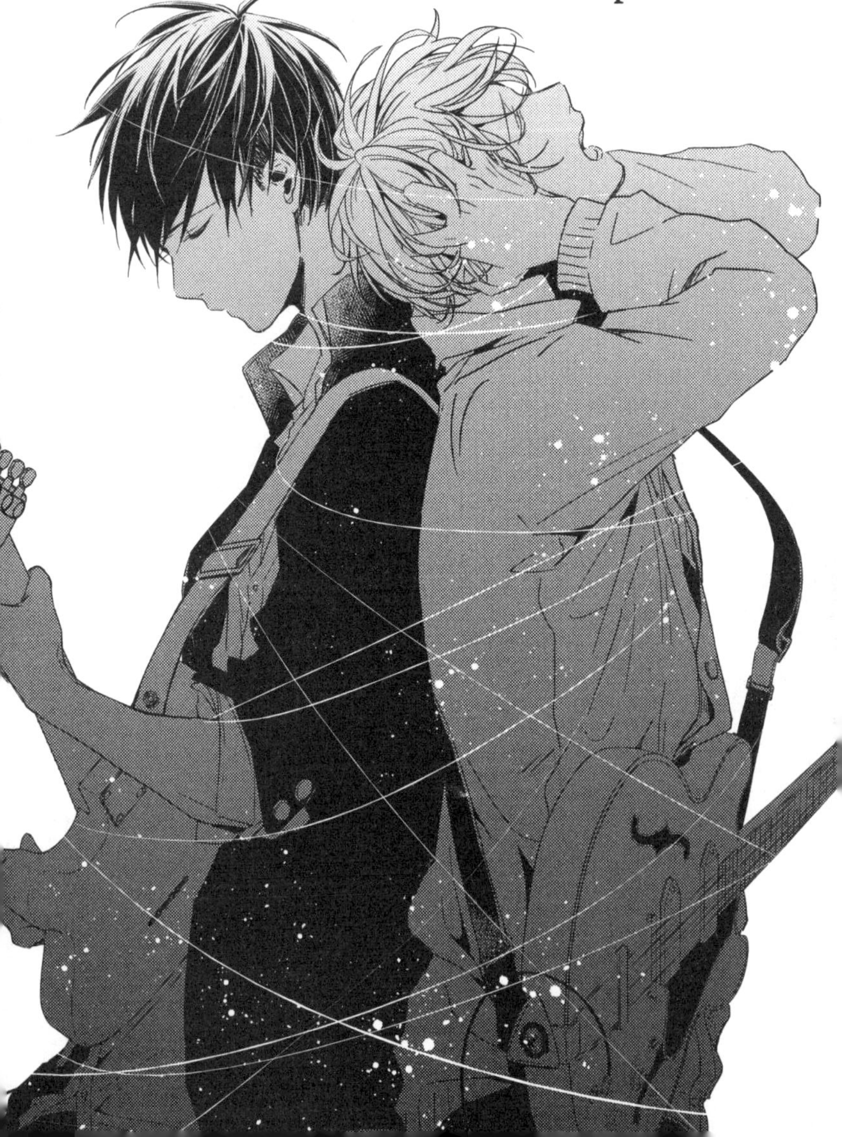

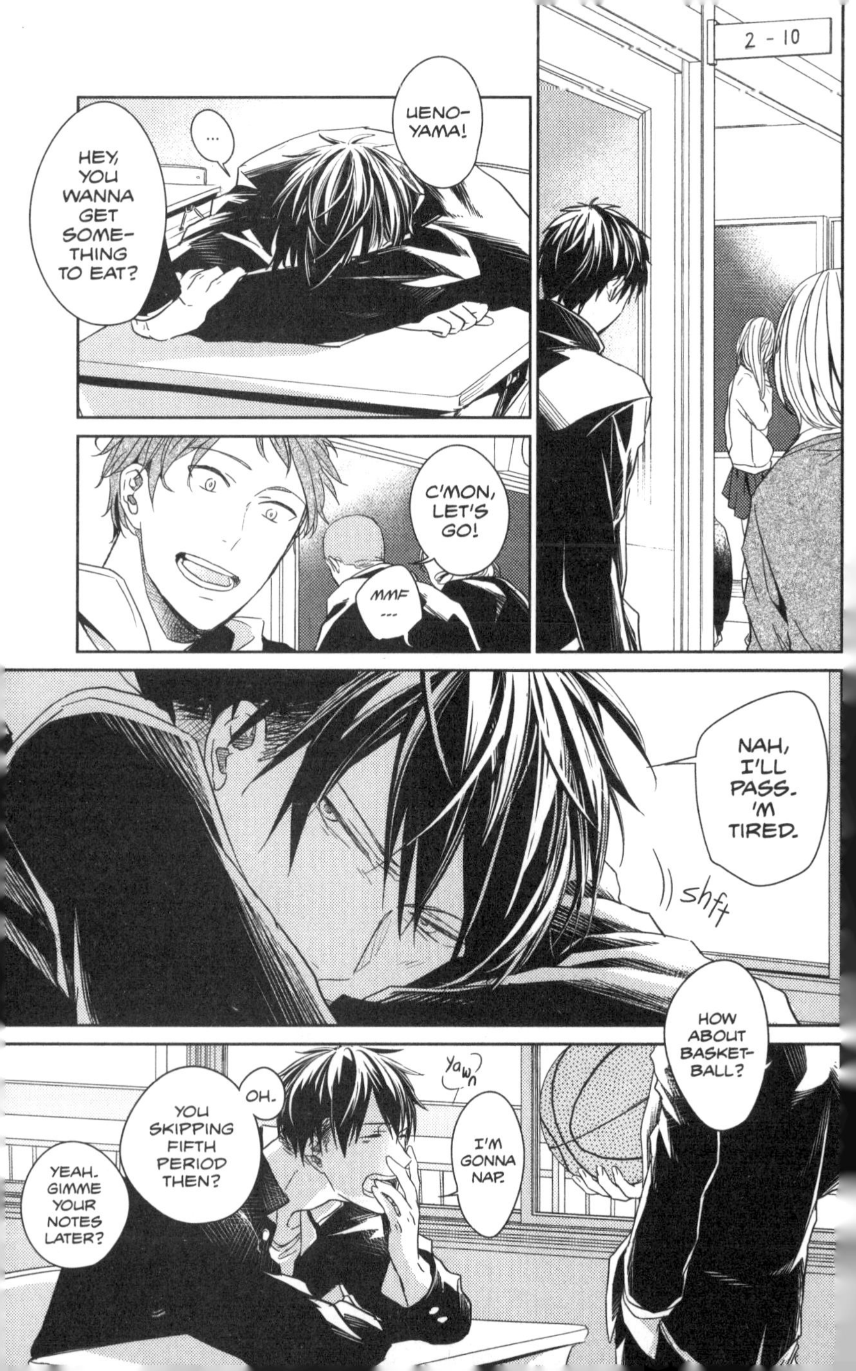
2 - 10
UENO-YAMA!
...
HEY, YOU WANNA GET SOME-THING TO EAT?
C'MON, LET'S GO!
MMF ...
NAH, I'LL PASS. 'M TIRED.
shft
HOW ABOUT BASKET-BALL?
I'M GONNA NAP.
Yawn
OH.
YOU SKIPPING FIFTH PERIOD THEN?
YEAH. GIMME YOUR NOTES LATER?

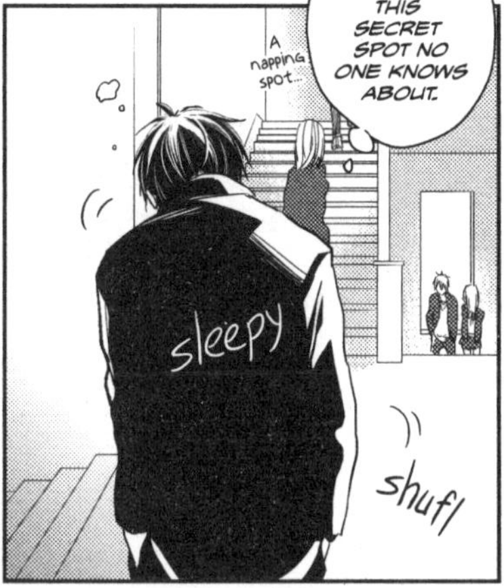
RECENTLY I FOUND THIS SECRET SPOT NO ONE KNOWS ABOUT.
A napping spot...
sleepy
shufl
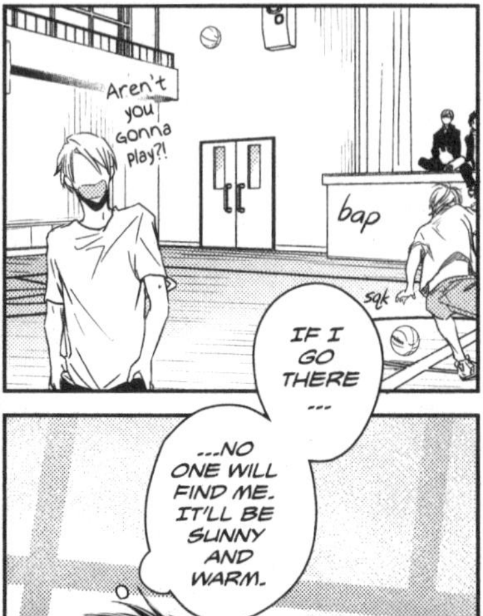
Aren't you gonna play?!
bap
sqk
IF I GO THERE ...
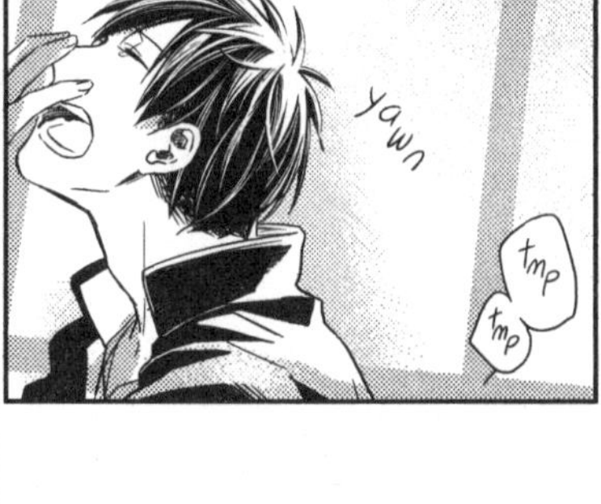
...NO ONE WILL FIND ME. IT'LL BE SUNNY AND WARM.
yawn
tmp
tmp
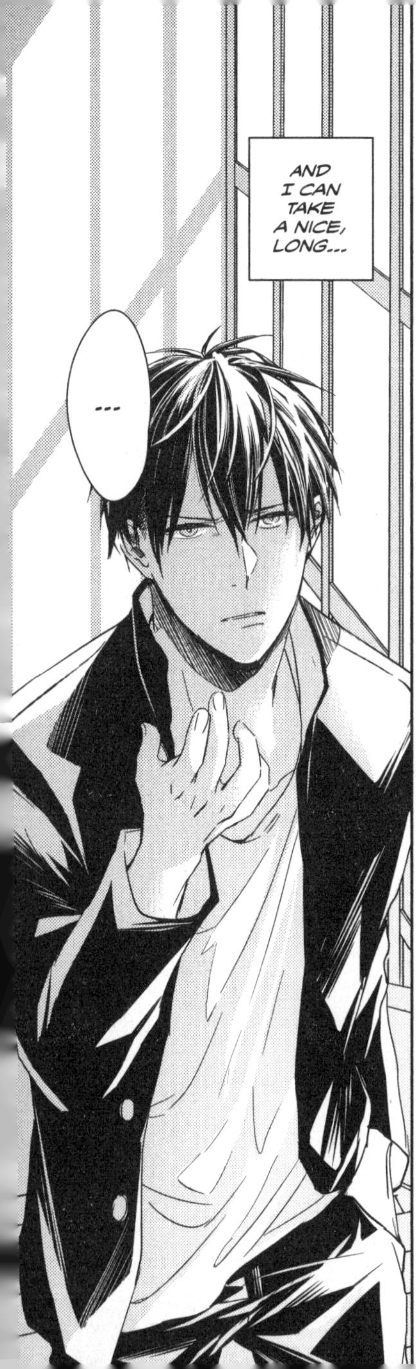
AND I CAN TAKE A NICE, LONG...
...

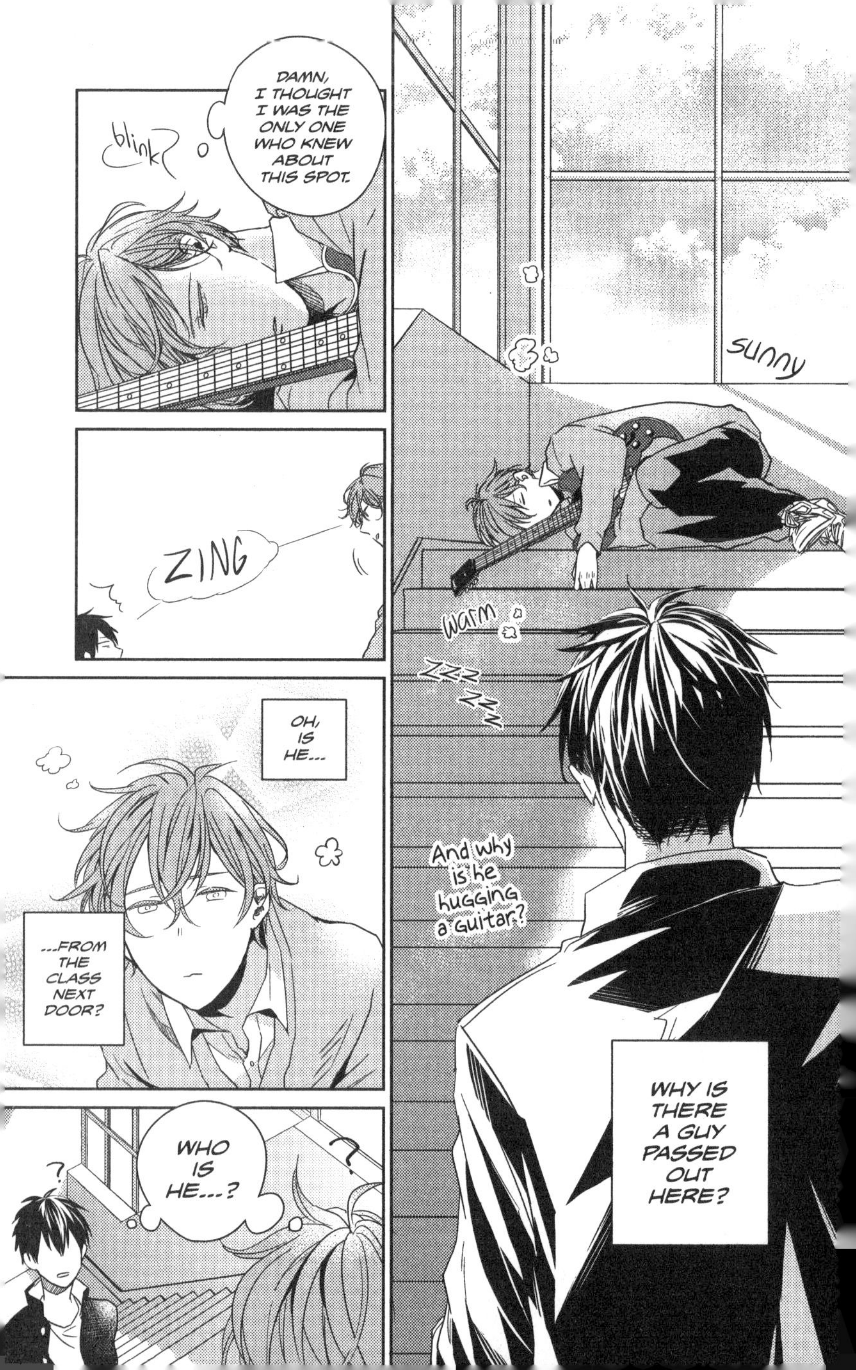
sunny
warm
ZZZ ZZZ
And why is he hugging a guitar?
WHY IS THERE A GUY PASSED OUT HERE?
DAMN, I THOUGHT I WAS THE ONLY ONE WHO KNEW ABOUT THIS SPOT.
blink
ZING
OH, IS HE...
...FROM THE CLASS NEXT DOOR?
WHO IS HE...?

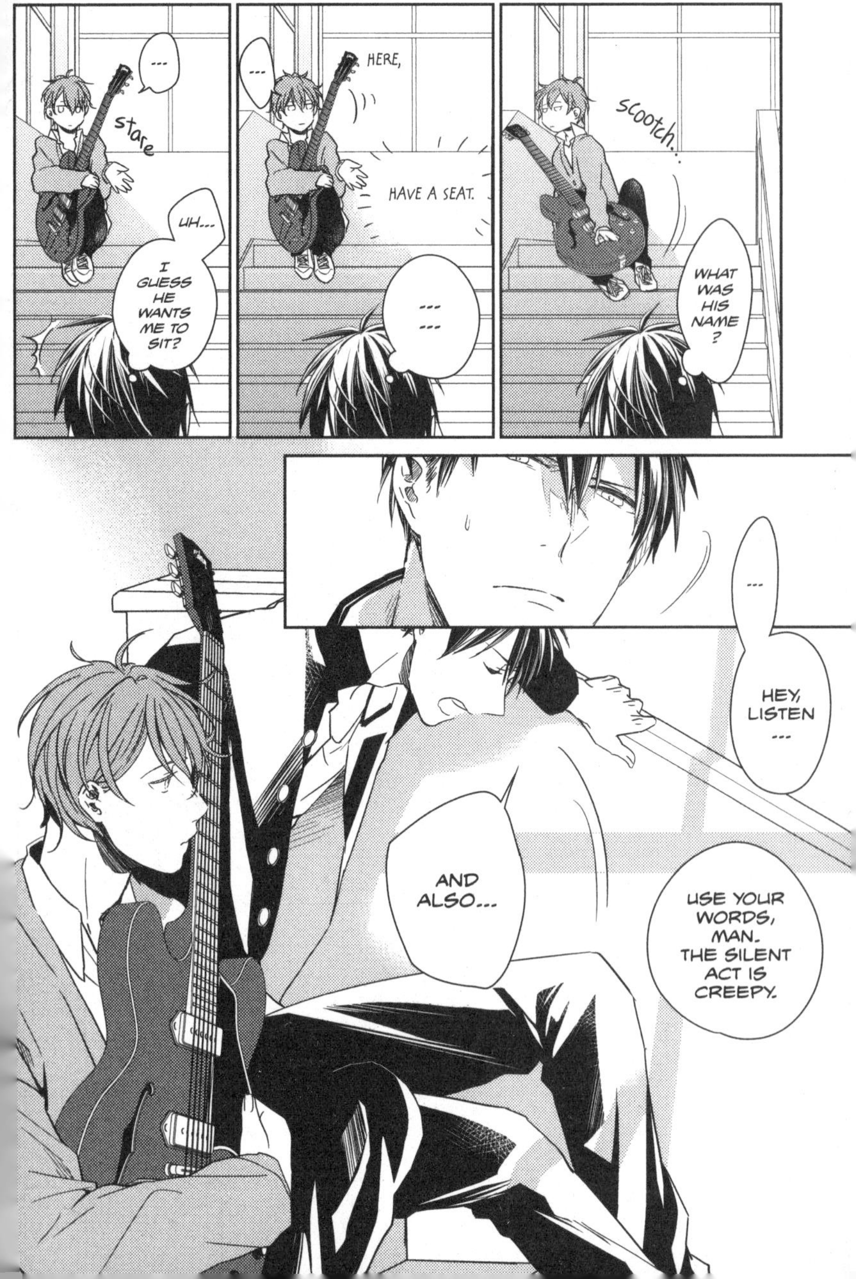
...
stare
UH...
I GUESS HE WANTS ME TO SIT?
...
HERE,
HAVE A SEAT.
...
...
scootch...
WHAT WAS HIS NAME?
...
HEY, LISTEN...
AND ALSO...
USE YOUR WORDS, MAN. THE SILENT ACT IS CREEPY.

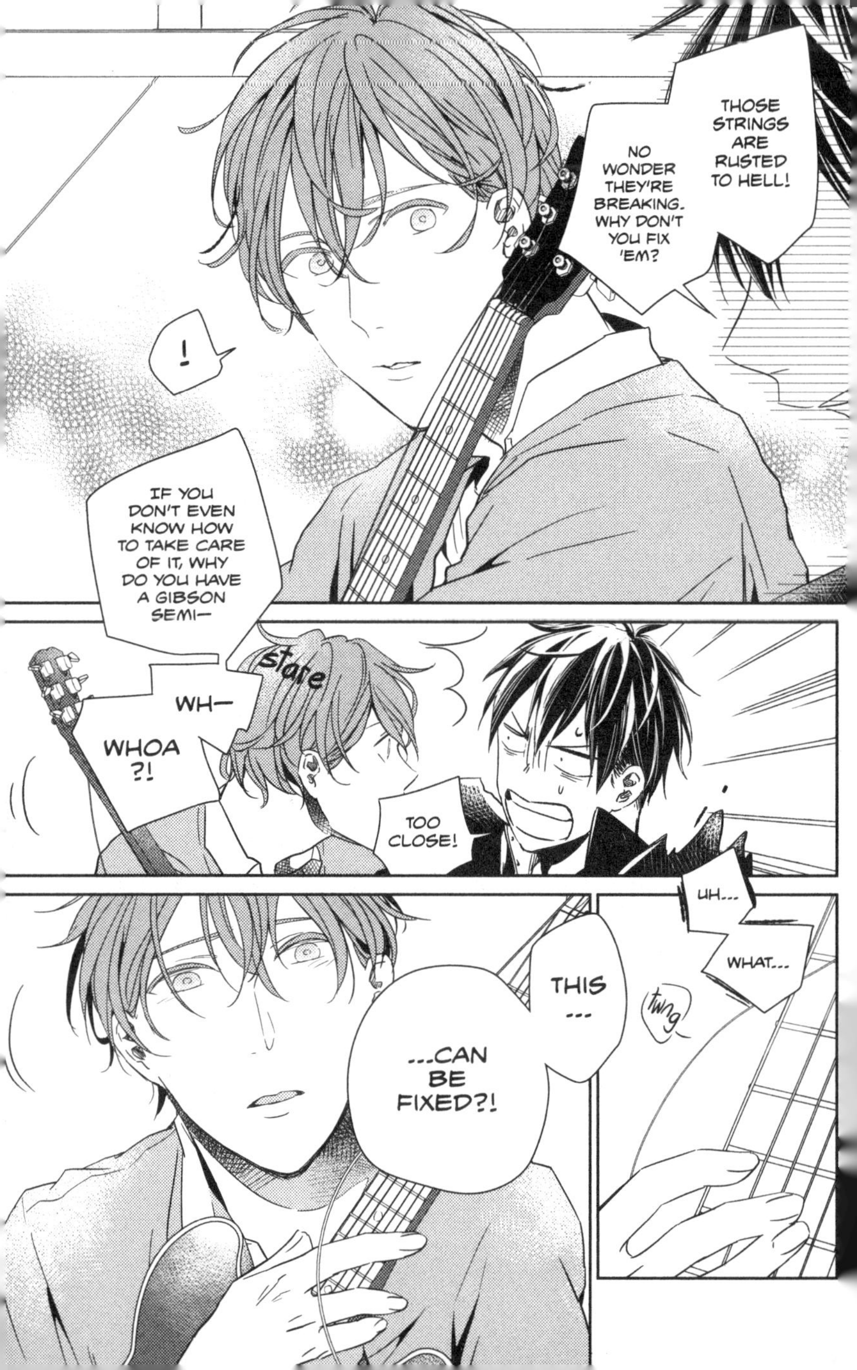
THOSE STRINGS ARE RUSTED TO HELL!
NO WONDER THEY'RE BREAKING. WHY DON'T YOU FIX 'EM?
!
IF YOU DON'T EVEN KNOW HOW TO TAKE CARE OF IT, WHY DO YOU HAVE A GIBSON SEMI—
stare
TOO CLOSE!
WH— WHOA ?!
UH...
WHAT...
twng
THIS ...
...CAN BE FIXED?!

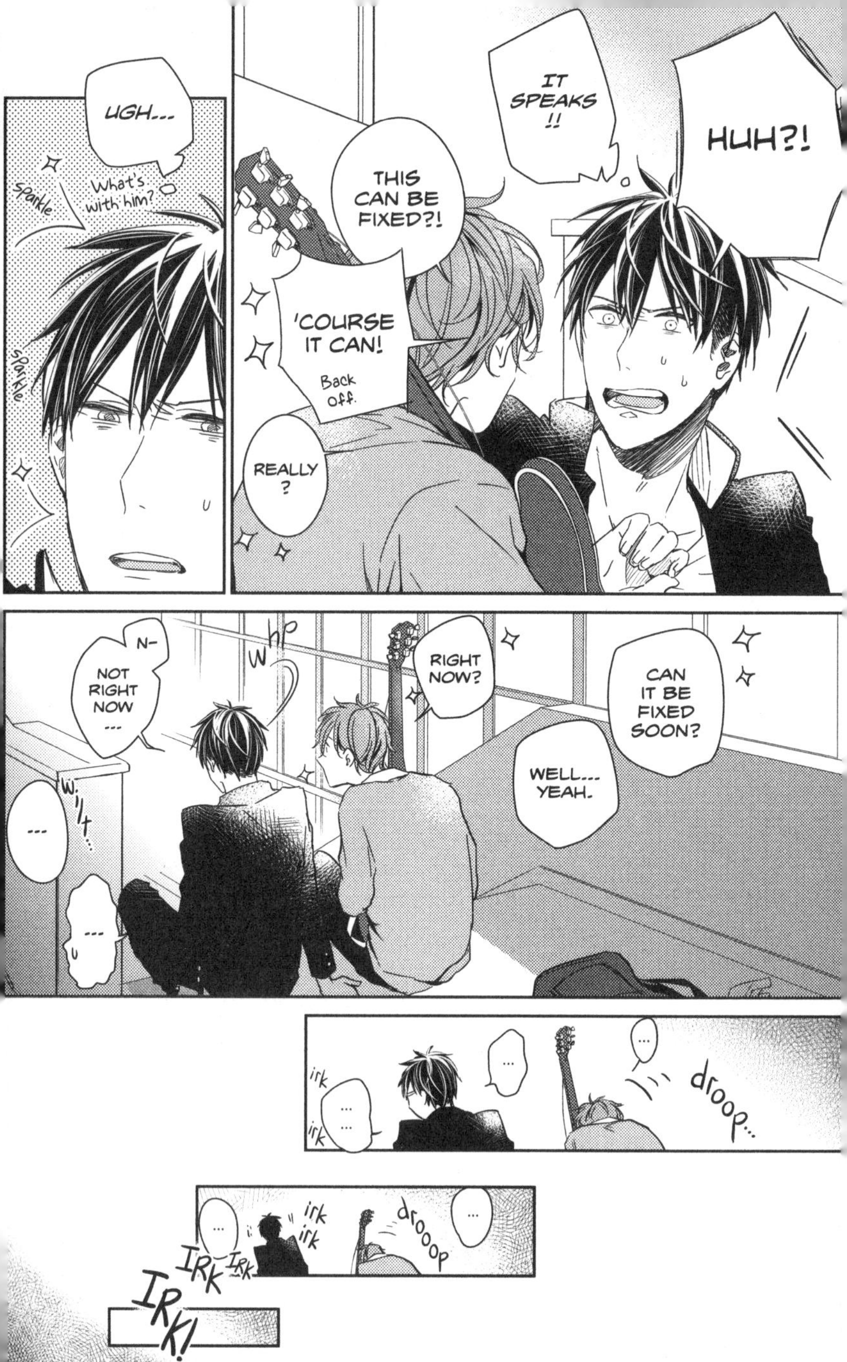
HUH?!
IT SPEAKS !!
THIS CAN BE FIXED?!
'COURSE IT CAN!
Back off.
REALLY ?
UGH...
What's with him?
sparkle
sparkle
CAN IT BE FIXED SOON?
WELL... YEAH.
RIGHT NOW?
whp
N-
NOT RIGHT NOW ...
wilt...
...
...
droop...
...
...
... ...
irk
irk
...
droooop
irk
irk
...
IRK
IRK
IRK!

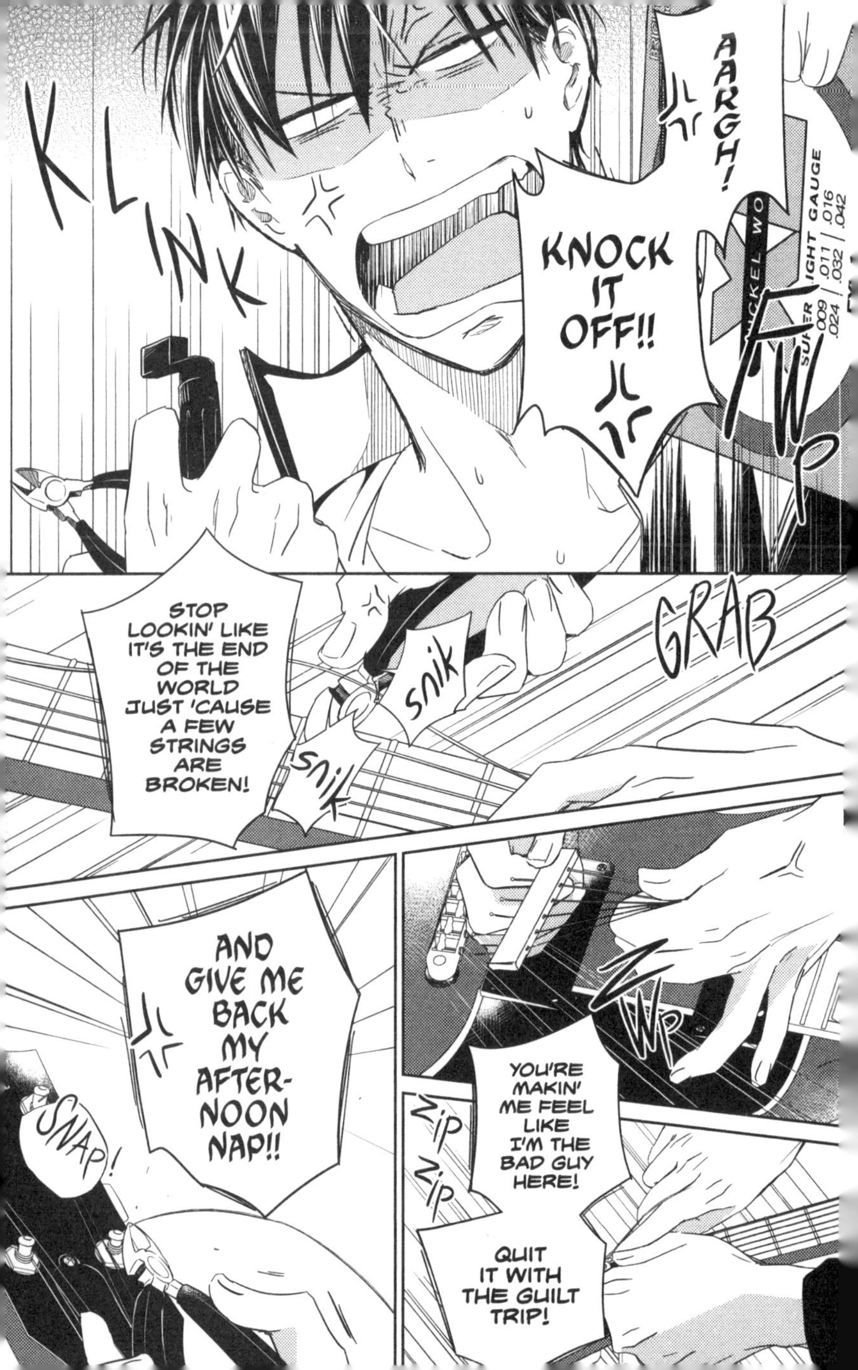
AARGH!
KNOCK IT OFF!!
KLINK
FWP
SUPER LIGHT GAUGE
.009 | .011 | .016
.024 | .032 | .042
GRAB
snik
snik
STOP LOOKIN' LIKE IT'S THE END OF THE WORLD JUST 'CAUSE A FEW STRINGS ARE BROKEN!
ZWP
YOU'RE MAKIN' ME FEEL LIKE I'M THE BAD GUY HERE!
Zip
Zip
QUIT IT WITH THE GUILT TRIP!
AND GIVE ME BACK MY AFTER-NOON NAP!!
SNAP!

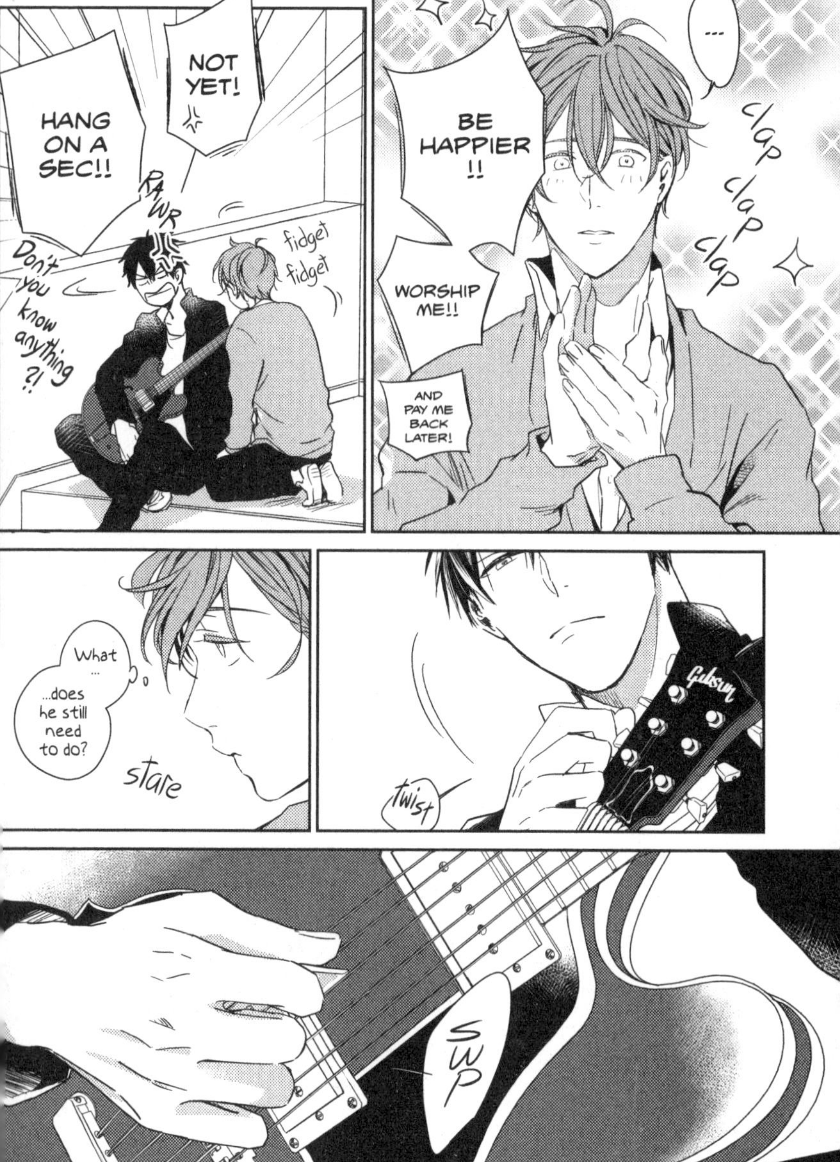
...
clap clap clap
BE HAPPIER !!
WORSHIP ME!!
AND PAY ME BACK LATER!
NOT YET!
HANG ON A SEC!!
RAWR
Don't you know anything ?!
fidget fidget
twist
What ... ...does he still need to do?
stare
SWP

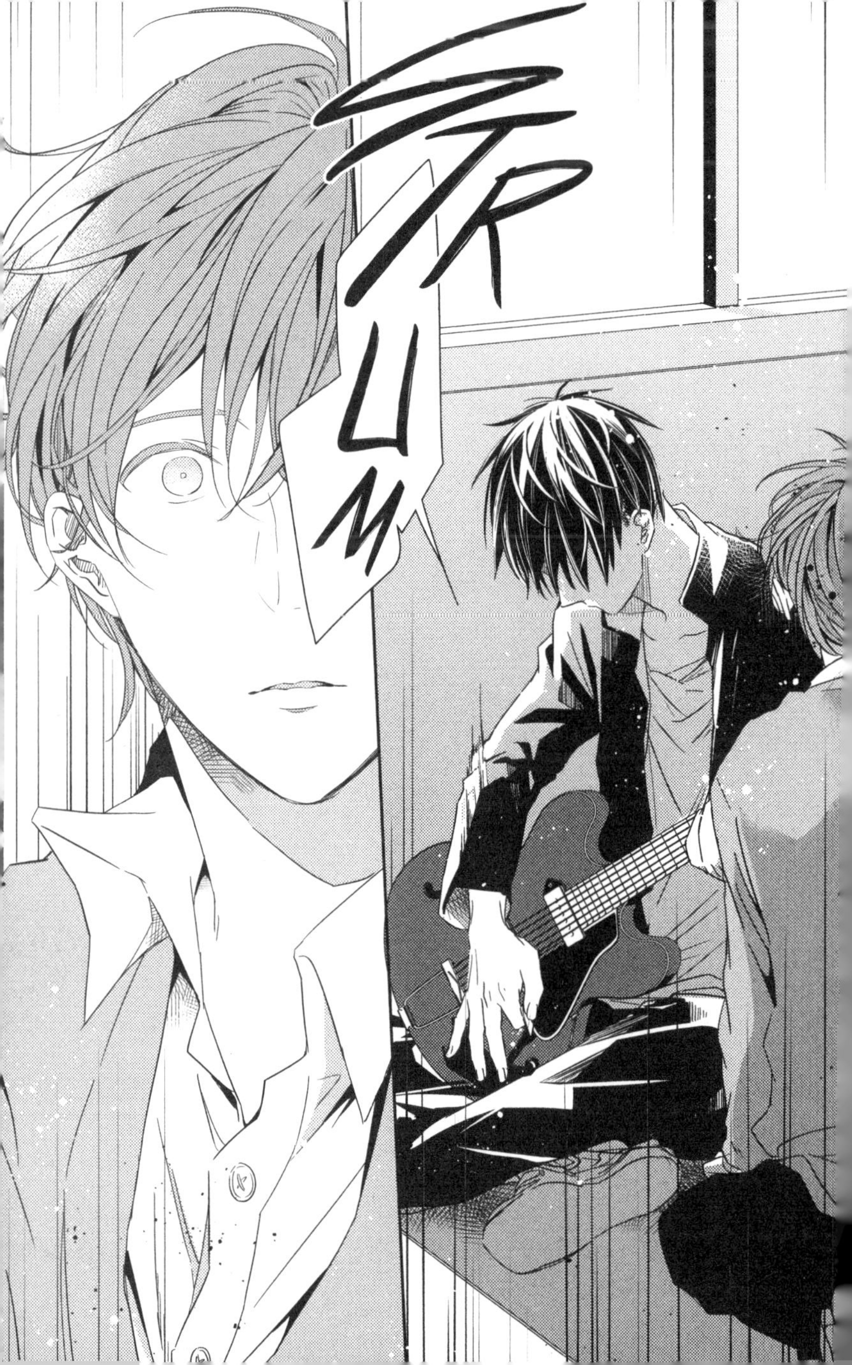
STRUM

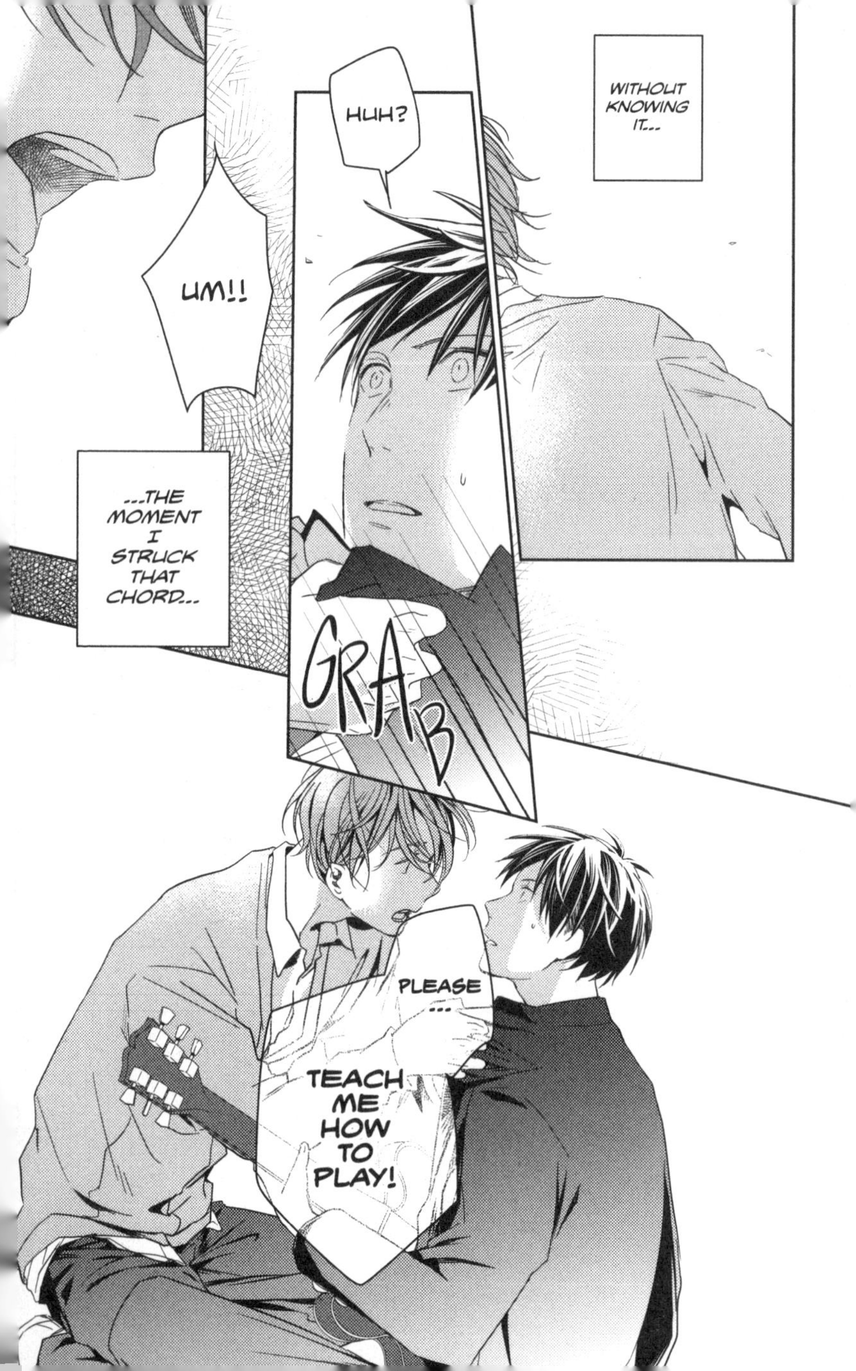
WITHOUT KNOWING IT...
HUH?
UM!!
...THE MOMENT I STRUCK THAT CHORD...
GRAB
PLEASE ...
TEACH ME HOW TO PLAY!

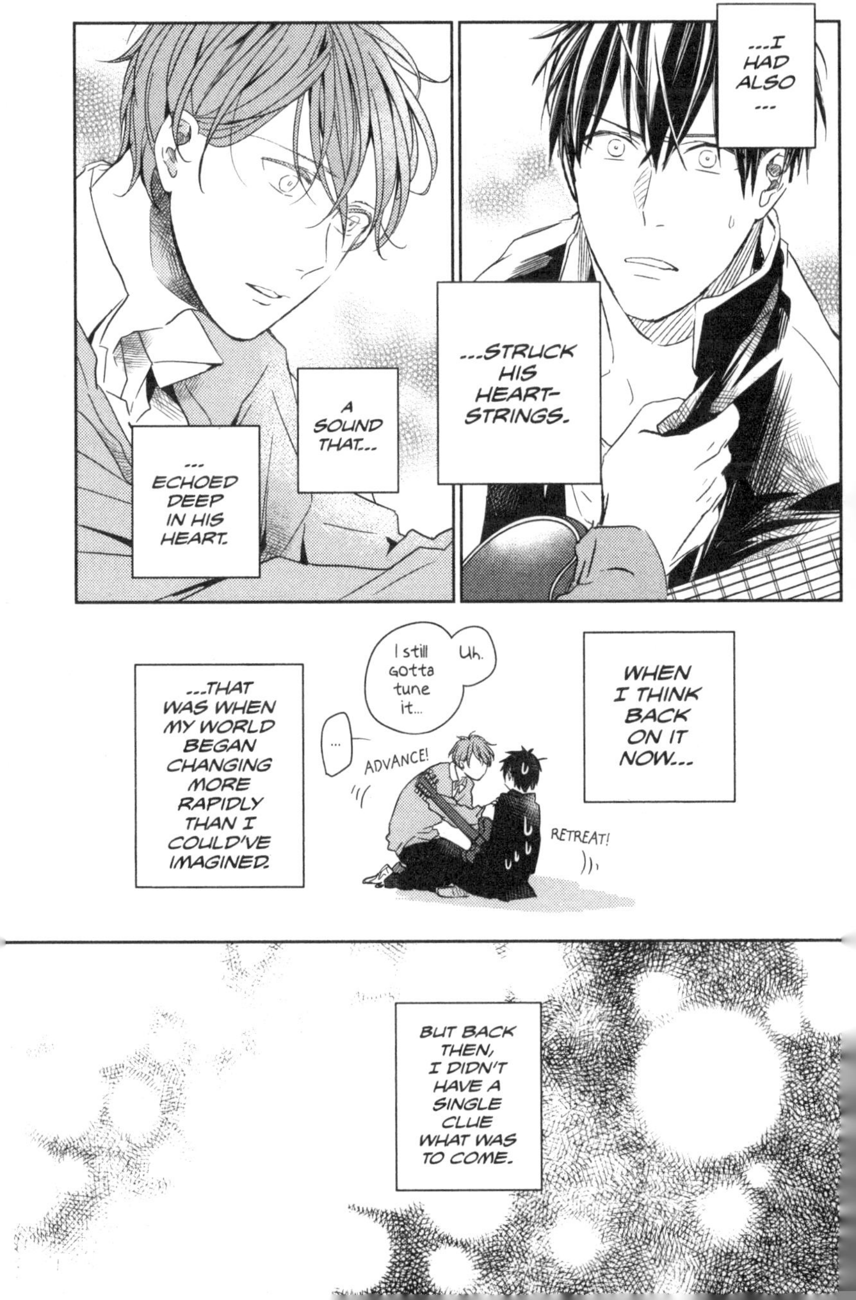
...I HAD ALSO ...
...STRUCK HIS HEART-STRINGS.
A SOUND THAT...
...ECHOED DEEP IN HIS HEART.
WHEN I THINK BACK ON IT NOW...
Uh.
I still gotta tune it...
...
ADVANCE!
RETREAT!
...THAT WAS WHEN MY WORLD BEGAN CHANGING MORE RAPIDLY THAN I COULD'VE IMAGINED.
BUT BACK THEN, I DIDN'T HAVE A SINGLE CLUE WHAT WAS TO COME.

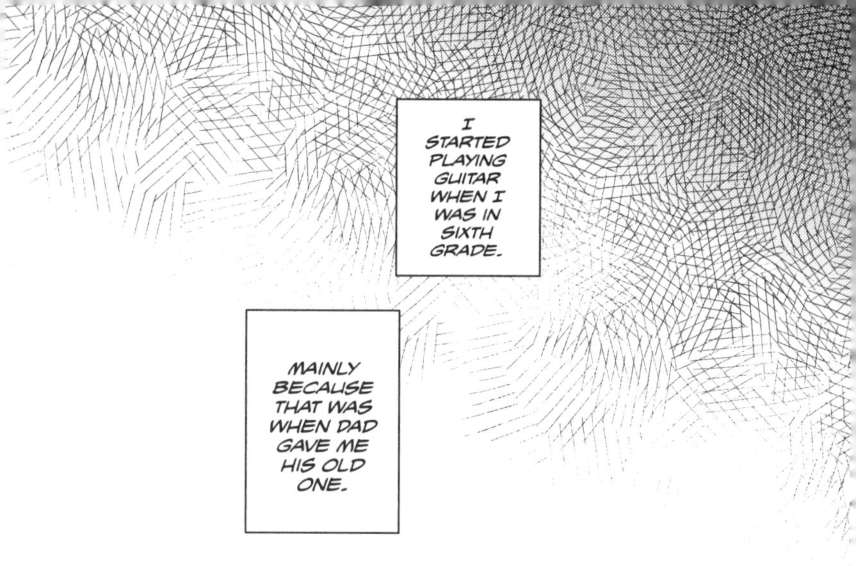
I STARTED PLAYING GUITAR WHEN I WAS IN SIXTH GRADE.
MAINLY BECAUSE THAT WAS WHEN DAD GAVE ME HIS OLD ONE.

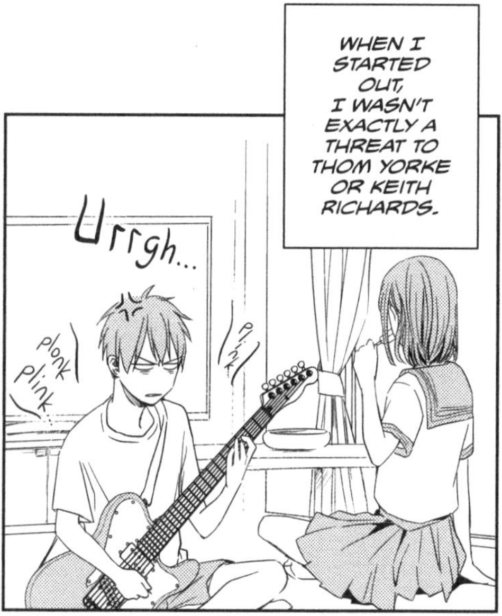
WHEN I STARTED OUT, I WASN'T EXACTLY A THREAT TO THOM YORKE OR KEITH RICHARDS.
Urrgh...
Plink
plonk plink

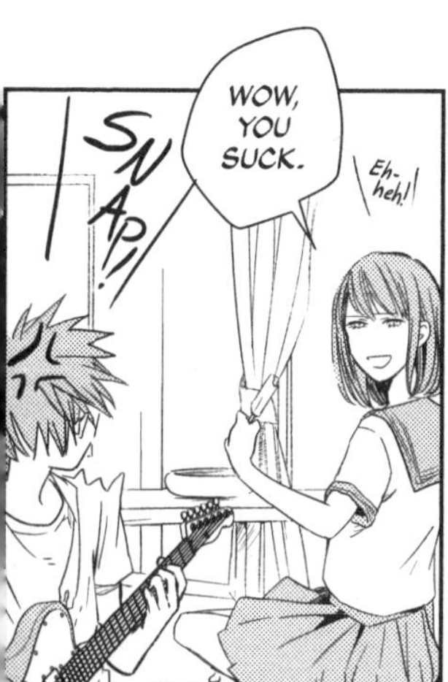
Eh-heh!
WOW, YOU SUCK.
SNAP!!

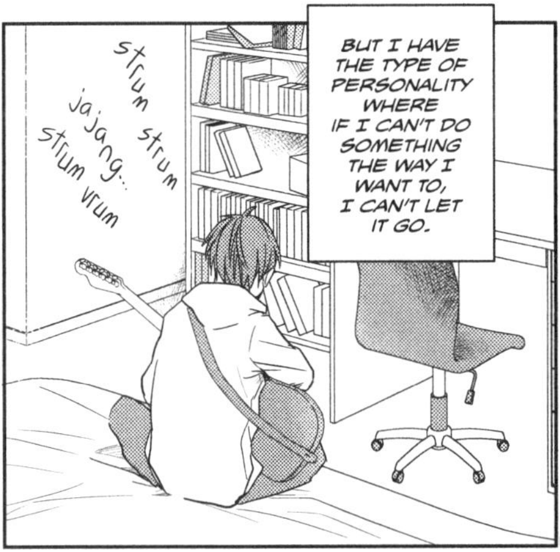
BUT I HAVE THE TYPE OF PERSONALITY WHERE IF I CAN'T DO SOMETHING THE WAY I WANT TO, I CAN'T LET IT GO.
strum strum
jajang...
strum vrum

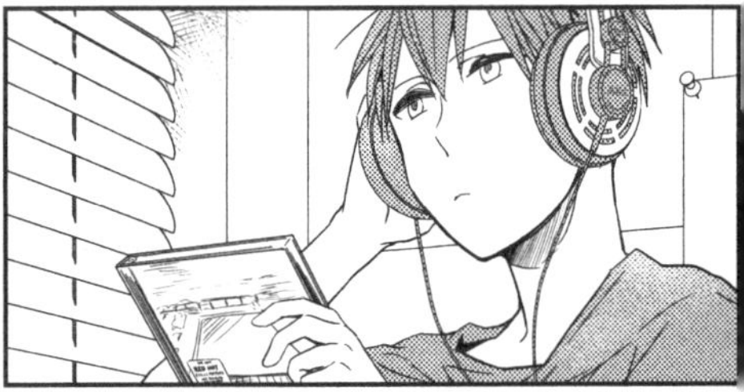

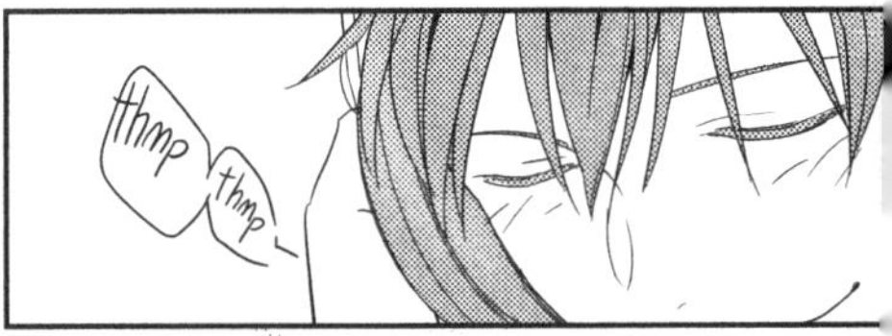
thmp
thmp

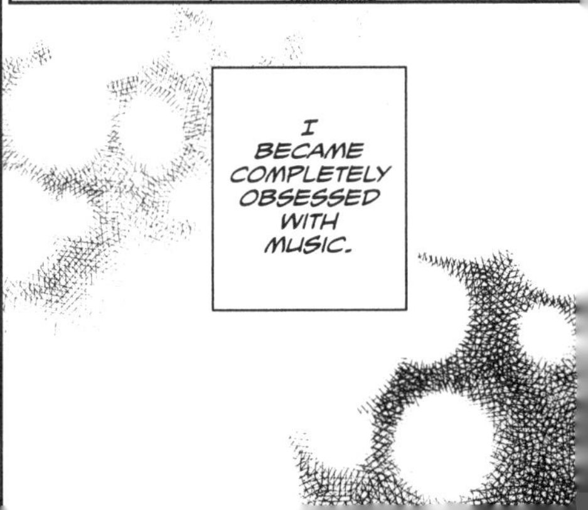
I BECAME COMPLETELY OBSESSED WITH MUSIC.

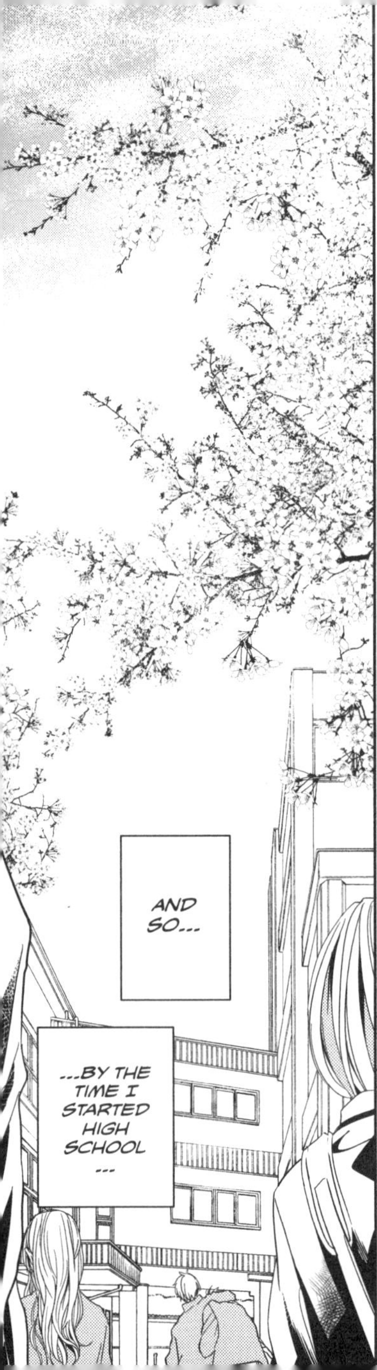
AND SO...
...BY THE TIME I STARTED HIGH SCHOOL ...

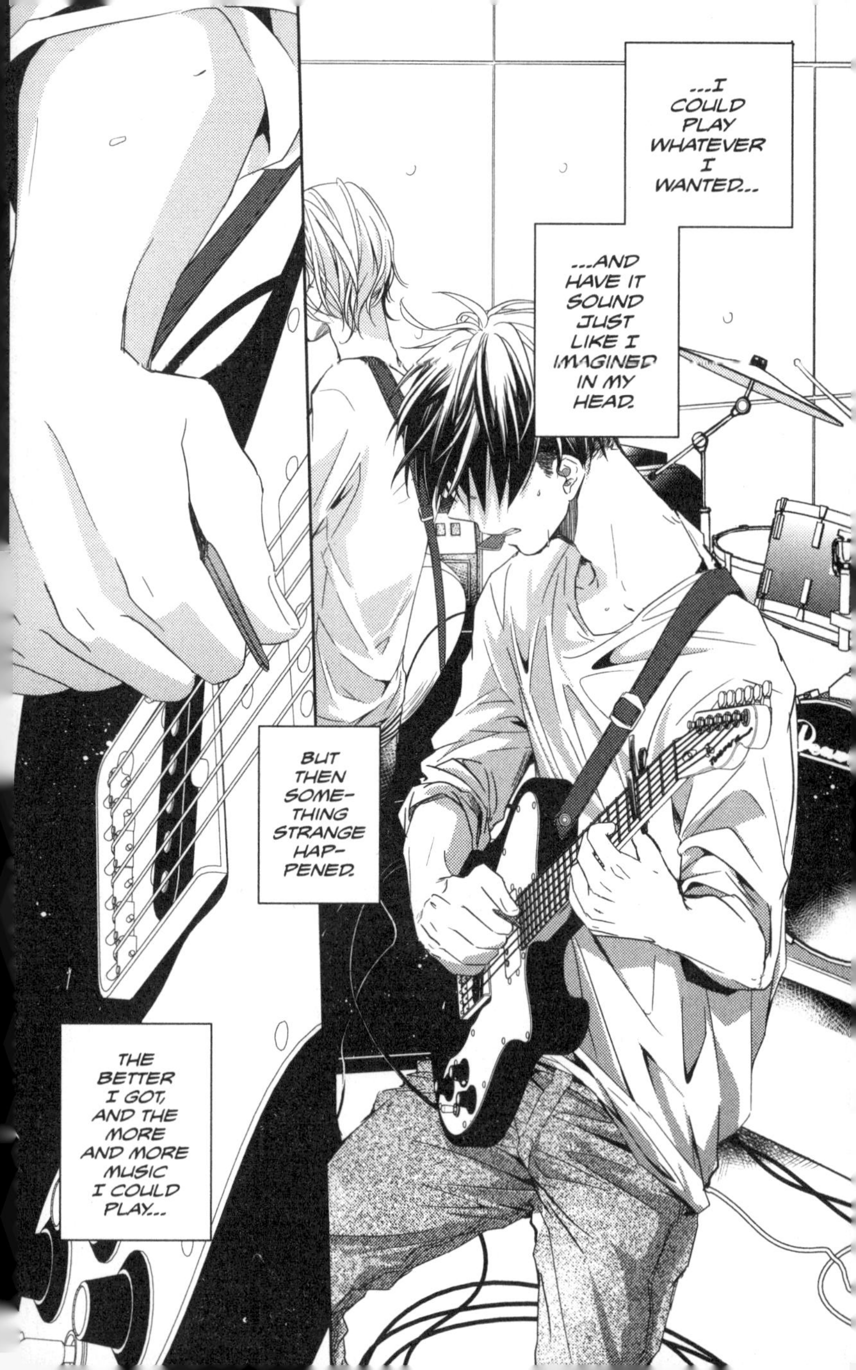
THE BETTER I GOT, AND THE MORE AND MORE MUSIC I COULD PLAY...
...I COULD PLAY WHATEVER I WANTED...
...AND HAVE IT SOUND JUST LIKE I IMAGINED IN MY HEAD.
BUT THEN SOME-THING STRANGE HAP-PENED.

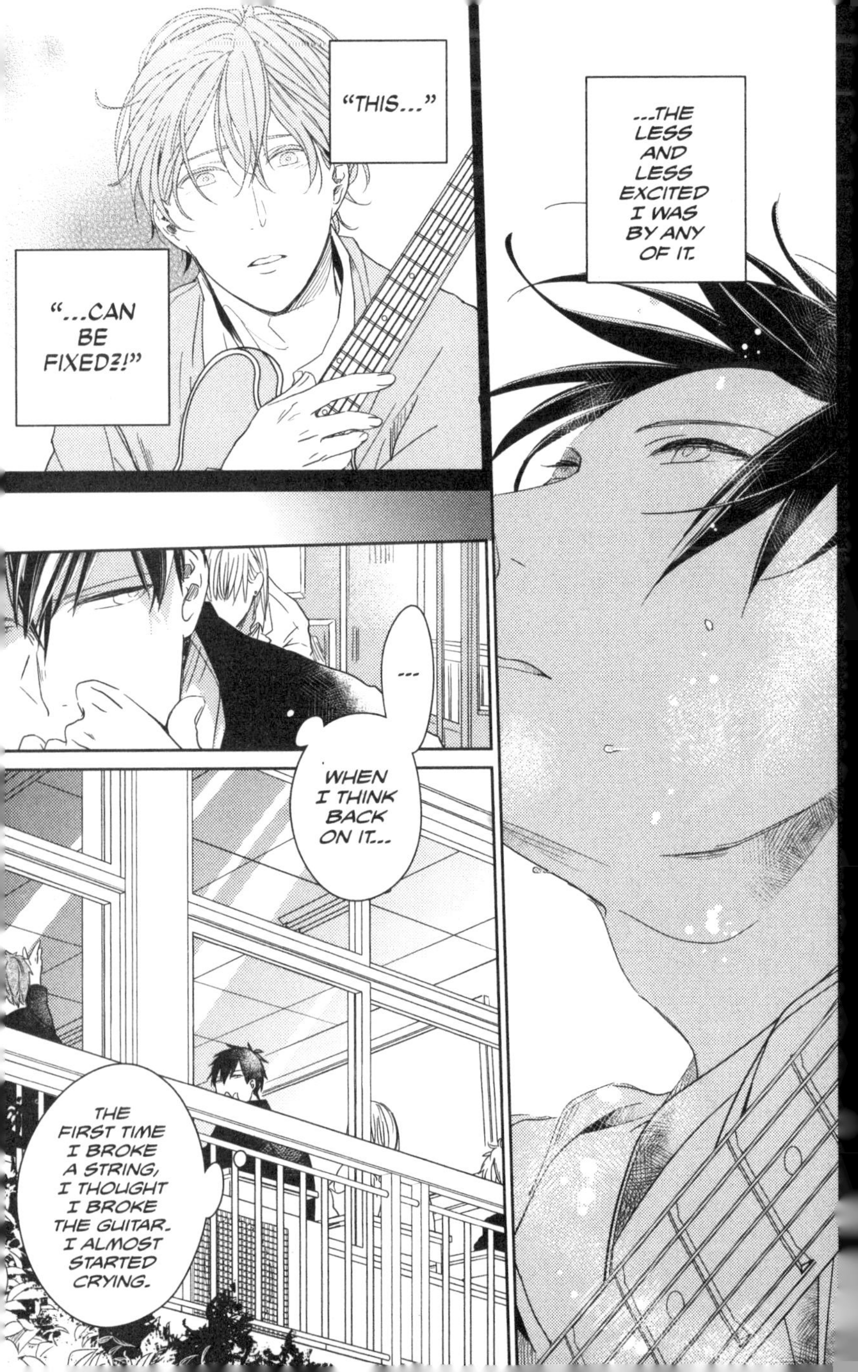
...THE LESS AND LESS EXCITED I WAS BY ANY OF IT.
"THIS..."
"...CAN BE FIXED?!"
...
WHEN I THINK BACK ON IT...
THE FIRST TIME I BROKE A STRING, I THOUGHT I BROKE THE GUITAR. I ALMOST STARTED CRYING.

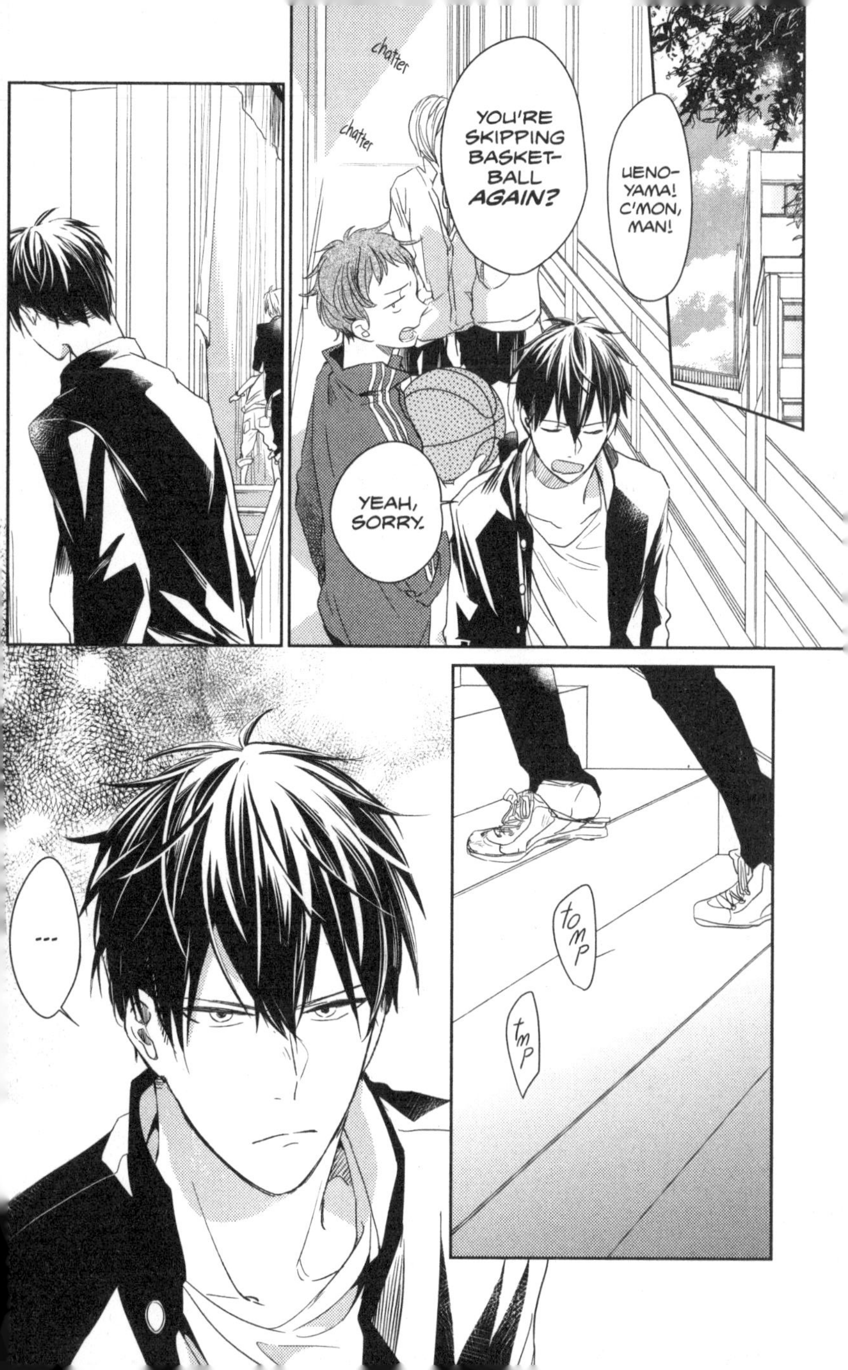
UENO-YAMA! C'MON, MAN!
YOU'RE SKIPPING BASKET-BALL AGAIN?
chatter
chatter
YEAH, SORRY.
tomp
tmp
...

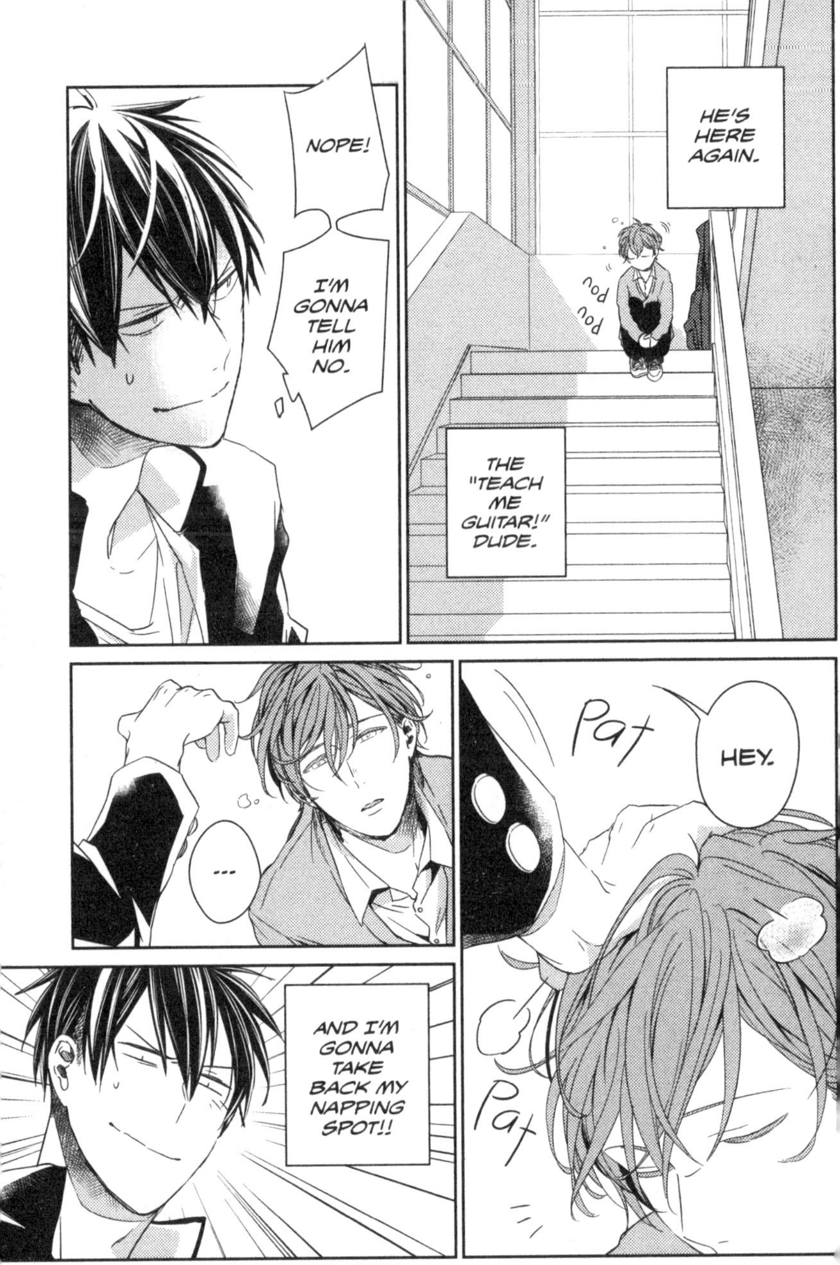
HE'S HERE AGAIN.
nod nod
THE "TEACH ME GUITAR!" DUDE.
NOPE!
I'M GONNA TELL HIM NO.
Pat
HEY.
Pat
...
AND I'M GONNA TAKE BACK MY NAPPING SPOT!!

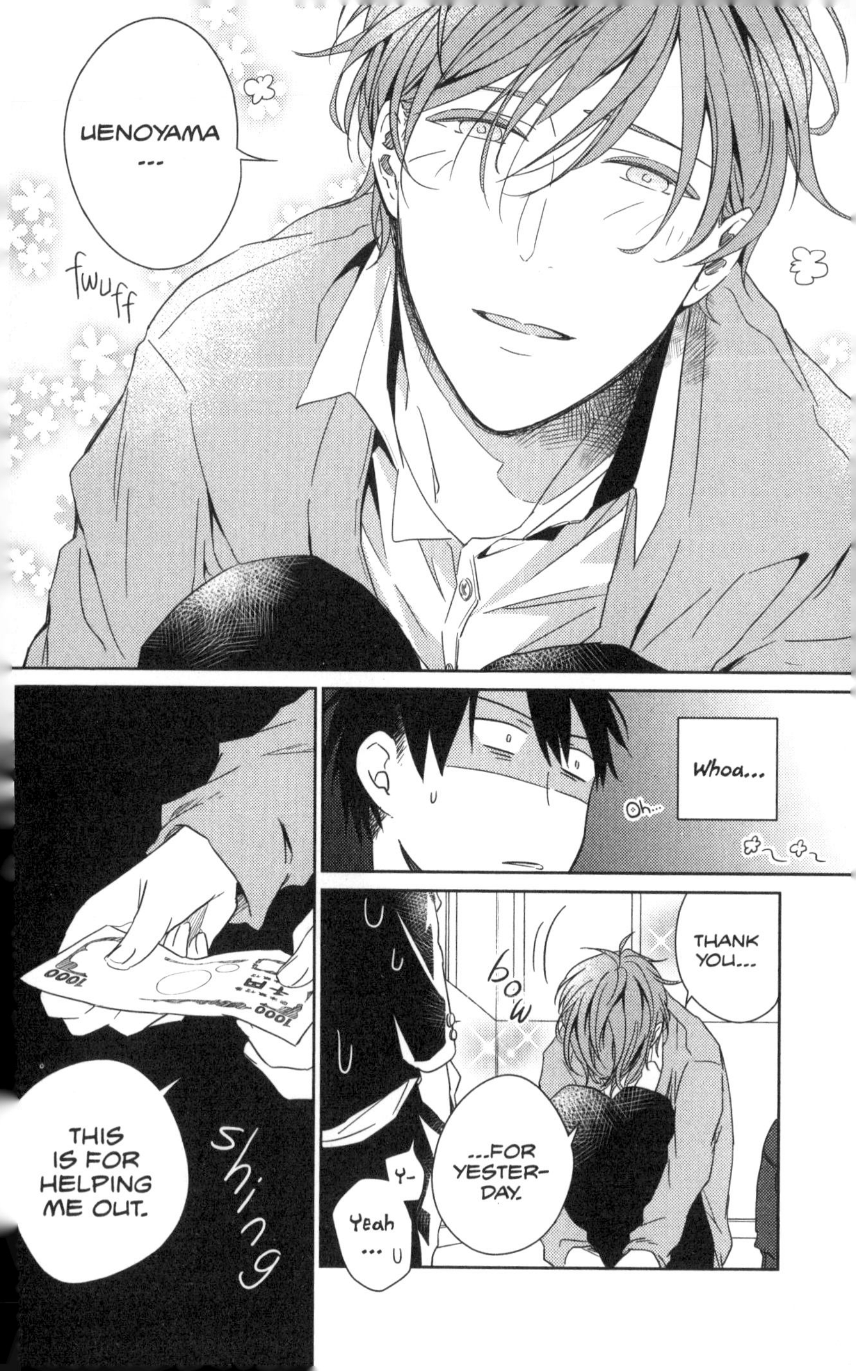
UENOYAMA
...
fwuff
Whoa...
Oh...
THANK YOU...
bow
...FOR YESTER-DAY.
Y-
Yeah ...
THIS IS FOR HELPING ME OUT.
shing

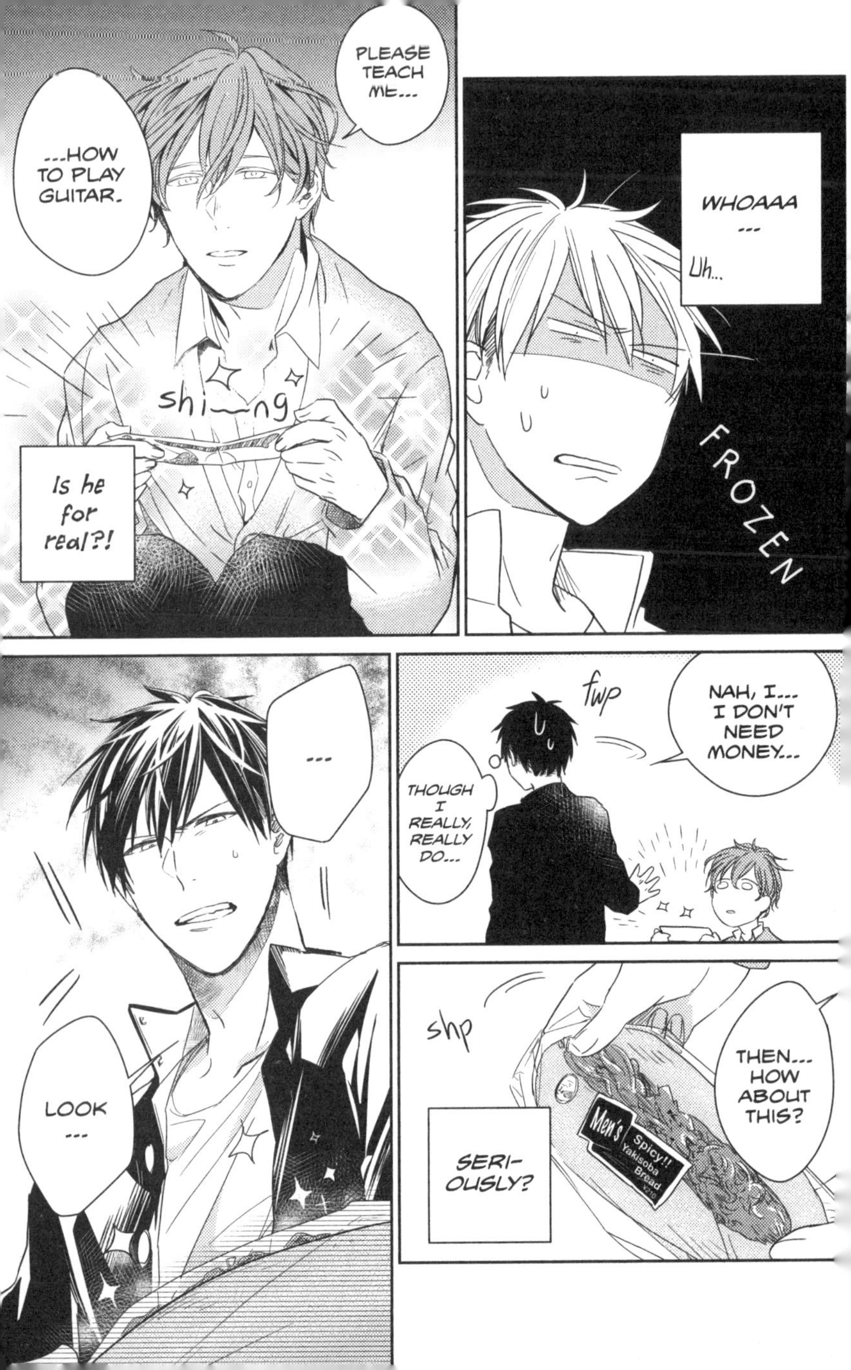
WHOAAA
...
Uh...
FROZEN
PLEASE TEACH ME...
...HOW TO PLAY GUITAR.
shi~ng
Is he for real?!
NAH, I... I DON'T NEED MONEY...
fwp
THOUGH I REALLY, REALLY DO...
THEN... HOW ABOUT THIS?
shp
Men's
Spicy!! Yakisoba Bread
SERI-OUSLY?
...
LOOK
...

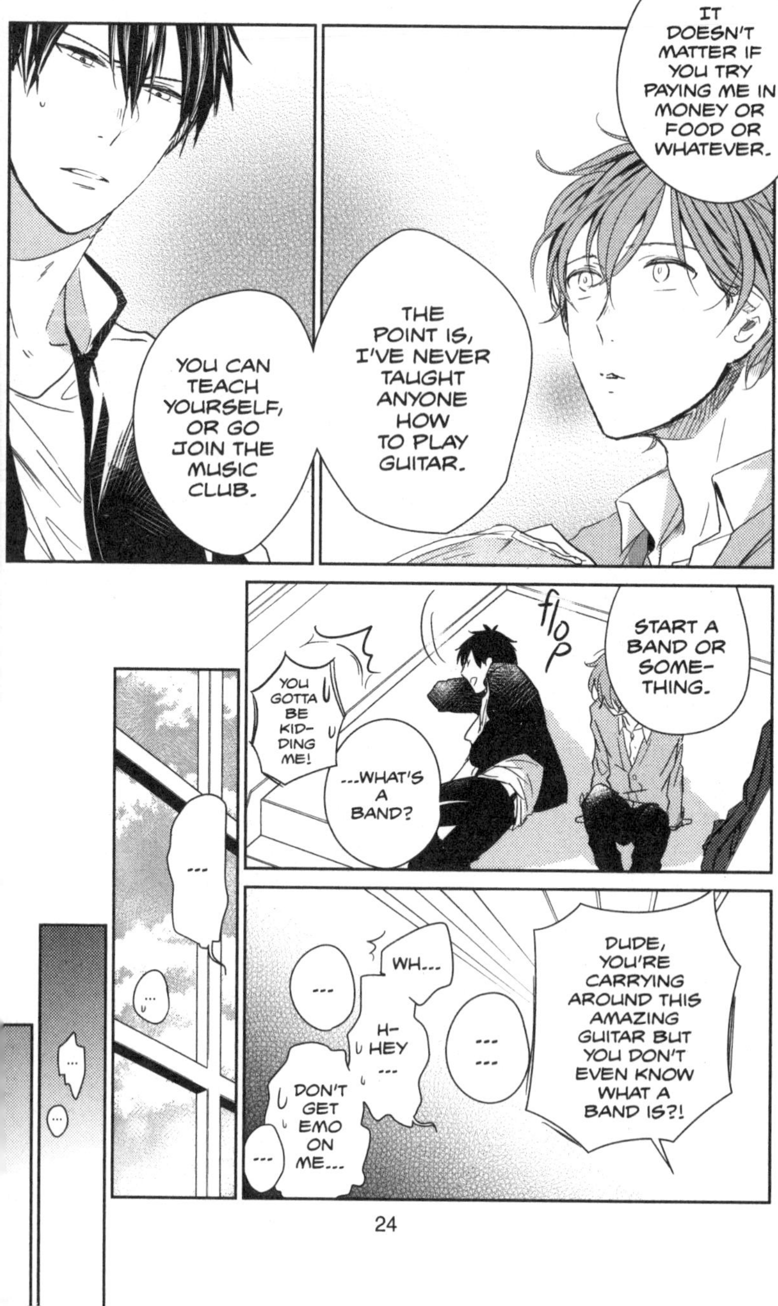
IT DOESN'T MATTER IF YOU TRY PAYING ME IN MONEY OR FOOD OR WHATEVER.
THE POINT IS, I'VE NEVER TAUGHT ANYONE HOW TO PLAY GUITAR.
YOU CAN TEACH YOURSELF, OR GO JOIN THE MUSIC CLUB.
START A BAND OR SOME-THING.
flop
...WHAT'S A BAND?
YOU GOTTA BE KID-DING ME!
DUDE, YOU'RE CARRYING AROUND THIS AMAZING GUITAR BUT YOU DON'T EVEN KNOW WHAT A BAND IS?!
...
...
WH...
...
H-HEY...
DON'T GET EMO ON ME...
...
...
...
...
...

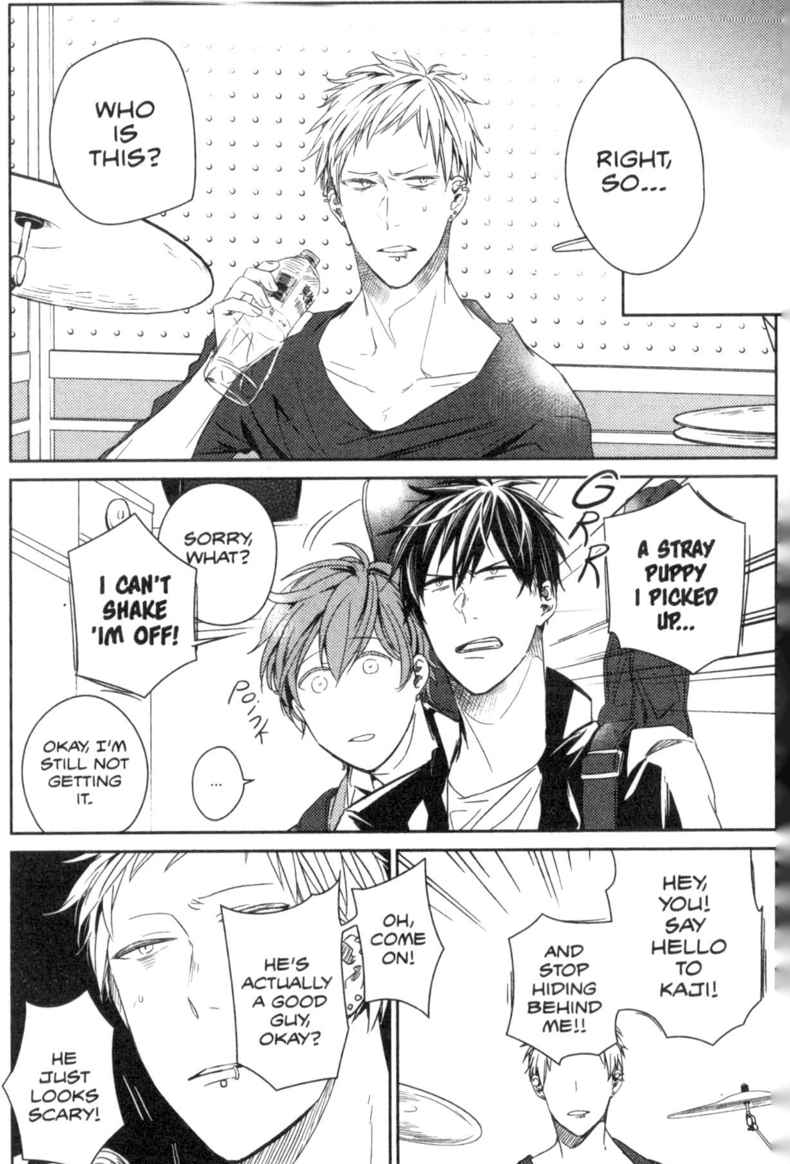
RIGHT, SO...
WHO IS THIS?
GRR
A STRAY PUPPY I PICKED UP...
SORRY, WHAT?
I CAN'T SHAKE 'IM OFF!
Poink
...
OKAY, I'M STILL NOT GETTING IT.
HEY, YOU! SAY HELLO TO KAJI!
AND STOP HIDING BEHIND ME!!
OH, COME ON!
HE'S ACTUALLY A GOOD GUY, OKAY?
HE JUST LOOKS SCARY!

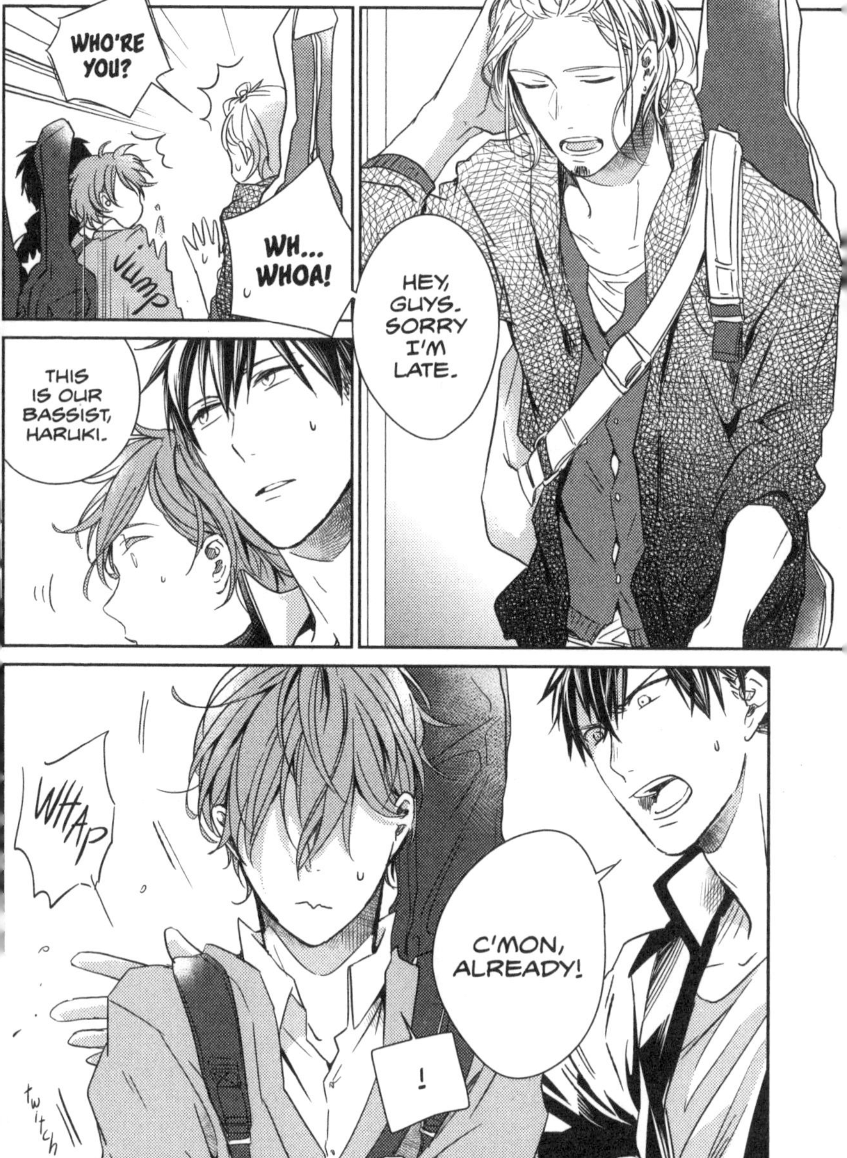
HEY, GUYS. SORRY I'M LATE.
WHO'RE YOU?
JUMP
WH... WHOA!
THIS IS OUR BASSIST, HARUKI.
C'MON, ALREADY!
!
WHAP
twitch

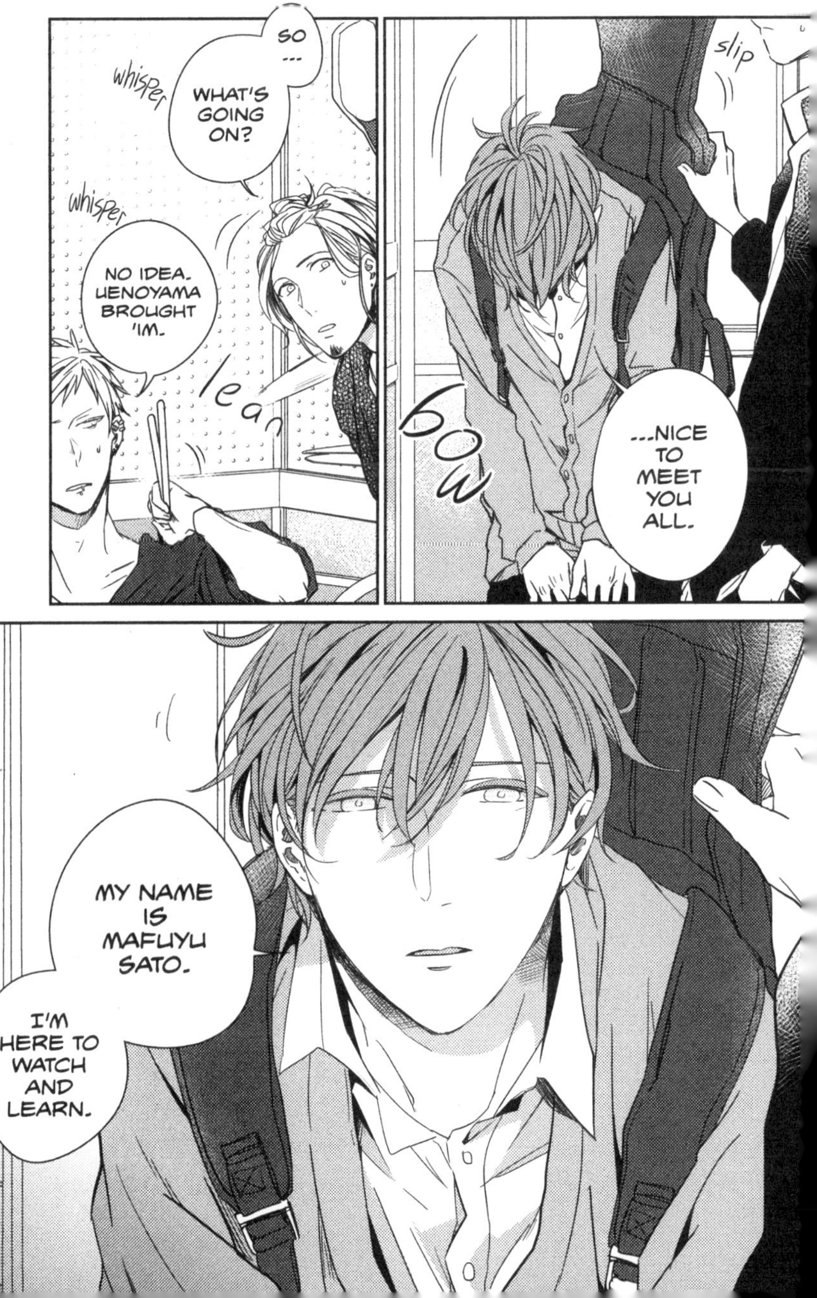
slip
bow
...NICE TO MEET YOU ALL.
SO ... WHAT'S GOING ON?
whisper
whisper
NO IDEA. UENOYAMA BROUGHT 'IM.
lean
MY NAME IS MAFUYU SATO.
I'M HERE TO WATCH AND LEARN.

Mafuyu Sato (16)

175 cm
(Second-year high school student)
Still growing

Birthday: 2/28 Sign: Pisces Blood Type: AB

Vocals & Guitar ← Gibson ES-330 (red)

I haven't decided on a lot
of his music things yet.
All he knows about music is
what he's learned in school.

Favorite Music: Unknown

Not a member of any clubs
in middle school or high school.
Good at studying. Doesn't do
horribly in science classes.

Family: Mother

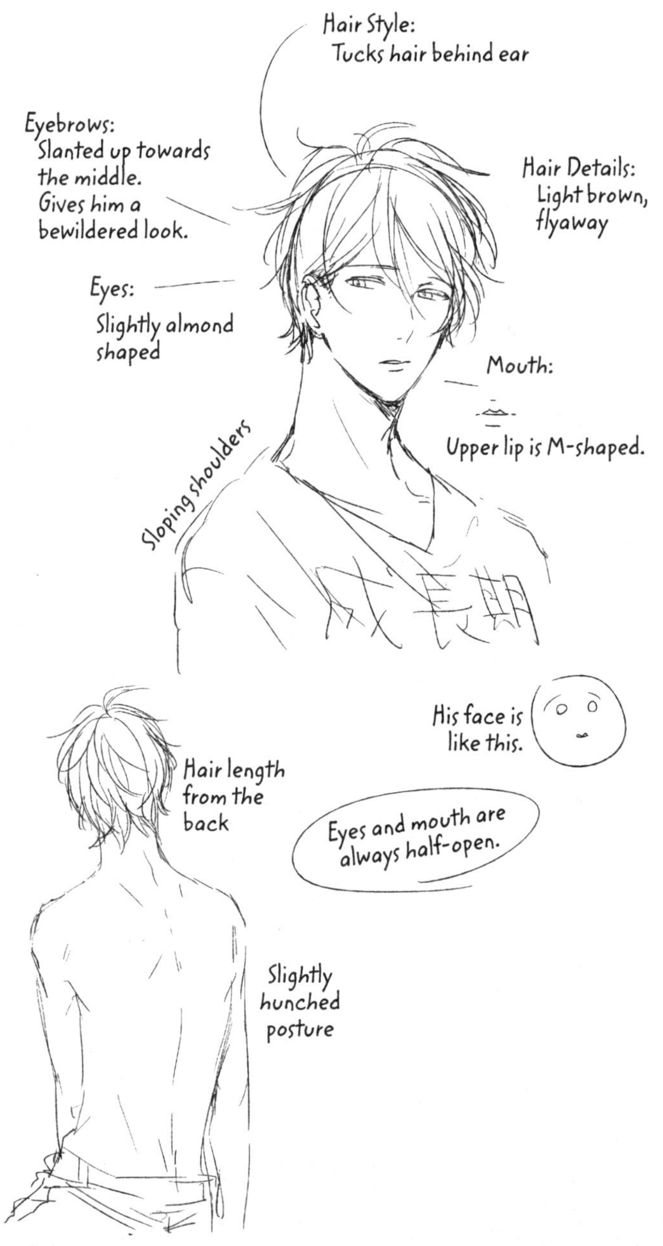
Hair Style:
Tucks hair behind ear
Eyebrows:
Slanted up towards the middle.
Gives him a bewildered look.
Hair Details:
Light brown, flyaway
Eyes:
Slightly almond shaped
Mouth:
Upper lip is M-shaped.
Sloping shoulders
His face is like this.
Hair length from the back
Eyes and mouth are always half-open.
Slightly hunched posture

given

by Natsuki Kizu

chapter 2

given

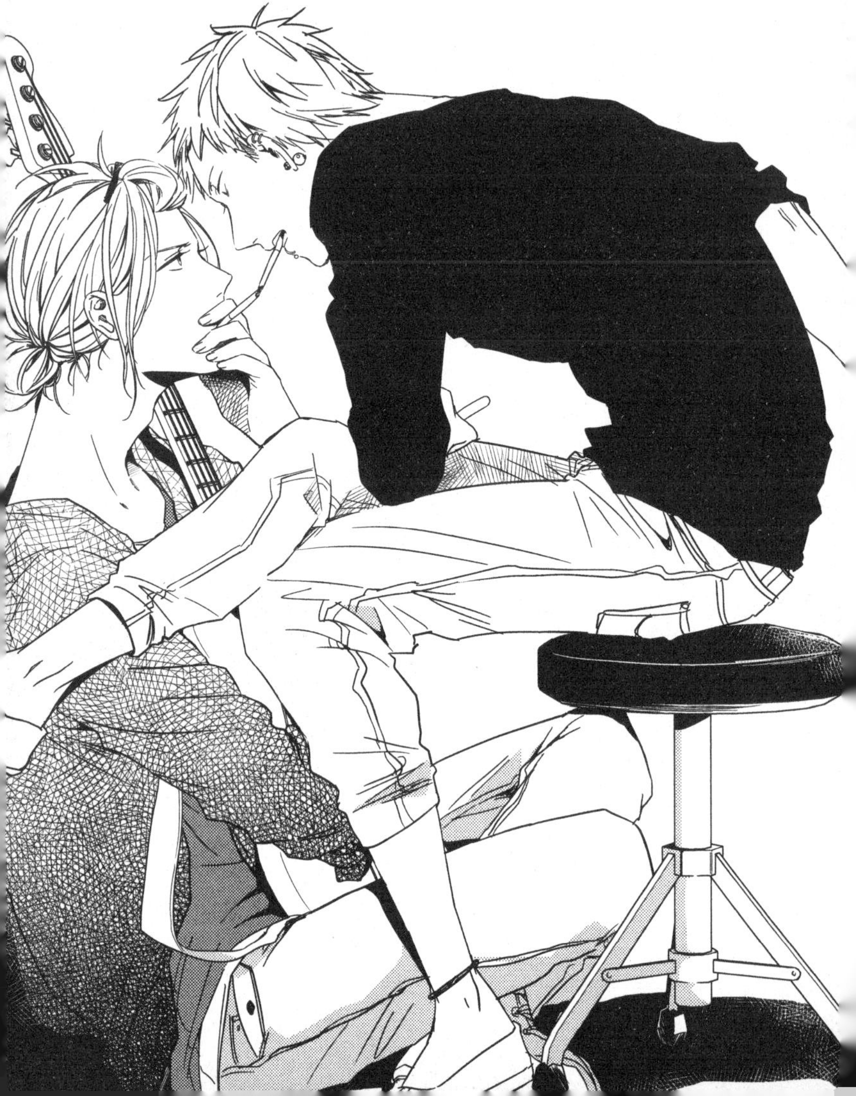

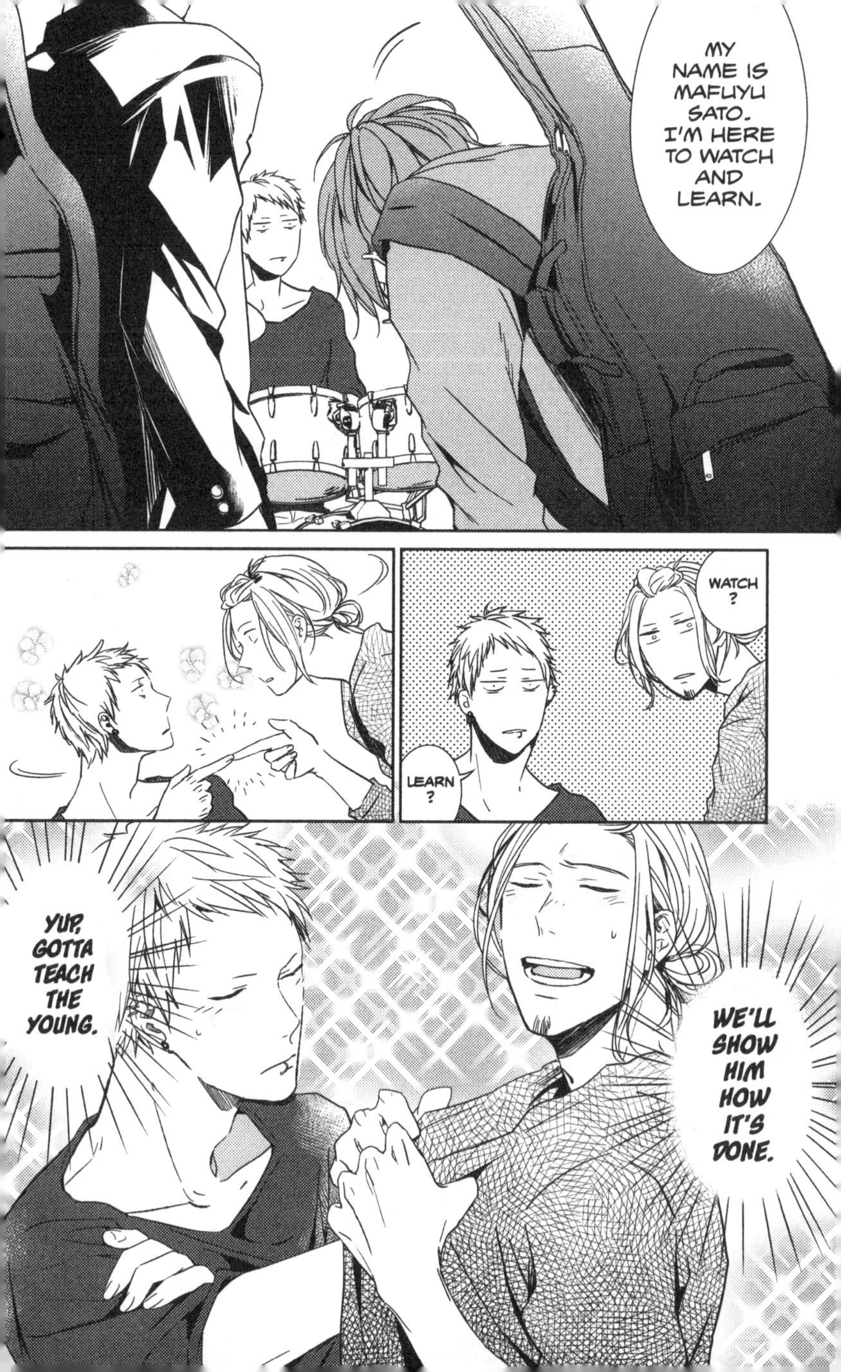
MY NAME IS MAFUYU SATO. I'M HERE TO WATCH AND LEARN.
WATCH?
LEARN?
WE'LL SHOW HIM HOW IT'S DONE.
YUP, GOTTA TEACH THE YOUNG.

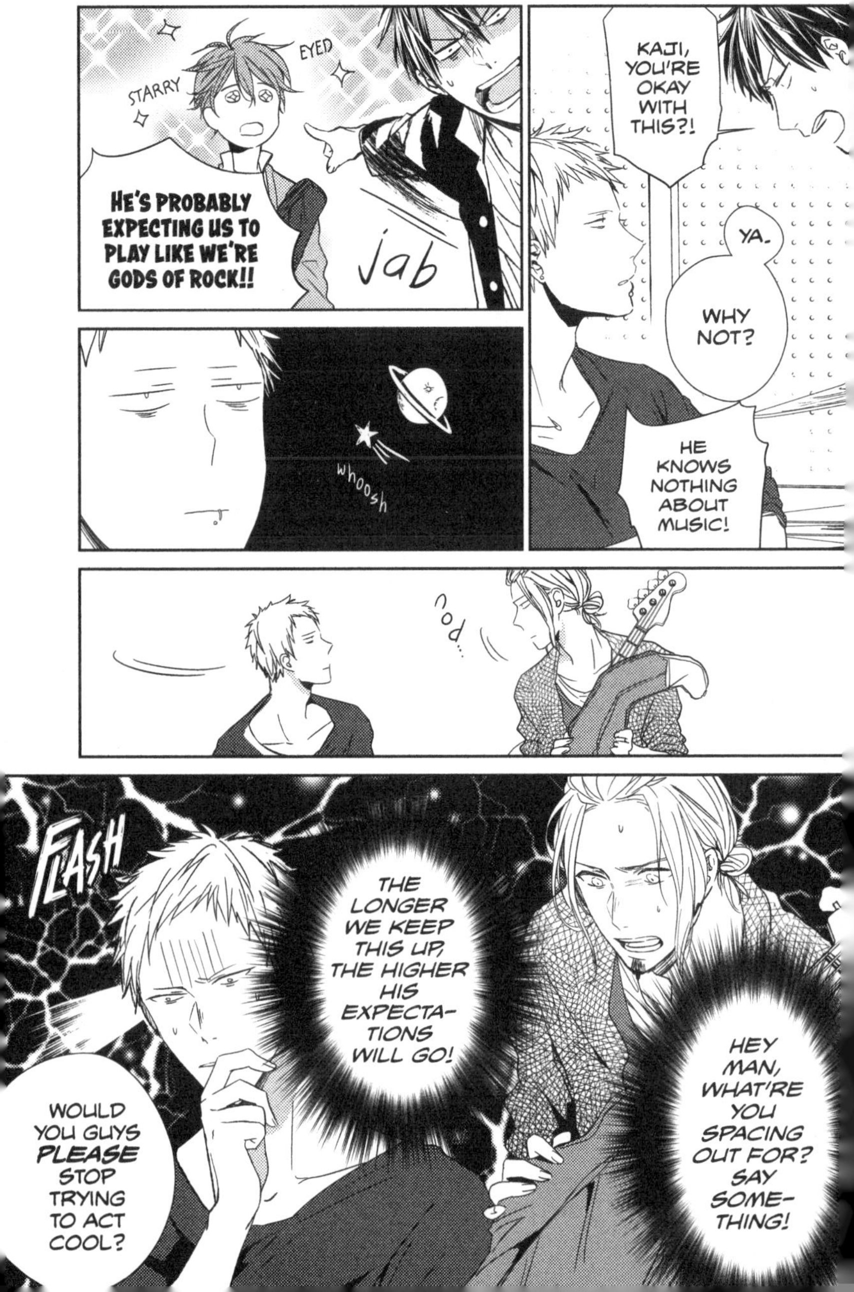
KAJI, YOU'RE OKAY WITH THIS?!
YA.
WHY NOT?
HE KNOWS NOTHING ABOUT MUSIC!
STARRY EYED
HE'S PROBABLY EXPECTING US TO PLAY LIKE WE'RE GODS OF ROCK!!
jab
whoosh
nod...
HEY MAN, WHAT'RE YOU SPACING OUT FOR? SAY SOME-THING!
THE LONGER WE KEEP THIS UP, THE HIGHER HIS EXPECTA-TIONS WILL GO!
FLASH
WOULD YOU GUYS PLEASE STOP TRYING TO ACT COOL?

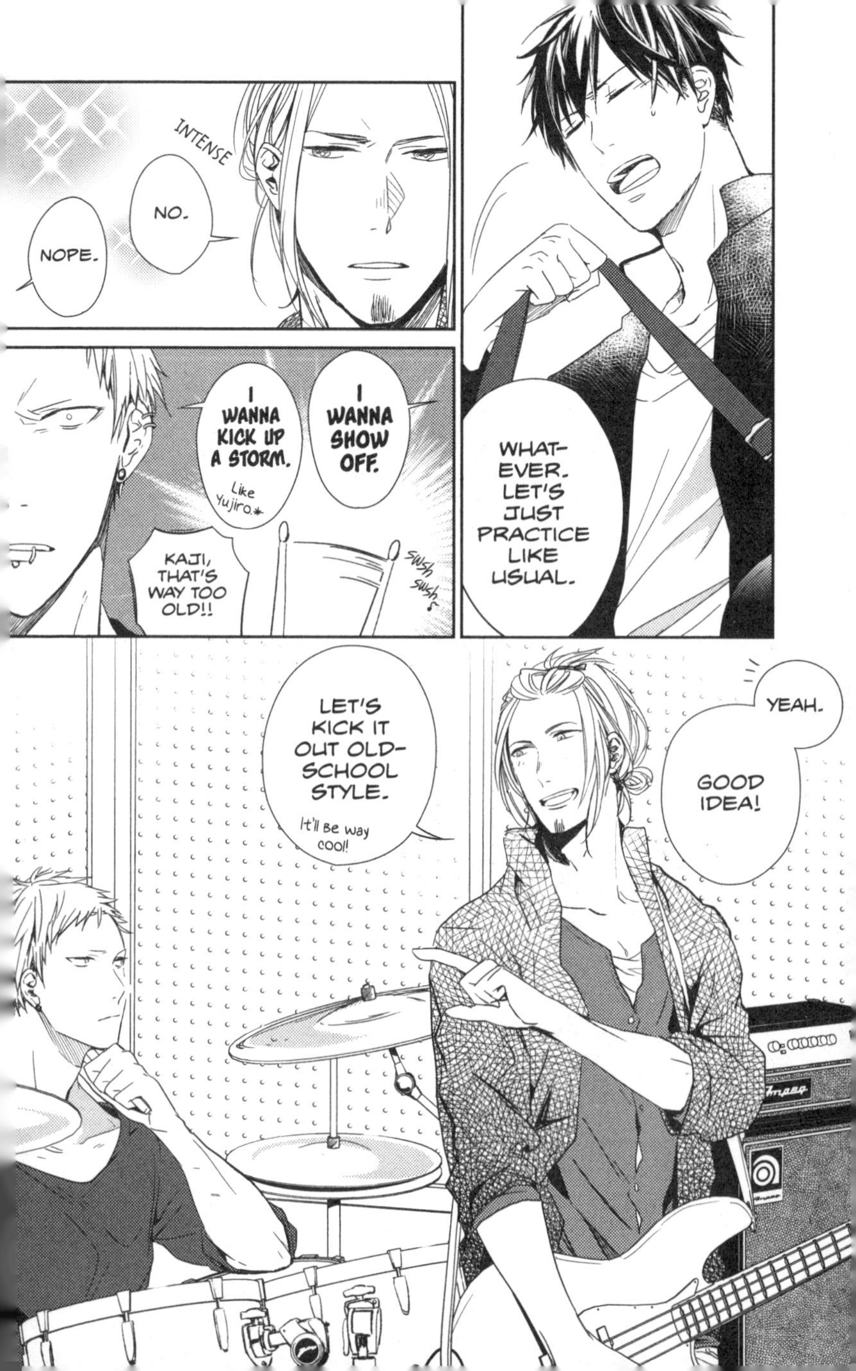
WHATEVER. LET'S JUST PRACTICE LIKE USUAL.
INTENSE
NO.
NOPE.
I WANNA SHOW OFF.
I WANNA KICK UP A STORM.
Like Yujiro.*
KAJI, THAT'S WAY TOO OLD!!
SWSH SWSH
YEAH.
GOOD IDEA!
LET'S KICK IT OUT OLD-SCHOOL STYLE.
It'll Be way cool!

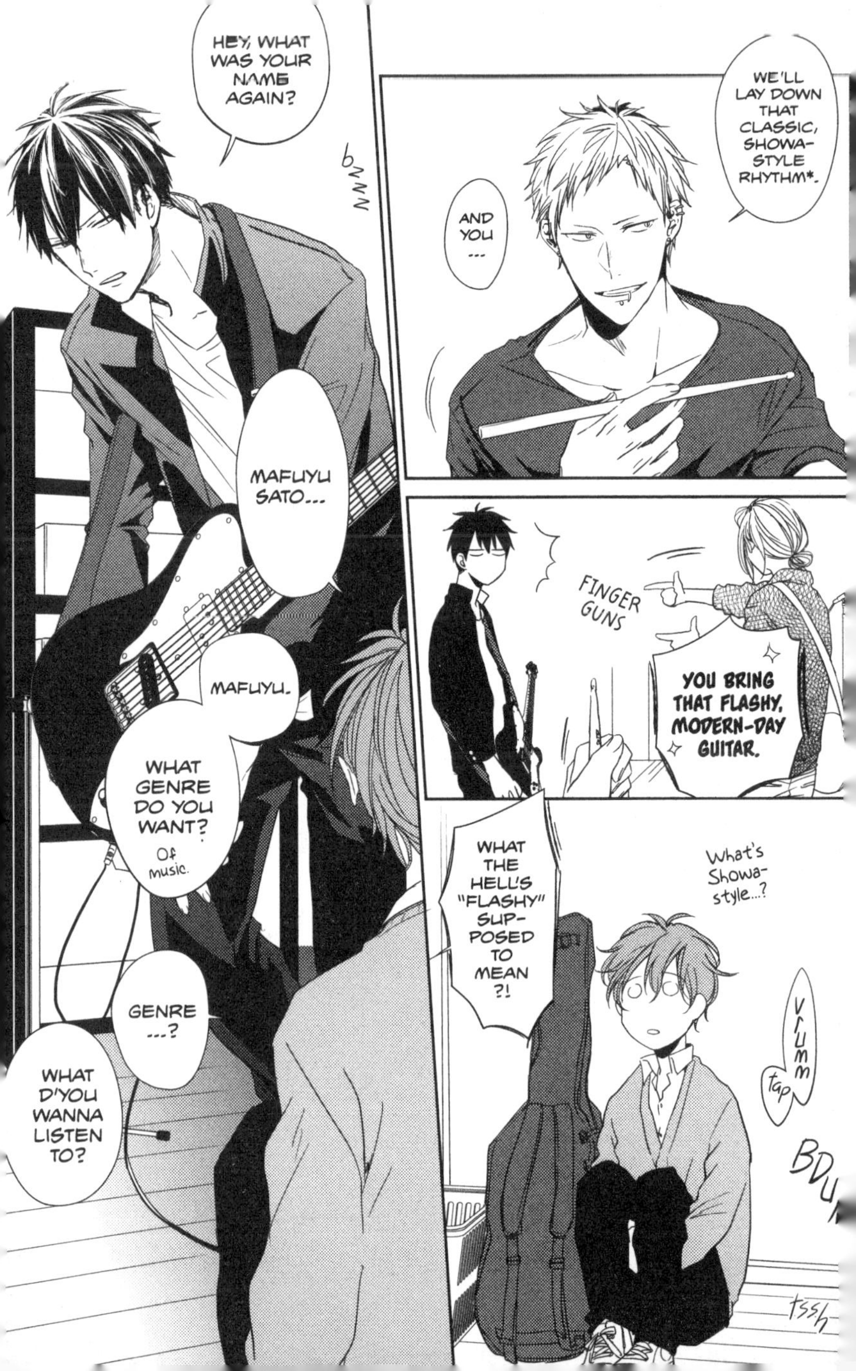
WE'LL LAY DOWN THAT CLASSIC, SHOWA-STYLE RHYTHM*.
AND YOU ...
FINGER GUNS
YOU BRING THAT FLASHY, MODERN-DAY GUITAR.
What's Showa-style...?
vrumm
tap
BDUN
tssh
WHAT THE HELL'S "FLASHY" SUP-POSED TO MEAN ?!
HEY, WHAT WAS YOUR NAME AGAIN?
bzzz
MAFUYU SATO...
MAFUYU.
WHAT GENRE DO YOU WANT?
Of music.
GENRE ...?
WHAT D'YOU WANNA LISTEN TO?

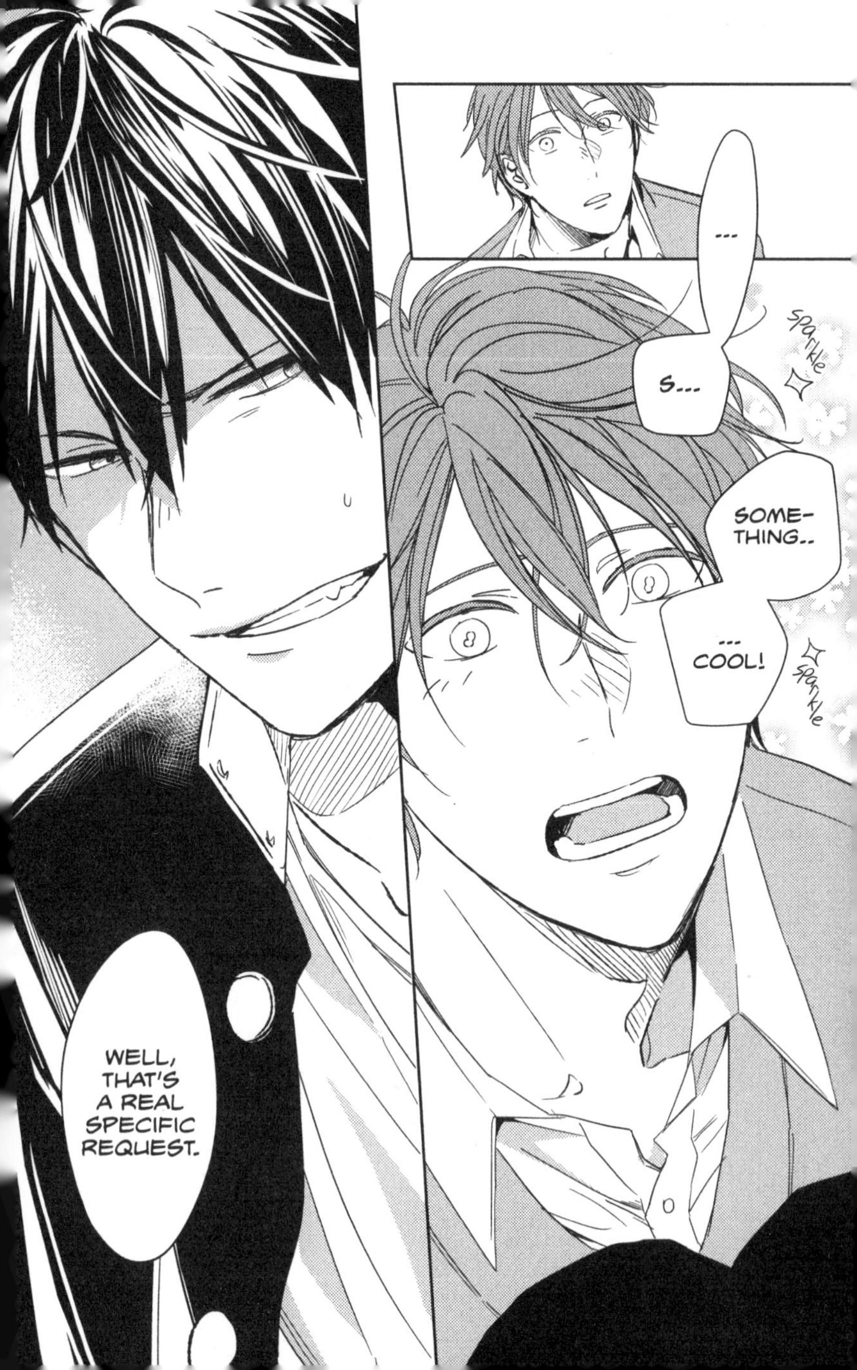
...
S...
sparkle
SOME-THING..
...COOL!
sparkle
WELL, THAT'S A REAL SPECIFIC REQUEST.

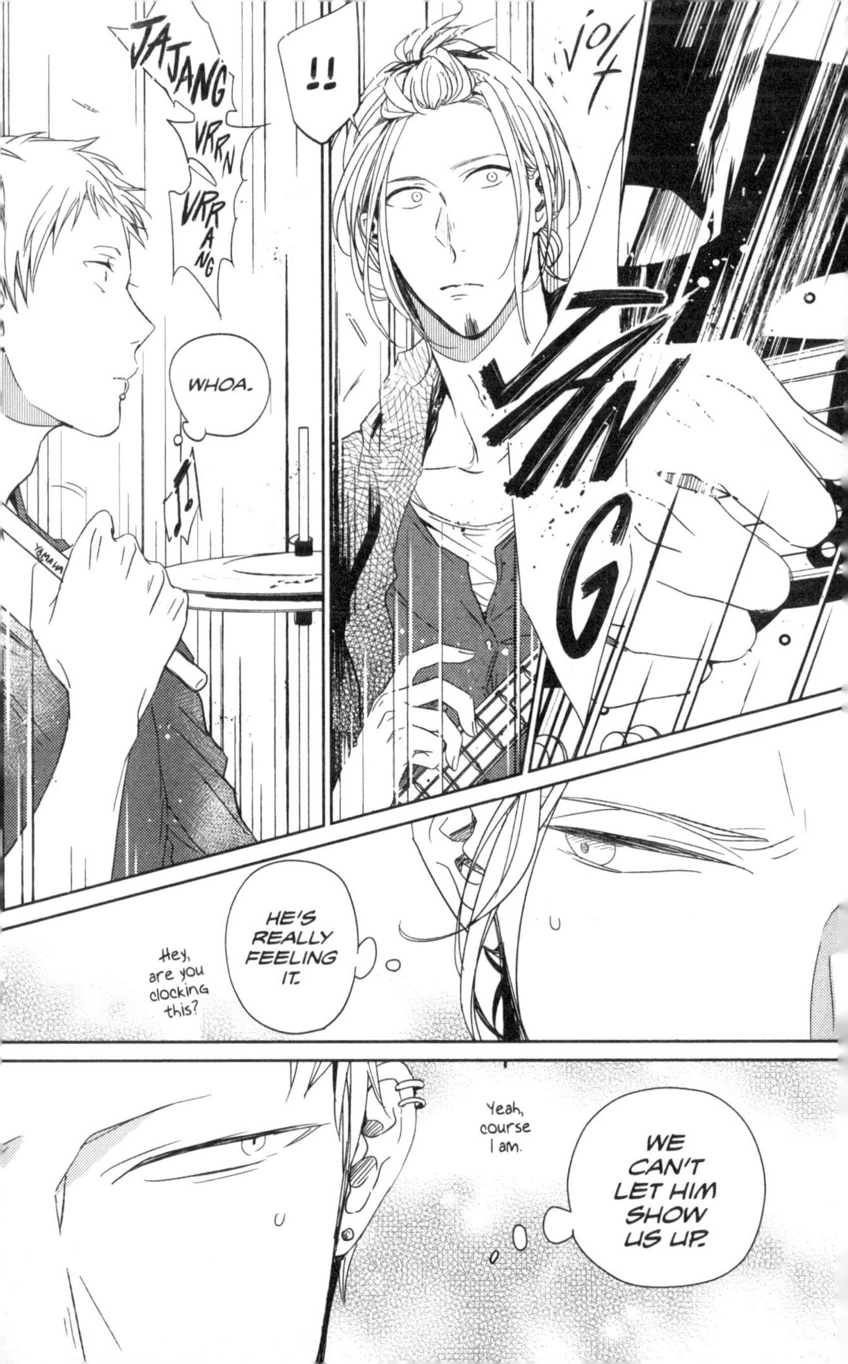
JOLT
!!
JAJANG
VRRN
VRRANG
WHOA.
JANG
HE'S REALLY FEELING IT.
Hey, are you clocking this?
WE CAN'T LET HIM SHOW US UP.
Yeah, course I am.

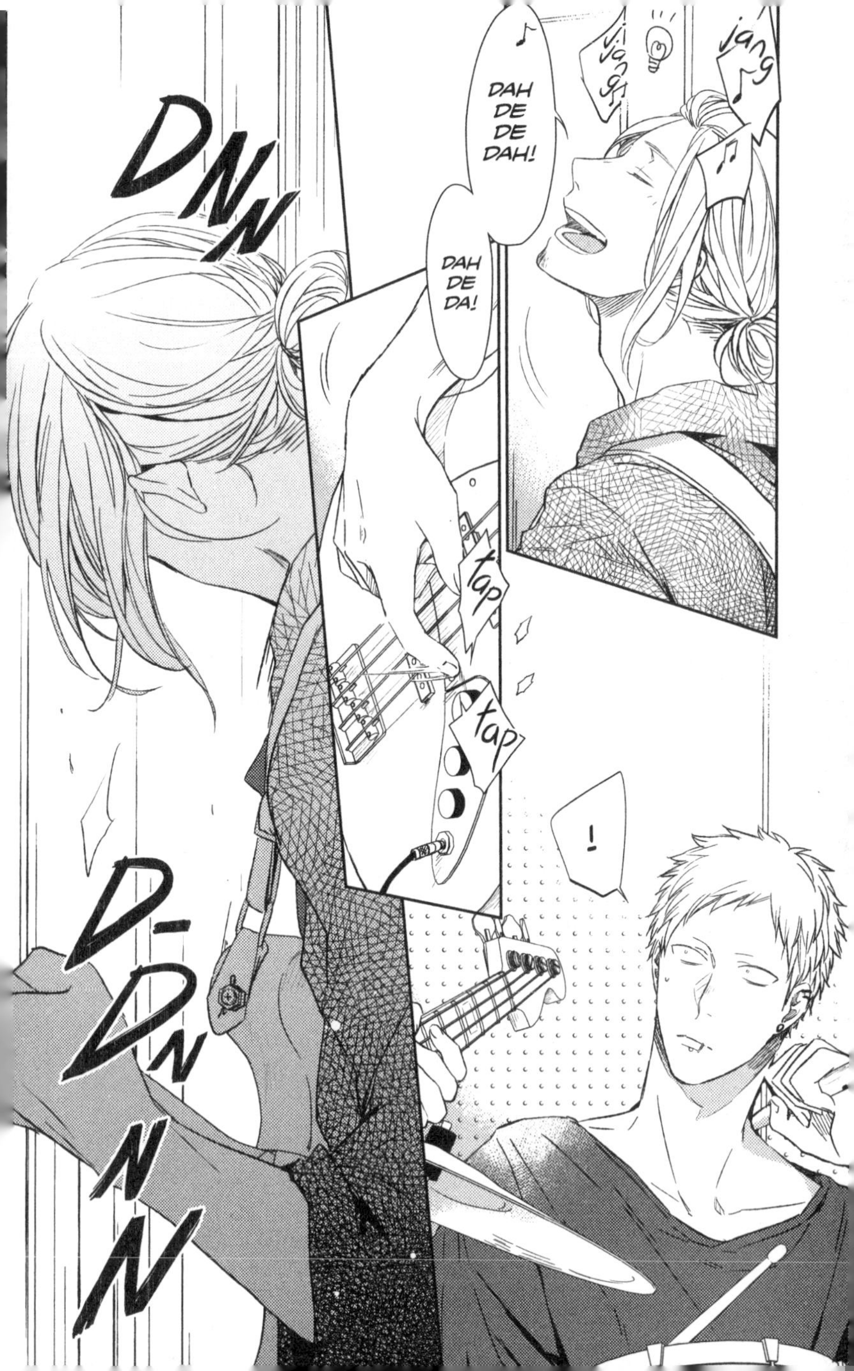
jang
jang!!
DAH DE DE DAH!
DAH DE DA!
DNN
tap
tap
!
D-DN NNN

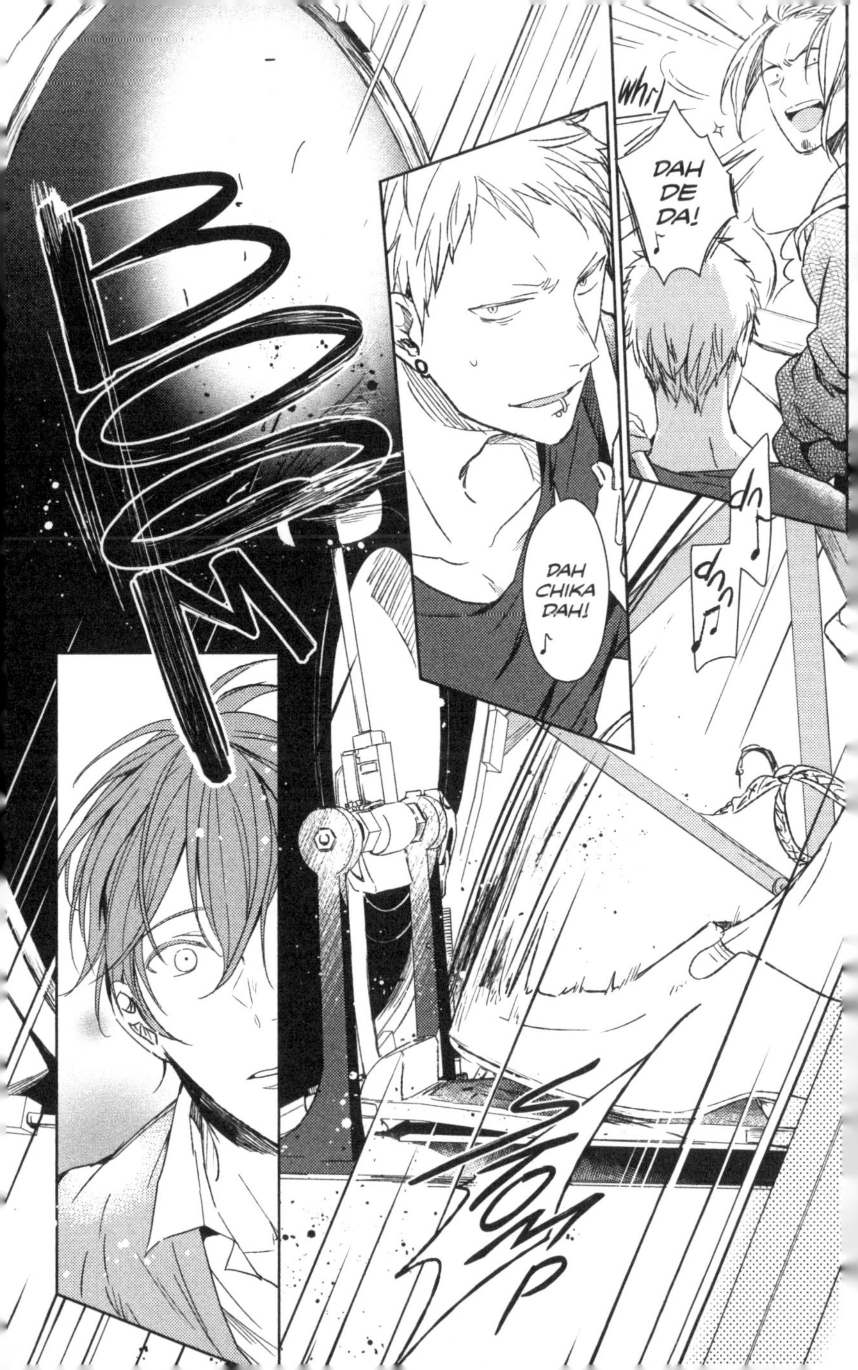
whrl
DAH DE DA! ♪
dn dnn ♪
DAH CHIKA DAH! ♪
BOOM
STOMP

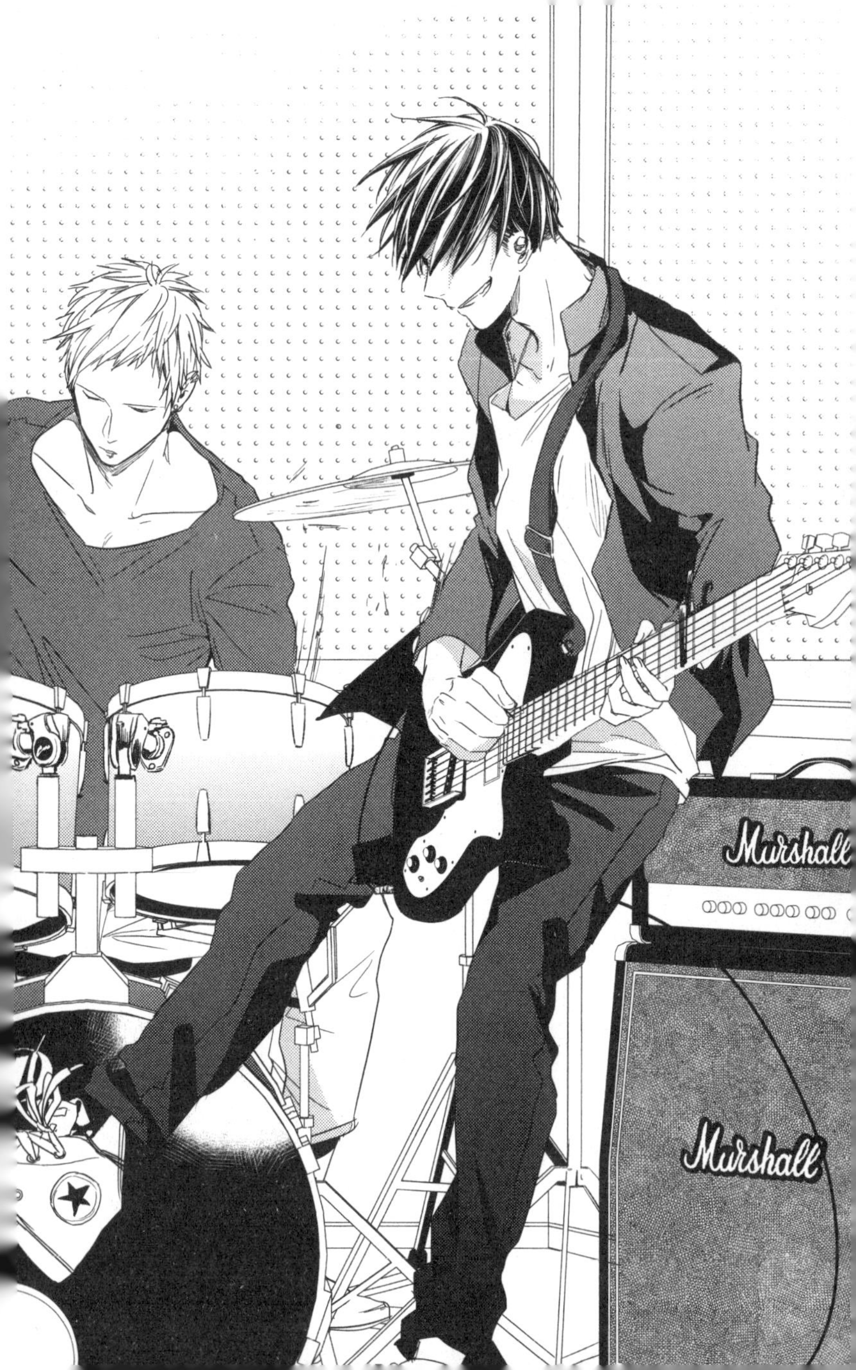
Marshall
Marshall

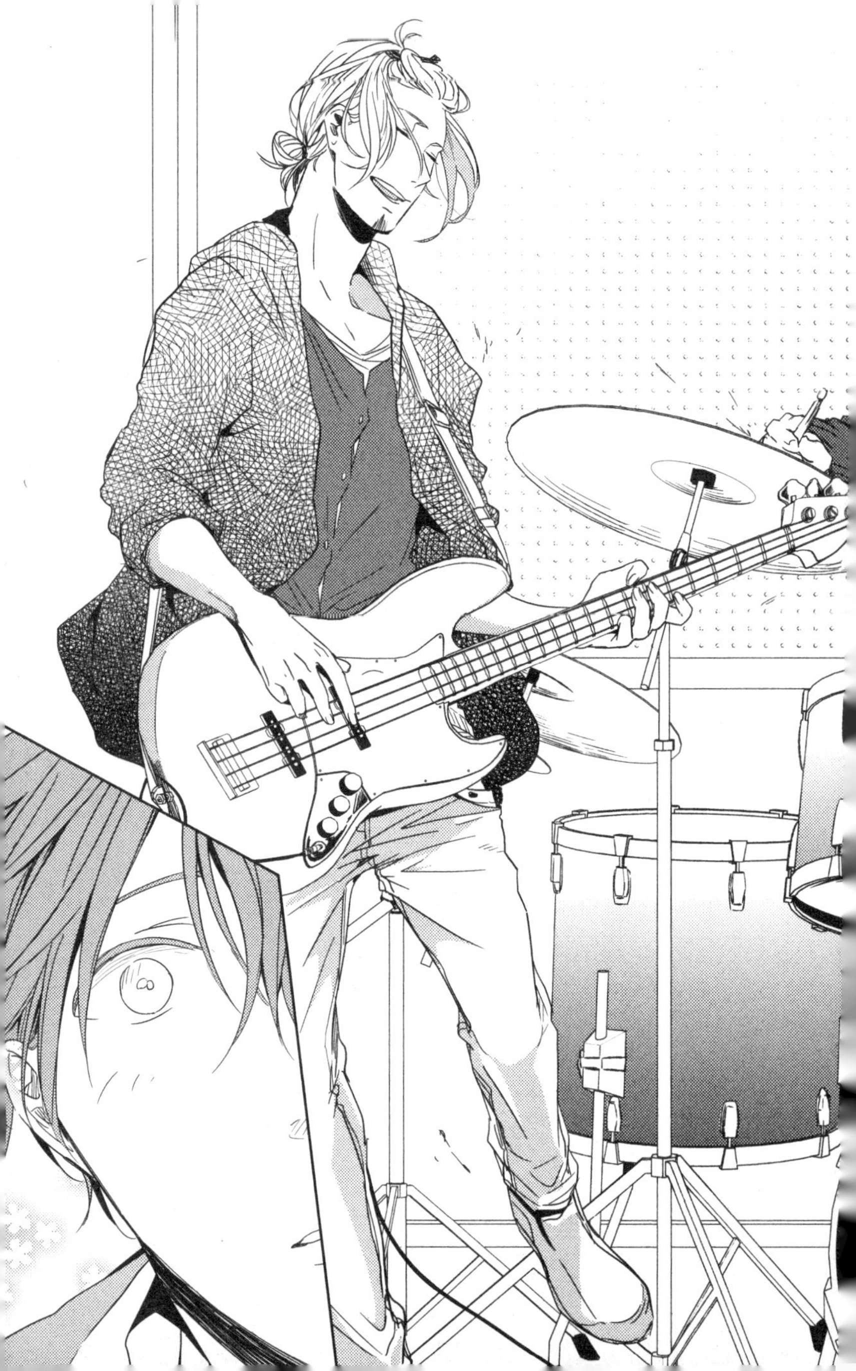

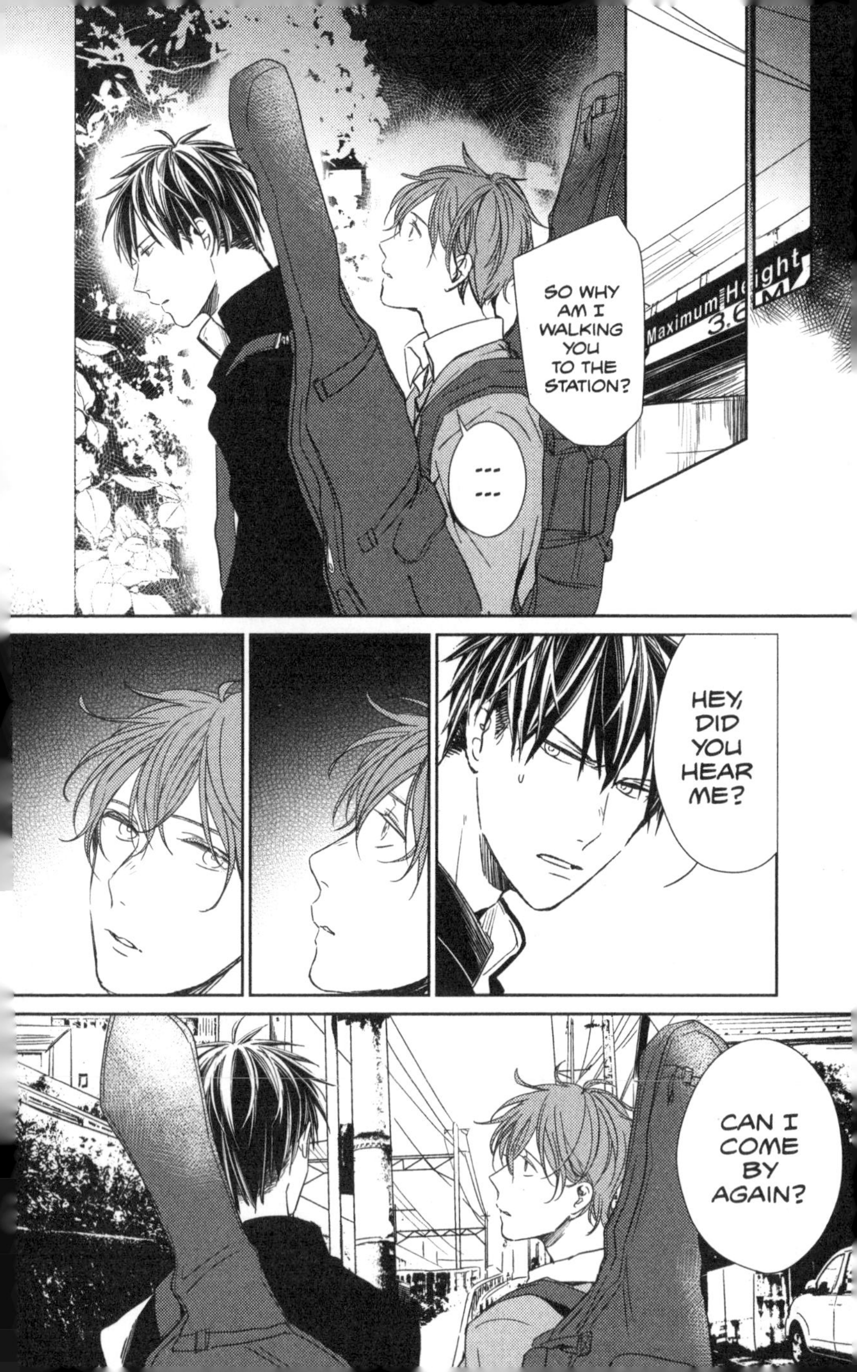
Maximum Height
3.6 M
SO WHY AM I WALKING YOU TO THE STATION?
......
HEY, DID YOU HEAR ME?
CAN I COME BY AGAIN?

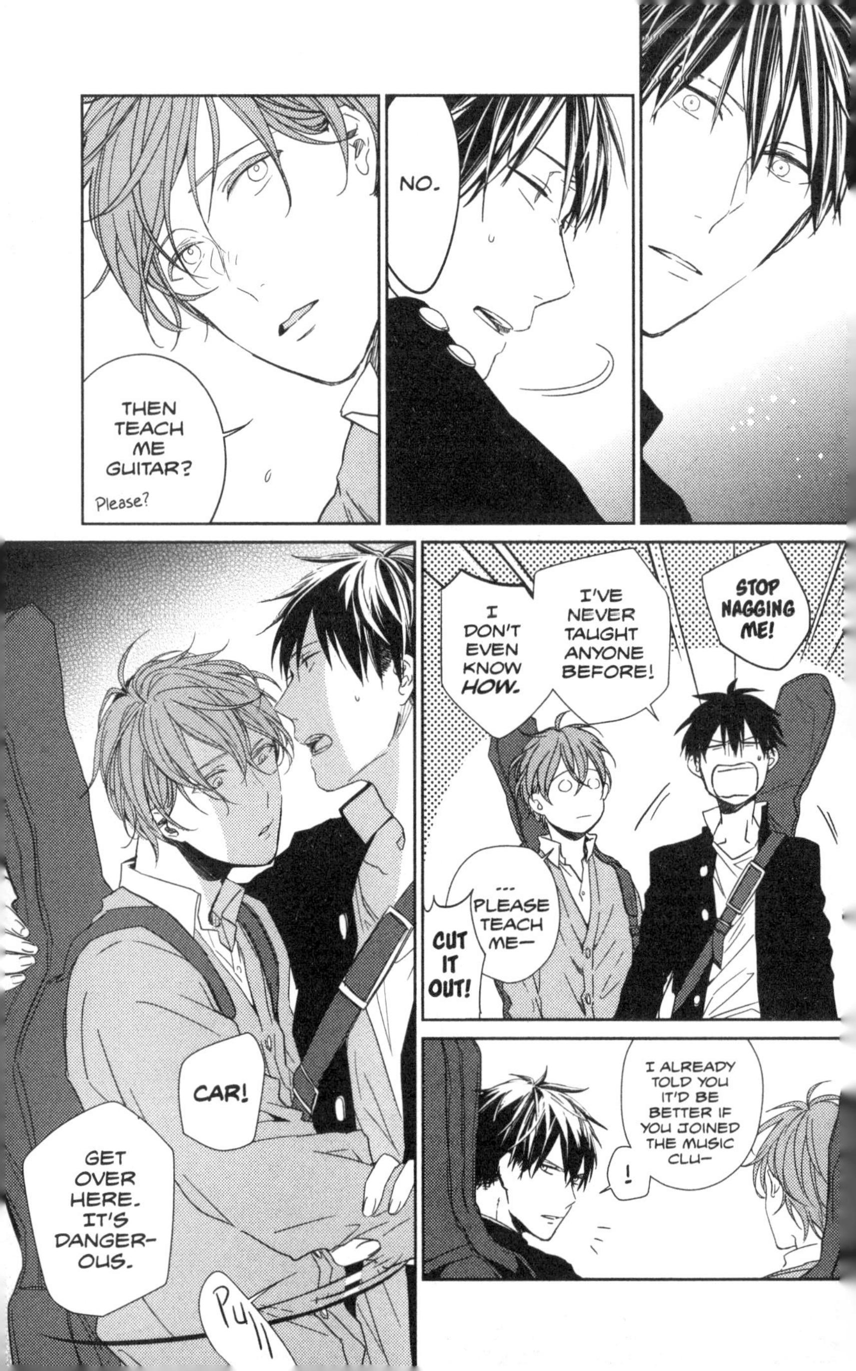
NO.
THEN TEACH ME GUITAR?
Please?
STOP NAGGING ME!
I'VE NEVER TAUGHT ANYONE BEFORE!
I DON'T EVEN KNOW *HOW.*
...PLEASE TEACH ME—
CUT IT OUT!
I ALREADY TOLD YOU IT'D BE BETTER IF YOU JOINED THE MUSIC CLU—
!
CAR!
GET OVER HERE. IT'S DANGEROUS.
Pull

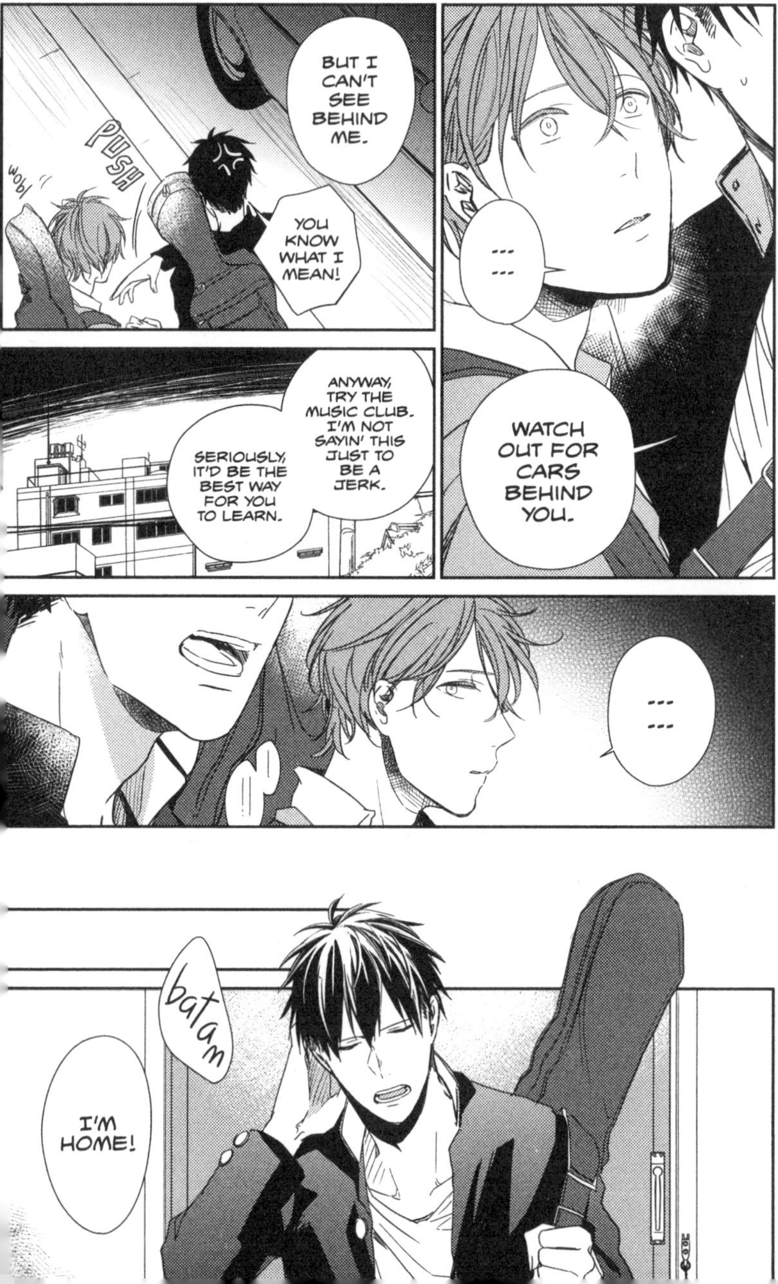
...
...
WATCH OUT FOR CARS BEHIND YOU.
BUT I CAN'T SEE BEHIND ME.
PUSH
YOU KNOW WHAT I MEAN!
wob
ANYWAY, TRY THE MUSIC CLUB. I'M NOT SAYIN' THIS JUST TO BE A JERK.
SERIOUSLY, IT'D BE THE BEST WAY FOR YOU TO LEARN.
...
...
batam
I'M HOME!

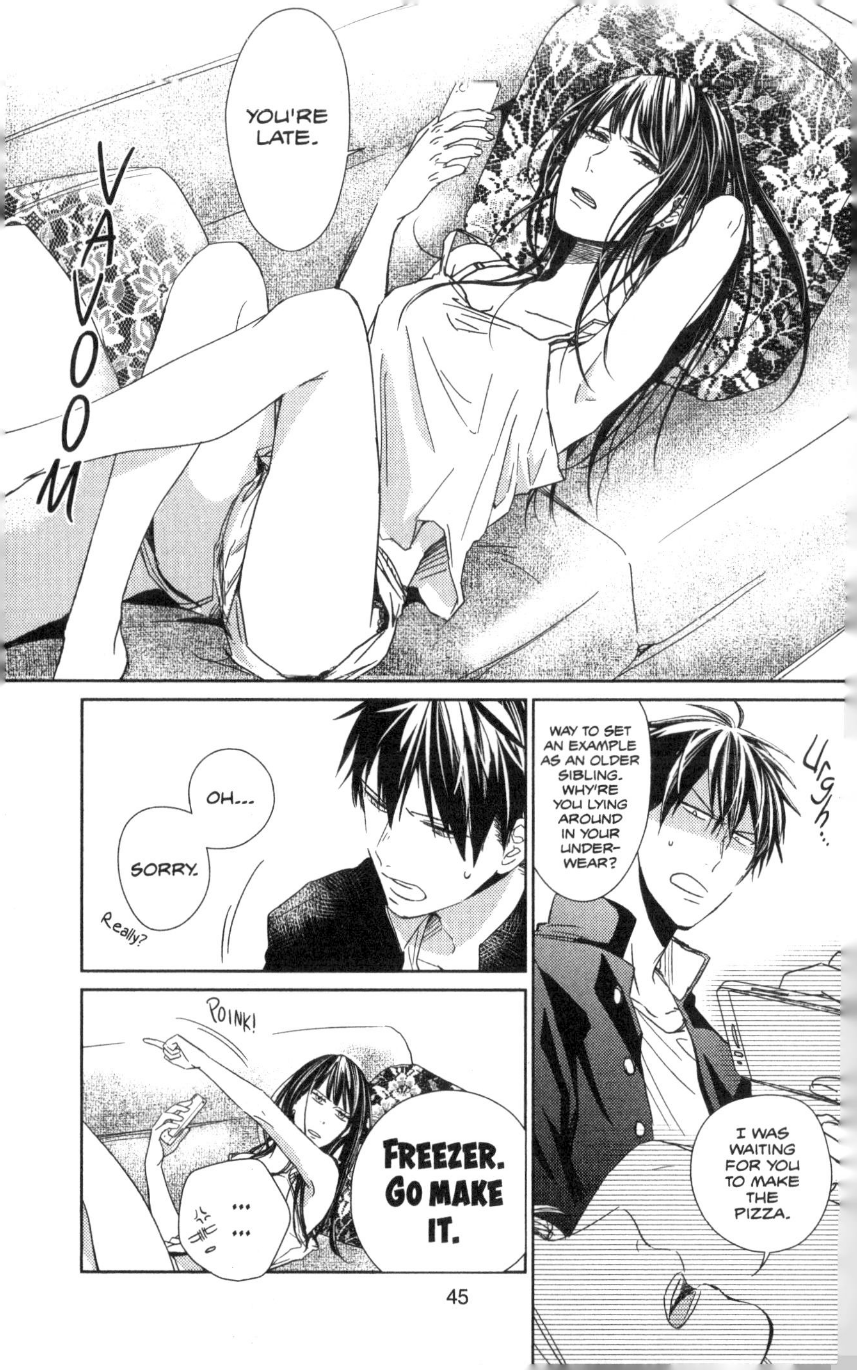
YOU'RE LATE.
VAVOOOM
URGH...
WAY TO SET AN EXAMPLE AS AN OLDER SIBLING. WHY'RE YOU LYING AROUND IN YOUR UNDER-WEAR?
I WAS WAITING FOR YOU TO MAKE THE PIZZA.
OH...
SORRY.
Really?
POINK!
FREEZER. GO MAKE IT.
... ...

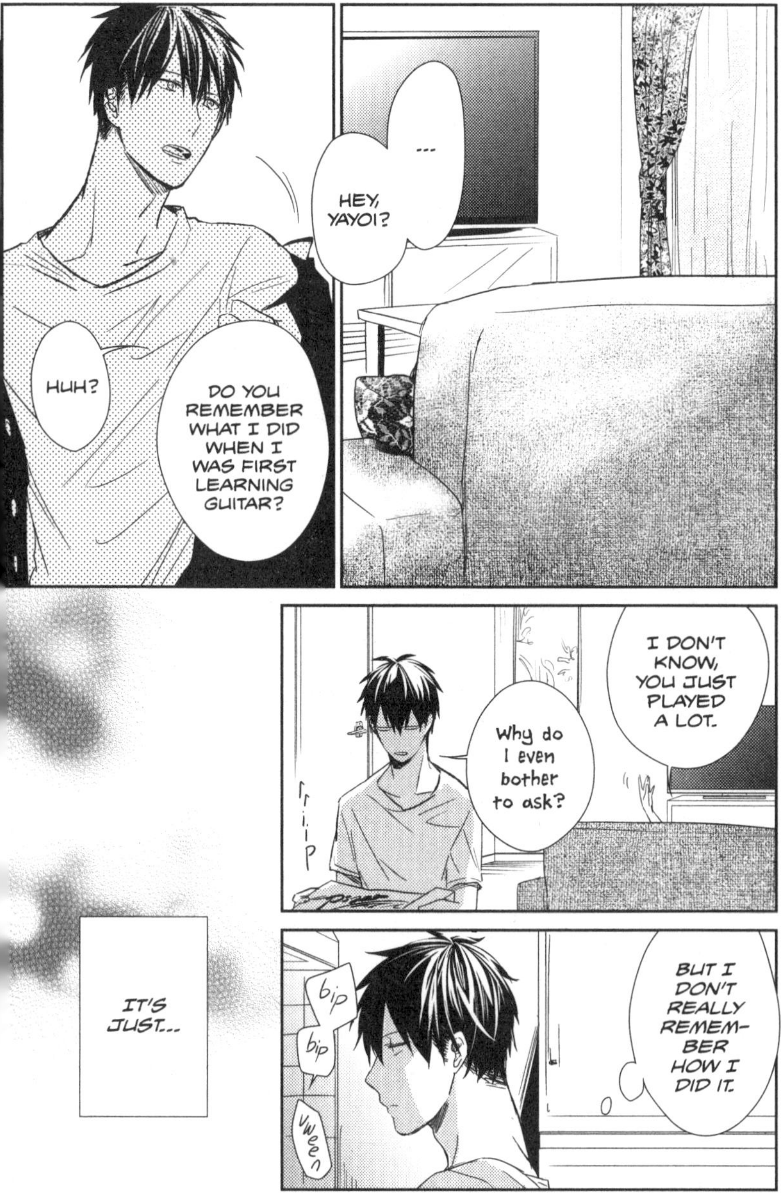
...
HEY, YAYOI?
DO YOU REMEMBER WHAT I DID WHEN I WAS FIRST LEARNING GUITAR?
HUH?
I DON'T KNOW, YOU JUST PLAYED A LOT.
Why do I even bother to ask?
rr.i.i.p
BUT I DON'T REALLY REMEMBER HOW I DID IT.
bip
bip
vween
IT'S JUST...

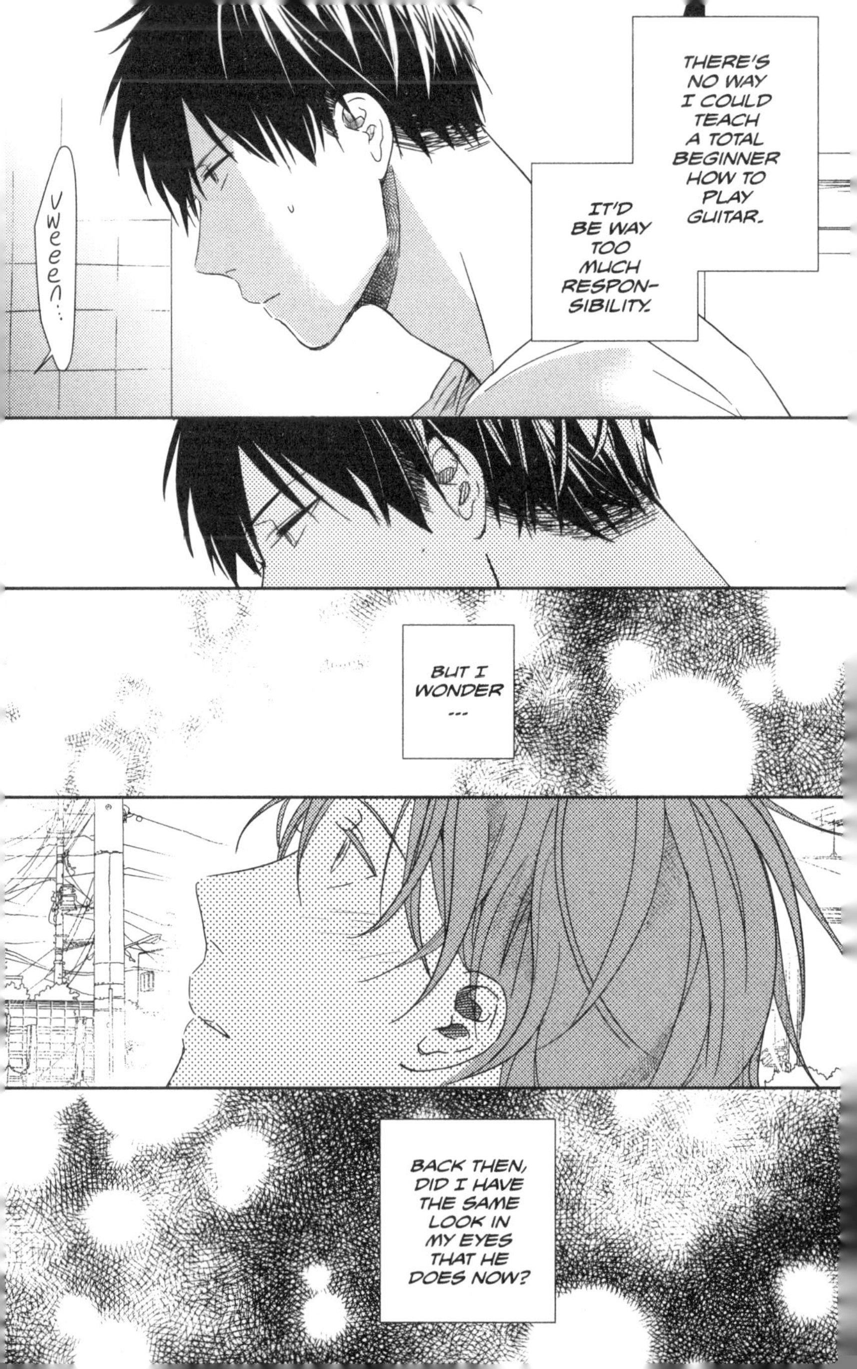
THERE'S NO WAY I COULD TEACH A TOTAL BEGINNER HOW TO PLAY GUITAR.
IT'D BE WAY TOO MUCH RESPON-SIBILITY.
Vweeen...
BUT I WONDER ...
BACK THEN, DID I HAVE THE SAME LOOK IN MY EYES THAT HE DOES NOW?

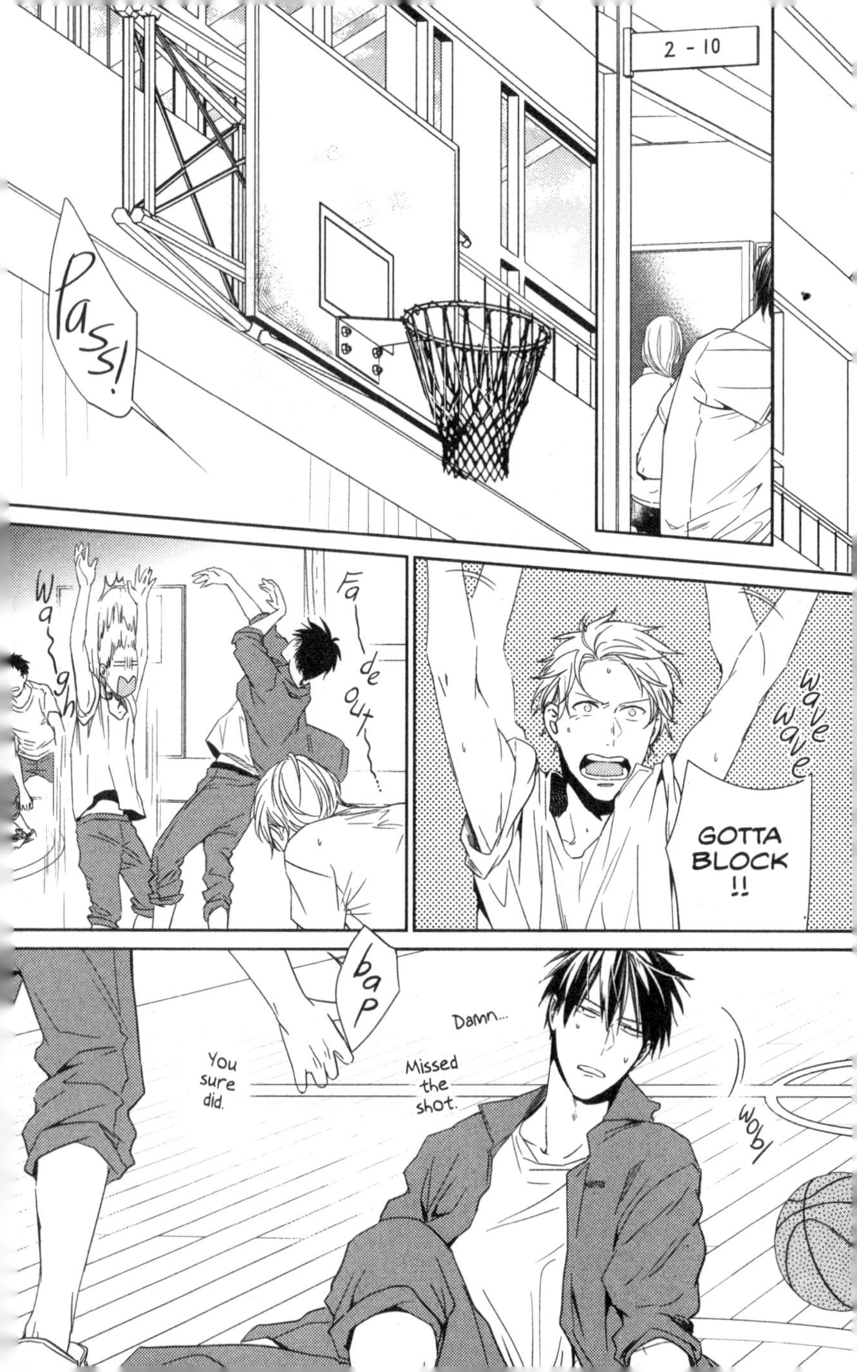
2 - 10
Pass!
wave wave
GOTTA BLOCK !!
Fa-de out...
Wa~gh
bap
Damn...
Missed the shot.
You sure did.
wobl

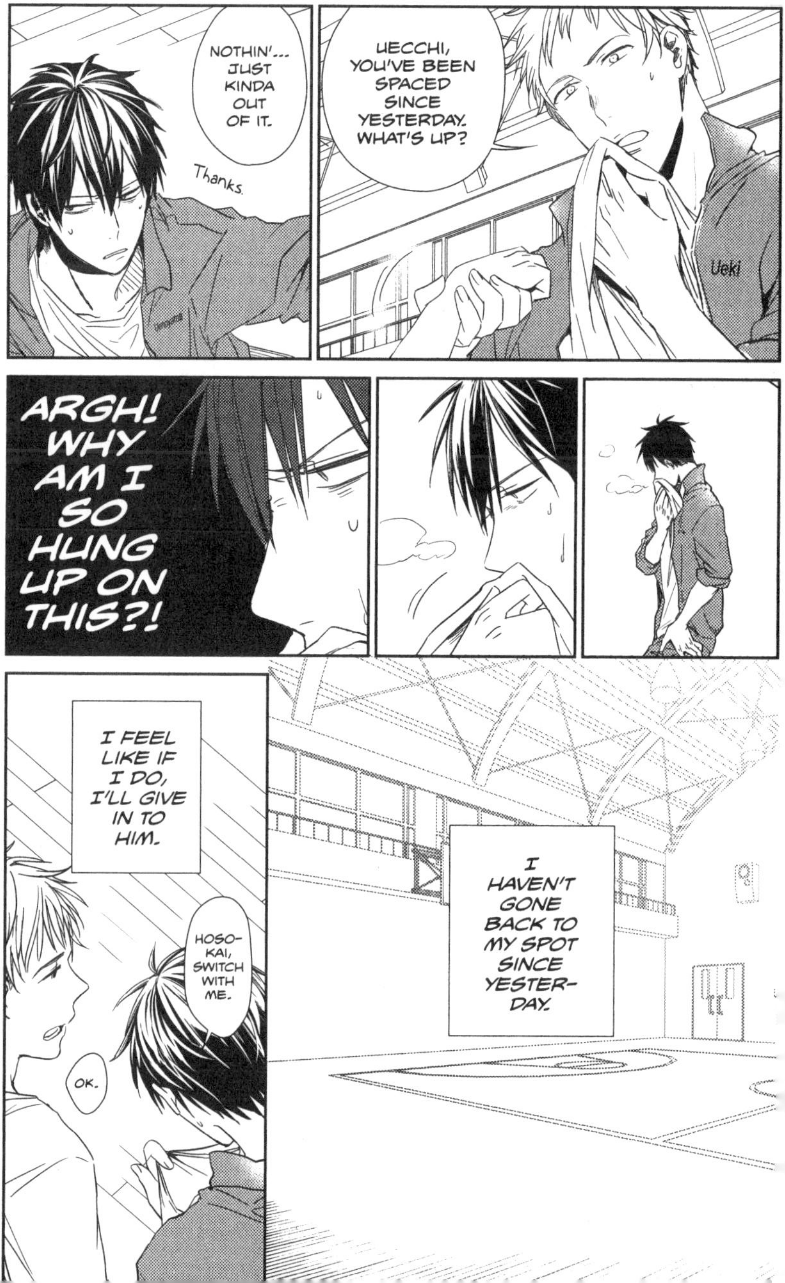
Ueki
UECCHI, YOU'VE BEEN SPACED SINCE YESTERDAY. WHAT'S UP?
NOTHIN'... JUST KINDA OUT OF IT.
Thanks.
ARGH! WHY AM I SO HUNG UP ON THIS?!
I HAVEN'T GONE BACK TO MY SPOT SINCE YESTER-DAY.
I FEEL LIKE IF I DO, I'LL GIVE IN TO HIM.
HOSO-KAI, SWITCH WITH ME.
OK.

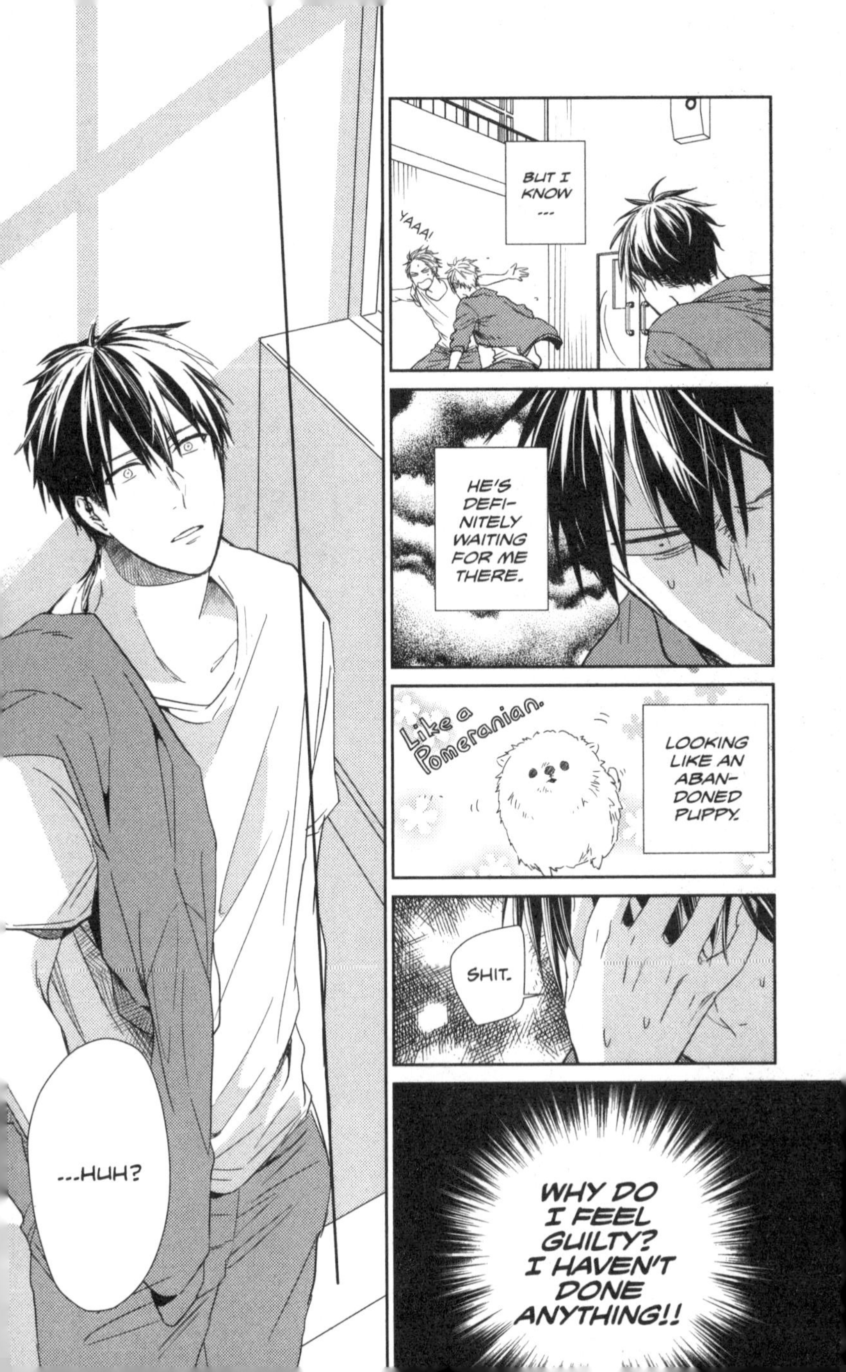
BUT I KNOW ---
YAAA!
HE'S DEFI-NITELY WAITING FOR ME THERE.
LOOKING LIKE AN ABAN-DONED PUPPY.
Like a Pomeranian.
SHIT.
WHY DO I FEEL GUILTY? I HAVEN'T DONE ANYTHING!!
---HUH?

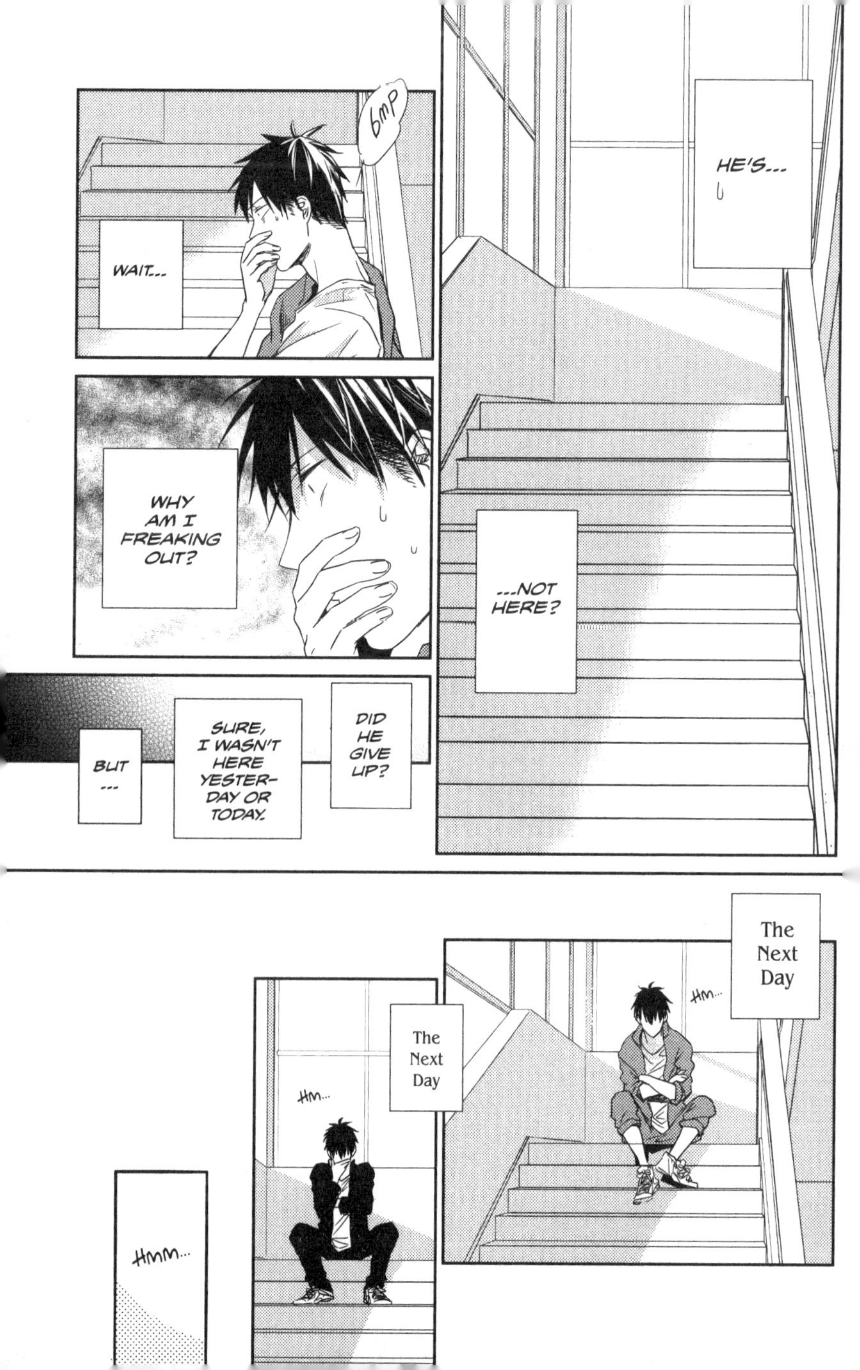
HE'S...
...NOT HERE?
bmp
WAIT...
WHY AM I FREAKING OUT?
DID HE GIVE UP?
SURE, I WASN'T HERE YESTER-DAY OR TODAY.
BUT ...
The Next Day
Hm...
The Next Day
Hm...
Hmm...

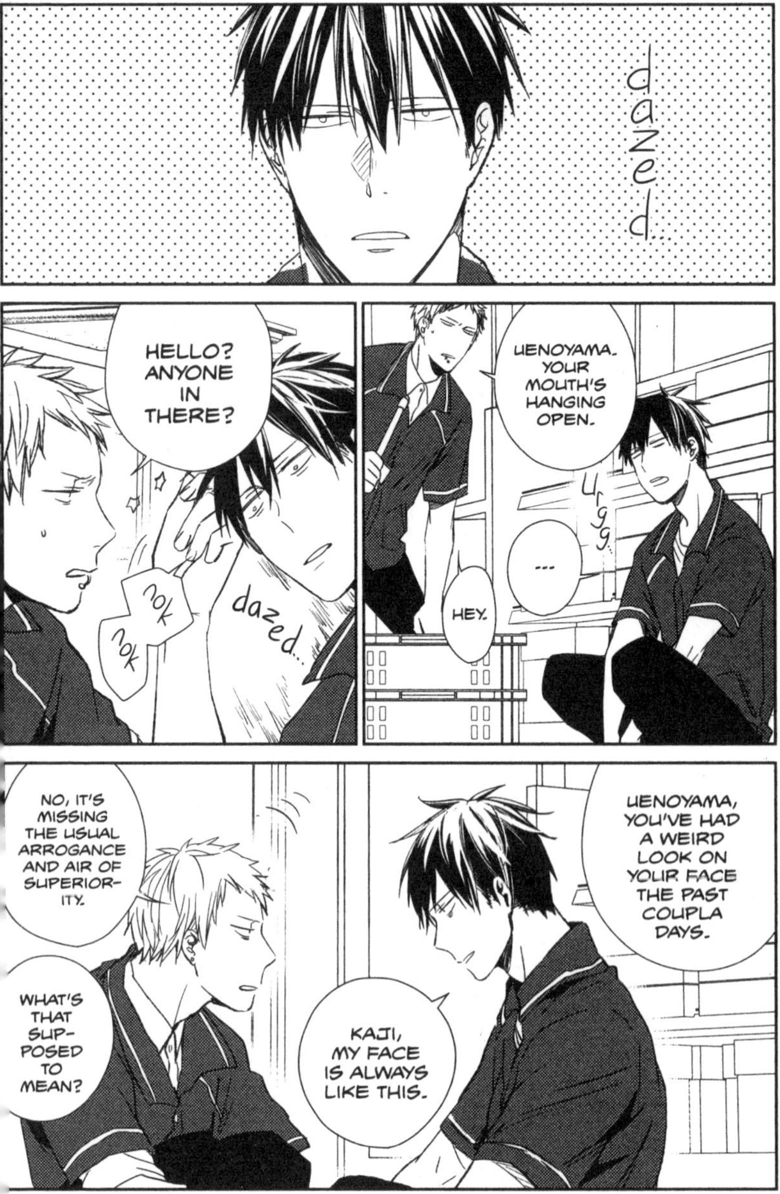
dazed...
UENOYAMA. YOUR MOUTH'S HANGING OPEN.
Urgg...
...
HEY.
HELLO? ANYONE IN THERE?
pok pok
dazed...
UENOYAMA, YOU'VE HAD A WEIRD LOOK ON YOUR FACE THE PAST COUPLA DAYS.
KAJI, MY FACE IS ALWAYS LIKE THIS.
NO, IT'S MISSING THE USUAL ARROGANCE AND AIR OF SUPERIOR-ITY.
WHAT'S THAT SUP-POSED TO MEAN?

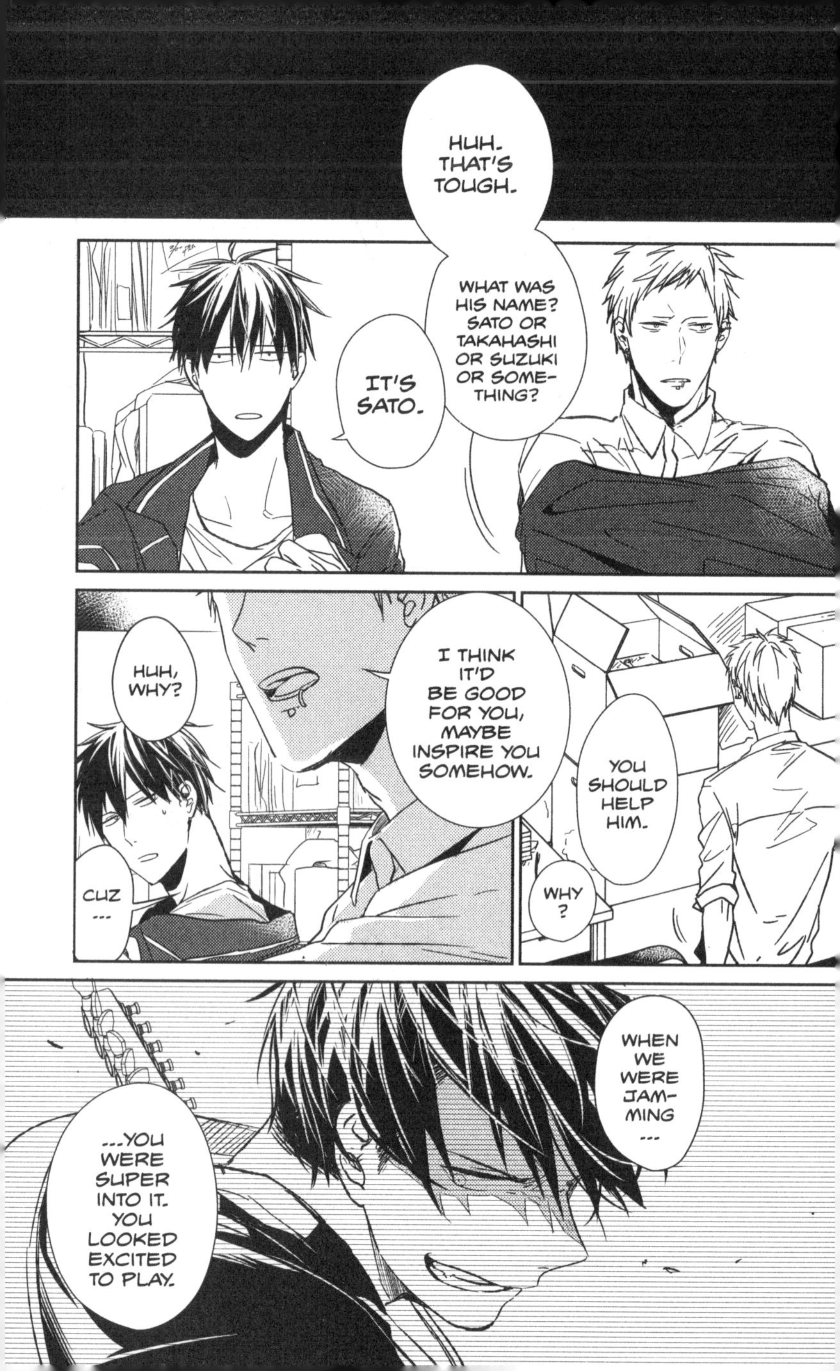
HUH. THAT'S TOUGH.
WHAT WAS HIS NAME? SATO OR TAKAHASHI OR SUZUKI OR SOME-THING?
IT'S SATO.
YOU SHOULD HELP HIM.
WHY?
I THINK IT'D BE GOOD FOR YOU, MAYBE INSPIRE YOU SOMEHOW.
HUH, WHY?
CUZ ...
WHEN WE WERE JAM-MING ...
...YOU WERE SUPER INTO IT. YOU LOOKED EXCITED TO PLAY.

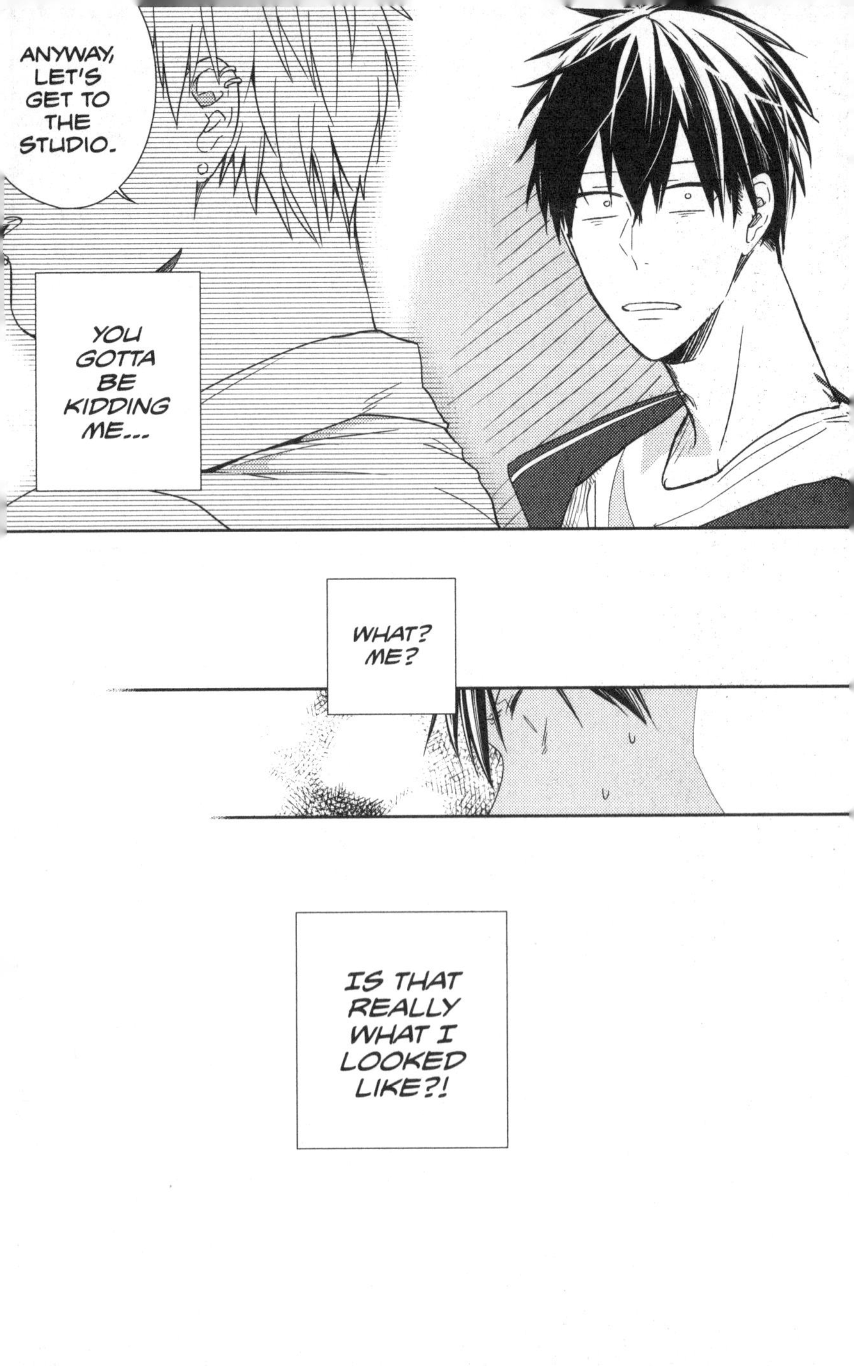
ANYWAY, LET'S GET TO THE STUDIO.
YOU GOTTA BE KIDDING ME...
WHAT? ME?
IS THAT REALLY WHAT I LOOKED LIKE?!

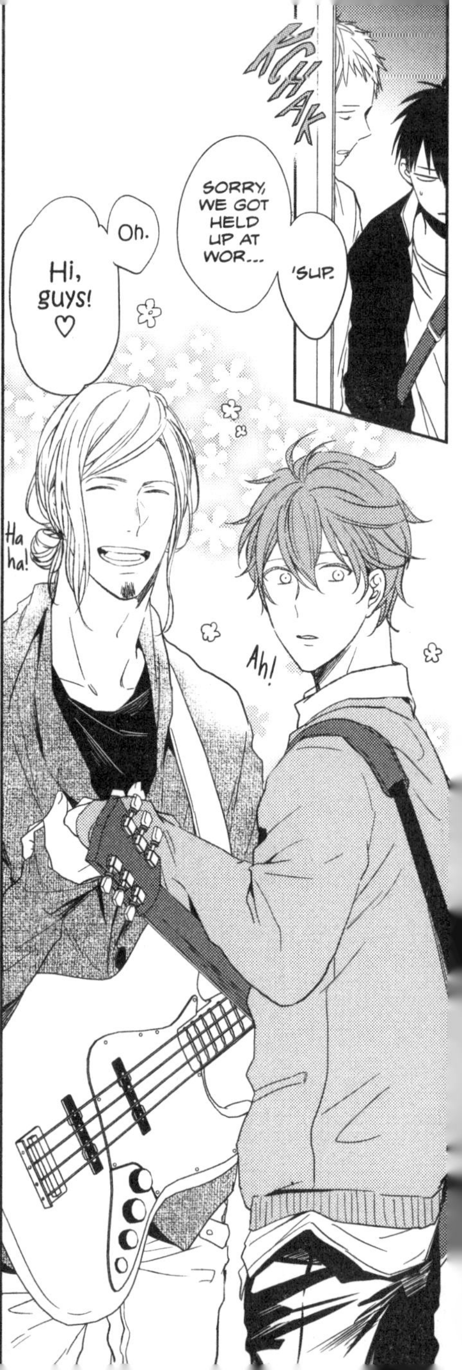
KCHAK
SORRY, WE GOT HELD UP AT WOR...
'SUP.
Oh.
Hi, guys! ♡
Ha ha!
Ah!

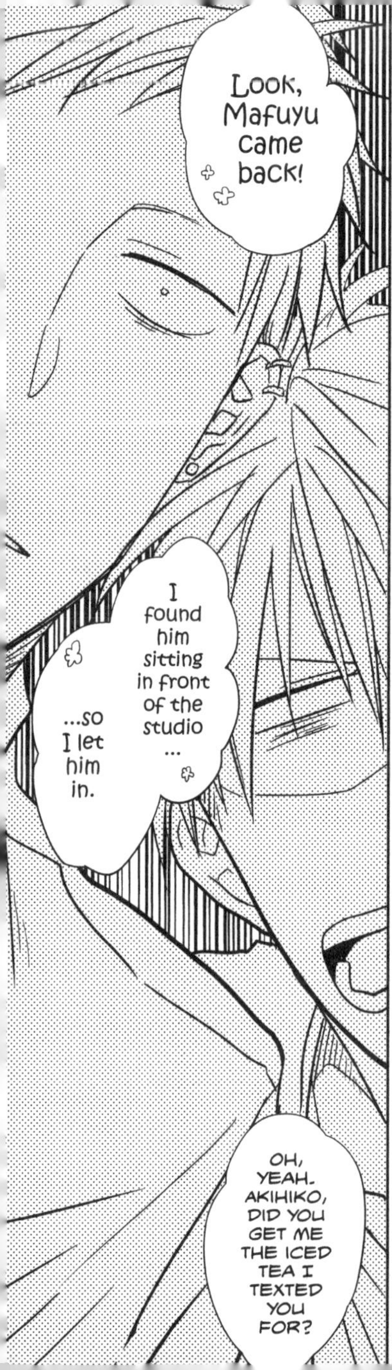
Look, Mafuyu came back!
I found him sitting in front of the studio ...
...so I let him in.
OH, YEAH. AKIHIKO, DID YOU GET ME THE ICED TEA I TEXTED YOU FOR?

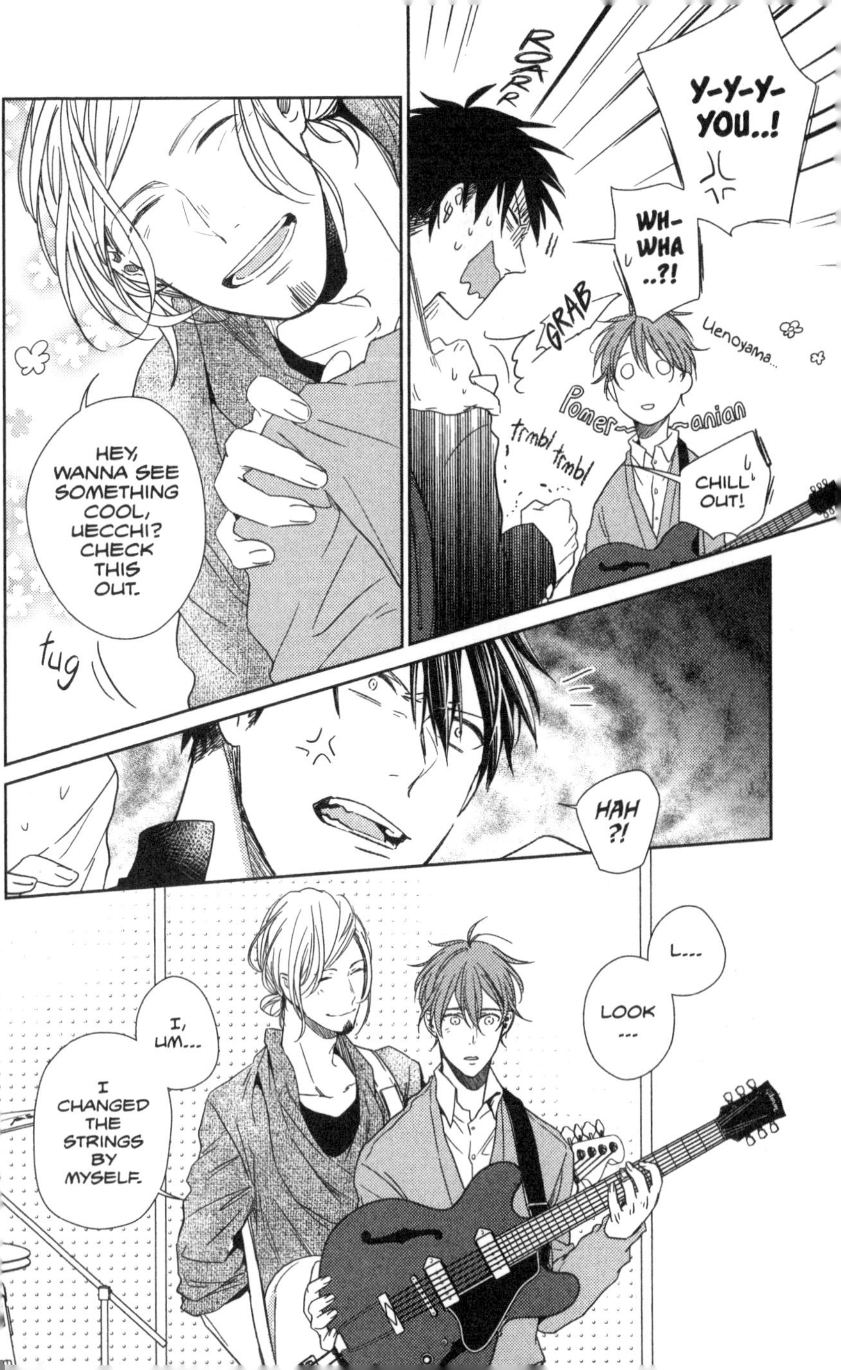
Y-Y-Y-YOU..!
ROARR
WH-WHA..?!
GRAB
Uenoyama...
Pomer~~anian
trmbl trmbl
CHILL OUT!
HEY, WANNA SEE SOMETHING COOL, UECCHI? CHECK THIS OUT.
tug
HAH?!
L...
LOOK...
I, UM...
I CHANGED THE STRINGS BY MYSELF.

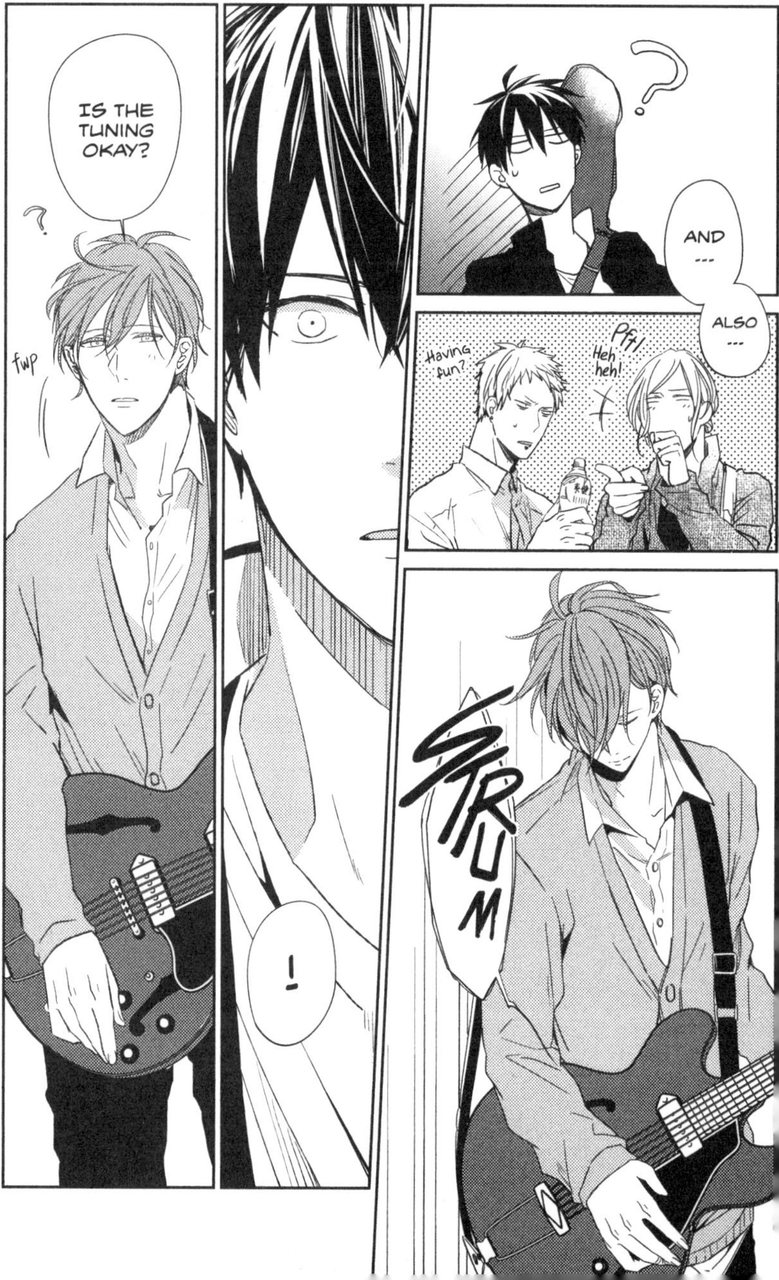
AND ---
ALSO ---
Having fun?
Pft!
Heh heh!
STRUM
!
IS THE TUNING OKAY?
?
fwp

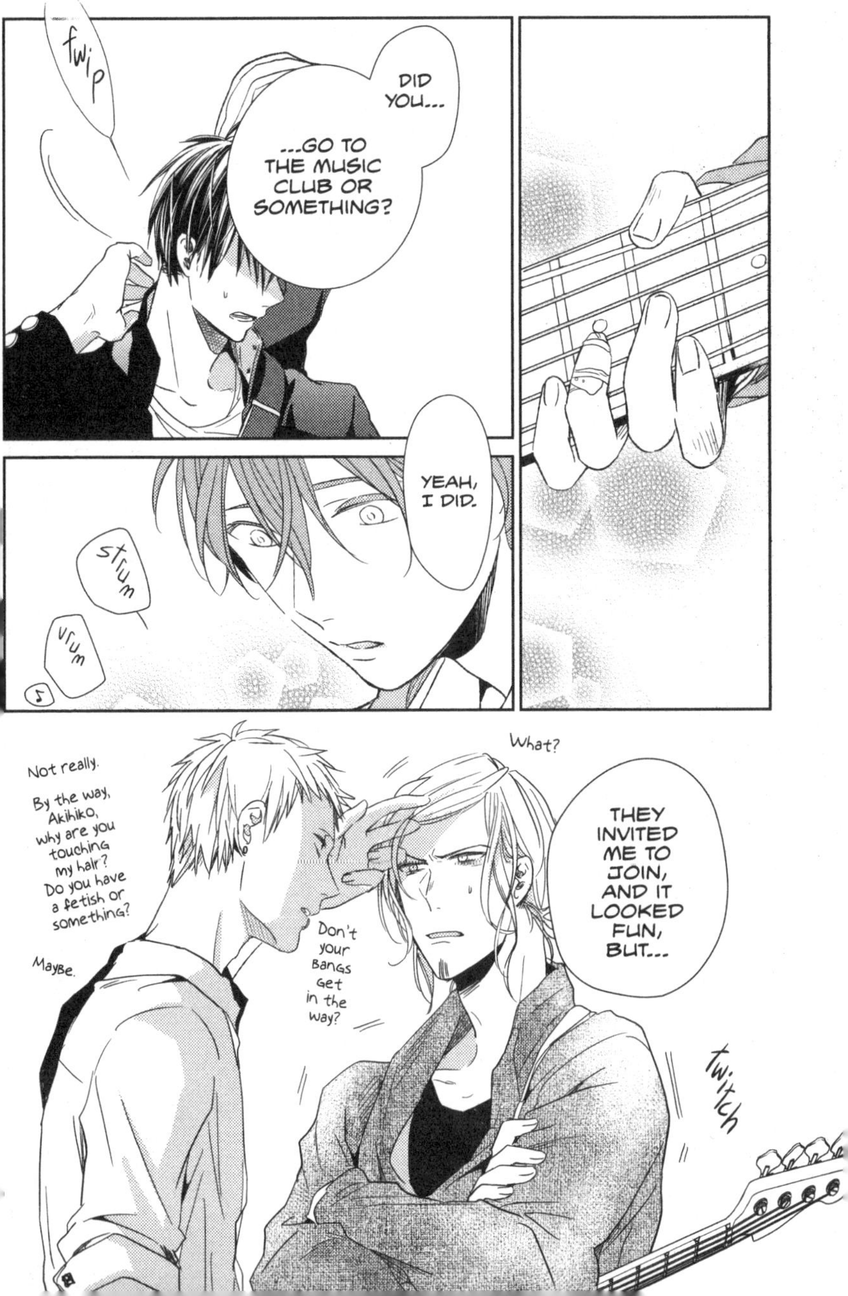
fwip
DID YOU...
...GO TO THE MUSIC CLUB OR SOMETHING?
YEAH, I DID.
strum
vrum
♪
What?
THEY INVITED ME TO JOIN, AND IT LOOKED FUN, BUT...
Don't your Bangs get in the way?
Not really.
By the way, Akihiko, why are you touching my hair? Do you have a fetish or something?
Maybe.
twitch

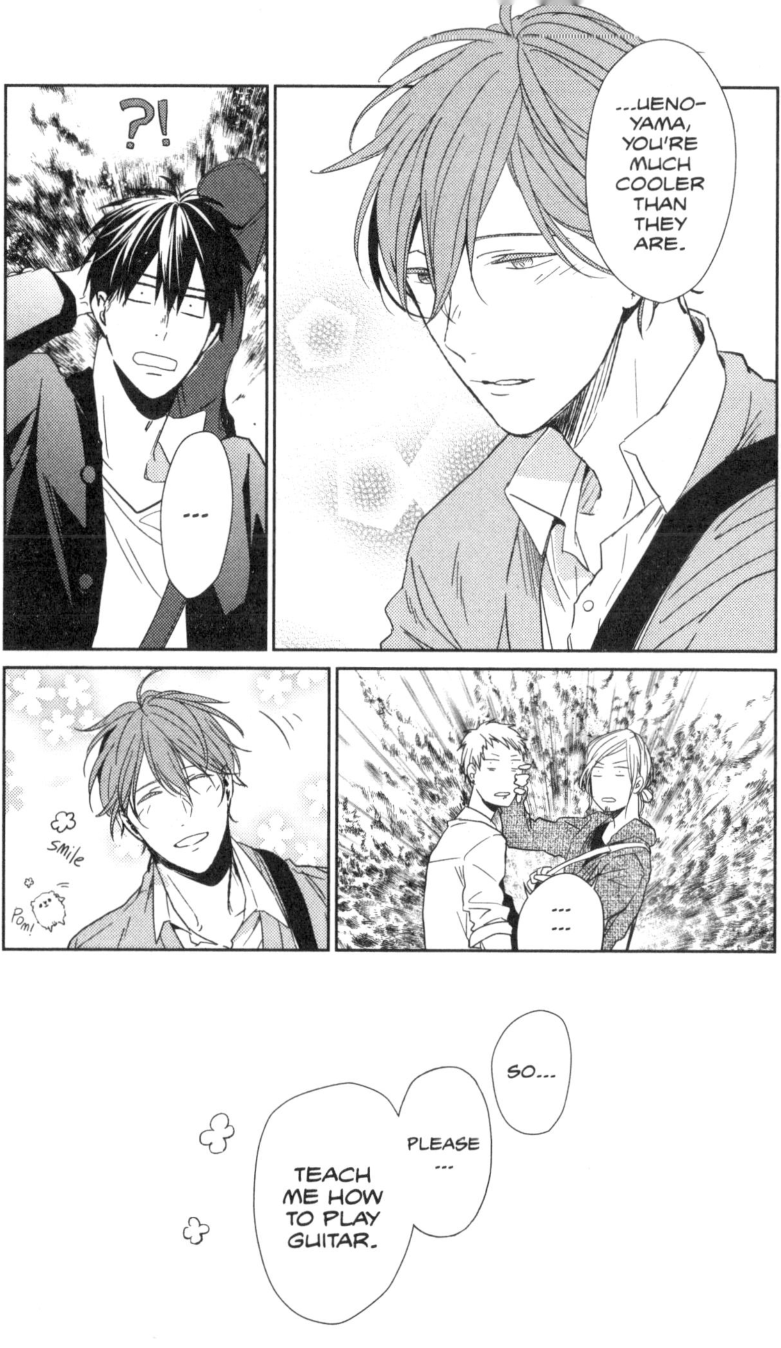
...UENO-YAMA, YOU'RE MUCH COOLER THAN THEY ARE.
?!
...
...
...
smile
Pom!
SO...
PLEASE ...
TEACH ME HOW TO PLAY GUITAR.

Ritsuka Uenoyama (16)

175 cm
(Second-year high school student)

Birthday: 8/1 Sign: Leo Blood Type: B

Guitar ← Telecaster Custom
(black) (customized a little)
Uses cheap triangle picks
↑
(If forced to choose) Easy-grip type
Headphones are AKG
Open-backed

Favorite Music:
Likes a wide variety, including old,
new, Asian, and Western.

In the rock genre: alternative, grunge,
emo, screamo, electronica, ambient,
dubstep. (The list goes on.)

His father is a music geek and
has been a big influence on him.
(And because of this, he's pretty cool
for a high schooler.)

He was in the basketball club in
middle school. (position: small forward).

Family: Dad, mom, older sister

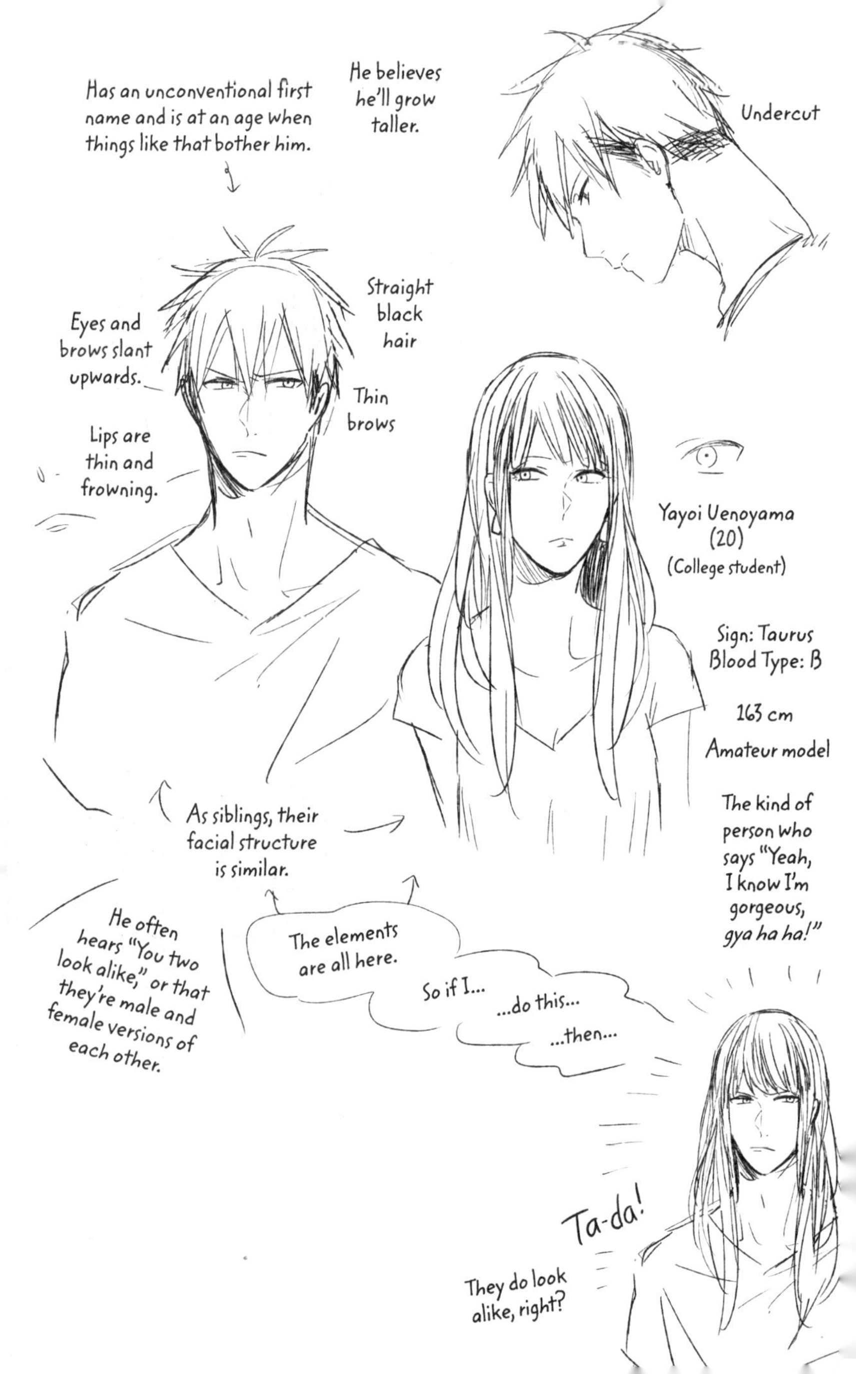
Has an unconventional first name and is at an age when things like that bother him.
He believes he'll grow taller.
Undercut
Straight black hair
Eyes and brows slant upwards.
Thin brows
Lips are thin and frowning.
Yayoi Uenoyama (20) (College student)
Sign: Taurus
Blood Type: B
163 cm
Amateur model
The kind of person who says "Yeah, I know I'm gorgeous, gya ha ha!"
As siblings, their facial structure is similar.
He often hears "You two look alike," or that they're male and female versions of each other.
The elements are all here.
So if I...
...do this...
...then...
Ta-da!
They do look alike, right?

given

by Natsuki Kizu

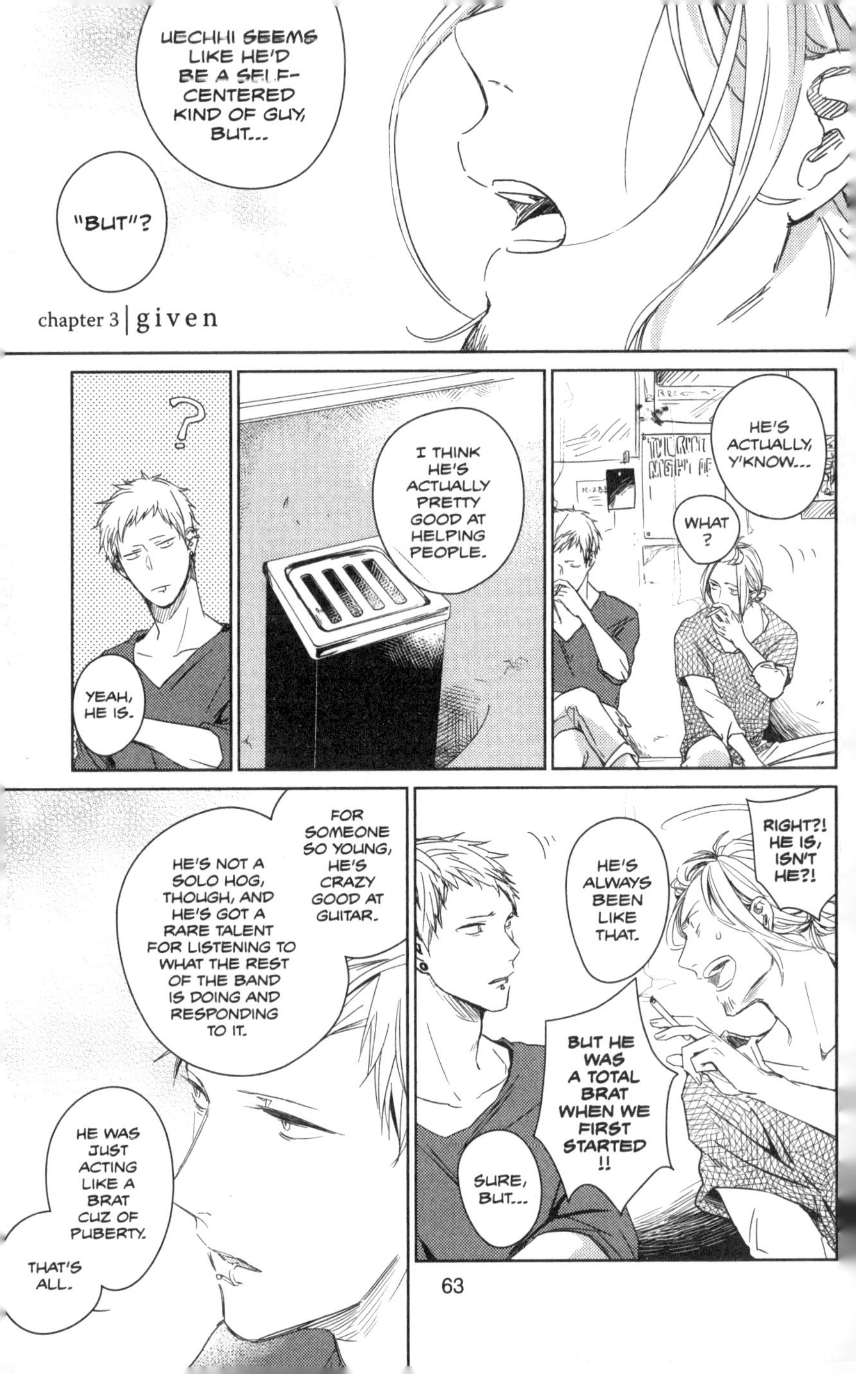
UECHHI SEEMS LIKE HE'D BE A SELF-CENTERED KIND OF GUY, BUT...
"BUT"?
HE'S ACTUALLY, Y'KNOW...
WHAT?
I THINK HE'S ACTUALLY PRETTY GOOD AT HELPING PEOPLE.
YEAH, HE IS.
RIGHT?! HE IS, ISN'T HE?!
HE'S ALWAYS BEEN LIKE THAT.
BUT HE WAS A TOTAL BRAT WHEN WE FIRST STARTED!!
SURE, BUT...
FOR SOMEONE SO YOUNG, HE'S CRAZY GOOD AT GUITAR.
HE'S NOT A SOLO HOG, THOUGH, AND HE'S GOT A RARE TALENT FOR LISTENING TO WHAT THE REST OF THE BAND IS DOING AND RESPONDING TO IT.
HE WAS JUST ACTING LIKE A BRAT CUZ OF PUBERTY.
THAT'S ALL.

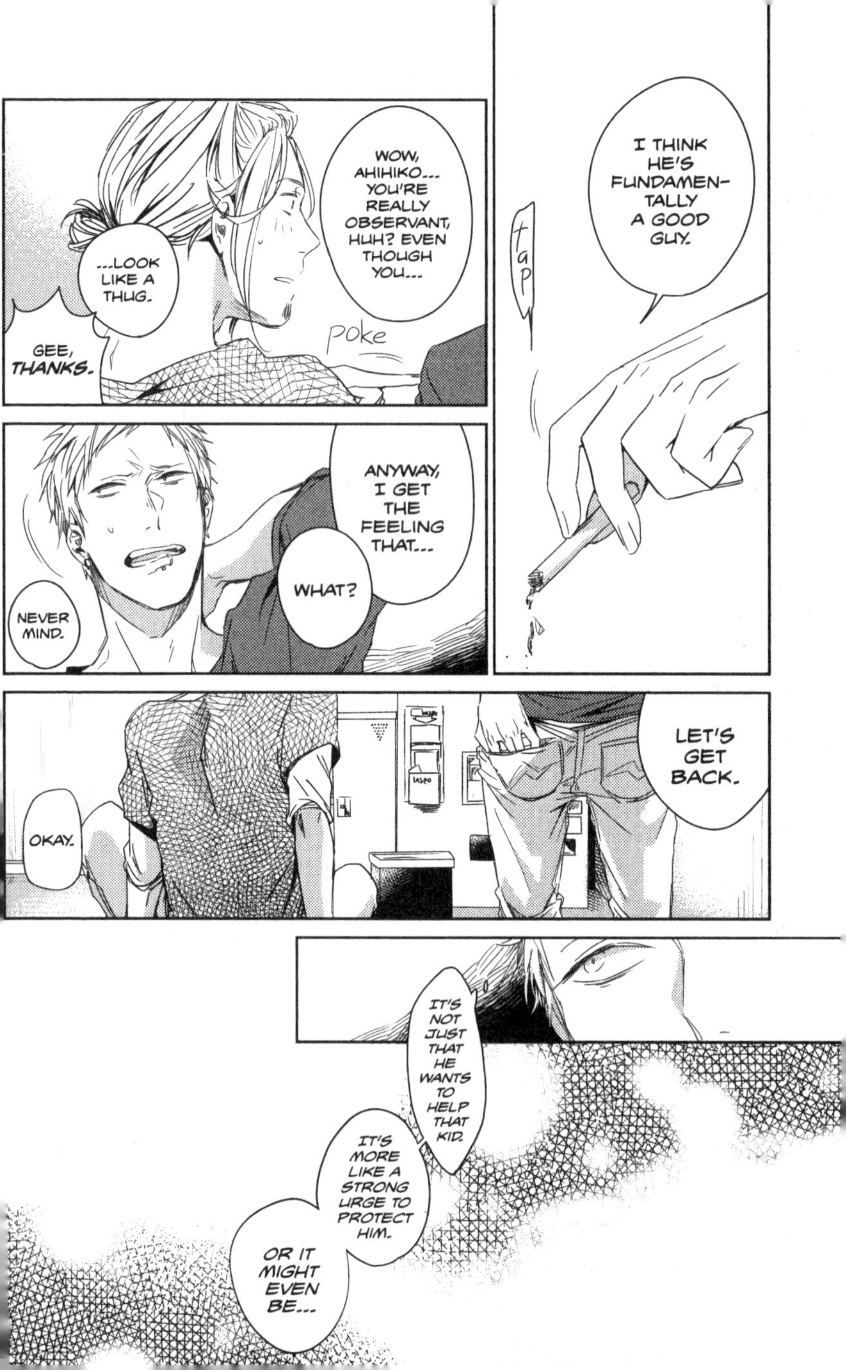
I THINK HE'S FUNDAMENTALLY A GOOD GUY.
tap
WOW, AHIHIKO... YOU'RE REALLY OBSERVANT, HUH? EVEN THOUGH YOU...
...LOOK LIKE A THUG.
poke
GEE, THANKS.
ANYWAY, I GET THE FEELING THAT...
WHAT?
NEVER MIND.
LET'S GET BACK.
OKAY.
IT'S NOT JUST THAT HE WANTS TO HELP THAT KID.
IT'S MORE LIKE A STRONG URGE TO PROTECT HIM.
OR IT MIGHT EVEN BE...

chapter 3

given

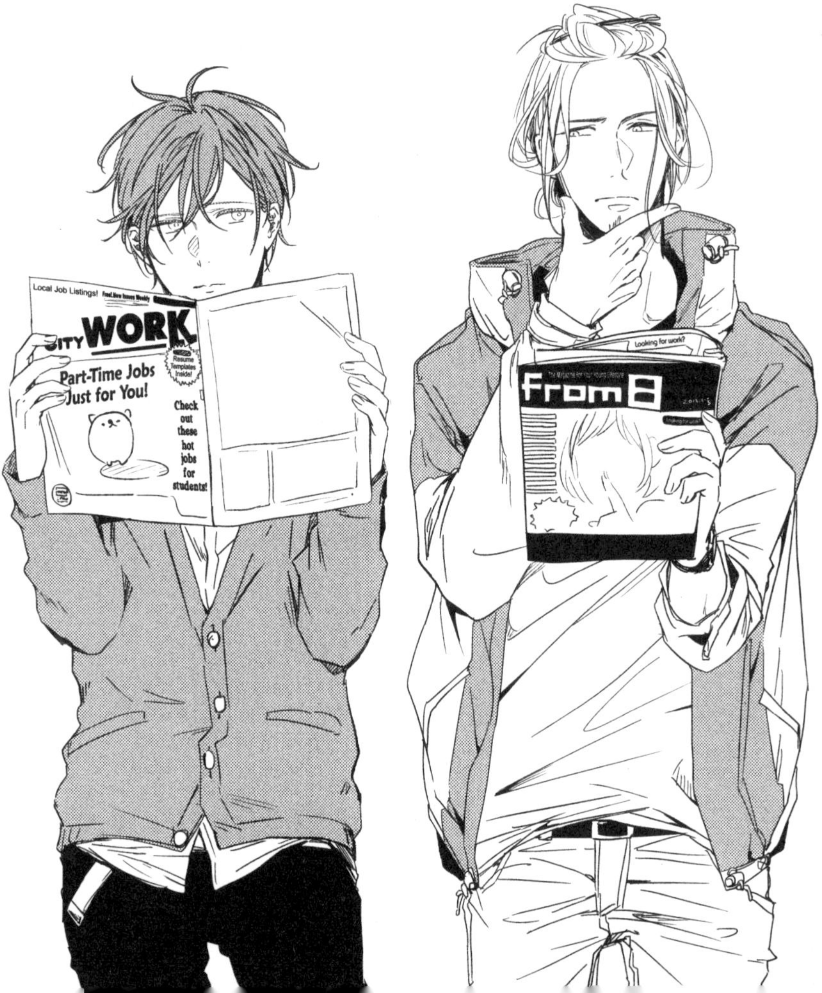
Local Job Listings!
CITY WORK
Resume Templates Inside!
Part-Time Jobs Just for You!
Check out these hot jobs for students!
Looking for work?
From B

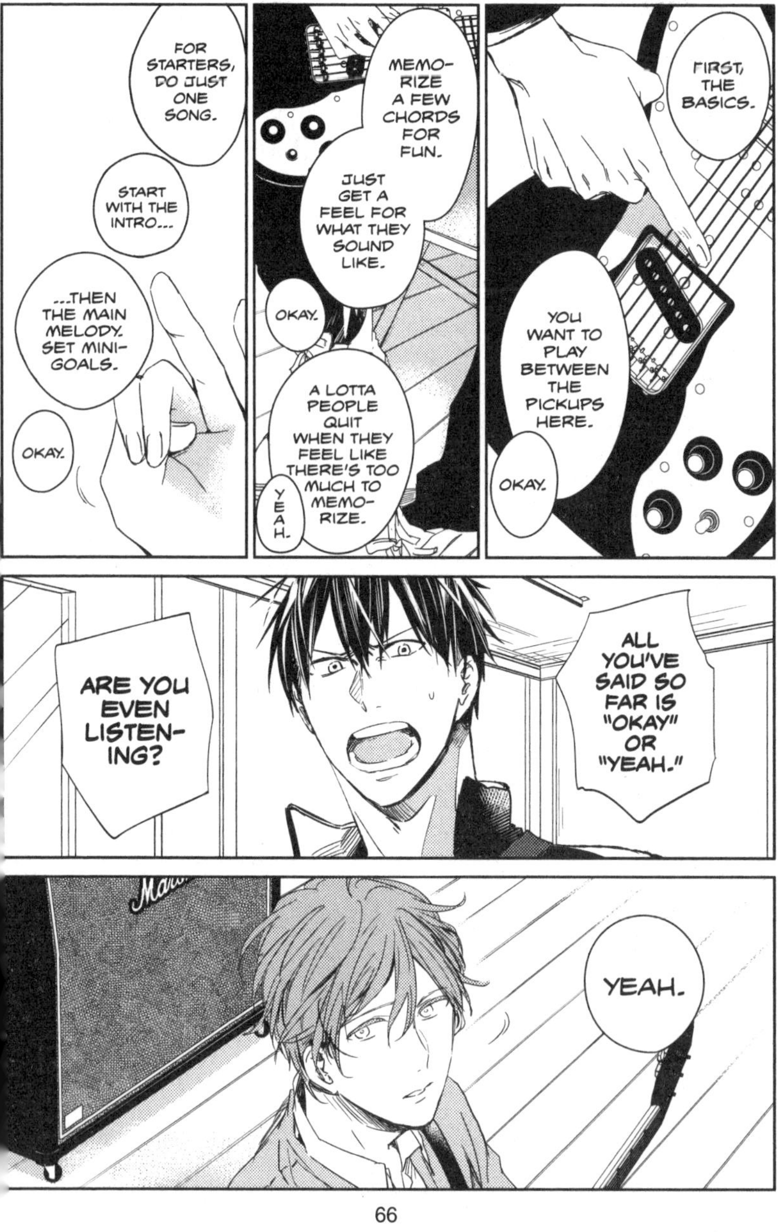
FIRST, THE BASICS.
YOU WANT TO PLAY BETWEEN THE PICKUPS HERE.
OKAY.
MEMORIZE A FEW CHORDS FOR FUN.
JUST GET A FEEL FOR WHAT THEY SOUND LIKE.
OKAY.
A LOTTA PEOPLE QUIT WHEN THEY FEEL LIKE THERE'S TOO MUCH TO MEMORIZE.
YEAH.
FOR STARTERS, DO JUST ONE SONG.
START WITH THE INTRO...
...THEN THE MAIN MELODY. SET MINI-GOALS.
OKAY.
ALL YOU'VE SAID SO FAR IS "OKAY" OR "YEAH."
ARE YOU EVEN LISTENING?
YEAH.

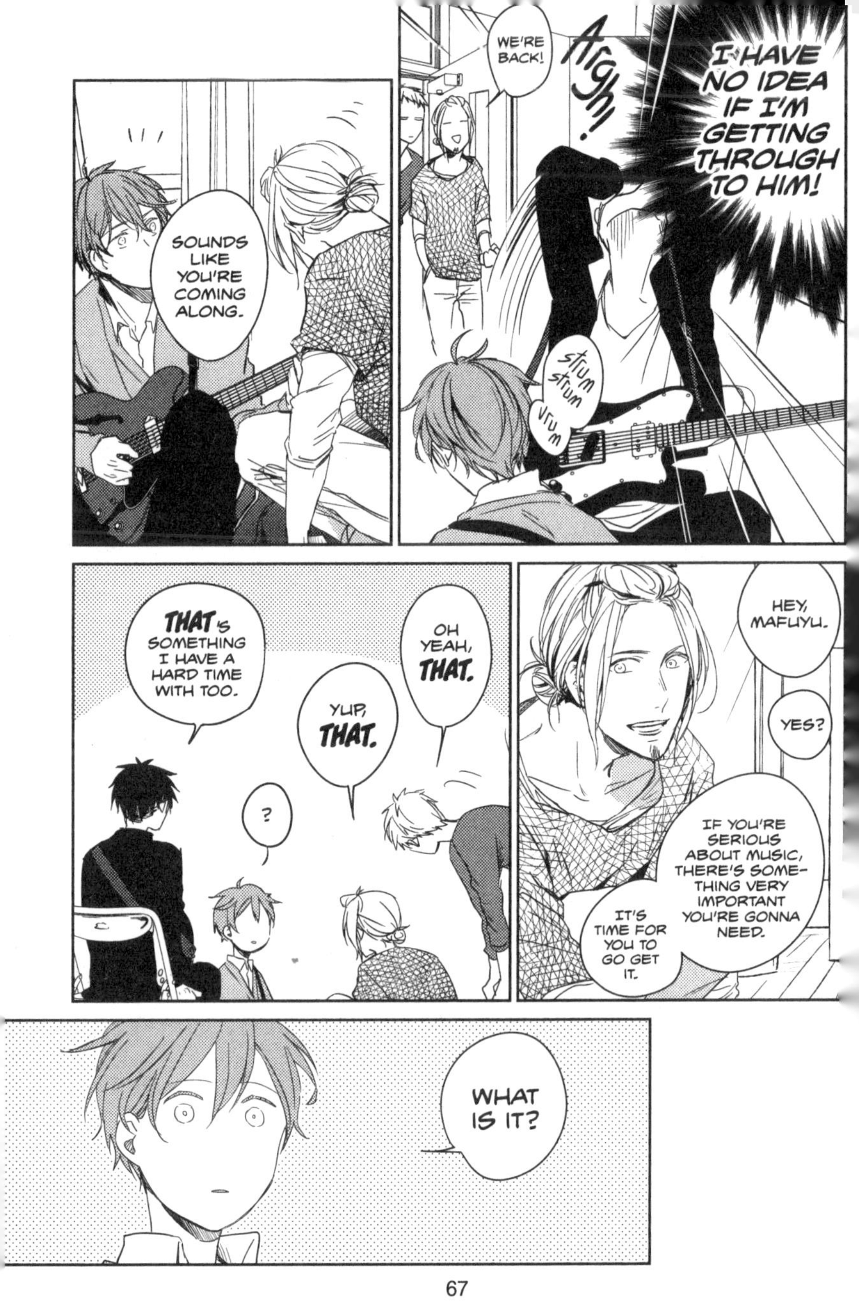
I HAVE NO IDEA IF I'M GETTING THROUGH TO HIM!
Argh!
WE'RE BACK!
strum strum
vrum
SOUNDS LIKE YOU'RE COMING ALONG.
HEY, MAFUYU.
YES?
IF YOU'RE SERIOUS ABOUT MUSIC, THERE'S SOMETHING VERY IMPORTANT YOU'RE GONNA NEED.
IT'S TIME FOR YOU TO GO GET IT.
OH YEAH, THAT.
YUP, THAT.
THAT'S SOMETHING I HAVE A HARD TIME WITH TOO.
?
WHAT IS IT?

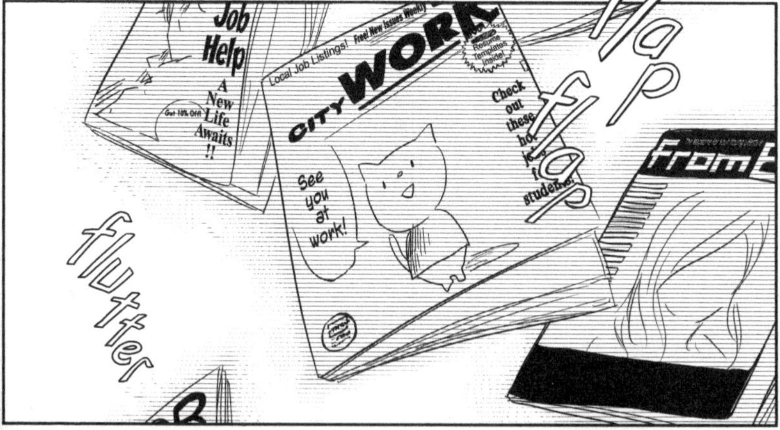
flap flap
Job Help
A New Life Awaits!!
Get 10% Off
Local Job Listings! Free! New Issues Weekly
CITY WORK
Check out these
See you at work!
flutter

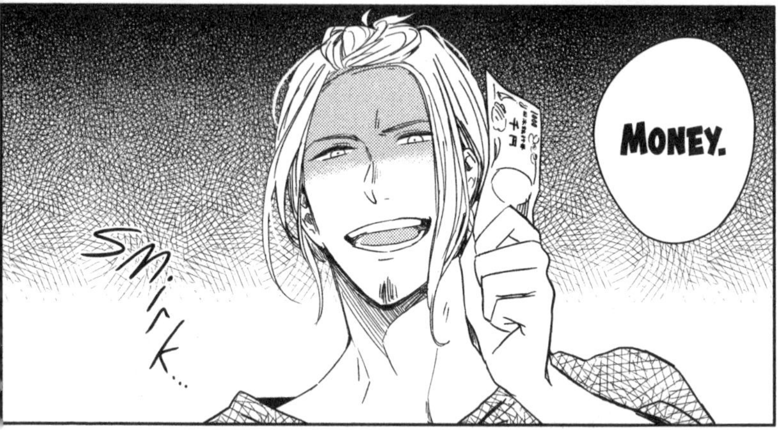
MONEY.
Smirk...

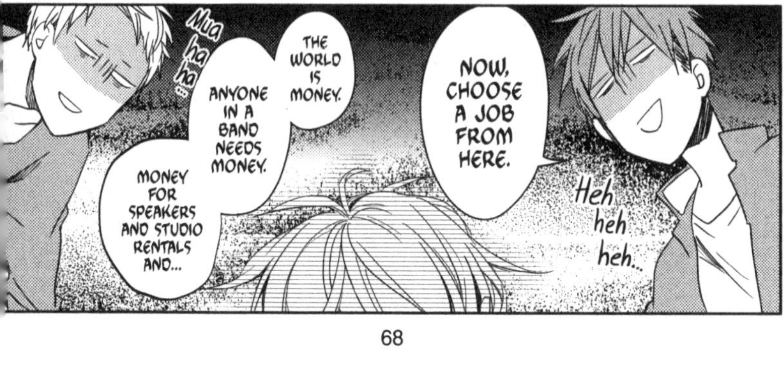
NOW, CHOOSE A JOB FROM HERE.
Heh heh heh...
THE WORLD IS MONEY.
ANYONE IN A BAND NEEDS MONEY.
MONEY FOR SPEAKERS AND STUDIO RENTALS AND...
Mua ha ha...

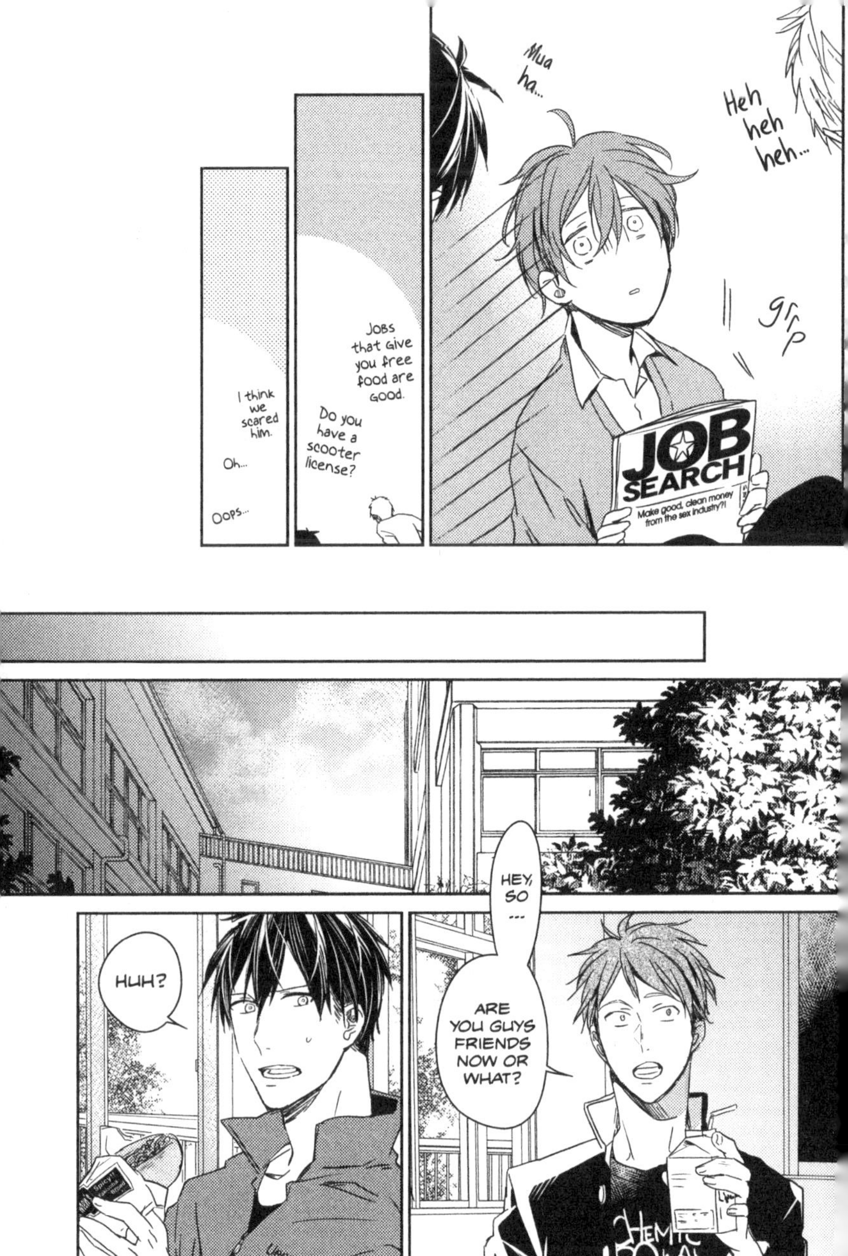
Heh heh heh...
Mua ha...
grip
JOB SEARCH
Make good, clean money from the sex industry?!
Jobs that give you free food are good.
Do you have a scooter license?
I think we scared him.
Oh...
Oops...
HEY, SO ...
ARE YOU GUYS FRIENDS NOW OR WHAT?
HUH?

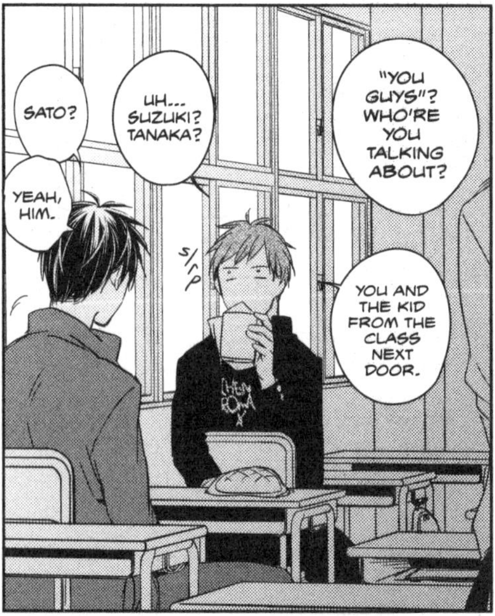
"YOU GUYS"? WHO'RE YOU TALKING ABOUT?
UH... SUZUKI? TANAKA?
SATO?
YEAH, HIM.
s/rp
YOU AND THE KID FROM THE CLASS NEXT DOOR.

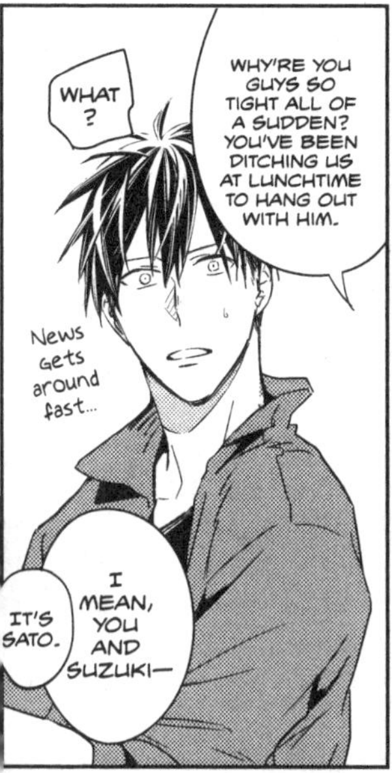
WHY'RE YOU GUYS SO TIGHT ALL OF A SUDDEN? YOU'VE BEEN DITCHING US AT LUNCHTIME TO HANG OUT WITH HIM.
WHAT?
News gets around fast...
I MEAN, YOU AND SUZUKI—
IT'S SATO.

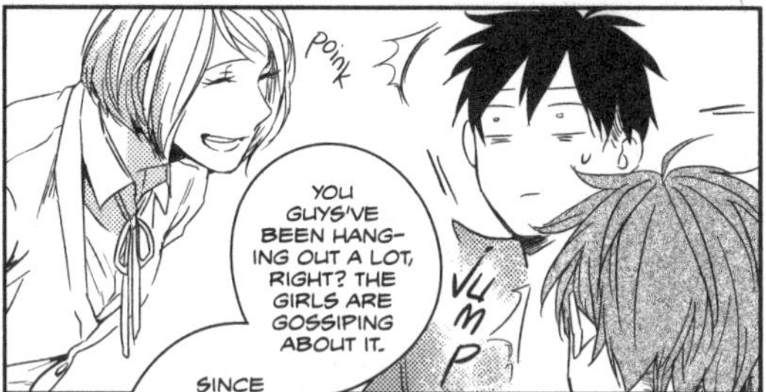
poink
YOU GUYS'VE BEEN HANGING OUT A LOT, RIGHT? THE GIRLS ARE GOSSIPING ABOUT IT.
JUMP

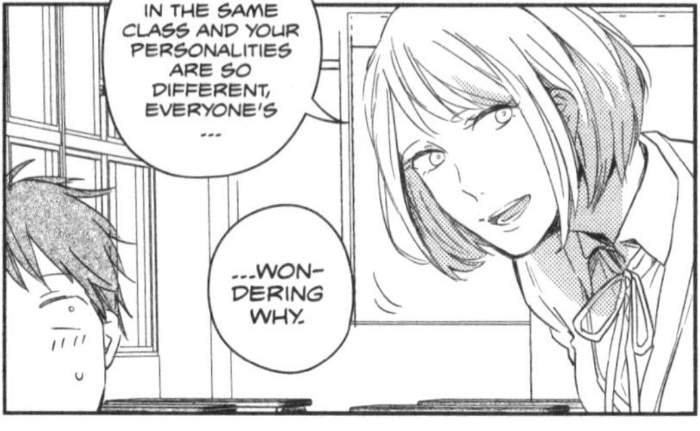
SINCE YOU'RE NOT IN THE SAME CLASS AND YOUR PERSONALITIES ARE SO DIFFERENT, EVERYONE'S ...
...WONDERING WHY.

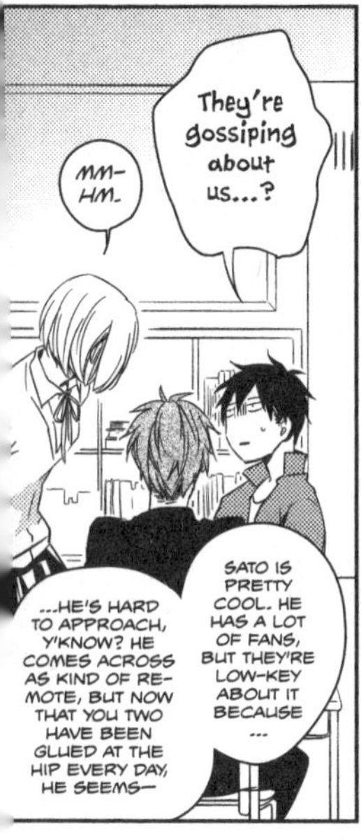
They're gossiping about us...?
MM-HM.
SATO IS PRETTY COOL. HE HAS A LOT OF FANS, BUT THEY'RE LOW-KEY ABOUT IT BECAUSE ...
...HE'S HARD TO APPROACH, Y'KNOW? HE COMES ACROSS AS KIND OF REMOTE, BUT NOW THAT YOU TWO HAVE BEEN GLUED AT THE HIP EVERY DAY, HE SEEMS—

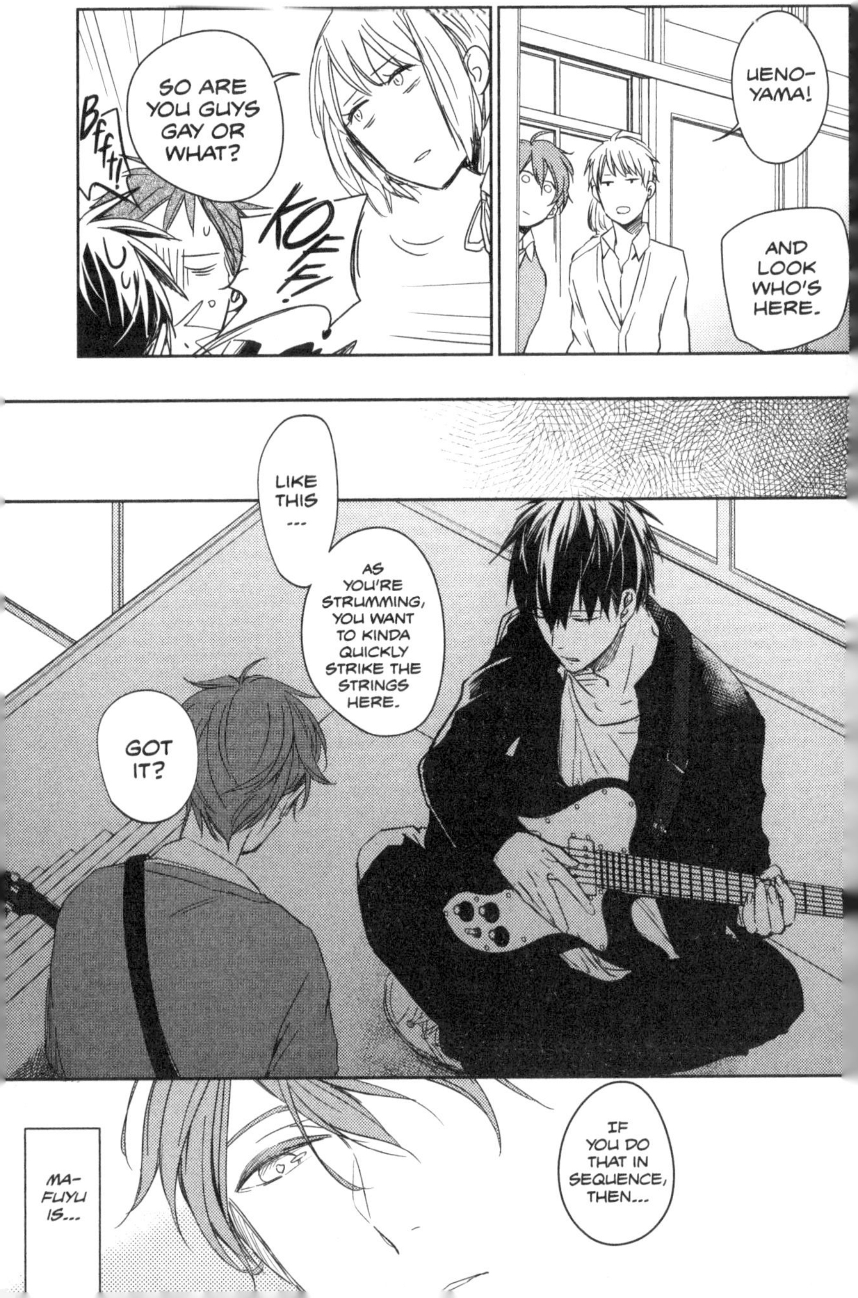
UENO-YAMA!
AND LOOK WHO'S HERE.
SO ARE YOU GUYS GAY OR WHAT?
KOFF!
Bffft!
LIKE THIS ...
AS YOU'RE STRUMMING, YOU WANT TO KINDA QUICKLY STRIKE THE STRINGS HERE.
GOT IT?
IF YOU DO THAT IN SEQUENCE, THEN...
MA-FUYU IS...

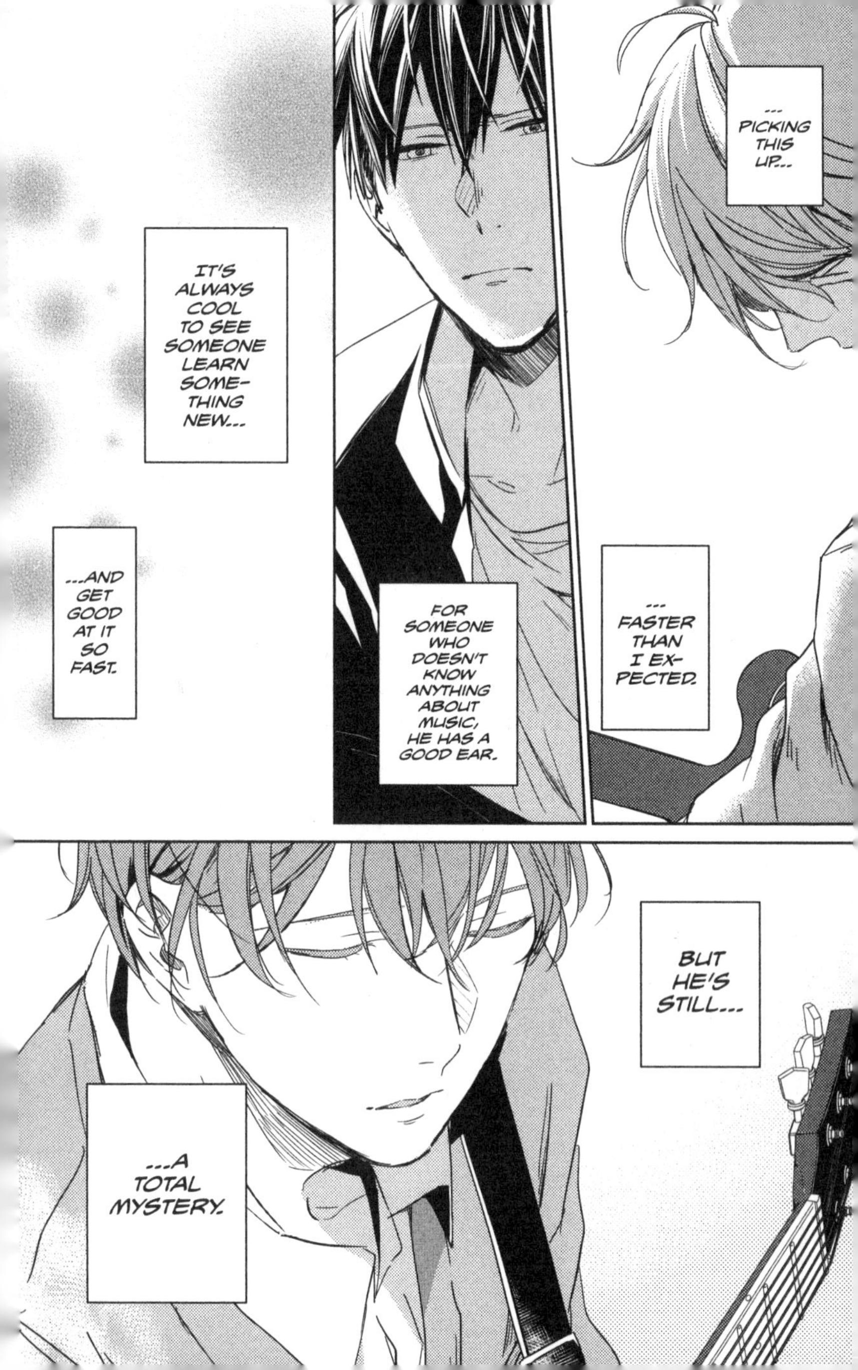
...PICKING THIS UP...
...FASTER THAN I EXPECTED.
FOR SOMEONE WHO DOESN'T KNOW ANYTHING ABOUT MUSIC, HE HAS A GOOD EAR.
IT'S ALWAYS COOL TO SEE SOMEONE LEARN SOMETHING NEW...
...AND GET GOOD AT IT SO FAST.
BUT HE'S STILL...
...A TOTAL MYSTERY.

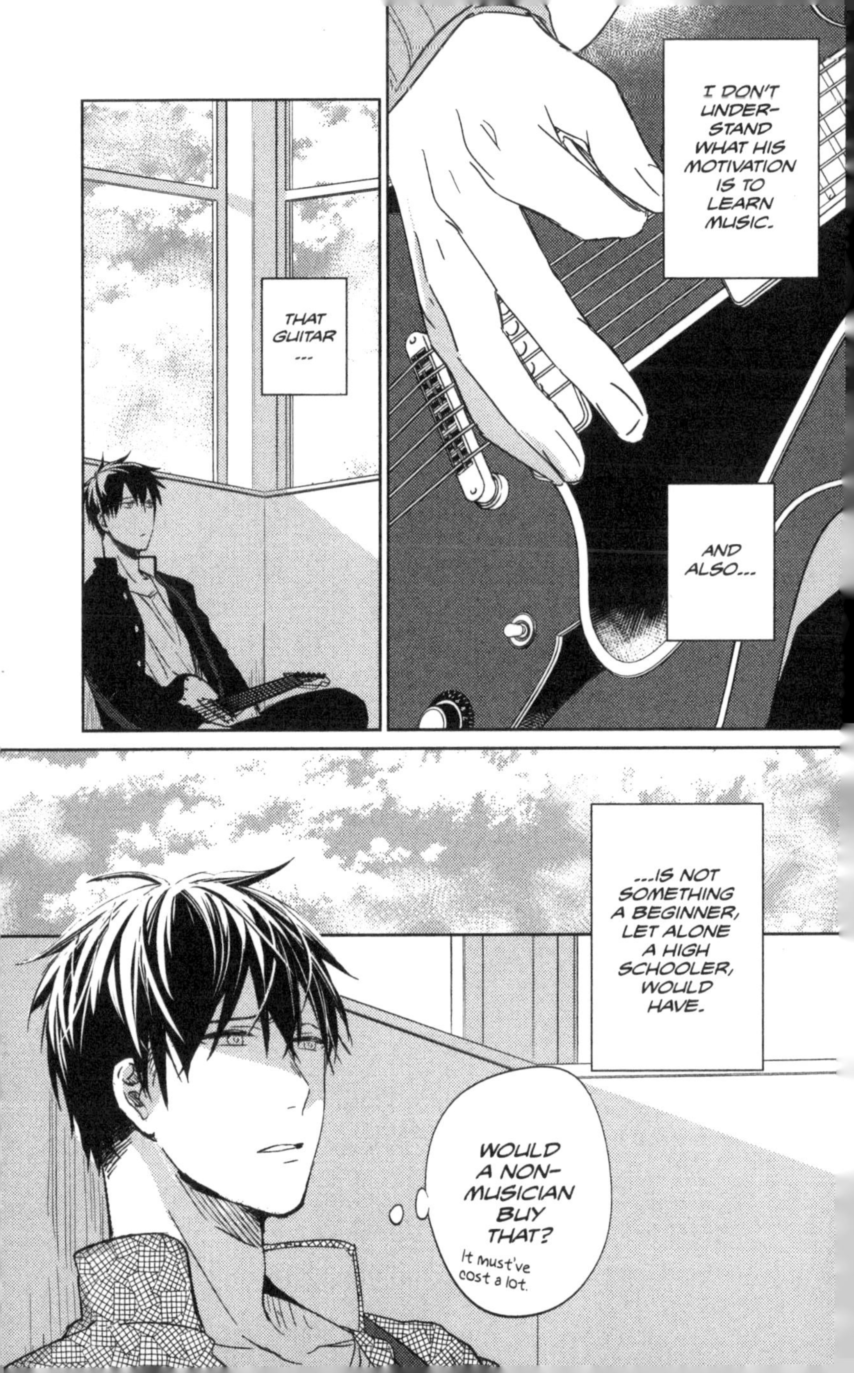
I DON'T UNDER-STAND WHAT HIS MOTIVATION IS TO LEARN MUSIC.
AND ALSO...
THAT GUITAR...
...IS NOT SOMETHING A BEGINNER, LET ALONE A HIGH SCHOOLER, WOULD HAVE.
WOULD A NON-MUSICIAN BUY THAT?
It must've cost a lot.

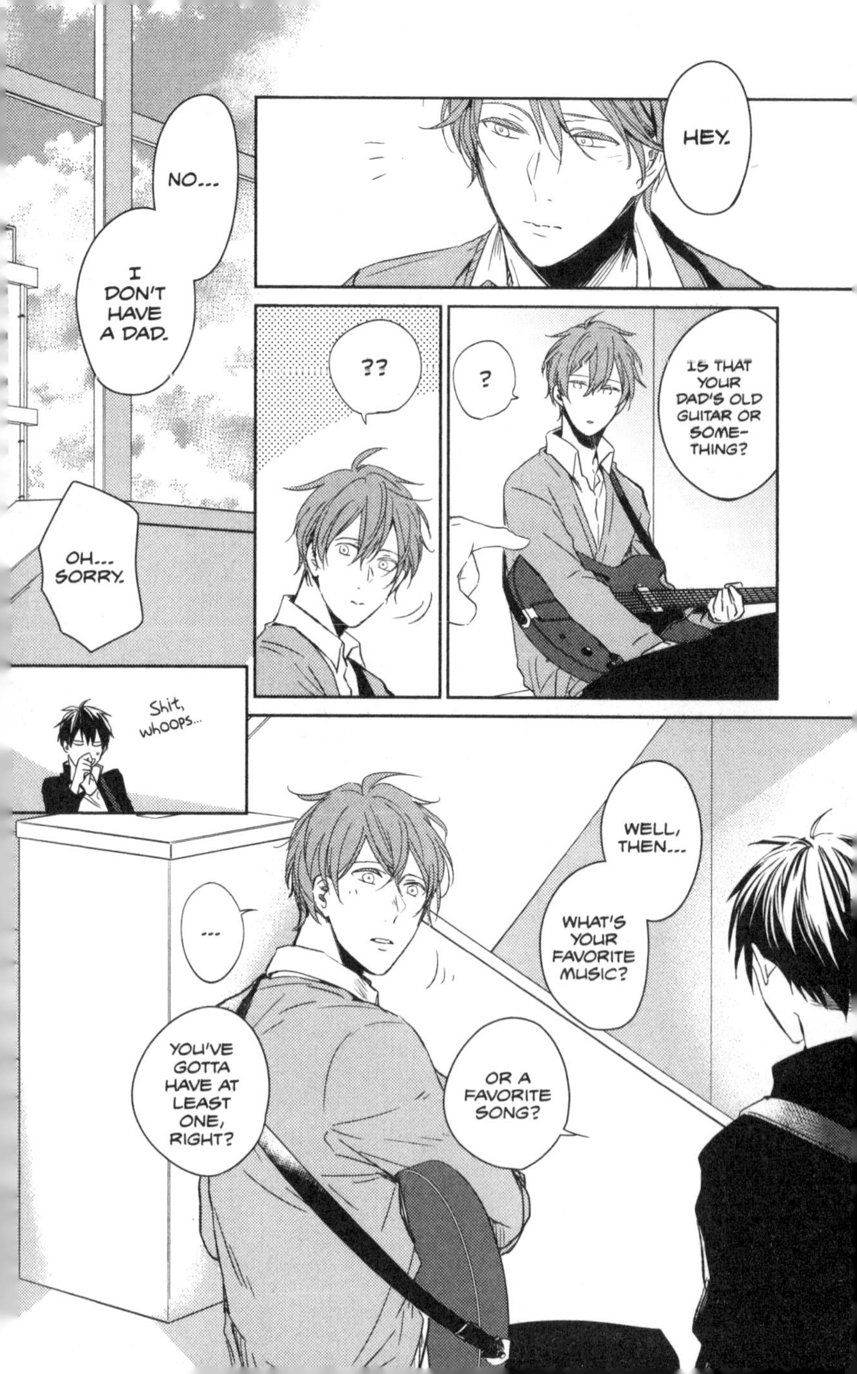
HEY.
IS THAT YOUR DAD'S OLD GUITAR OR SOME-THING?
?
??
NO...
I DON'T HAVE A DAD.
OH... SORRY.
Shit, whoops...
WELL, THEN...
WHAT'S YOUR FAVORITE MUSIC?
OR A FAVORITE SONG?
YOU'VE GOTTA HAVE AT LEAST ONE, RIGHT?
...

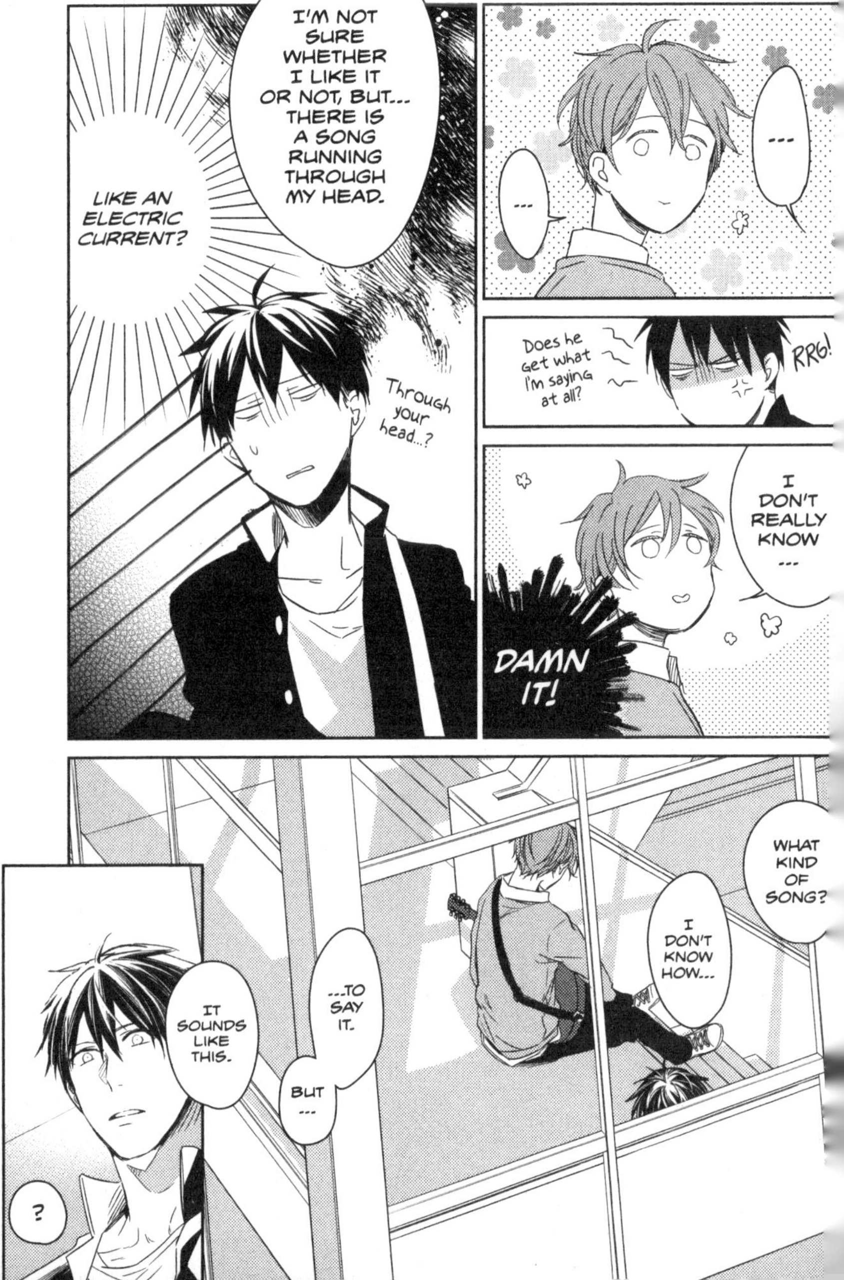
...
...
Does he get what I'm saying at all?
RRG!
I DON'T REALLY KNOW ...
DAMN IT!
I'M NOT SURE WHETHER I LIKE IT OR NOT, BUT... THERE IS A SONG RUNNING THROUGH MY HEAD.
LIKE AN ELECTRIC CURRENT?
Through your head...?
WHAT KIND OF SONG?
I DON'T KNOW HOW...
...TO SAY IT.
BUT ...
IT SOUNDS LIKE THIS.
?

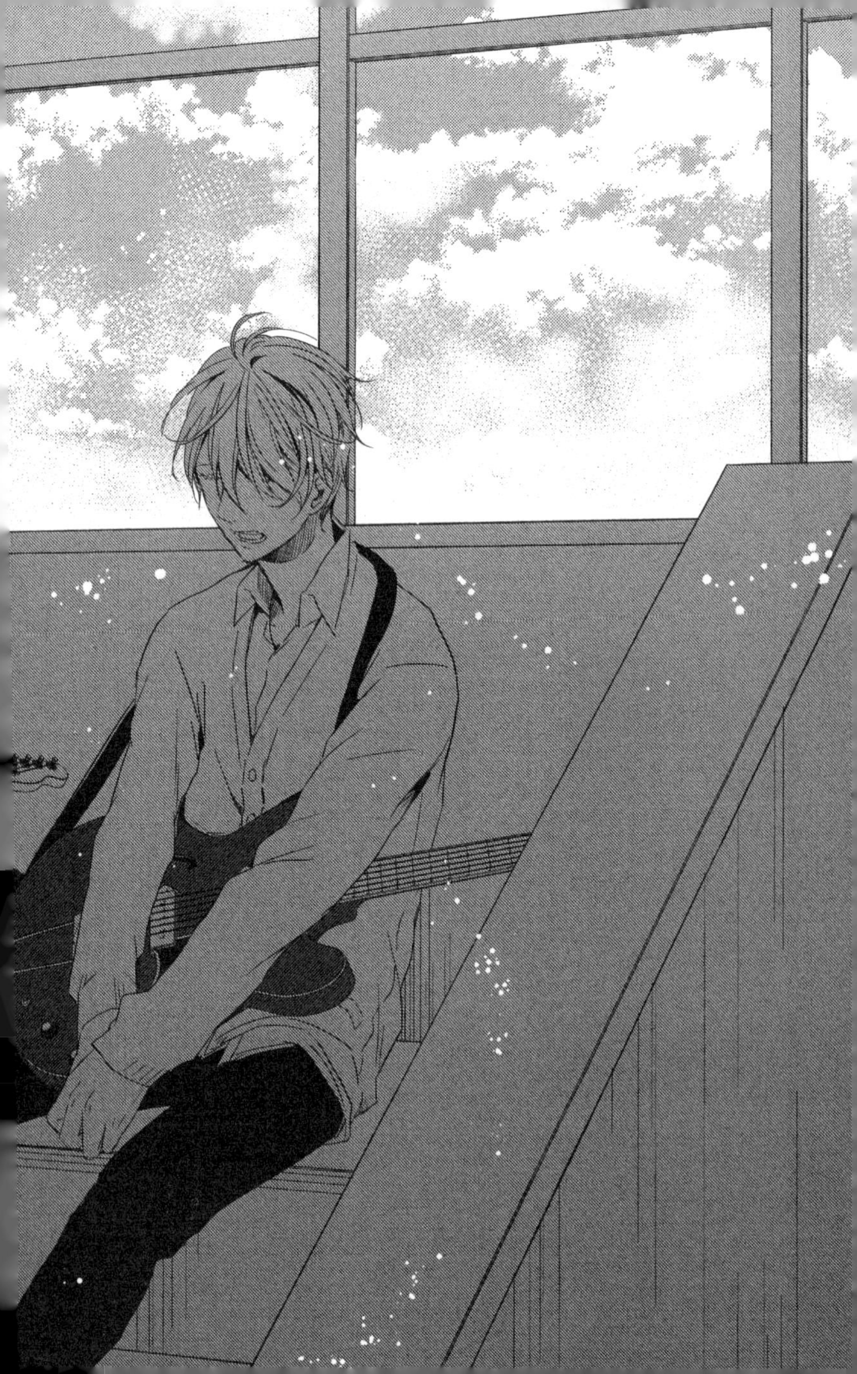

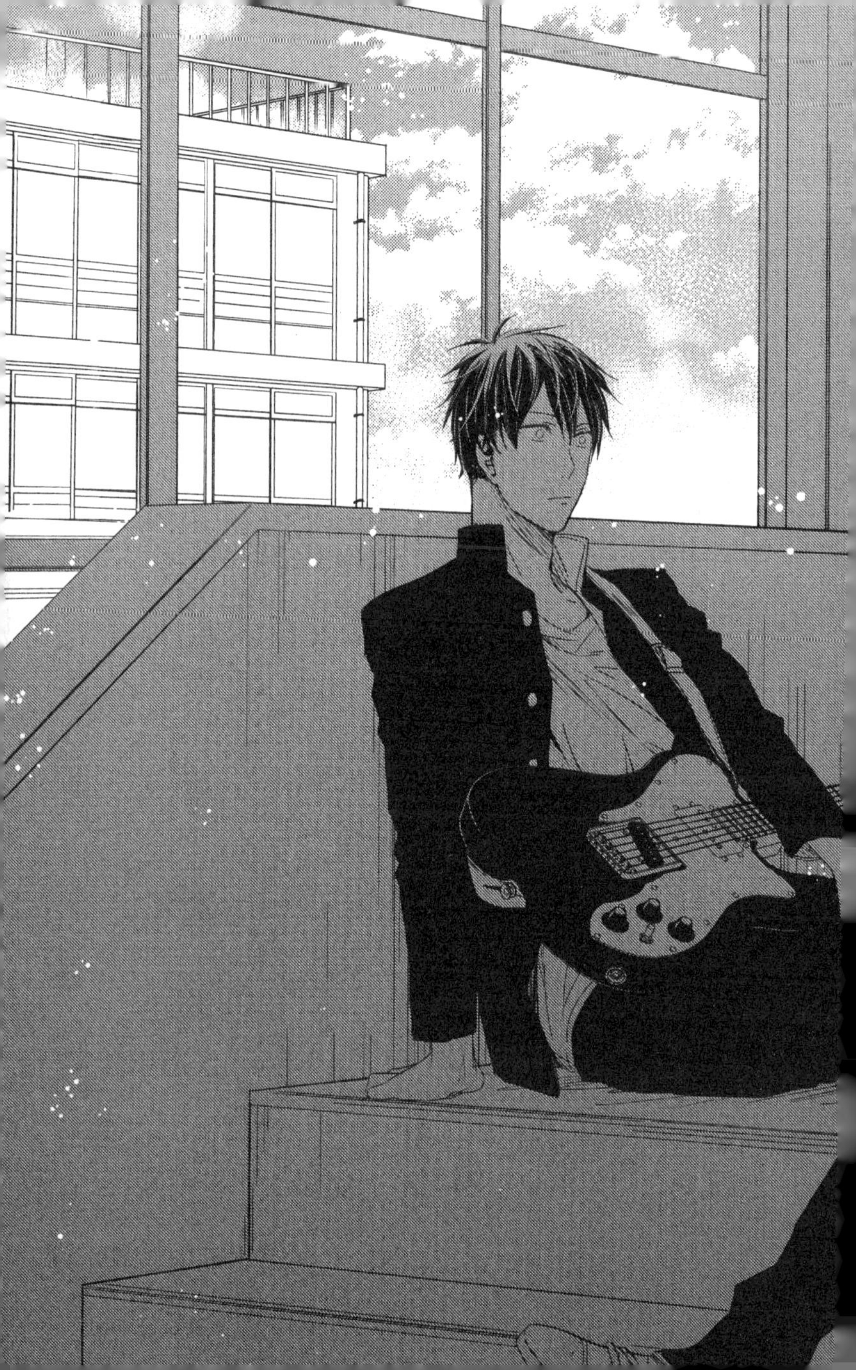

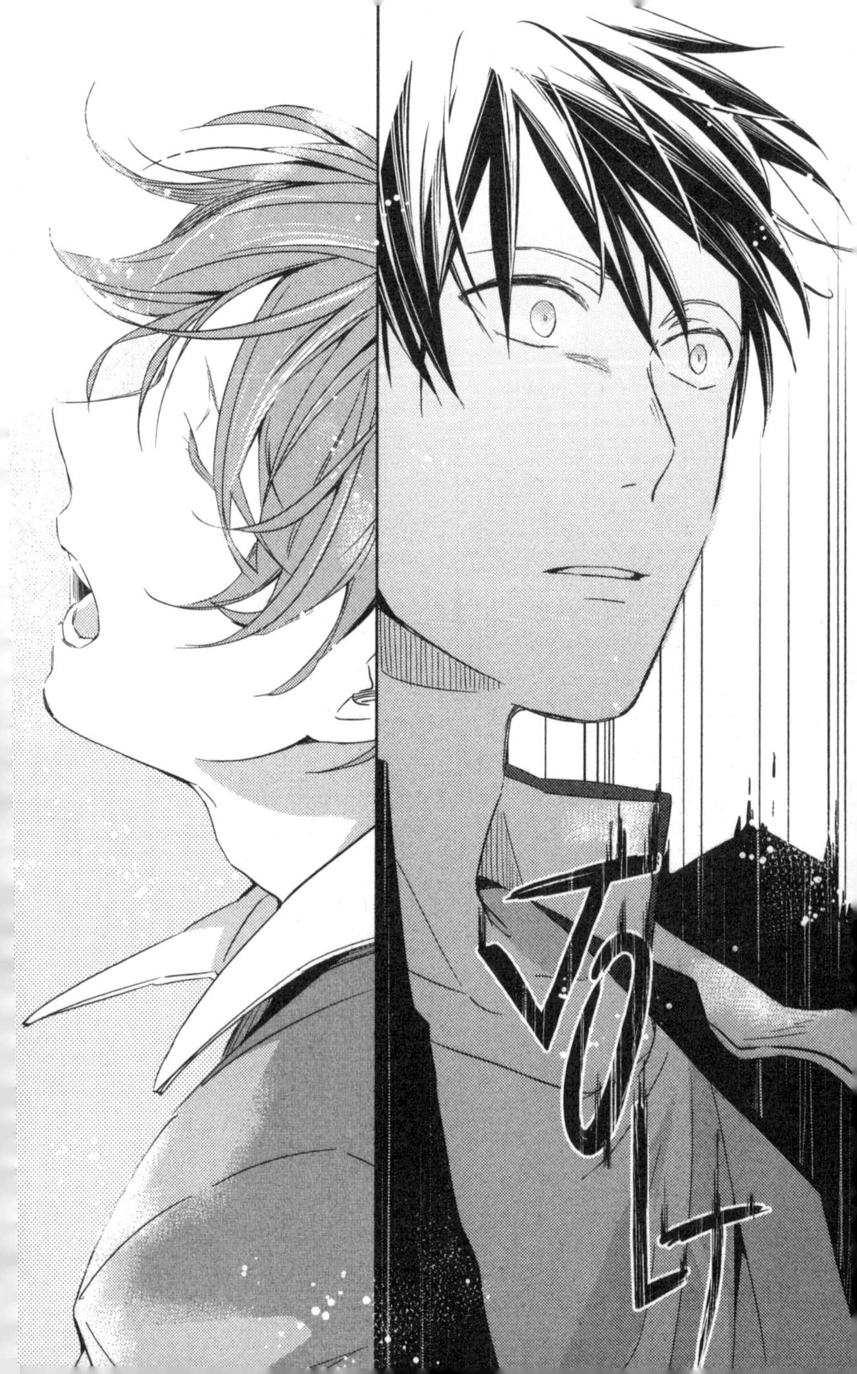
JOLT

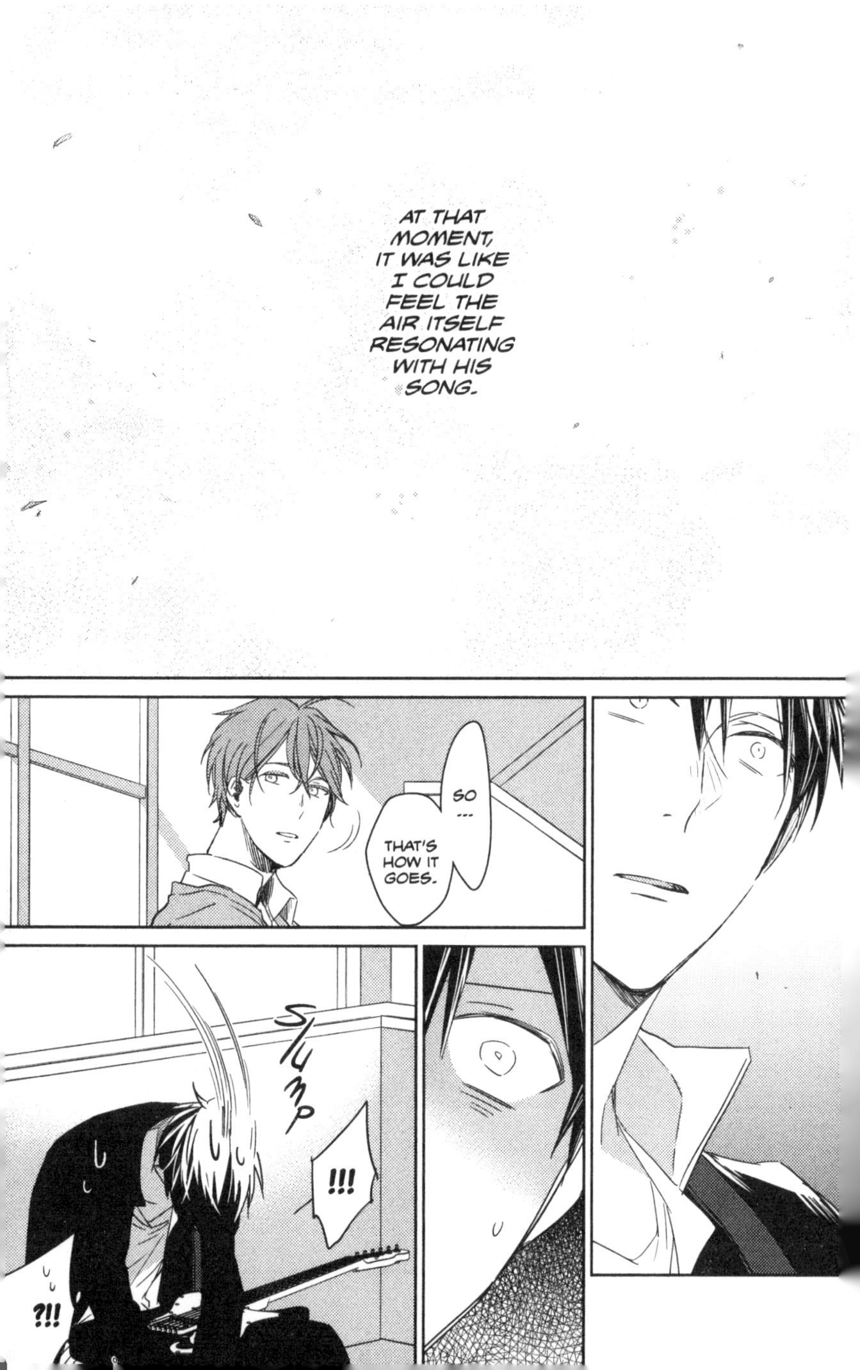
AT THAT MOMENT, IT WAS LIKE I COULD FEEL THE AIR ITSELF RESONATING WITH HIS SONG.
SO...
THAT'S HOW IT GOES.
!!!
SLUMP
?!!

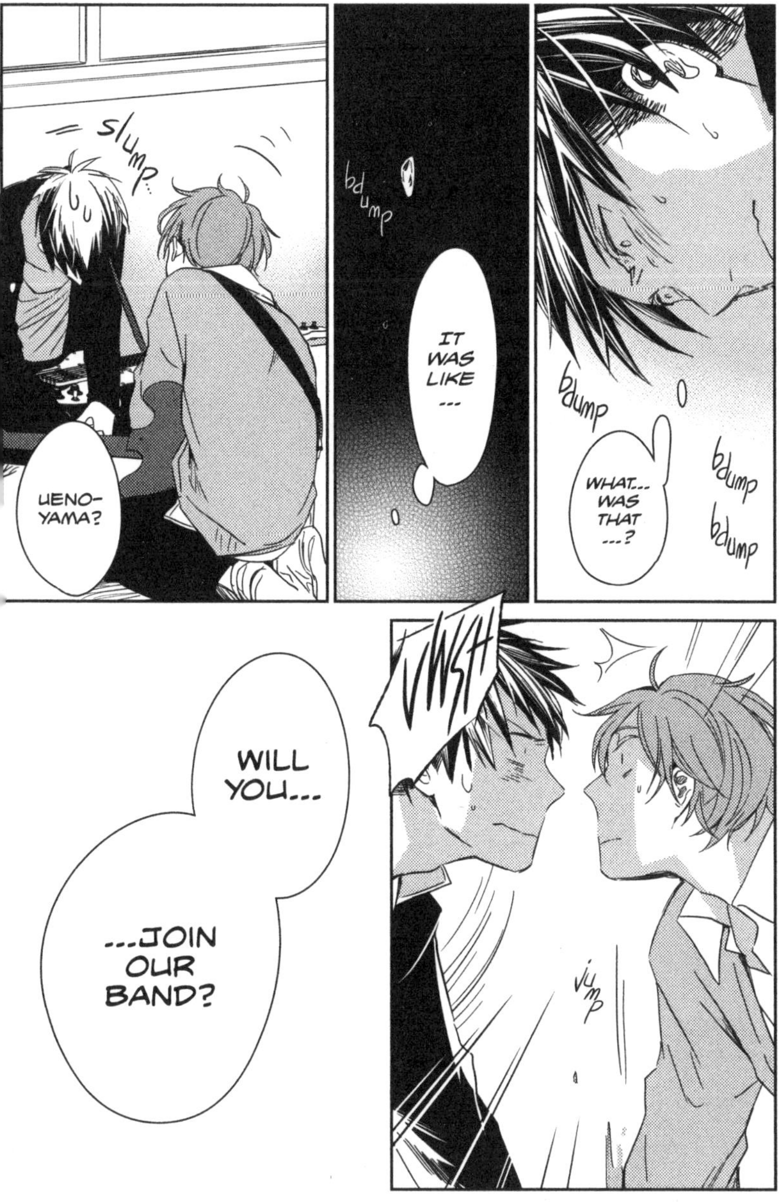
bdump
WHAT... WAS THAT ...?
bdump
bdump
bdump
IT WAS LIKE ...
slump...
UENO-YAMA?
VWSH
jump
WILL YOU...
...JOIN OUR BAND?

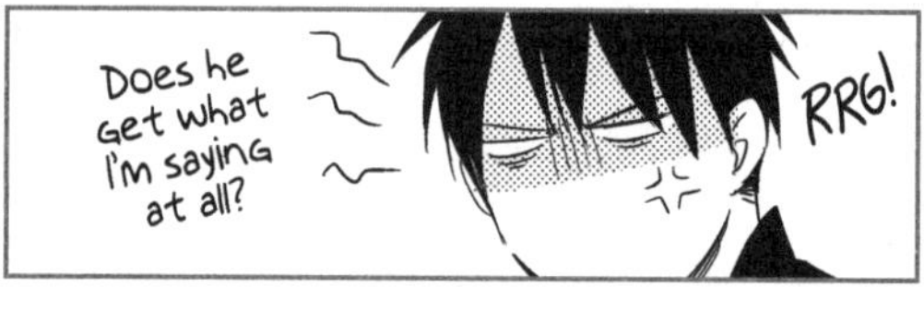
RRG!
Does he get what I'm saying at all?

given

by Natsuki Kizu

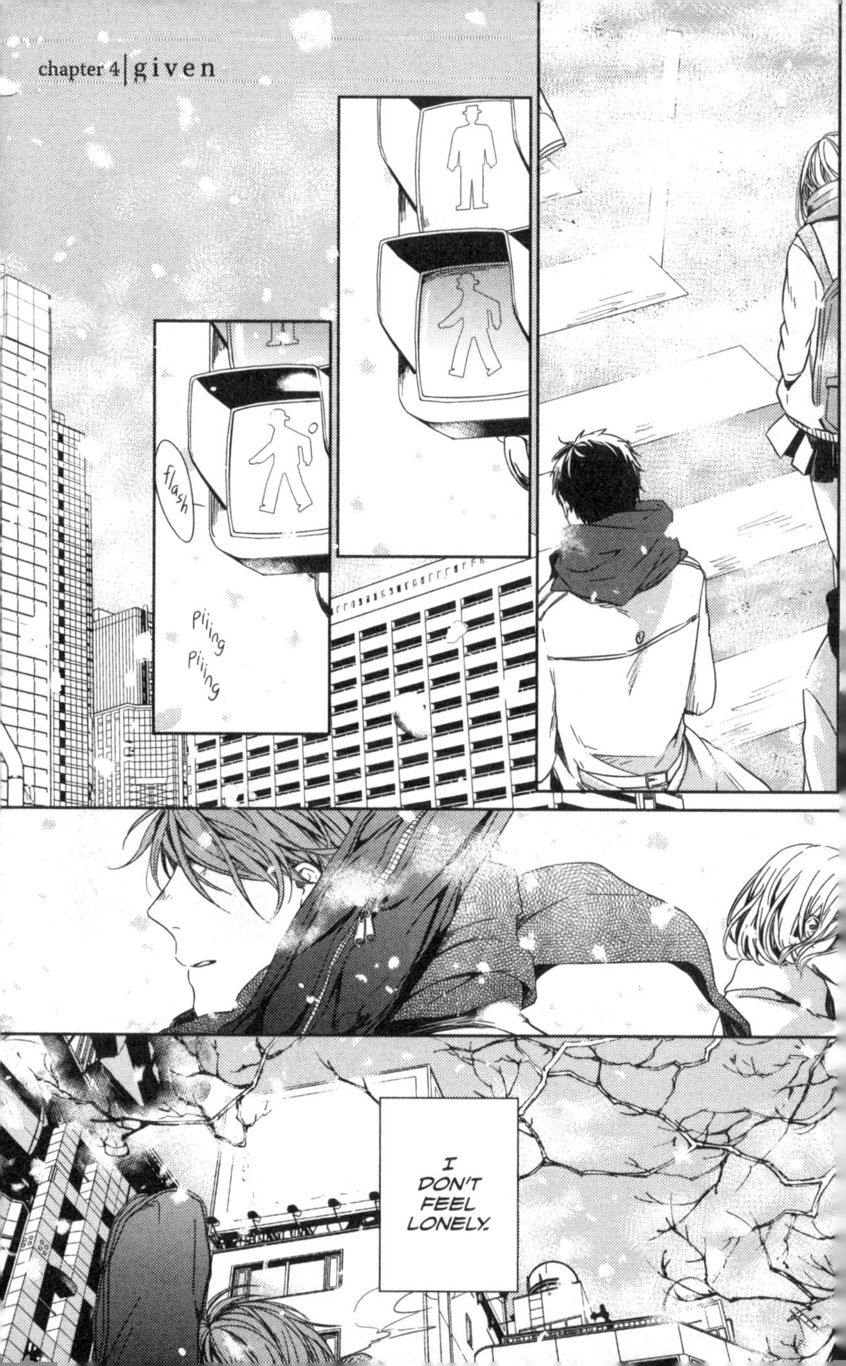
flash
piiing piiing
I DON'T FEEL LONELY.

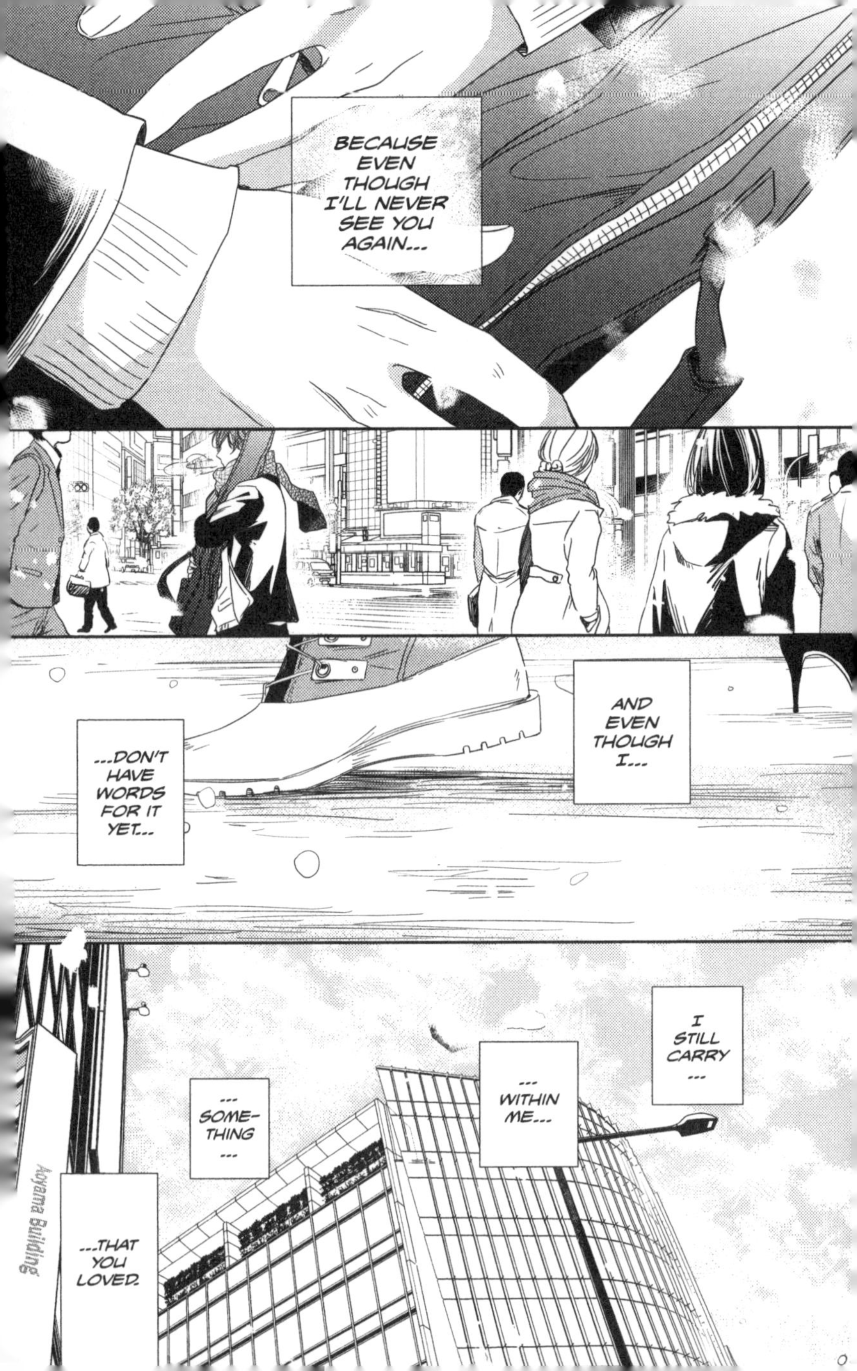
BECAUSE EVEN THOUGH I'LL NEVER SEE YOU AGAIN...
AND EVEN THOUGH I...
...DON'T HAVE WORDS FOR IT YET...
I STILL CARRY ...
... WITHIN ME...
... SOME-THING ...
Aoyama Building
...THAT YOU LOVED.

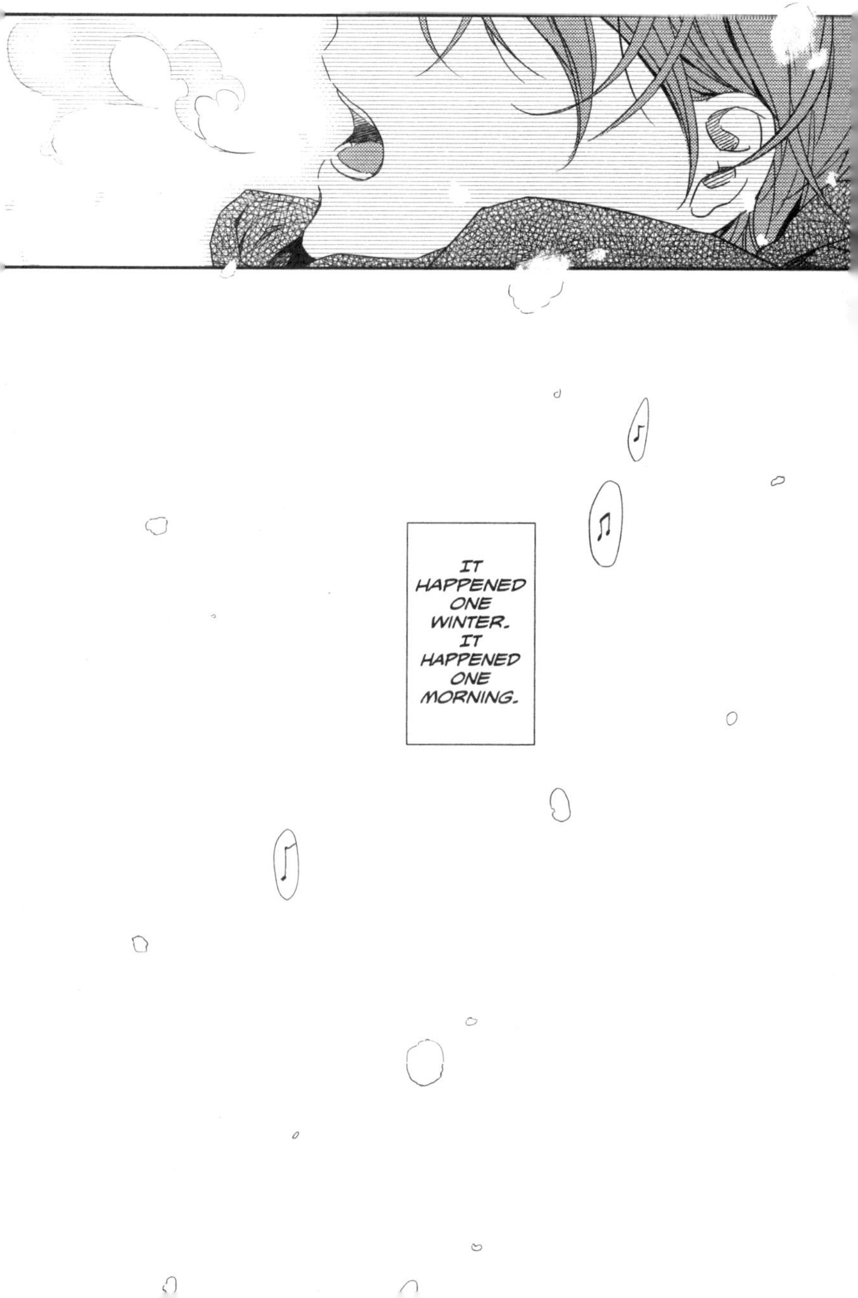
IT HAPPENED ONE WINTER. IT HAPPENED ONE MORNING.

chapter 4
given

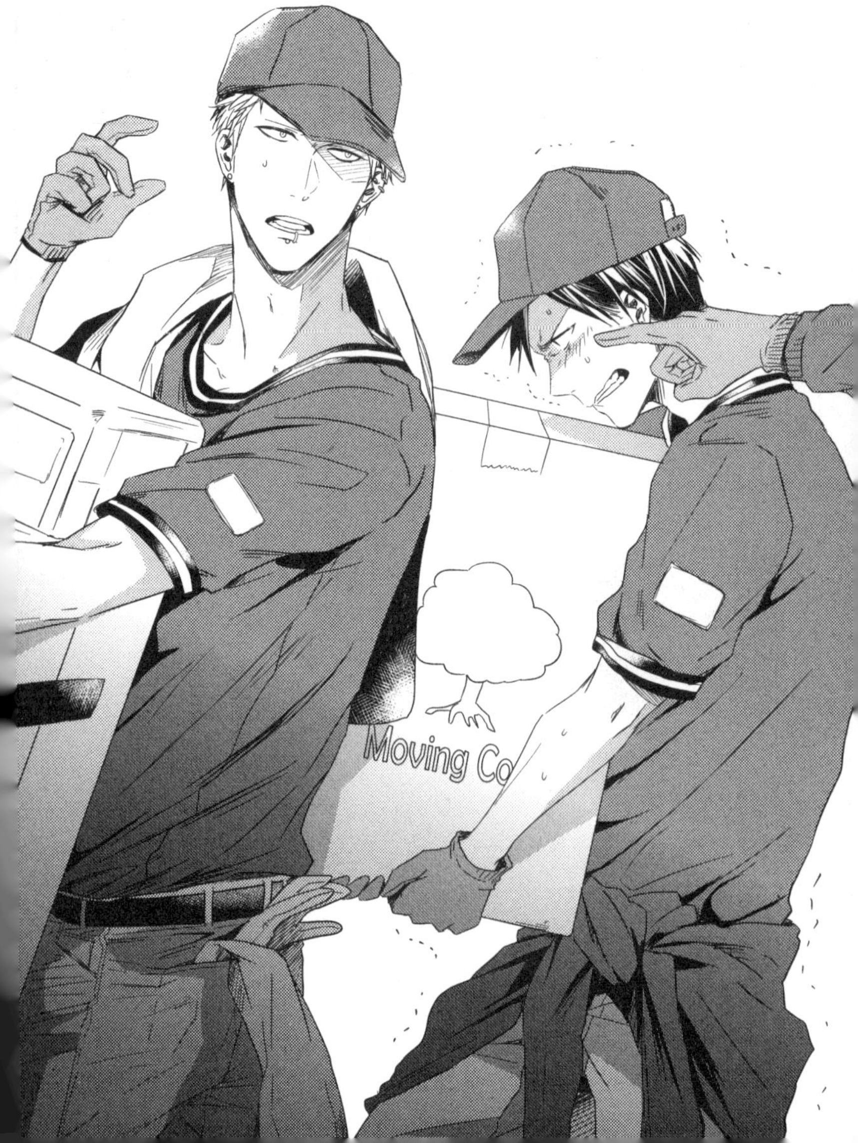
Moving Co

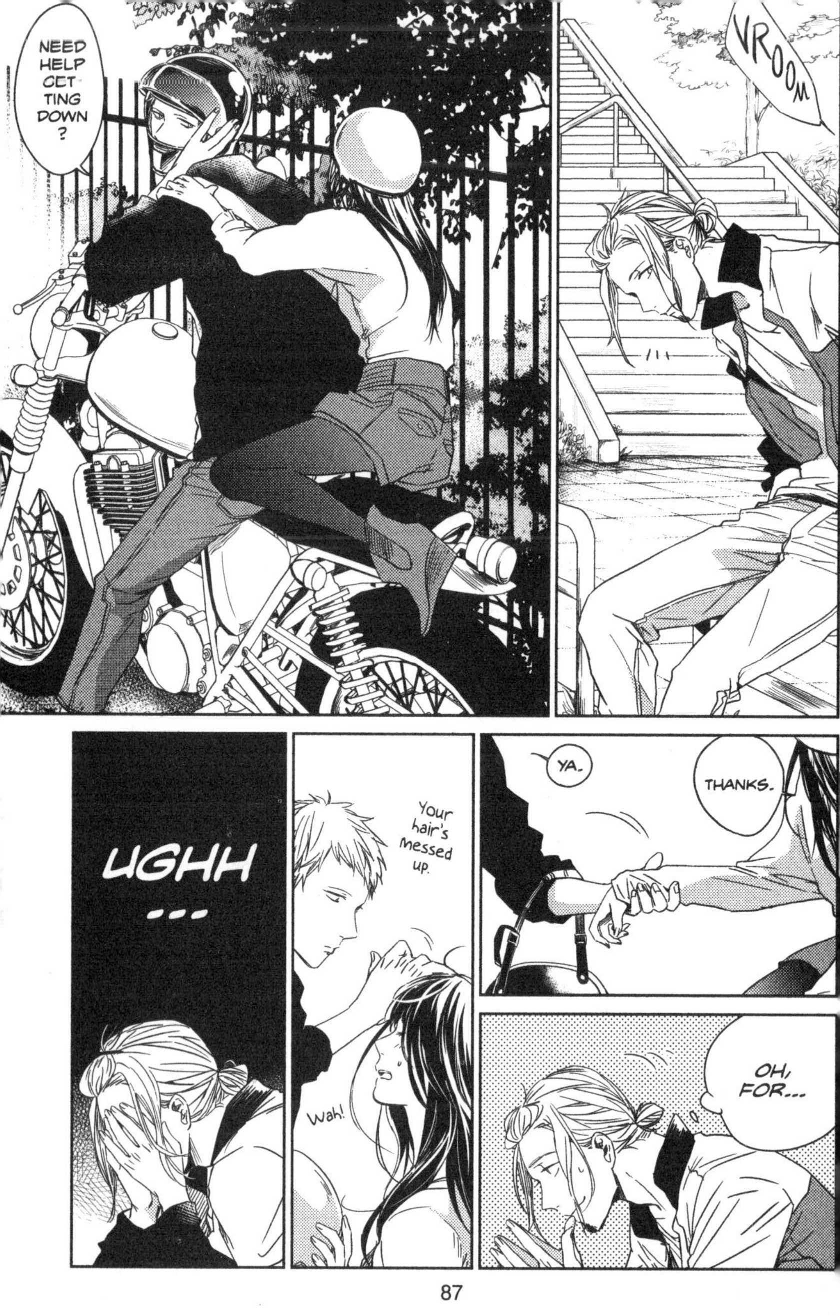
VROOM
NEED HELP GET-TING DOWN?
THANKS.
YA.
OH, FOR...
Your hair's messed up.
Wah!
UGHH...

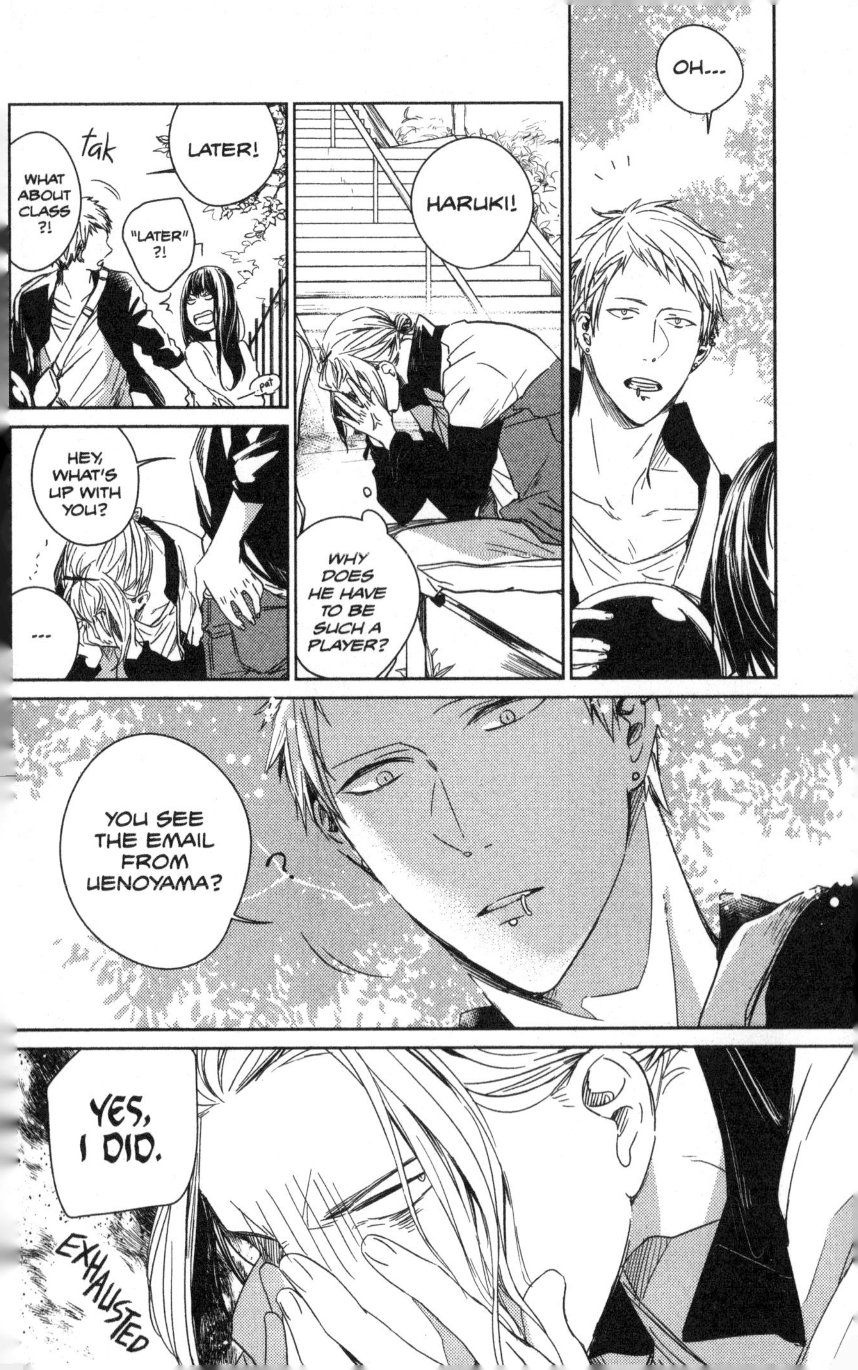
OH...
HARUKI!
WHY DOES HE HAVE TO BE SUCH A PLAYER?
LATER!
tak
WHAT ABOUT CLASS ?!
"LATER" ?!
pat
HEY, WHAT'S UP WITH YOU?
...
YOU SEE THE EMAIL FROM UENOYAMA?
YES, I DID.
EXHAUSTED

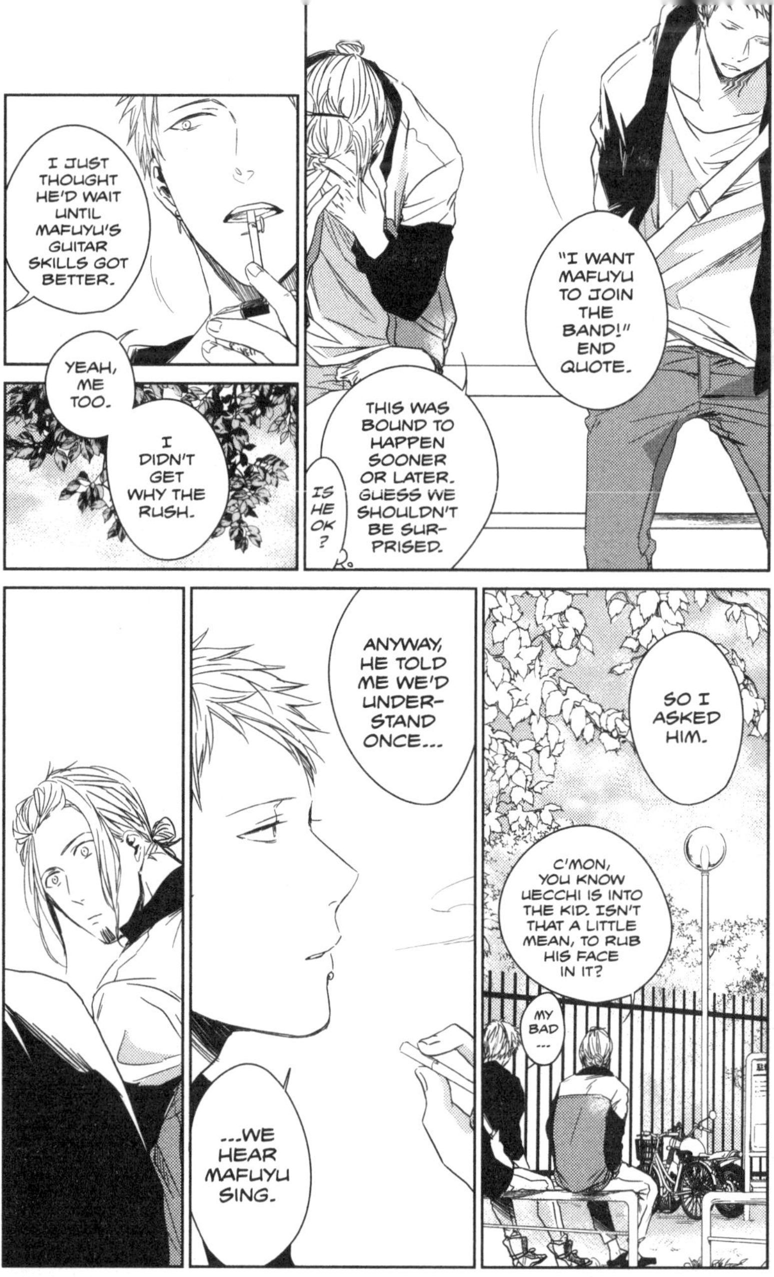
"I WANT MAFUYU TO JOIN THE BAND!" END QUOTE.
THIS WAS BOUND TO HAPPEN SOONER OR LATER. GUESS WE SHOULDN'T BE SURPRISED.
IS HE OK?
I JUST THOUGHT HE'D WAIT UNTIL MAFUYU'S GUITAR SKILLS GOT BETTER.
YEAH, ME TOO.
I DIDN'T GET WHY THE RUSH.
SO I ASKED HIM.
C'MON, YOU KNOW UECCHI IS INTO THE KID. ISN'T THAT A LITTLE MEAN, TO RUB HIS FACE IN IT?
MY BAD...
ANYWAY, HE TOLD ME WE'D UNDERSTAND ONCE...
...WE HEAR MAFUYU SING.

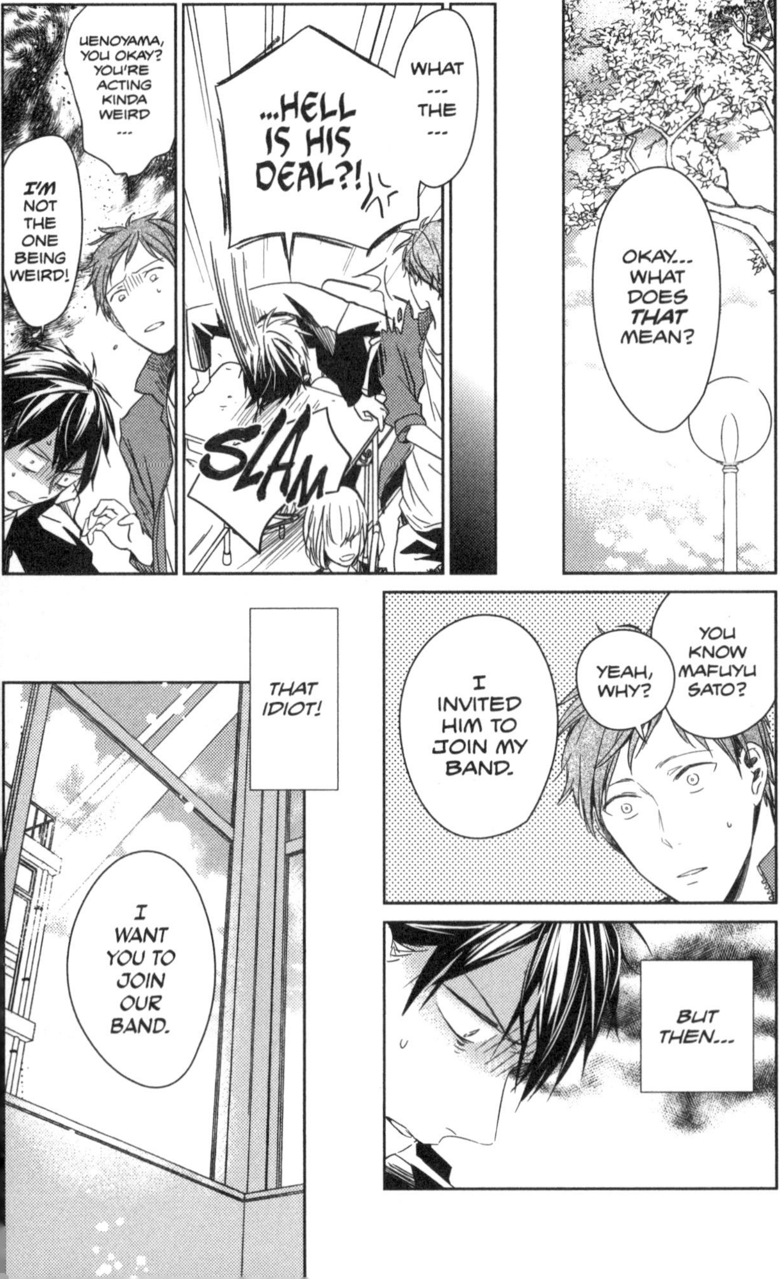
OKAY... WHAT DOES THAT MEAN?
WHAT --- THE ---
...HELL IS HIS DEAL?!
SLAM
UENOYAMA, YOU OKAY? YOU'RE ACTING KINDA WEIRD ---
I'M NOT THE ONE BEING WEIRD!
YOU KNOW MAFUYU SATO?
YEAH, WHY?
I INVITED HIM TO JOIN MY BAND.
BUT THEN...
THAT IDIOT!
I WANT YOU TO JOIN OUR BAND.

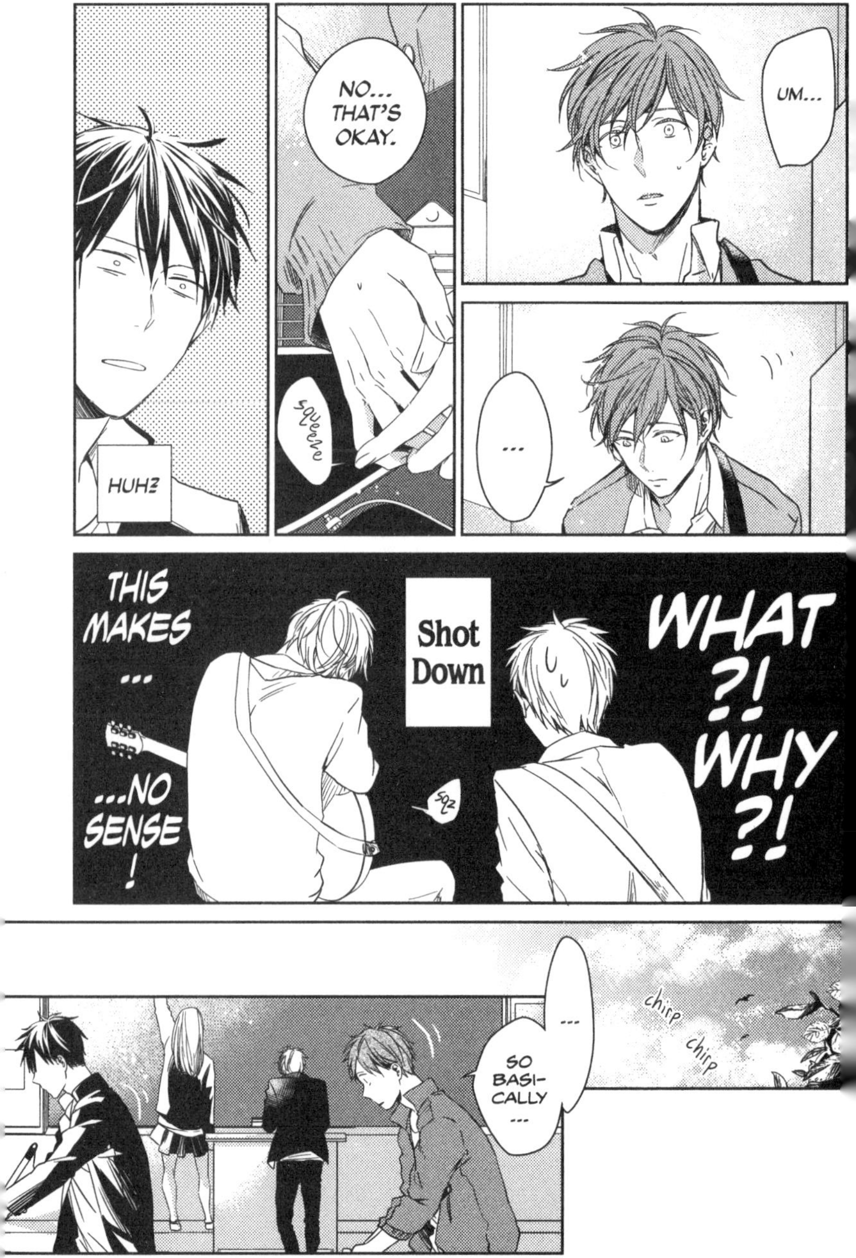
UM...
...
NO... THAT'S OKAY.
squeeze
HUH?
WHAT?! WHY?!
Shot Down
sqz
THIS MAKES... ...NO SENSE!
chirp
chirp
...
SO BASICALLY...

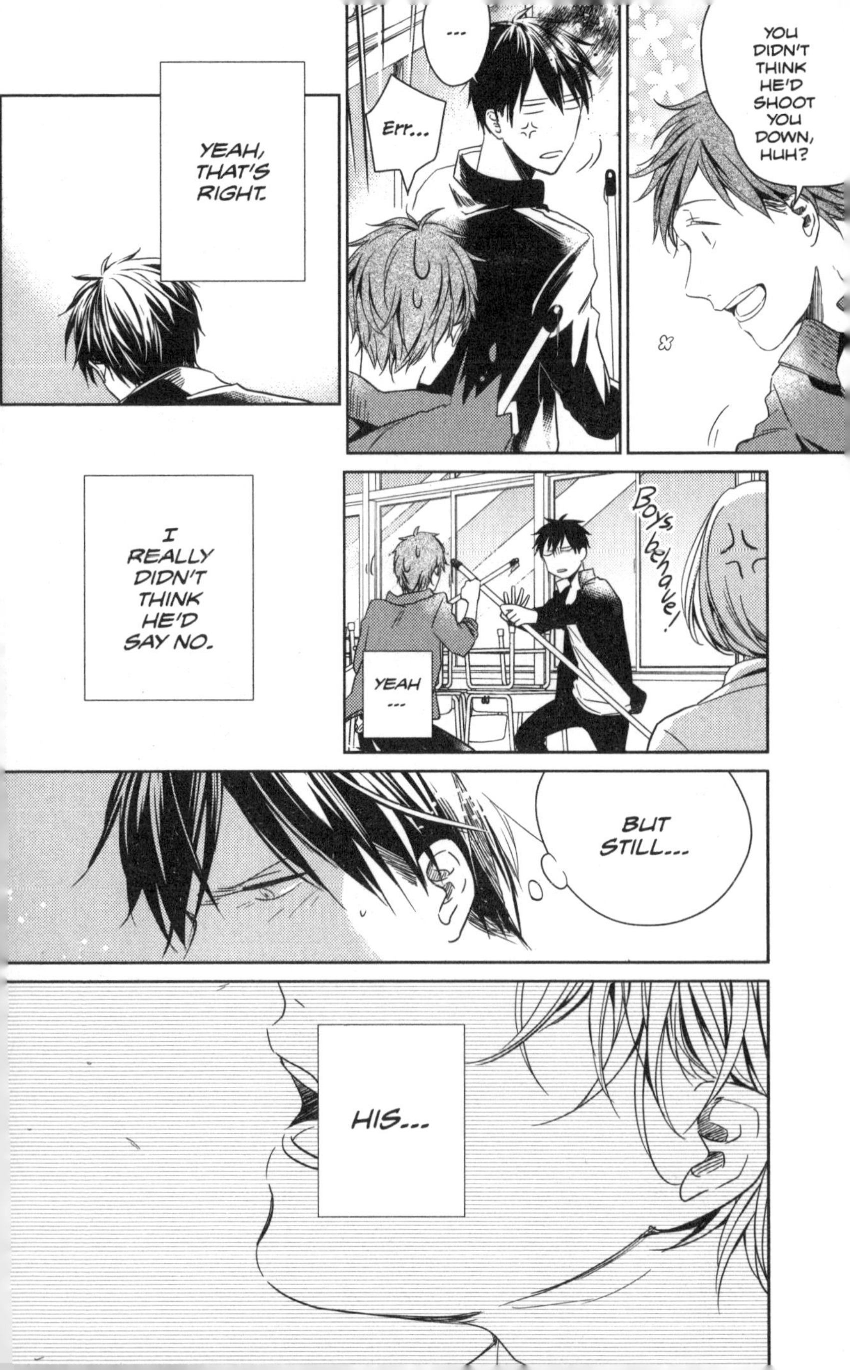
YOU DIDN'T THINK HE'D SHOOT YOU DOWN, HUH?
...
Err...
YEAH, THAT'S RIGHT.
Boys, behave!
YEAH ...
I REALLY DIDN'T THINK HE'D SAY NO.
BUT STILL...
HIS...

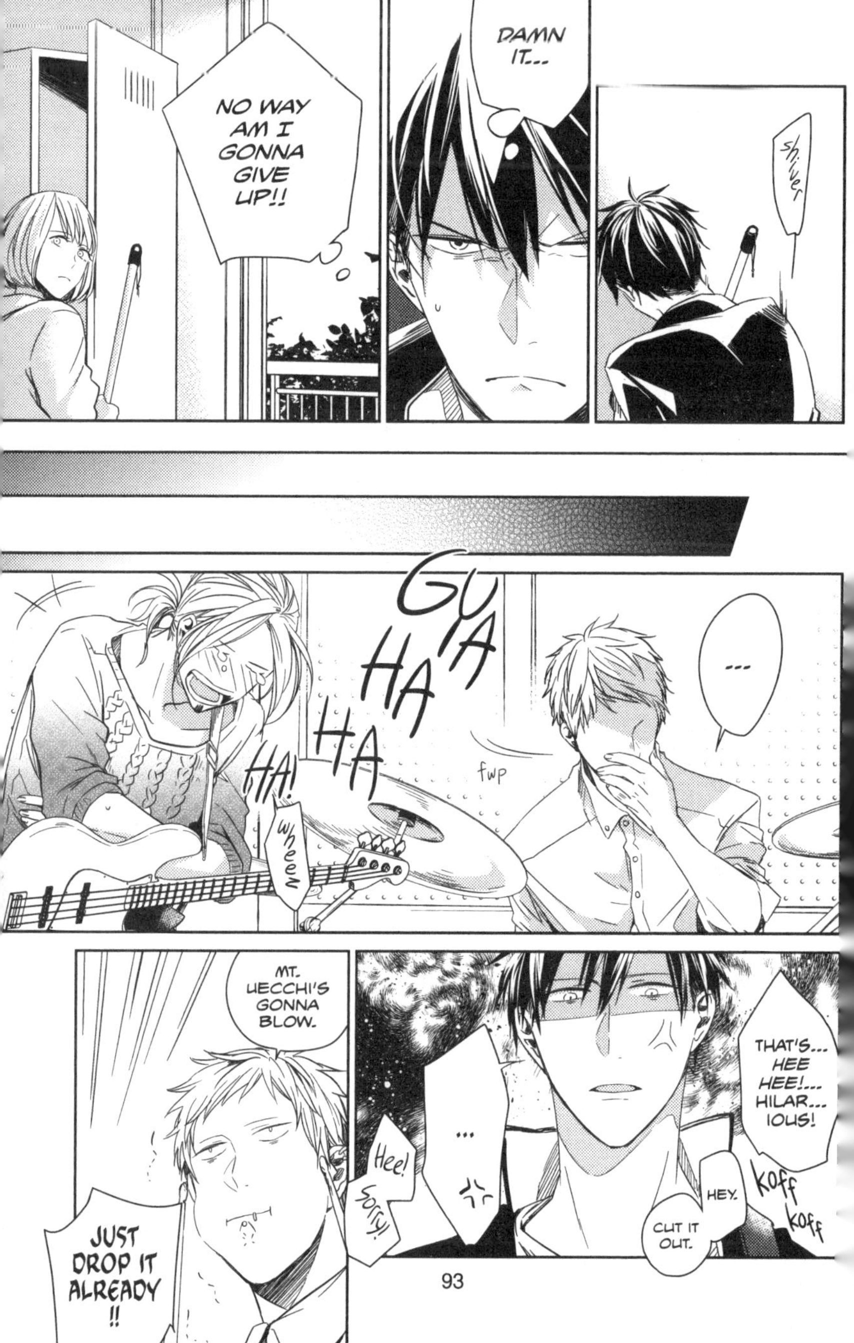
shiver
DAMN IT...
NO WAY AM I GONNA GIVE UP!!
GYAHAHAHA!
wheeze
fwp
...
THAT'S... HEE HEE!... HILAR... IOUS!
koff koff
HEY.
CUT IT OUT.
...
Hee! Sorry!
MT. UECCHI'S GONNA BLOW.
JUST DROP IT ALREADY!!

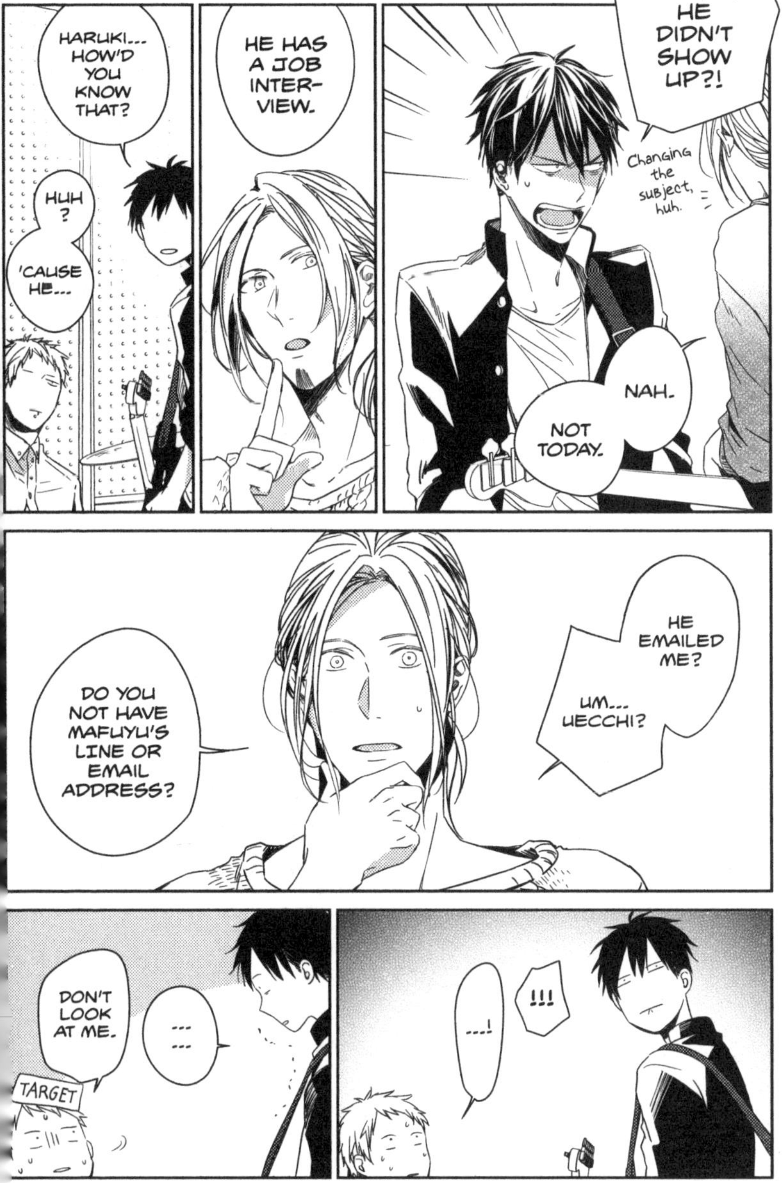
ANYWAY, HE DIDN'T SHOW UP?!
Changing the subject, huh.
NAH.
NOT TODAY.
HE HAS A JOB INTER-VIEW.
HARUKI... HOW'D YOU KNOW THAT?
HUH?
'CAUSE HE...
HE EMAILED ME?
UM... UECCHI?
DO YOU NOT HAVE MAFUYU'S LINE OR EMAIL ADDRESS?
!!!
...!
DON'T LOOK AT ME.
... ...
TARGET

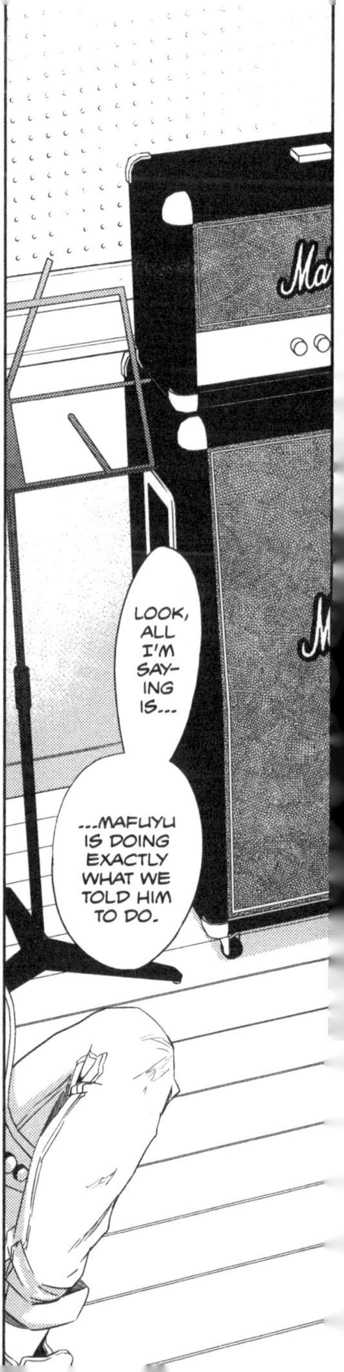
LOOK, ALL I'M SAY- ING IS...
...MAFUYU IS DOING EXACTLY WHAT WE TOLD HIM TO DO.
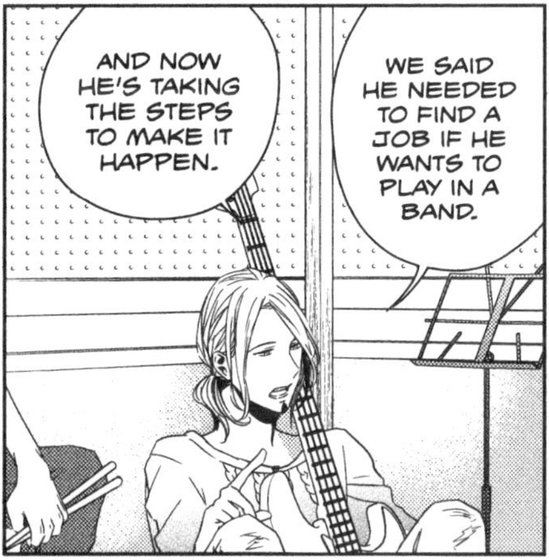
WE SAID HE NEEDED TO FIND A JOB IF HE WANTS TO PLAY IN A BAND.
AND NOW HE'S TAKING THE STEPS TO MAKE IT HAPPEN.
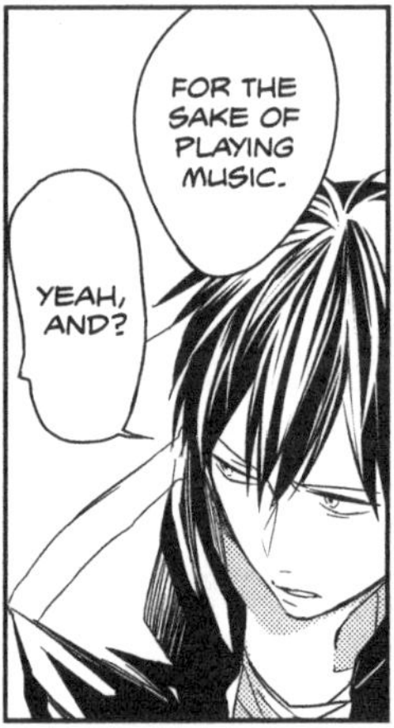
FOR THE SAKE OF PLAYING MUSIC.
YEAH, AND?
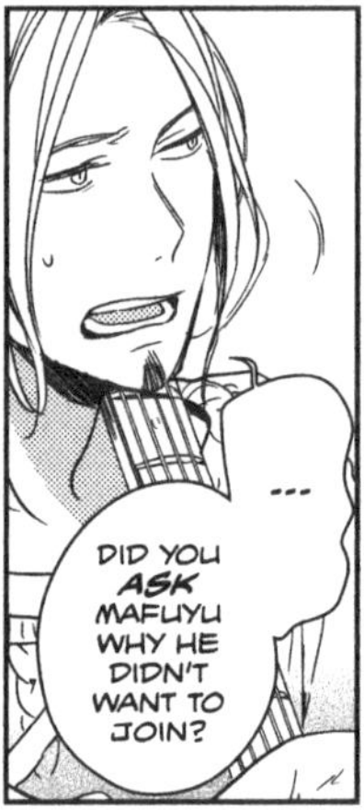
...
DID YOU ASK MAFUYU WHY HE DIDN'T WANT TO JOIN?
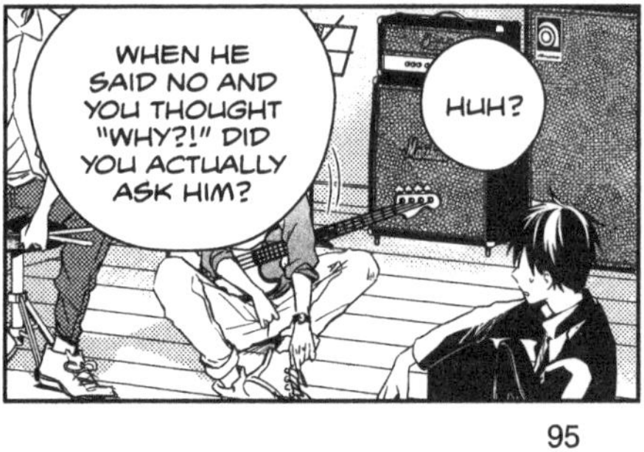
HUH?
WHEN HE SAID NO AND YOU THOUGHT "WHY?!" DID YOU ACTUALLY ASK HIM?

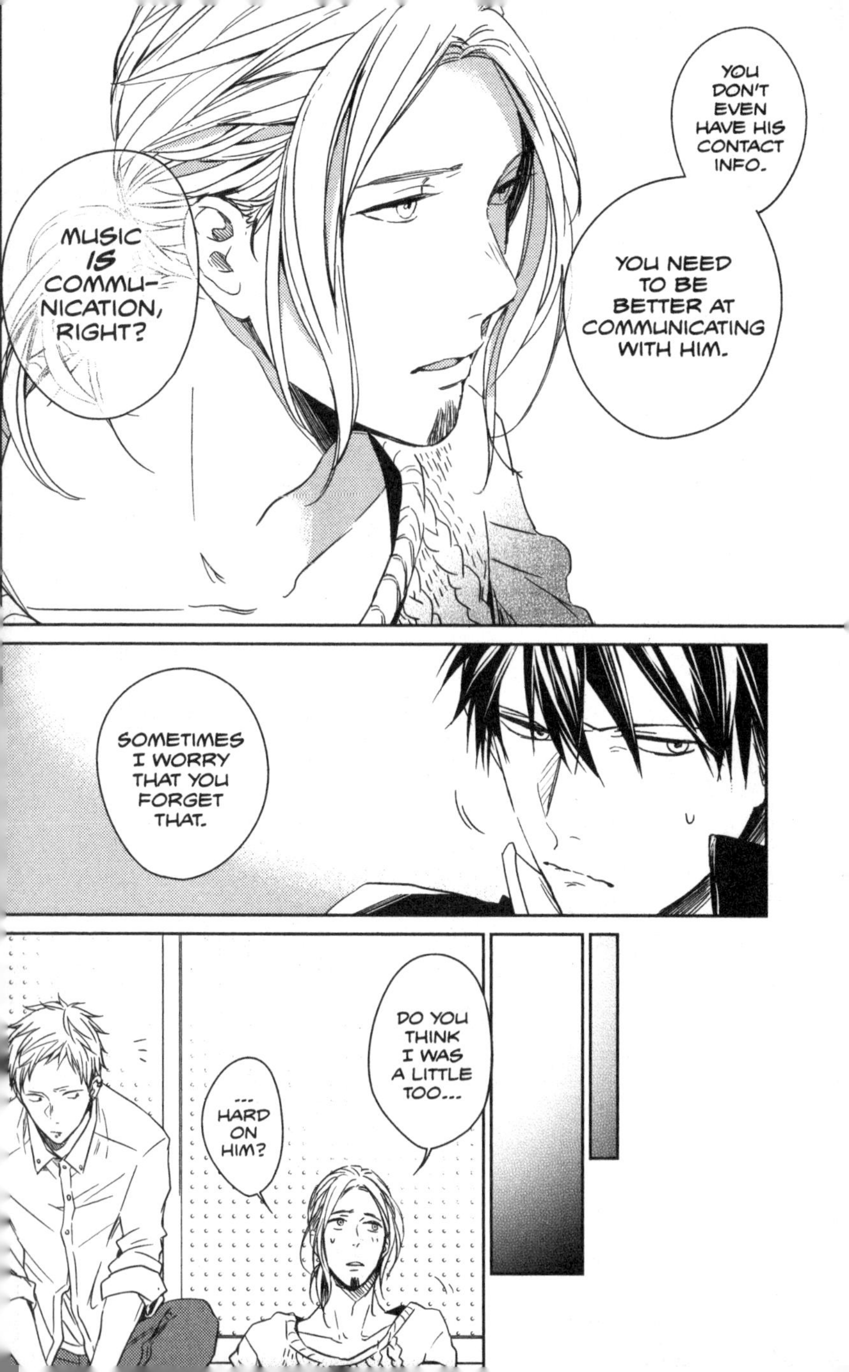
YOU DON'T EVEN HAVE HIS CONTACT INFO.
YOU NEED TO BE BETTER AT COMMUNICATING WITH HIM.
MUSIC *IS* COMMU-NICATION, RIGHT?
SOMETIMES I WORRY THAT YOU FORGET THAT.
DO YOU THINK I WAS A LITTLE TOO...
...HARD ON HIM?

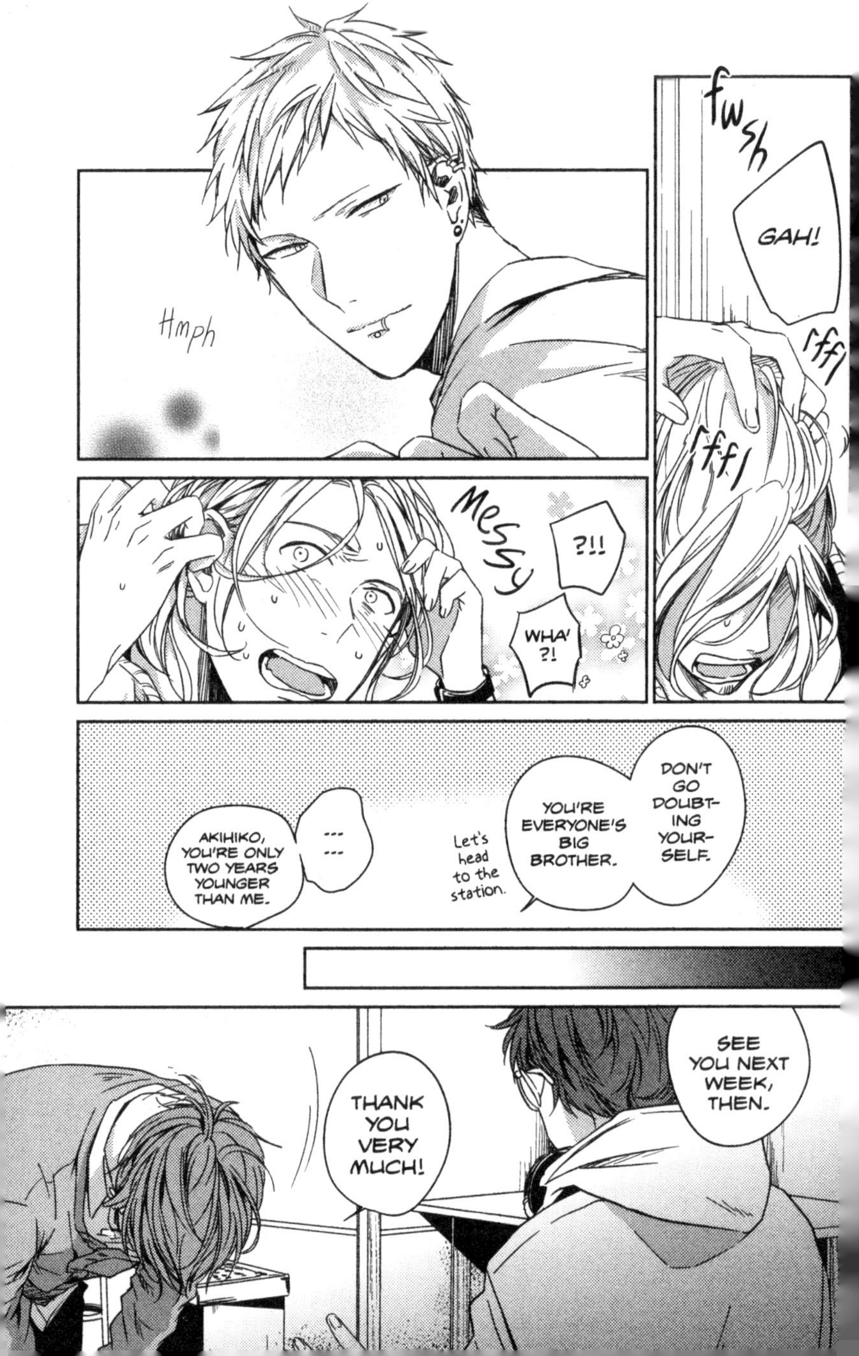
fwsh
GAH!
ruffle
ruffle
Hmph
Messy
?!!
WHA' ?!
DON'T GO DOUBTING YOURSELF.
YOU'RE EVERYONE'S BIG BROTHER.
Let's head to the station.
......
AKIHIKO, YOU'RE ONLY TWO YEARS YOUNGER THAN ME.
SEE YOU NEXT WEEK, THEN.
THANK YOU VERY MUCH!

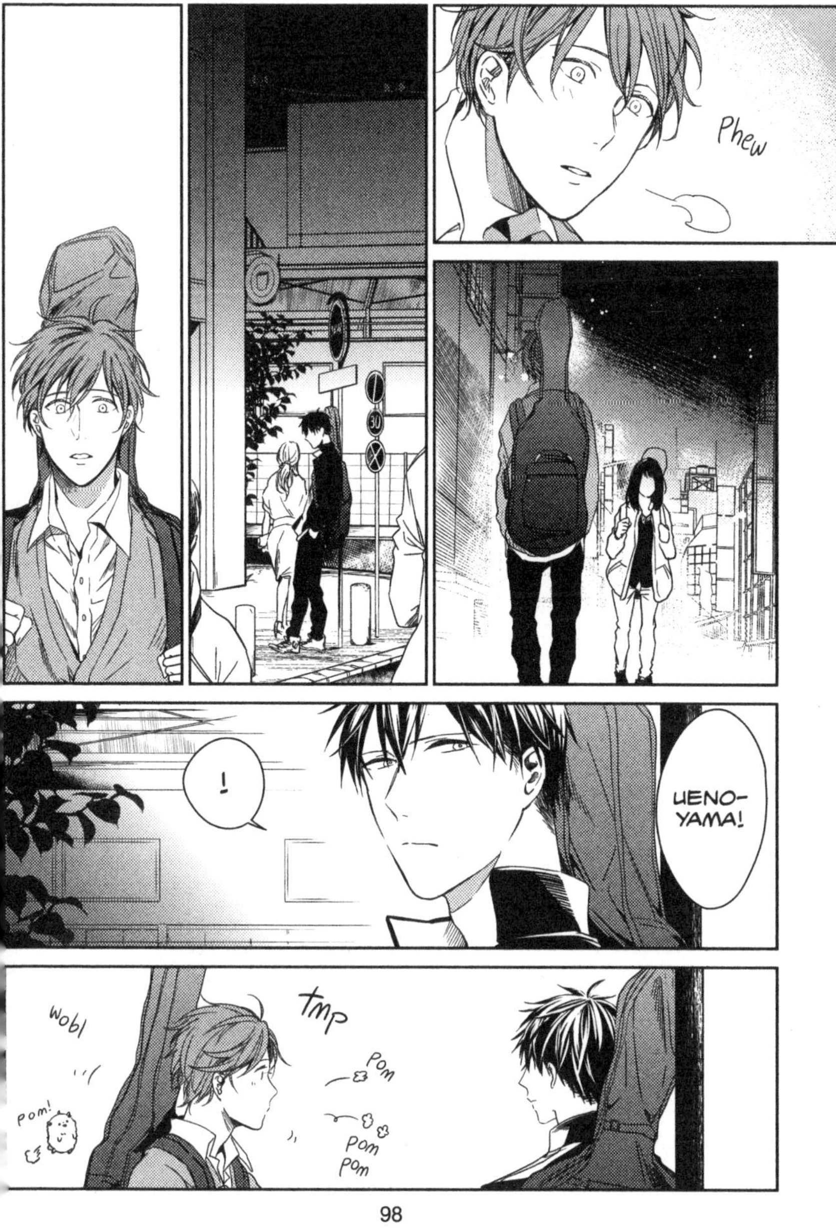
Phew
UENO-YAMA!
!
Pom
Pom
Pom
tmp
wobl
pom!

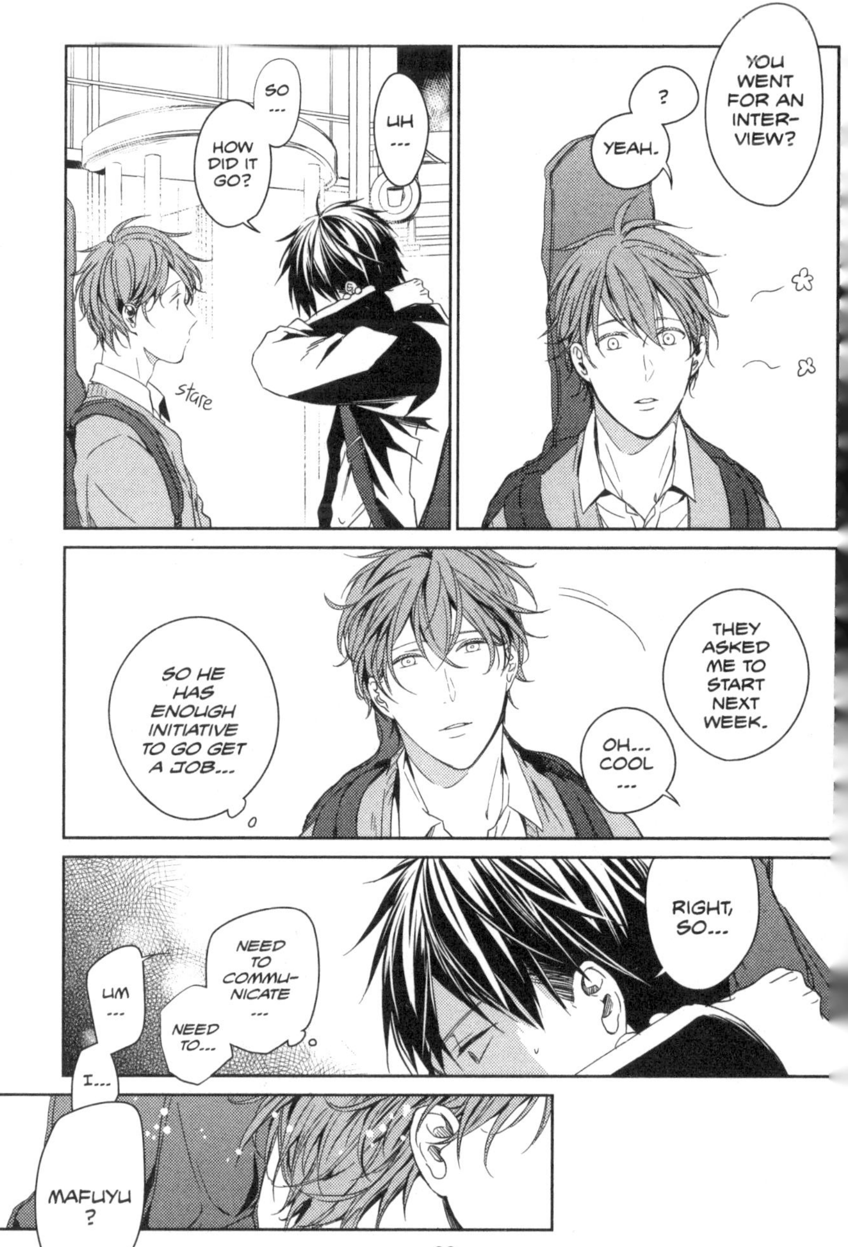
YOU WENT FOR AN INTER-VIEW?
?
YEAH.
UH ...
SO ...
HOW DID IT GO?
stare
THEY ASKED ME TO START NEXT WEEK.
OH... COOL ...
SO HE HAS ENOUGH INITIATIVE TO GO GET A JOB...
RIGHT, SO...
NEED TO COMMU-NICATE ...
NEED TO...
UM ...
I...
MAFUYU ?

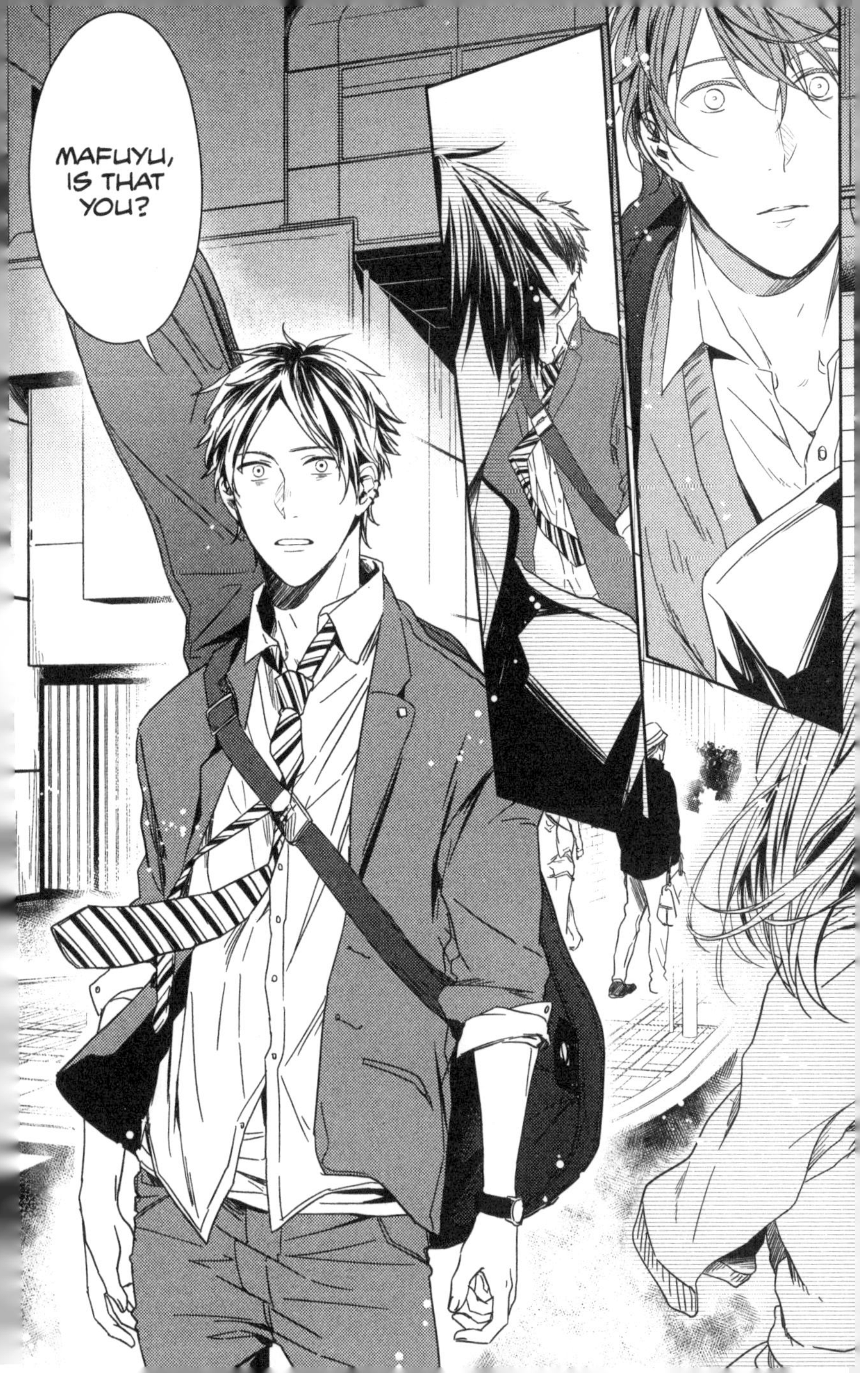
MAFUYU, IS THAT YOU?

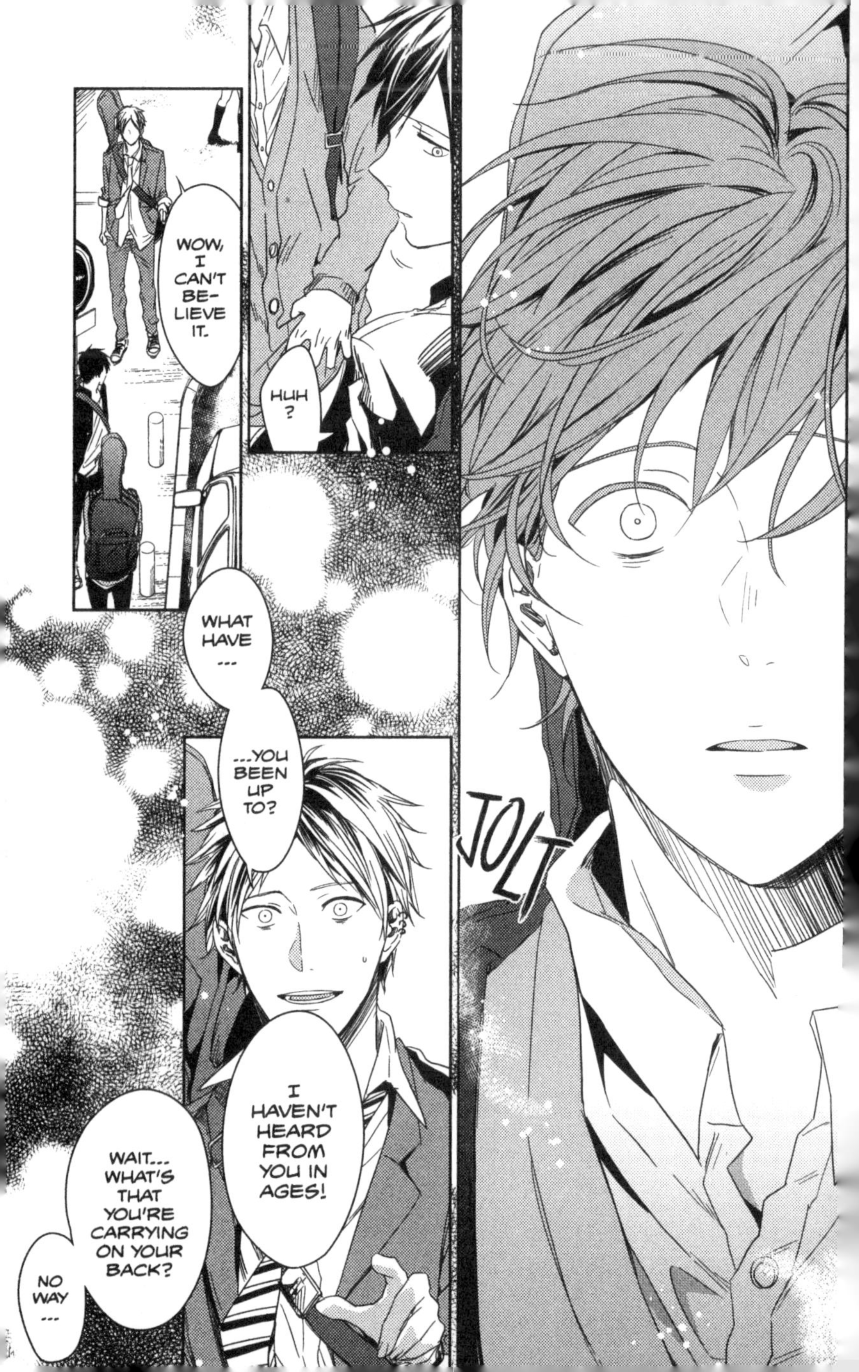
JOLT
WOW, I CAN'T BE-LIEVE IT.
HUH?
WHAT HAVE---
---YOU BEEN UP TO?
I HAVEN'T HEARD FROM YOU IN AGES!
WAIT... WHAT'S THAT YOU'RE CARRYING ON YOUR BACK?
NO WAY---

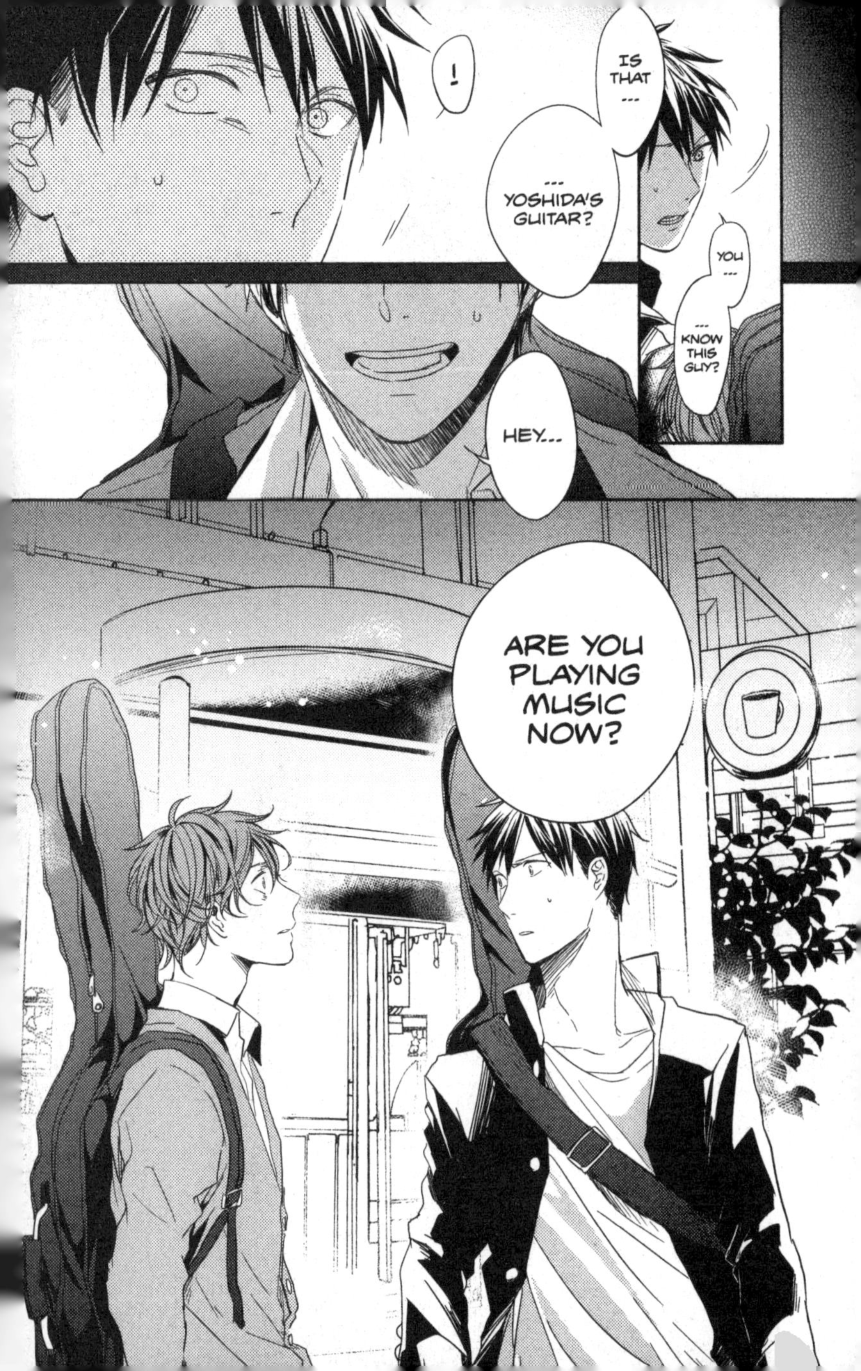
IS THAT ---
--- YOSHIDA'S GUITAR?
!
YOU ---
--- KNOW THIS GUY?
HEY...
ARE YOU PLAYING MUSIC NOW?

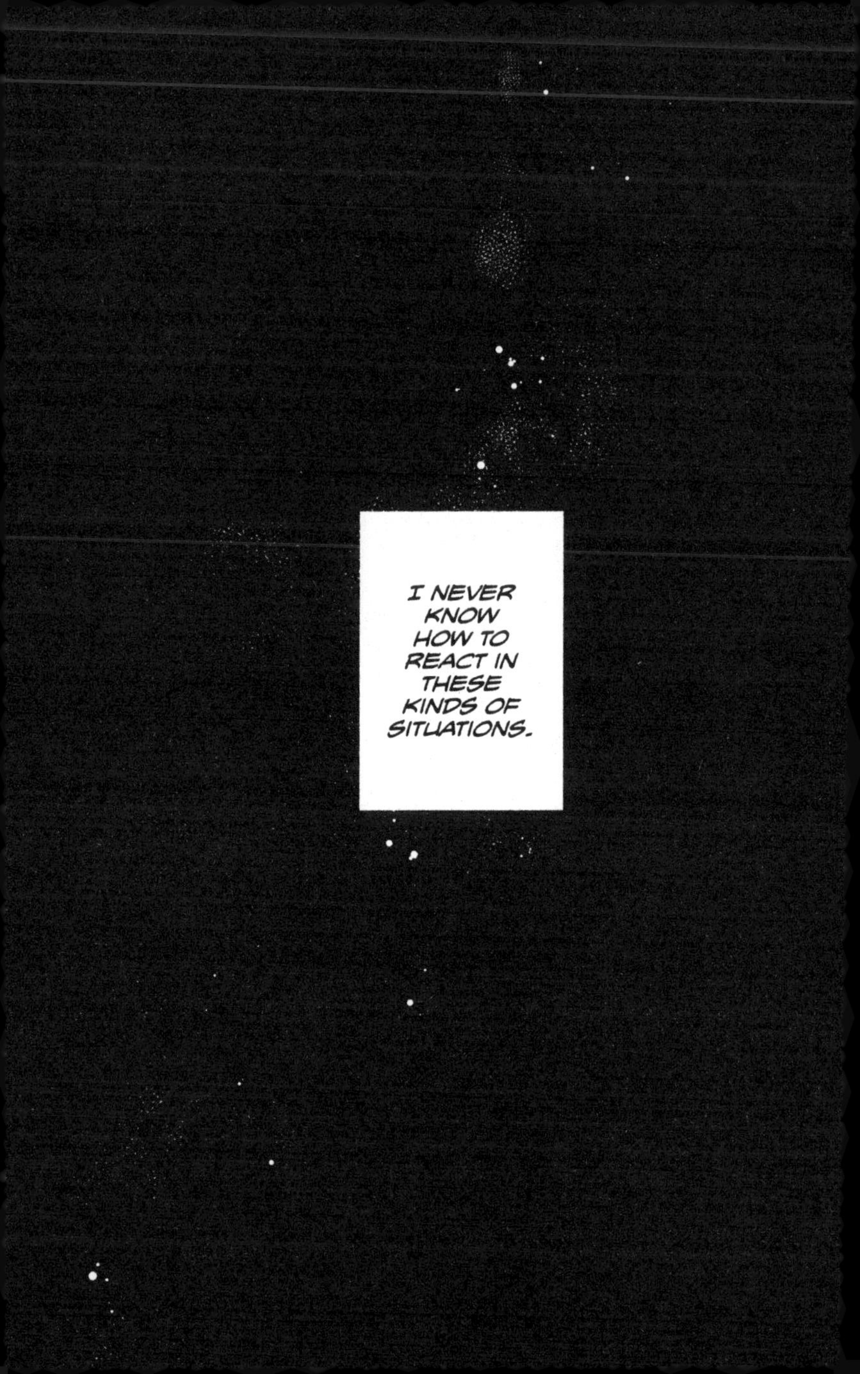
I NEVER KNOW HOW TO REACT IN THESE KINDS OF SITUATIONS.

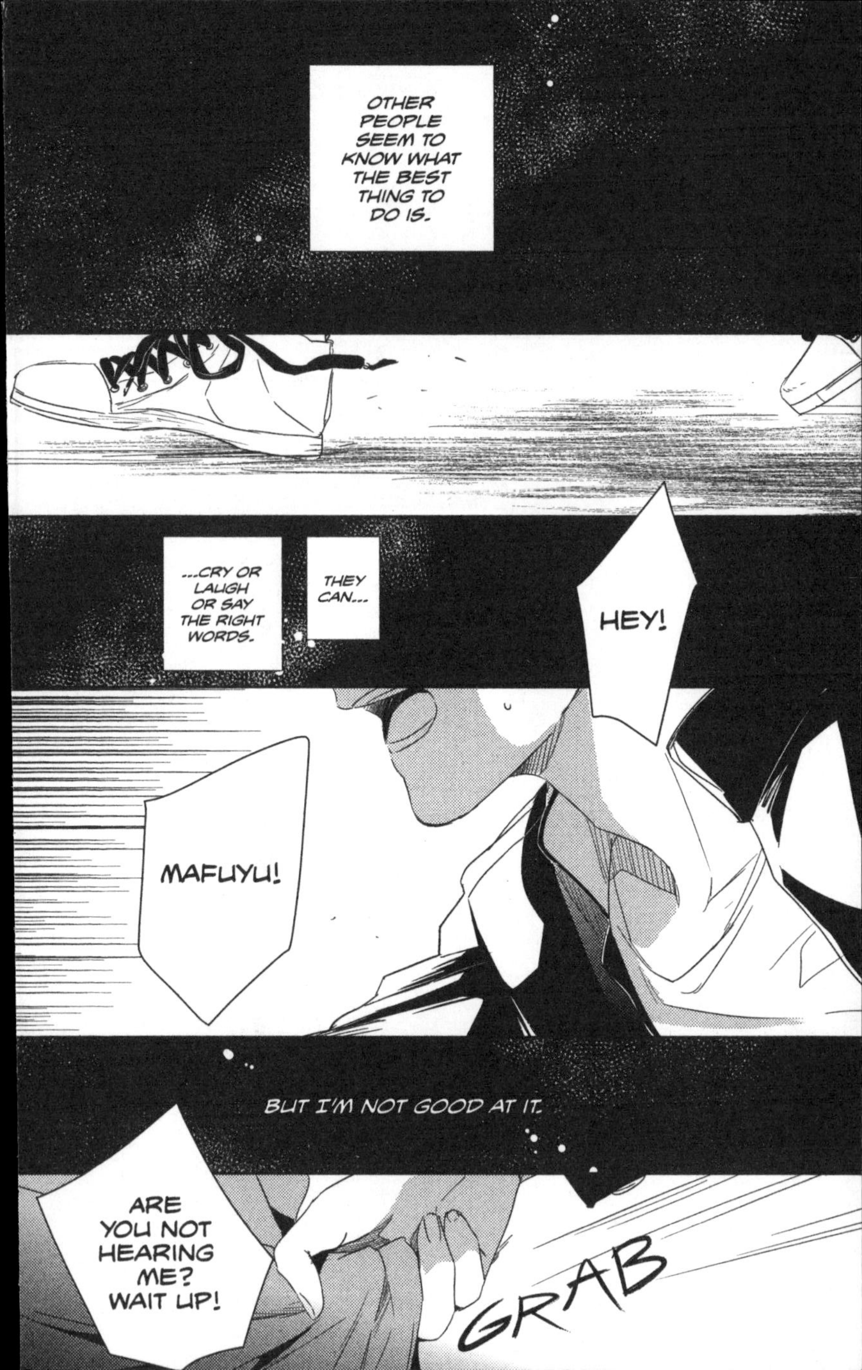
OTHER PEOPLE SEEM TO KNOW WHAT THE BEST THING TO DO IS.
HEY!
THEY CAN...
...CRY OR LAUGH OR SAY THE RIGHT WORDS.
MAFUYU!
BUT I'M NOT GOOD AT IT.
ARE YOU NOT HEARING ME? WAIT UP!
GRAB

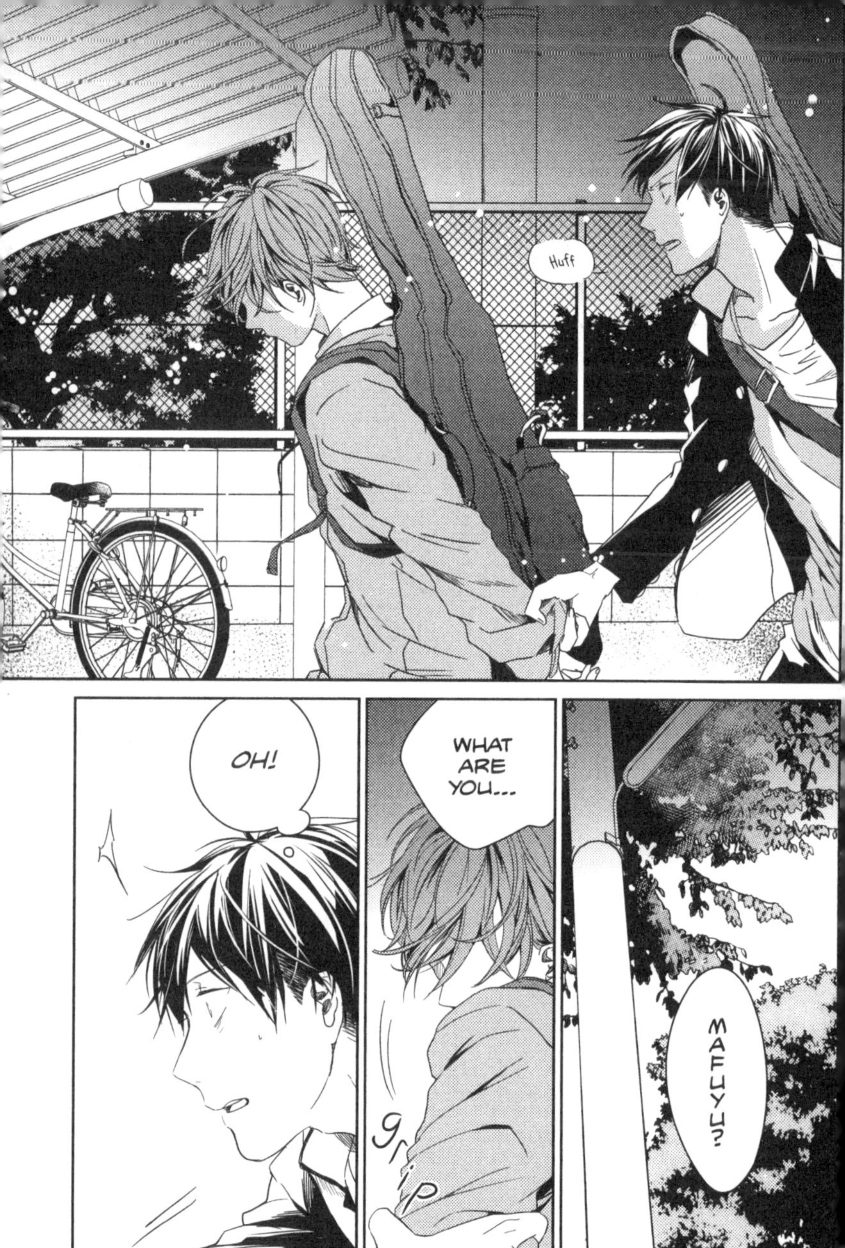
Huff
MAFUYU?
WHAT ARE YOU...
grip
OH!

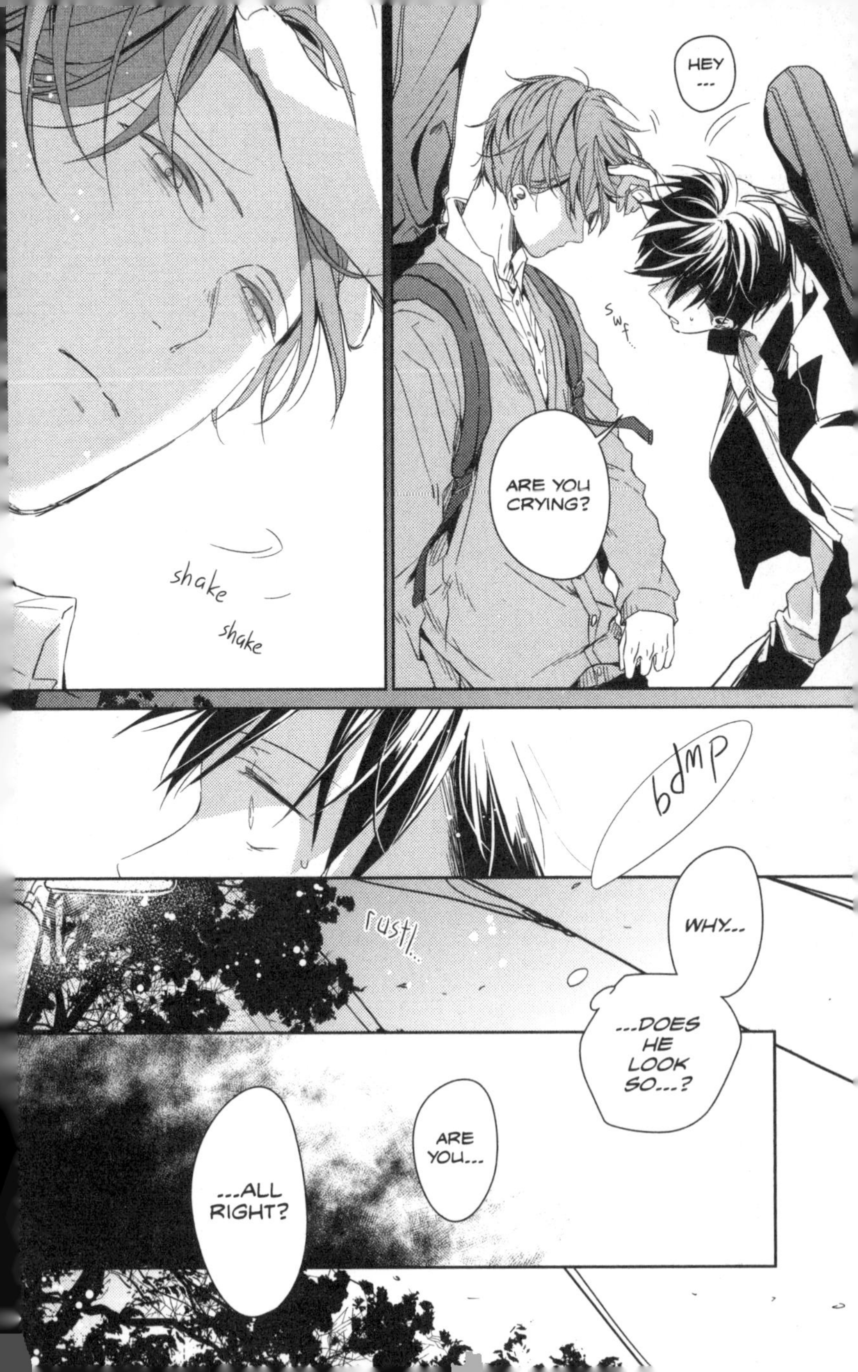
HEY ...
swf...
ARE YOU CRYING?
shake
shake
bdmp
WHY...
...DOES HE LOOK SO...?
rustl...
ARE YOU...
...ALL RIGHT?

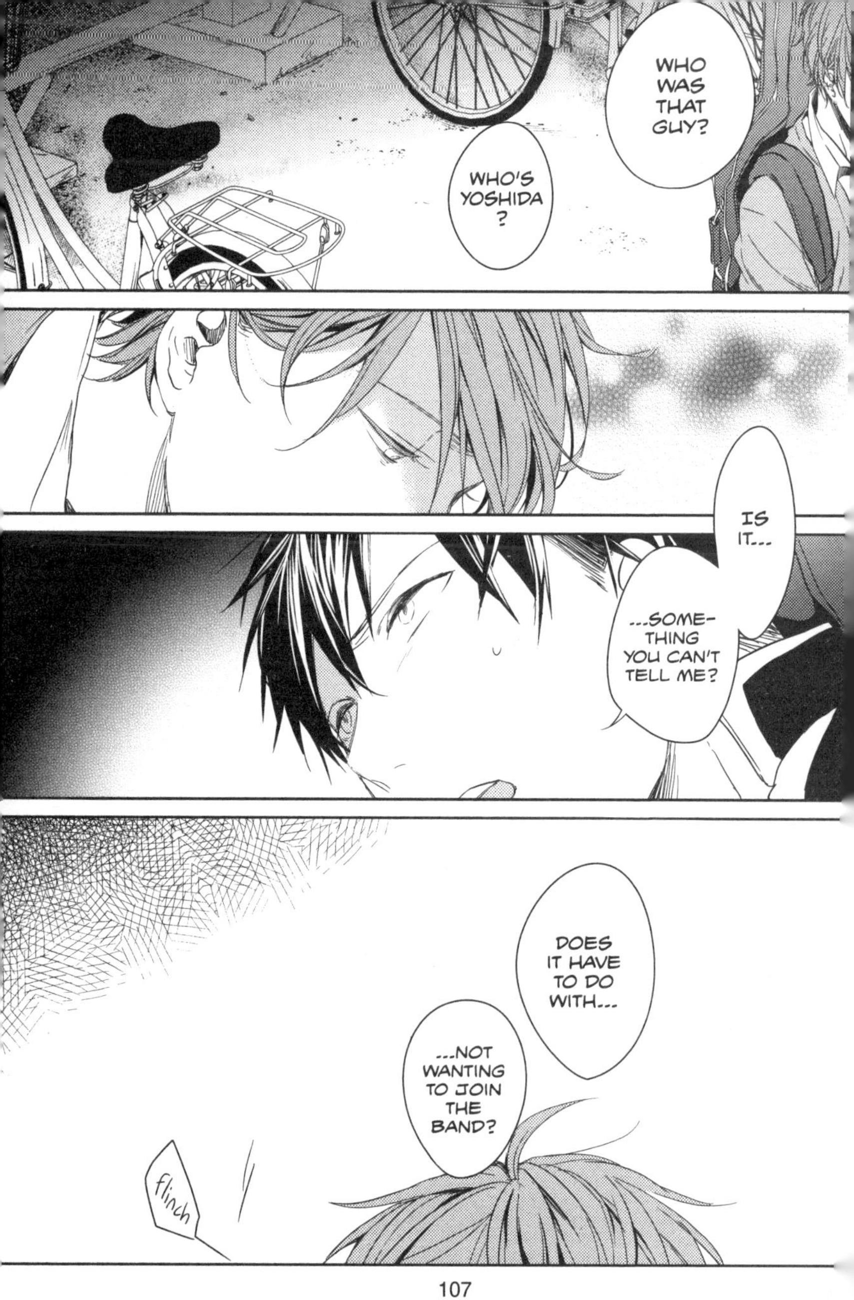
WHO WAS THAT GUY?
WHO'S YOSHIDA ?
IS IT...
...SOME-THING YOU CAN'T TELL ME?
DOES IT HAVE TO DO WITH...
...NOT WANTING TO JOIN THE BAND?
flinch

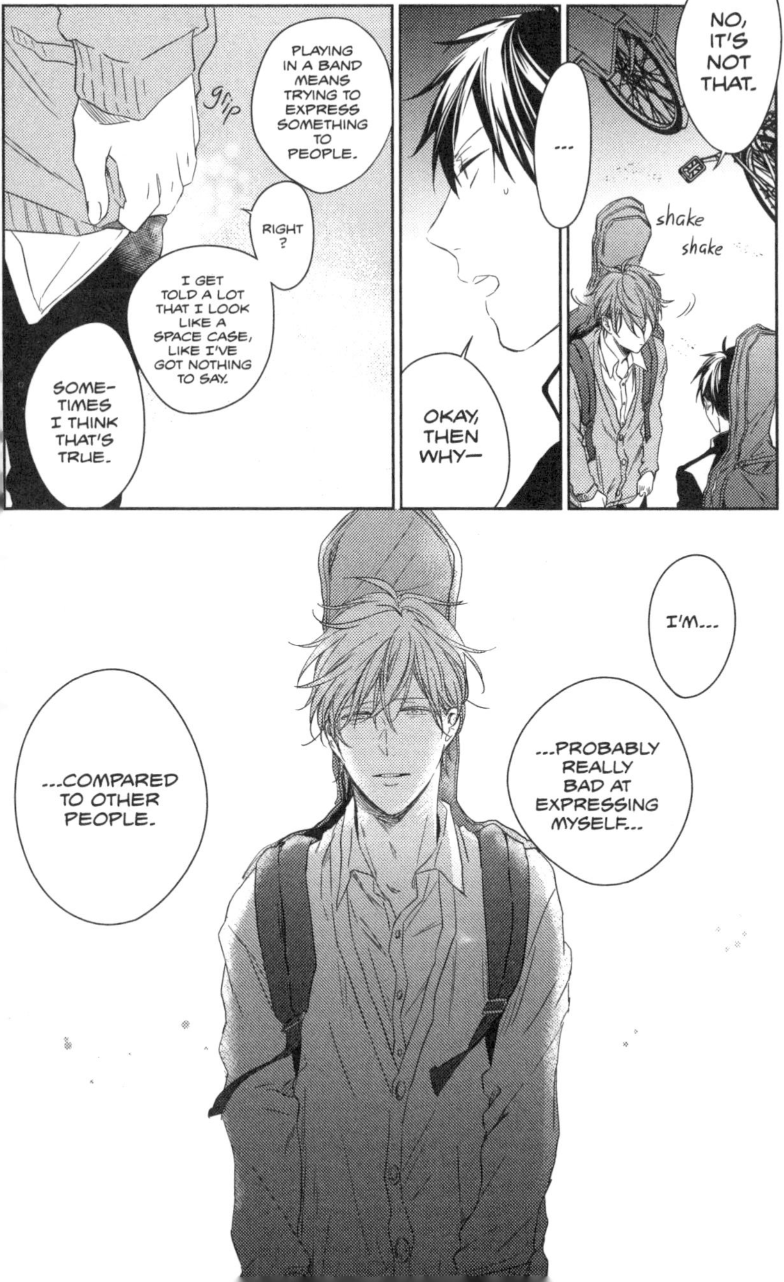
NO, IT'S NOT THAT.
shake shake
...
OKAY, THEN WHY—
PLAYING IN A BAND MEANS TRYING TO EXPRESS SOMETHING TO PEOPLE.
grip
RIGHT?
I GET TOLD A LOT THAT I LOOK LIKE A SPACE CASE, LIKE I'VE GOT NOTHING TO SAY.
SOME-TIMES I THINK THAT'S TRUE.
I'M...
...PROBABLY REALLY BAD AT EXPRESSING MYSELF...
...COMPARED TO OTHER PEOPLE.

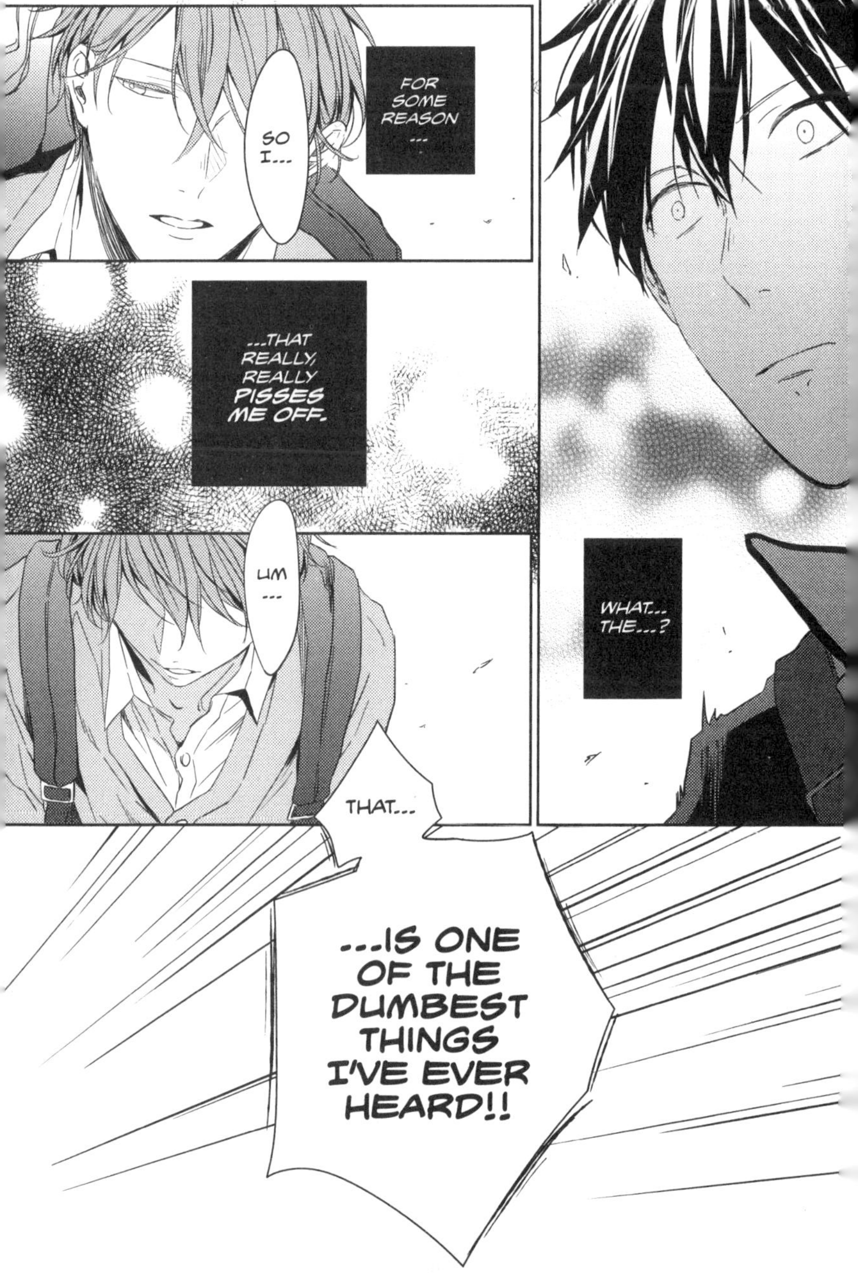
FOR SOME REASON ...
SO I...
...THAT REALLY, REALLY PISSES ME OFF.
WHAT... THE...?
UM ...
THAT...
...IS ONE OF THE DUMBEST THINGS I'VE EVER HEARD!!

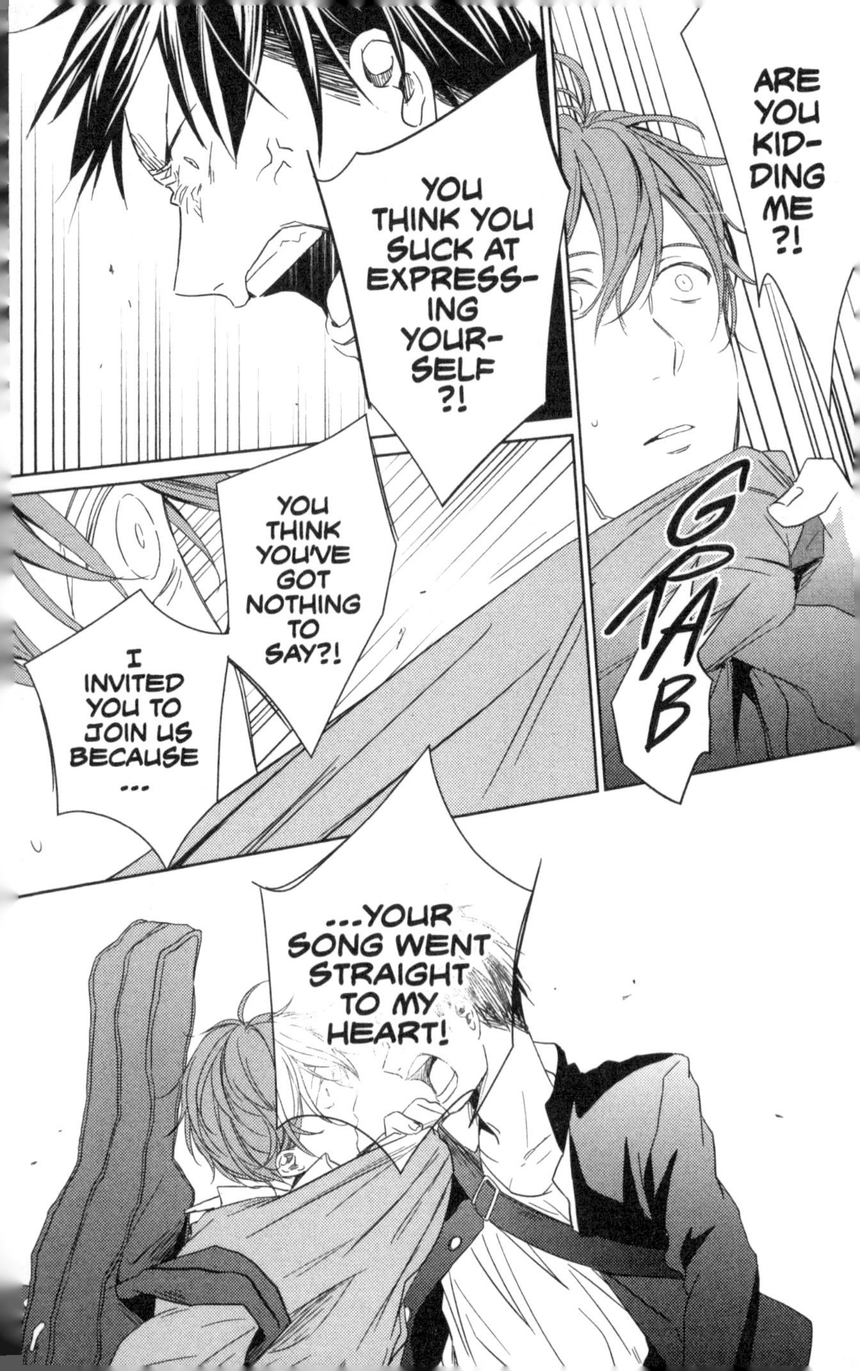
ARE YOU KID-DING ME?!
YOU THINK YOU SUCK AT EXPRESS-ING YOUR-SELF?!
GRAB
YOU THINK YOU'VE GOT NOTHING TO SAY?!
I INVITED YOU TO JOIN US BECAUSE...
...YOUR SONG WENT STRAIGHT TO MY HEART!

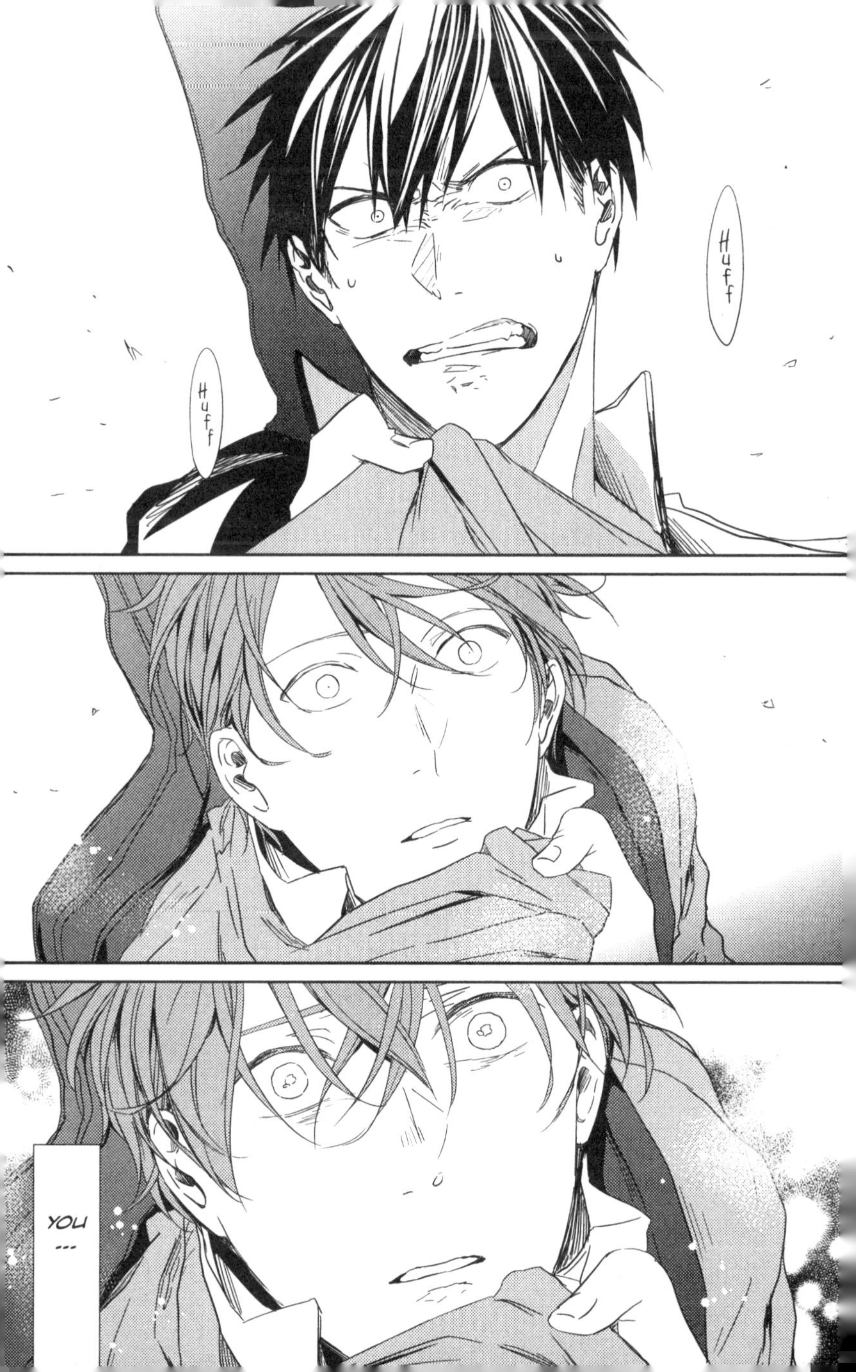
Huff
Huff
YOU ...

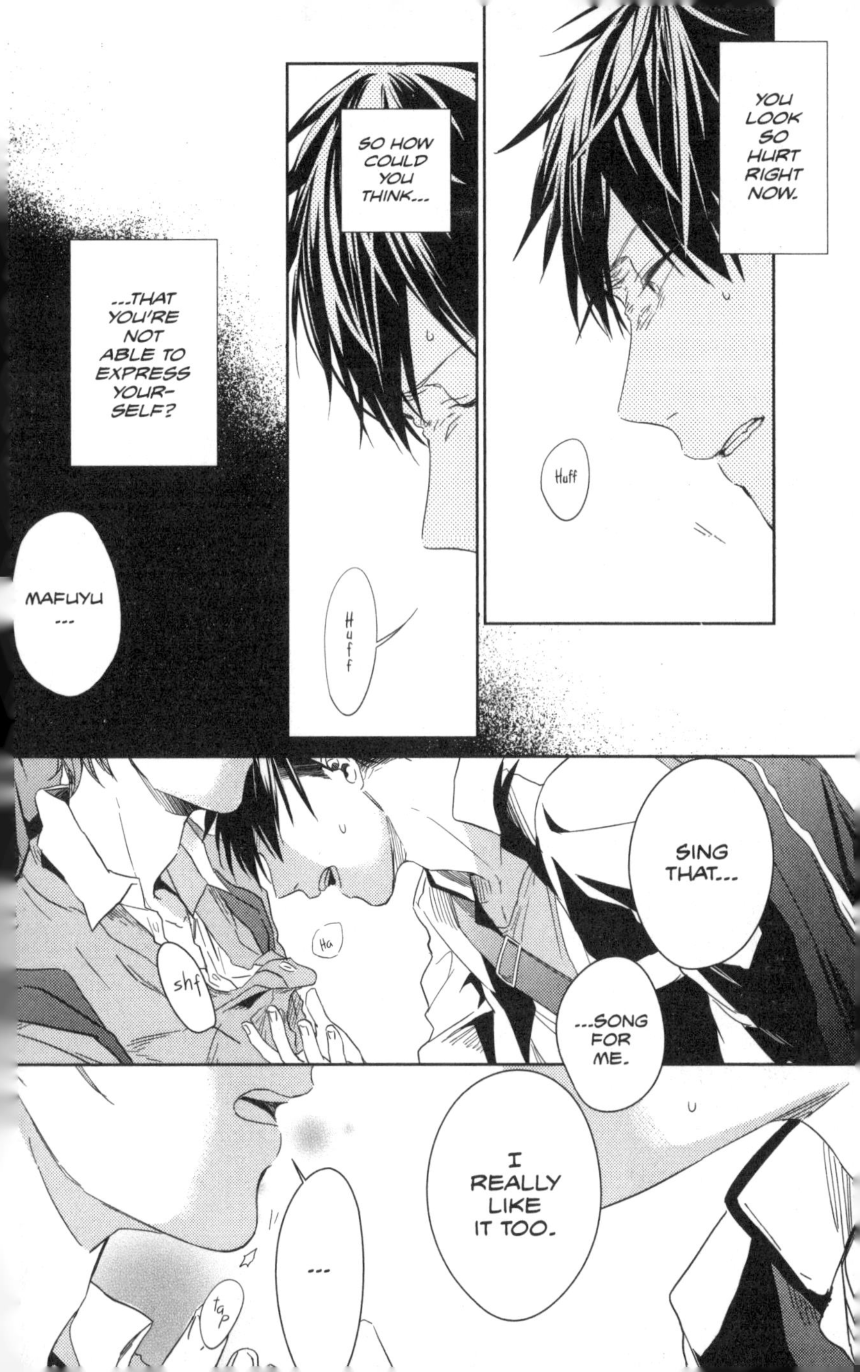
YOU LOOK SO HURT RIGHT NOW.
Huff
SO HOW COULD YOU THINK...
Huff
...THAT YOU'RE NOT ABLE TO EXPRESS YOUR-SELF?
MAFUYU...
SING THAT...
...SONG FOR ME.
Ha
shf
I REALLY LIKE IT TOO.
...
tap

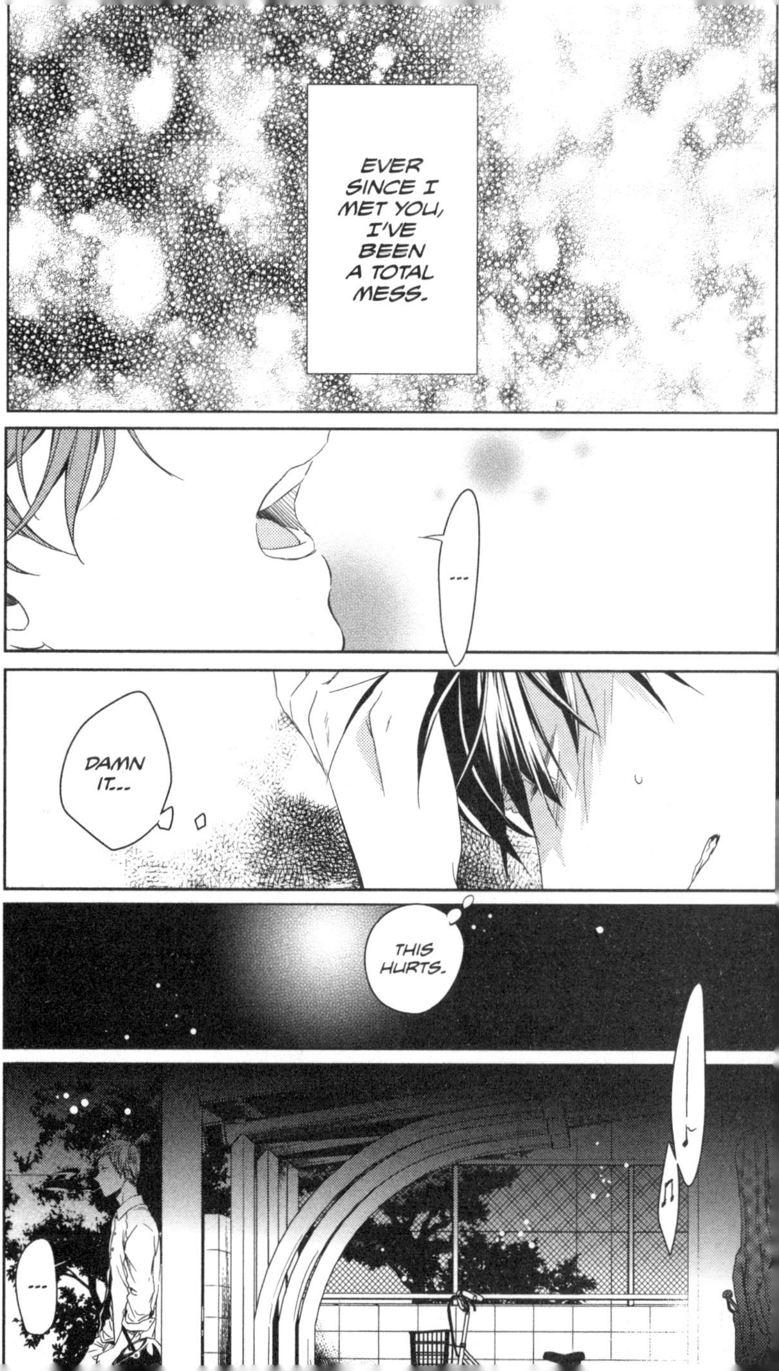
EVER SINCE I MET YOU, I'VE BEEN A TOTAL MESS.
...
DAMN IT...
THIS HURTS.
...

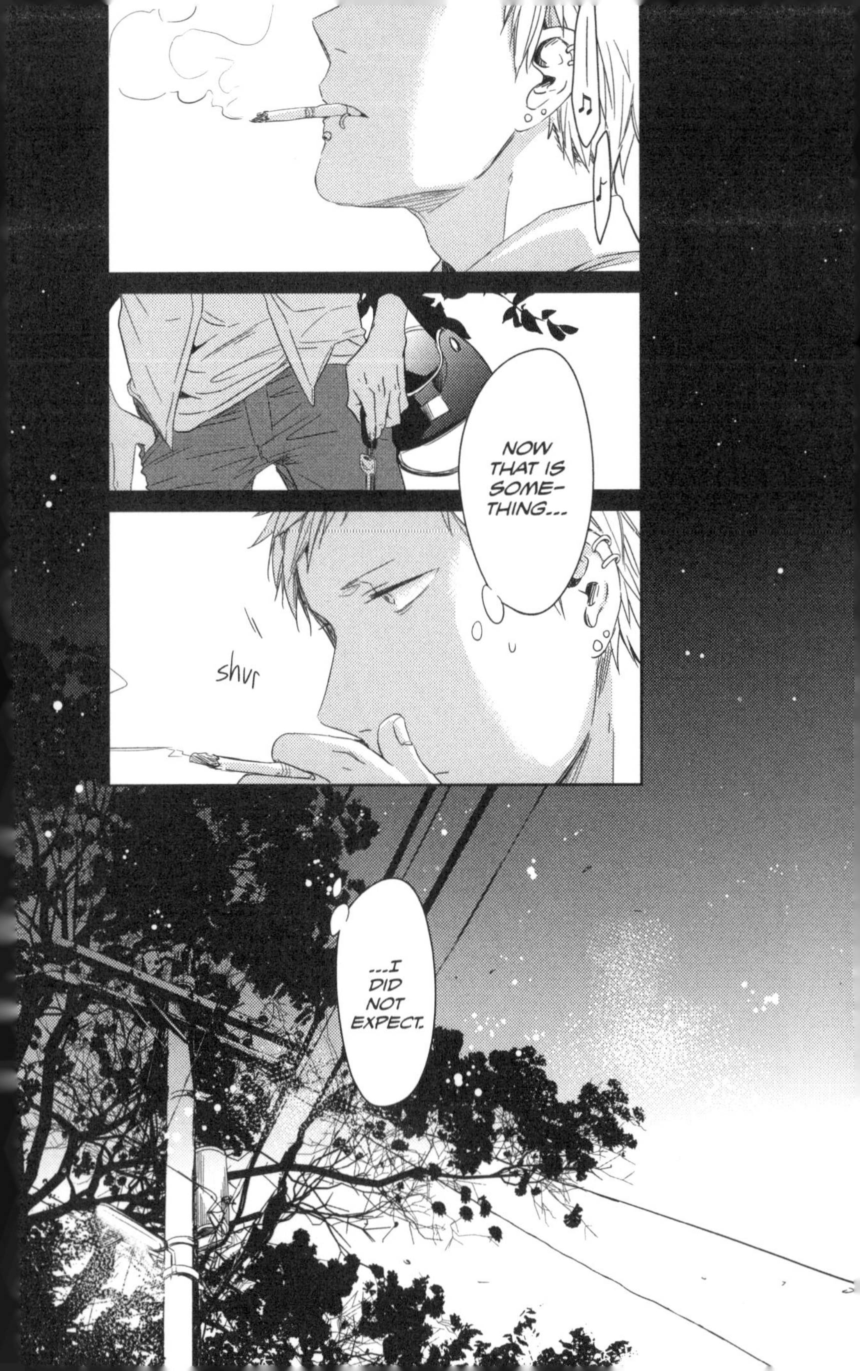
NOW THAT IS SOME-THING...
shvr
...I DID NOT EXPECT.

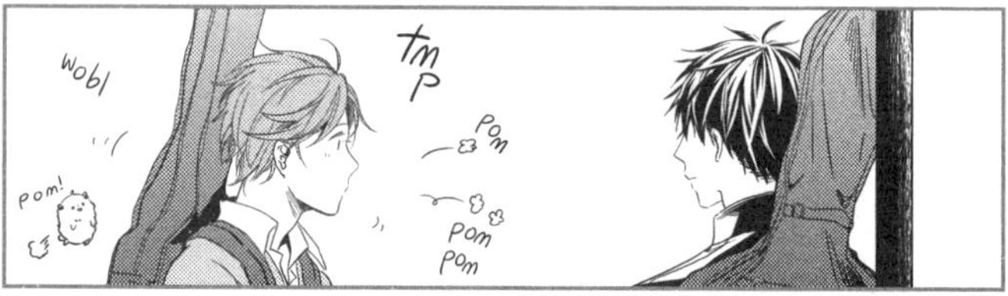
tmp
pom
pom
pom
wobl
pom!

given

by Natsuki Kizu

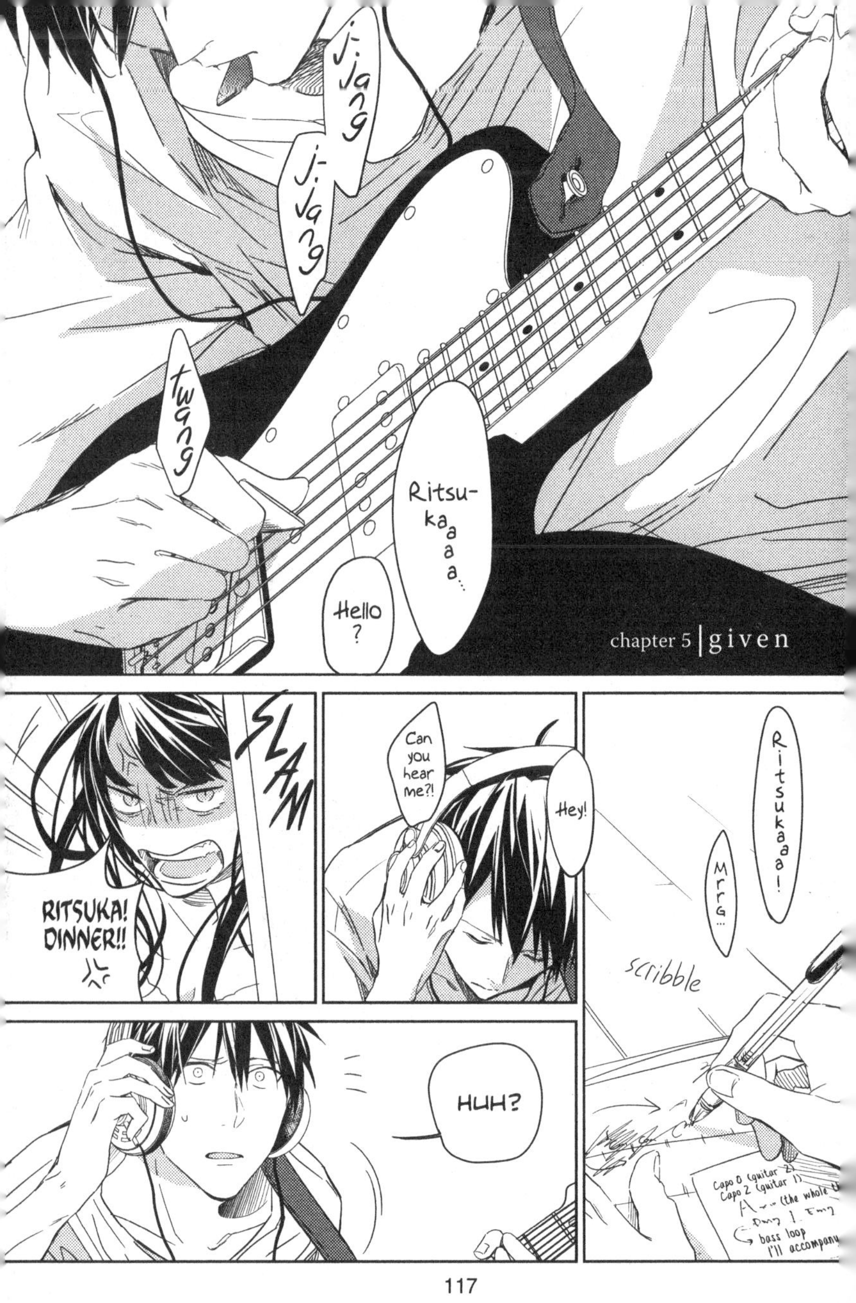
j-jang
j-jang
twang
Ritsu-kaaaa...
Hello?
chapter 5 | given
Ritsukaaa!
Mrrg..
scribble
Capo 0 (guitar 2)
Capo 2 (guitar 1)
bass loop
I'll accompany
Hey!
Can you hear me?!
SLAM
RITSUKA! DINNER!!
HUH?

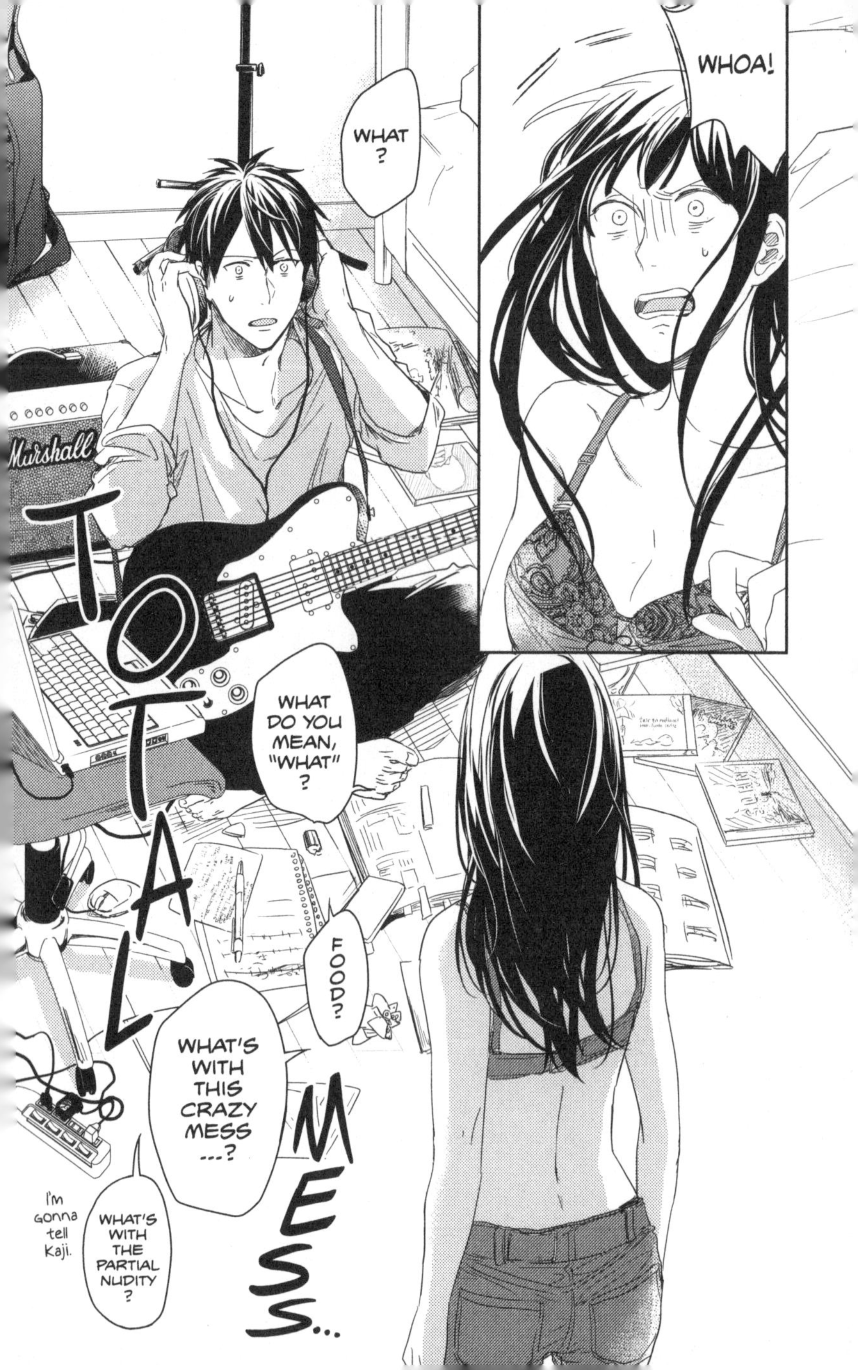
WHOA!
WHAT?
WHAT DO YOU MEAN, "WHAT"?
FOOD?
WHAT'S WITH THIS CRAZY MESS...?
WHAT'S WITH THE PARTIAL NUDITY?
I'm gonna tell Kaji.
TOTAL MESS...
Marshall

chapter 5

given

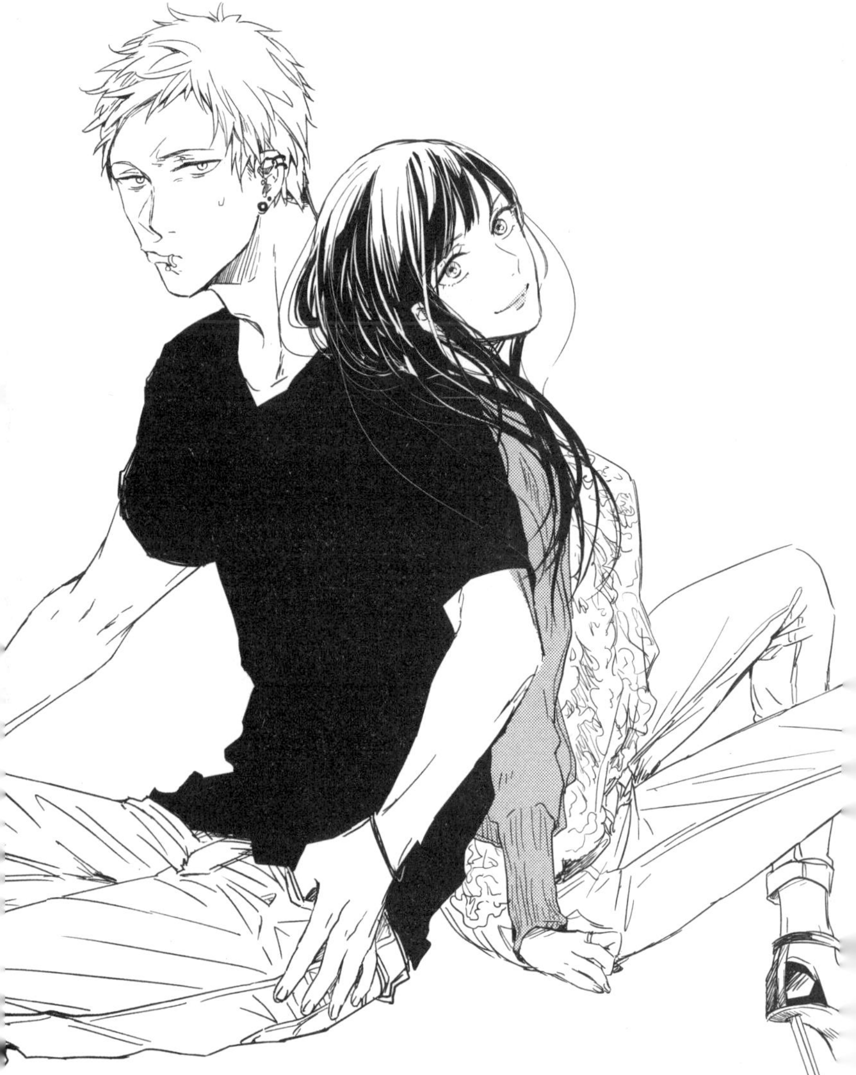

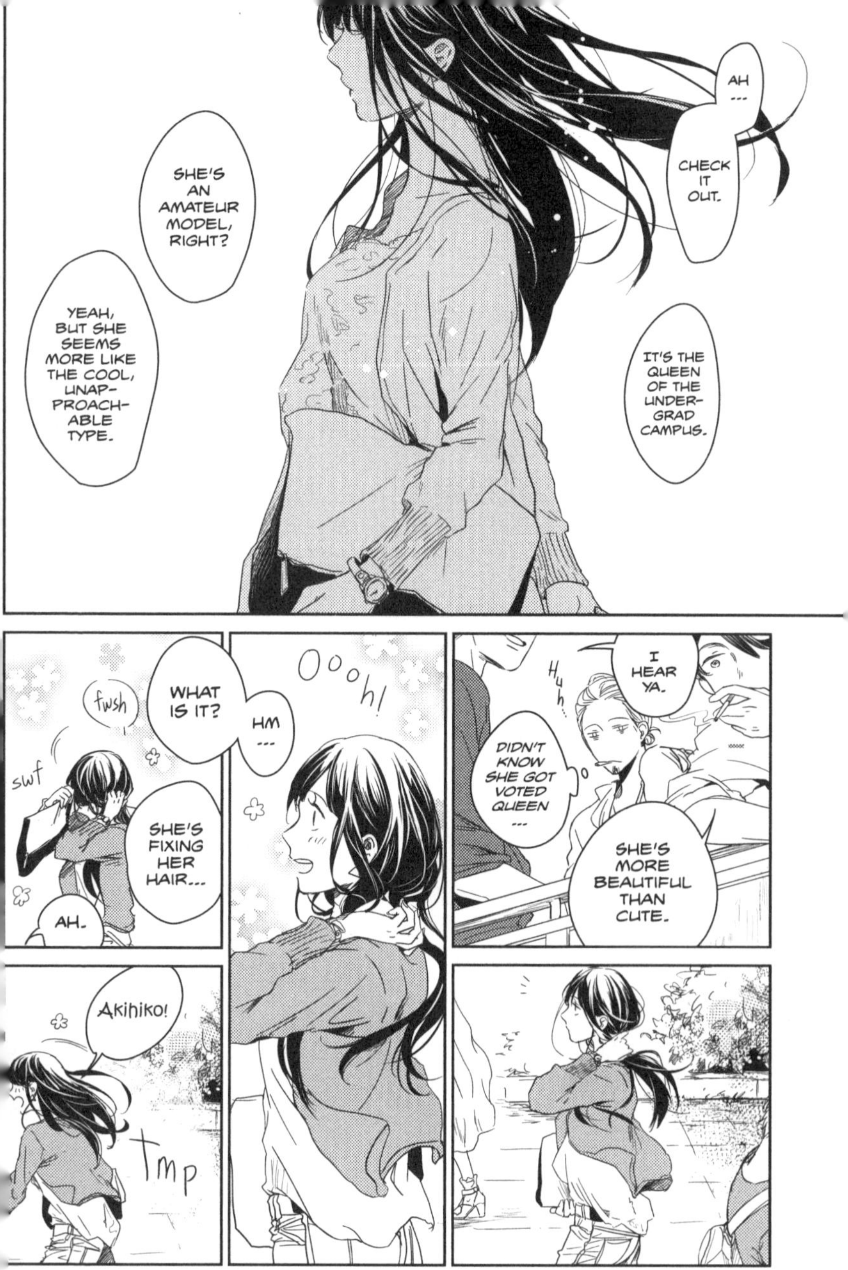
AH ---
CHECK IT OUT.
IT'S THE QUEEN OF THE UNDERGRAD CAMPUS.
SHE'S AN AMATEUR MODEL, RIGHT?
YEAH, BUT SHE SEEMS MORE LIKE THE COOL, UNAPPROACHABLE TYPE.
I HEAR YA.
Huh...
DIDN'T KNOW SHE GOT VOTED QUEEN ---
SHE'S MORE BEAUTIFUL THAN CUTE.
Oooh!
HM ---
WHAT IS IT?
fwsh
swf
SHE'S FIXING HER HAIR...
AH.
Akihiko!
Tmp

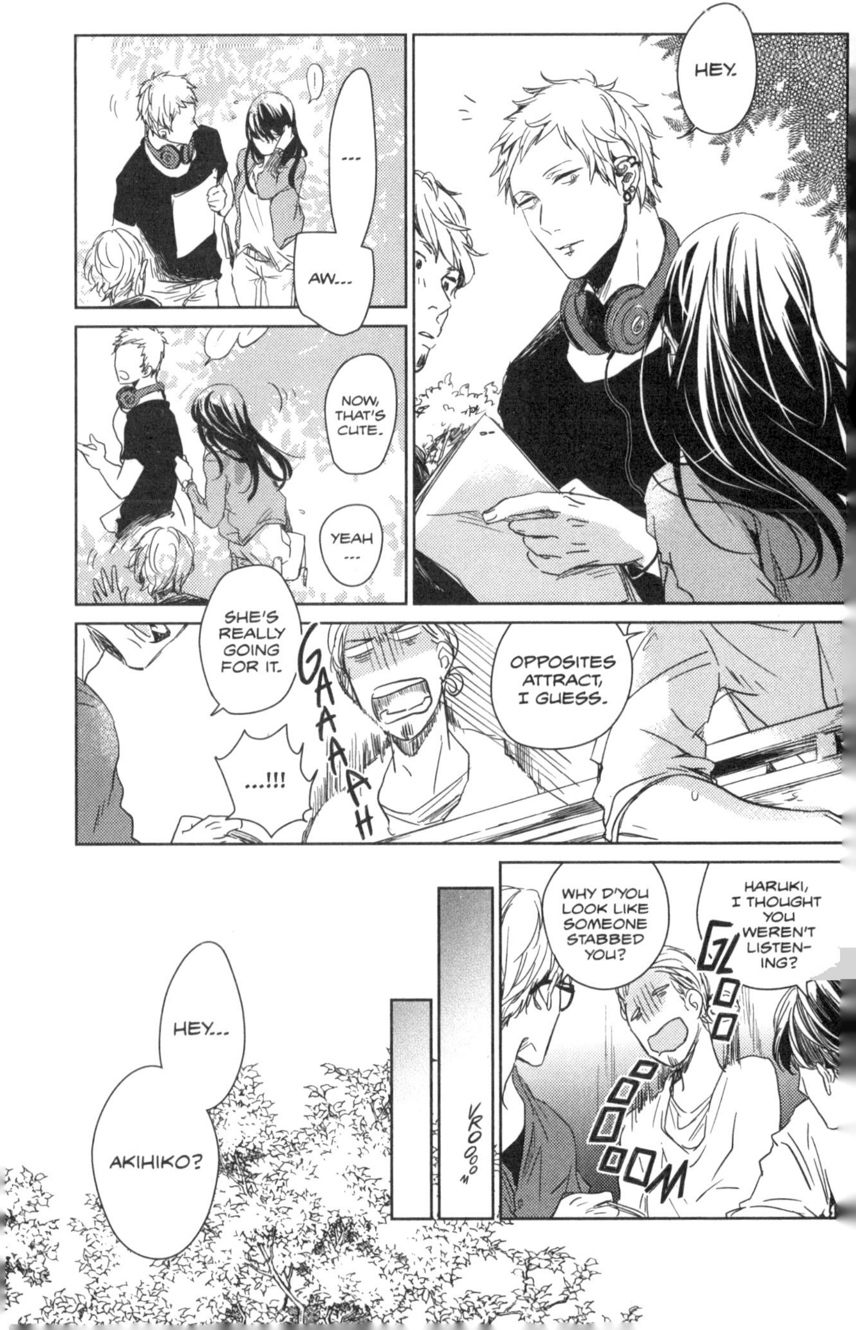
HEY.
--
!
...
AW...
NOW, THAT'S CUTE.
YEAH ...
OPPOSITES ATTRACT, I GUESS.
GAAAAH
SHE'S REALLY GOING FOR IT.
...!!!
HARUKI, I THOUGHT YOU WEREN'T LISTENING?
GLOOOOOOOM
WHY D'YOU LOOK LIKE SOMEONE STABBED YOU?
VROOOOM
HEY...
AKIHIKO?

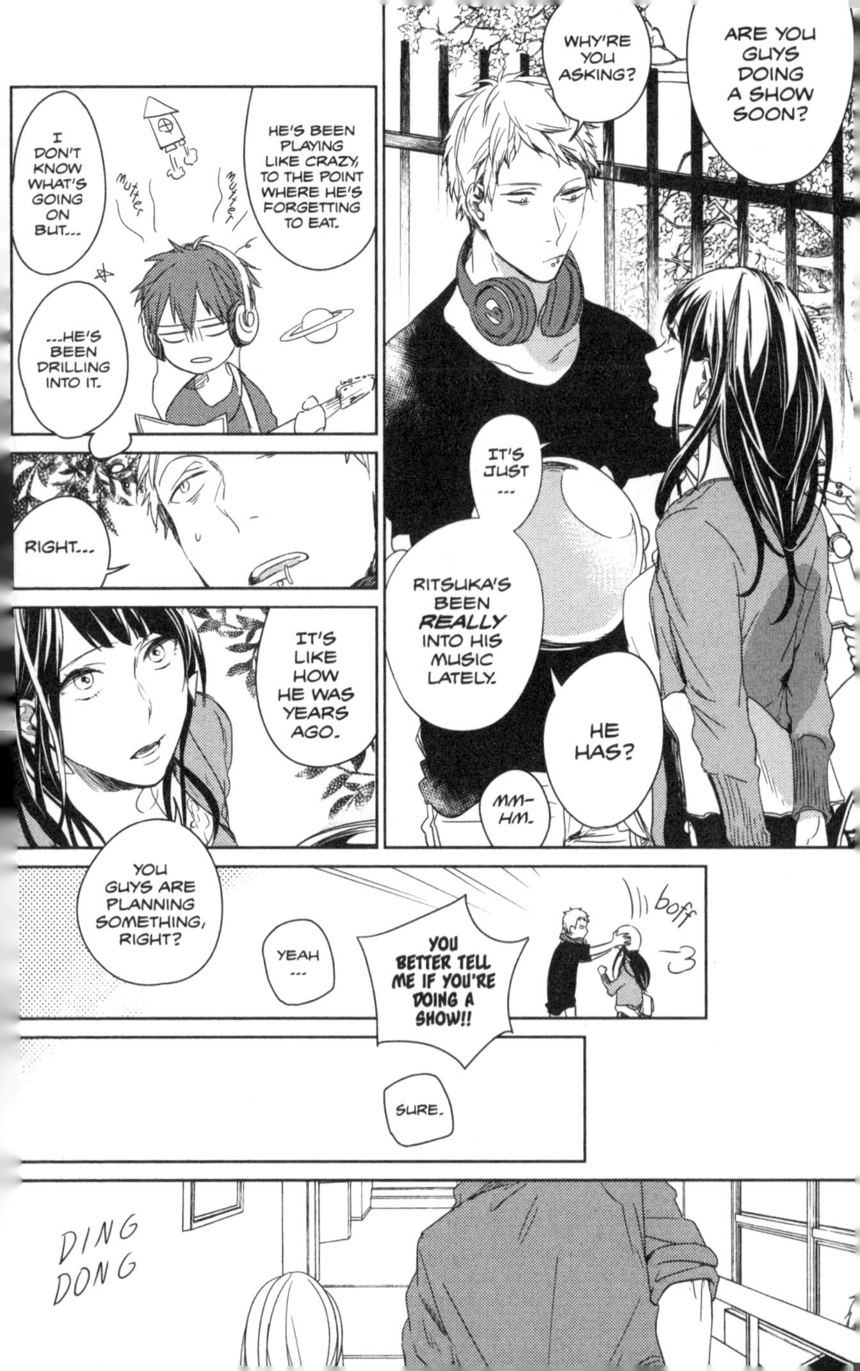
ARE YOU GUYS DOING A SHOW SOON?
WHY'RE YOU ASKING?
IT'S JUST ...
RITSUKA'S BEEN *REALLY* INTO HIS MUSIC LATELY.
HE HAS?
MM-HM.
HE'S BEEN PLAYING LIKE CRAZY, TO THE POINT WHERE HE'S FORGETTING TO EAT.
mutter
mutter
I DON'T KNOW WHAT'S GOING ON BUT...
...HE'S BEEN DRILLING INTO IT.
RIGHT...
IT'S LIKE HOW HE WAS YEARS AGO.
YOU GUYS ARE PLANNING SOMETHING, RIGHT?
YEAH ...
YOU BETTER TELL ME IF YOU'RE DOING A SHOW!!
boff
SURE.
DING DONG

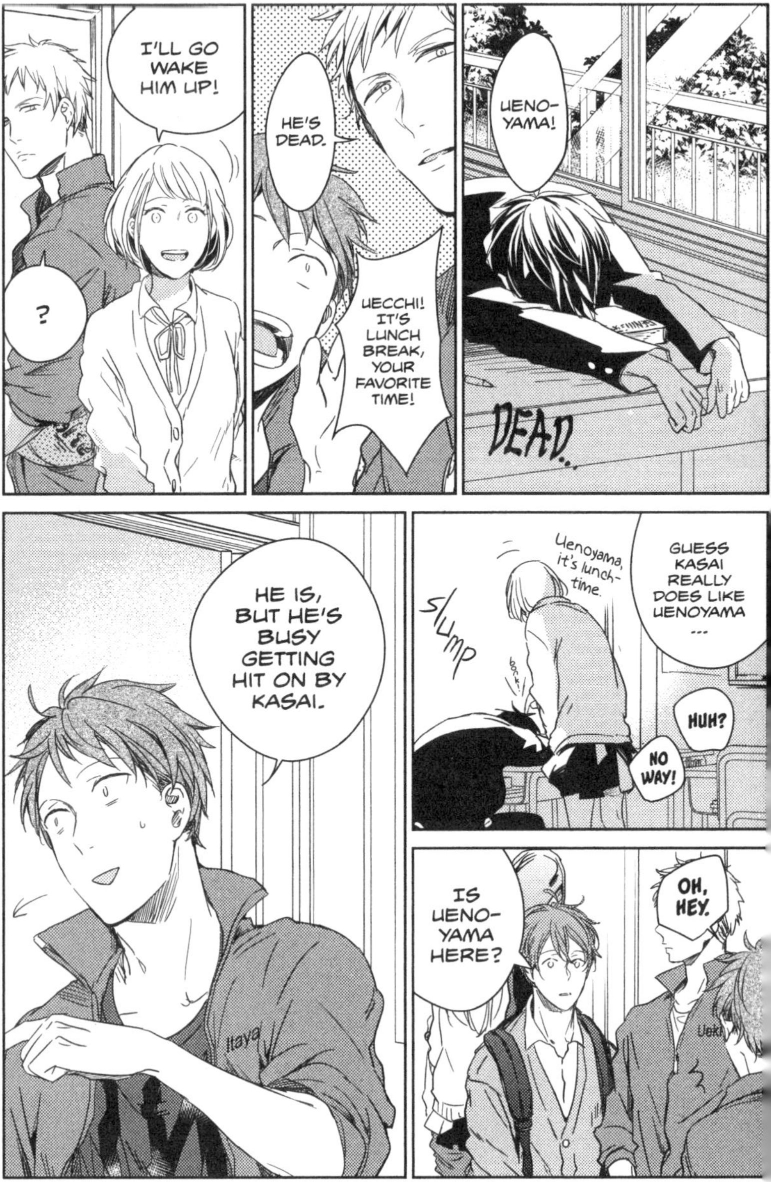
UENO-YAMA!
DEAD...
UECCHI! IT'S LUNCH BREAK, YOUR FAVORITE TIME!
HE'S DEAD.
I'LL GO WAKE HIM UP!
?
GUESS KASAI REALLY DOES LIKE UENOYAMA...
Uenoyama, it's lunch-time.
SLUMP
HUH?
NO WAY!
OH, HEY.
IS UENO-YAMA HERE?
HE IS, BUT HE'S BUSY GETTING HIT ON BY KASAI.
Itaya

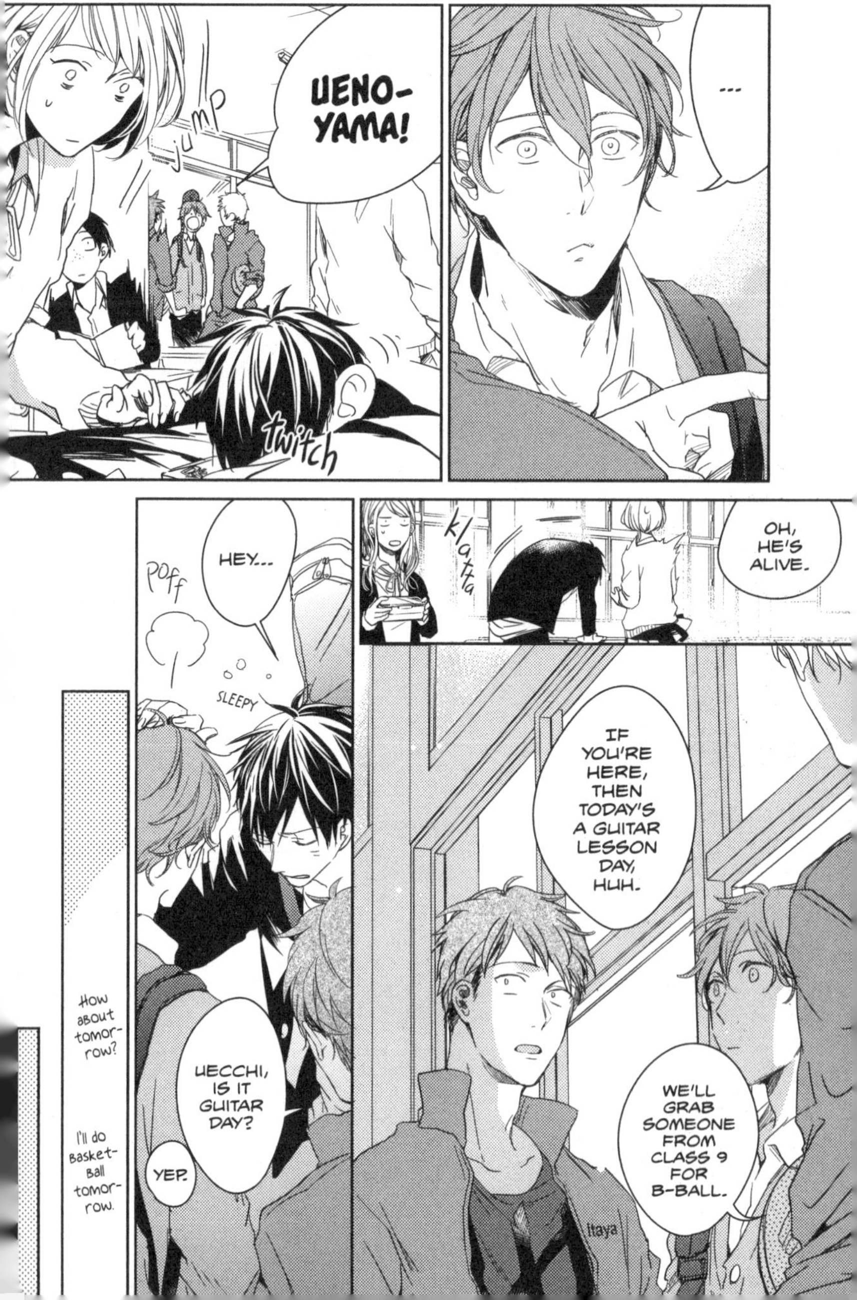
...
UENO-YAMA!
jump
twitch
OH, HE'S ALIVE.
klatta
HEY...
poff
SLEEPY
IF YOU'RE HERE, THEN TODAY'S A GUITAR LESSON DAY, HUH.
WE'LL GRAB SOMEONE FROM CLASS 9 FOR B-BALL.
UECCHI, IS IT GUITAR DAY?
YEP.
How about tomor-row?
I'll do Basket-Ball tomor-row.

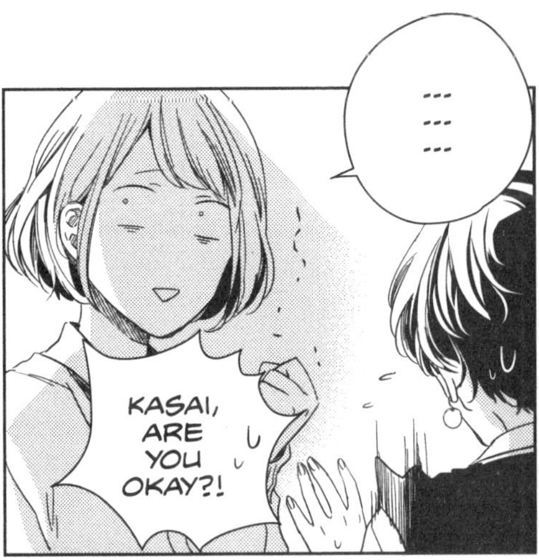
...
...
...
KASAI, ARE YOU OKAY?!
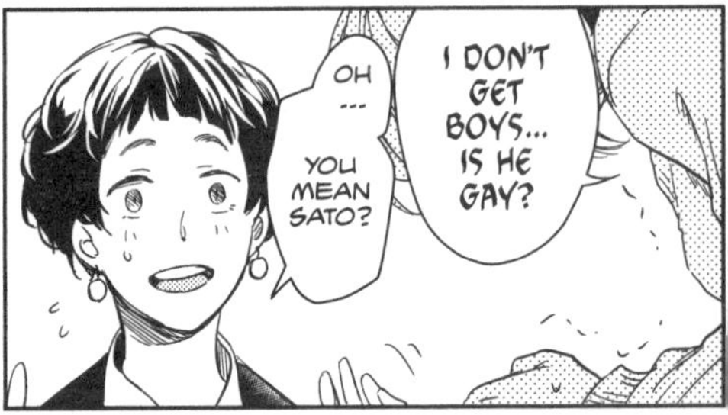
I DON'T GET BOYS... IS HE GAY?
OH... YOU MEAN SATO?
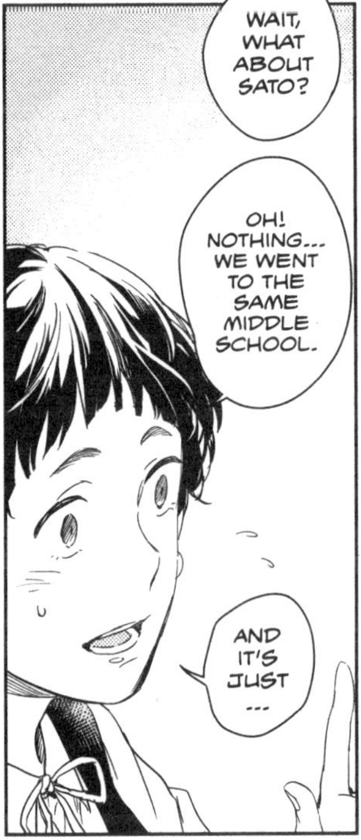
WAIT, WHAT ABOUT SATO?
OH! NOTHING... WE WENT TO THE SAME MIDDLE SCHOOL.
AND IT'S JUST...
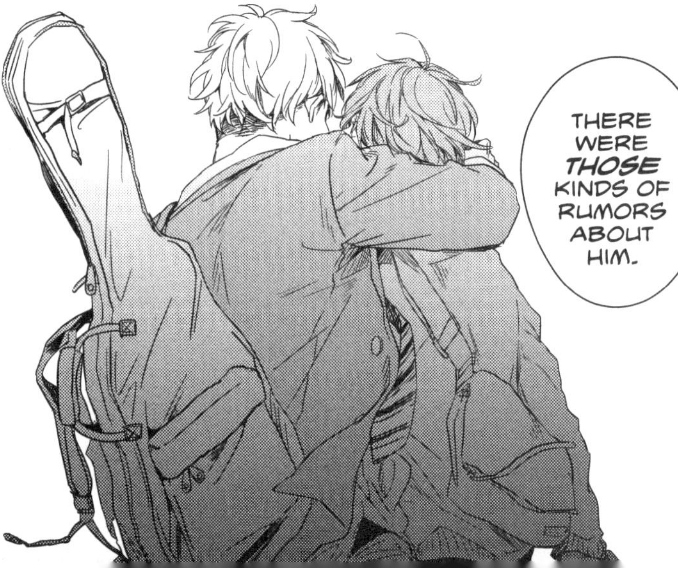
THERE WERE ***THOSE*** KINDS OF RUMORS ABOUT HIM.

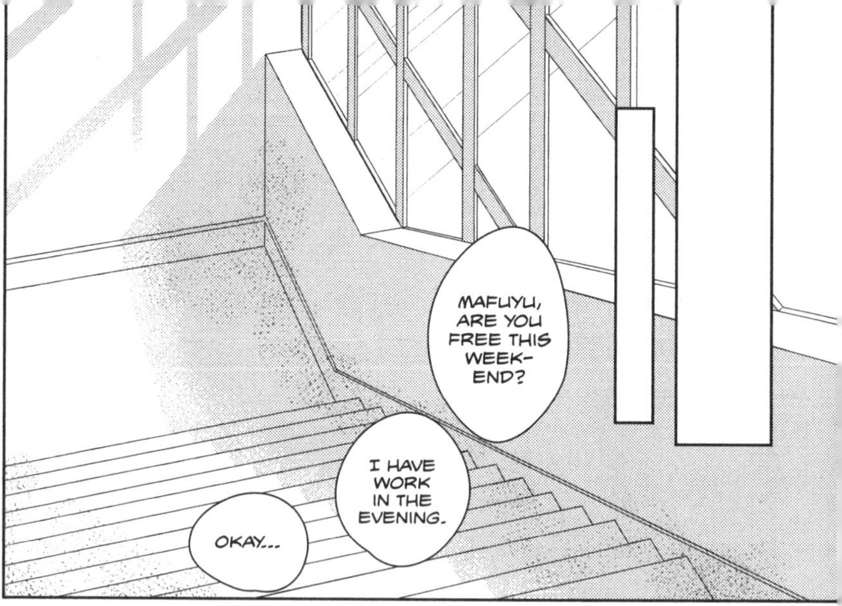
MAFUYU, ARE YOU FREE THIS WEEK-END?
I HAVE WORK IN THE EVENING.
OKAY...

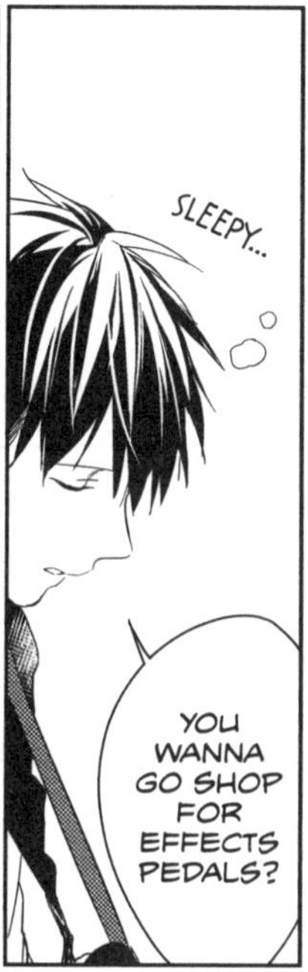
SLEEPY...
YOU WANNA GO SHOP FOR EFFECTS PEDALS?

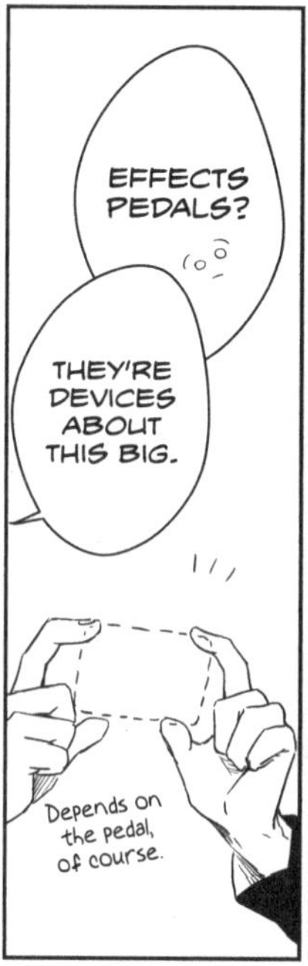
EFFECTS PEDALS?
THEY'RE DEVICES ABOUT THIS BIG.
Depends on the pedal, of course.

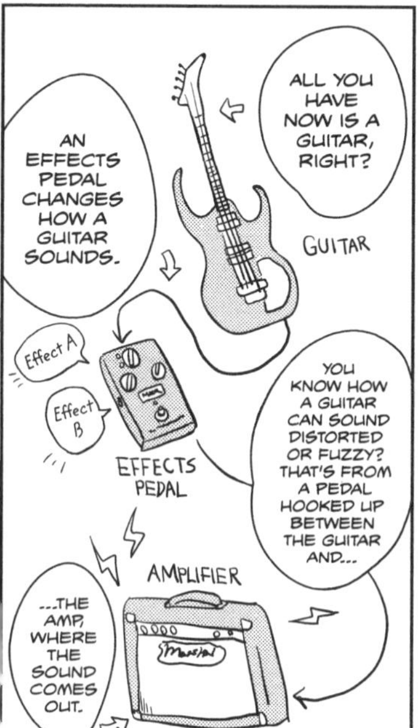
ALL YOU HAVE NOW IS A GUITAR, RIGHT?
AN EFFECTS PEDAL CHANGES HOW A GUITAR SOUNDS.
GUITAR
Effect A
Effect B
EFFECTS PEDAL
YOU KNOW HOW A GUITAR CAN SOUND DISTORTED OR FUZZY? THAT'S FROM A PEDAL HOOKED UP BETWEEN THE GUITAR AND...
AMPLIFIER
...THE AMP, WHERE THE SOUND COMES OUT.

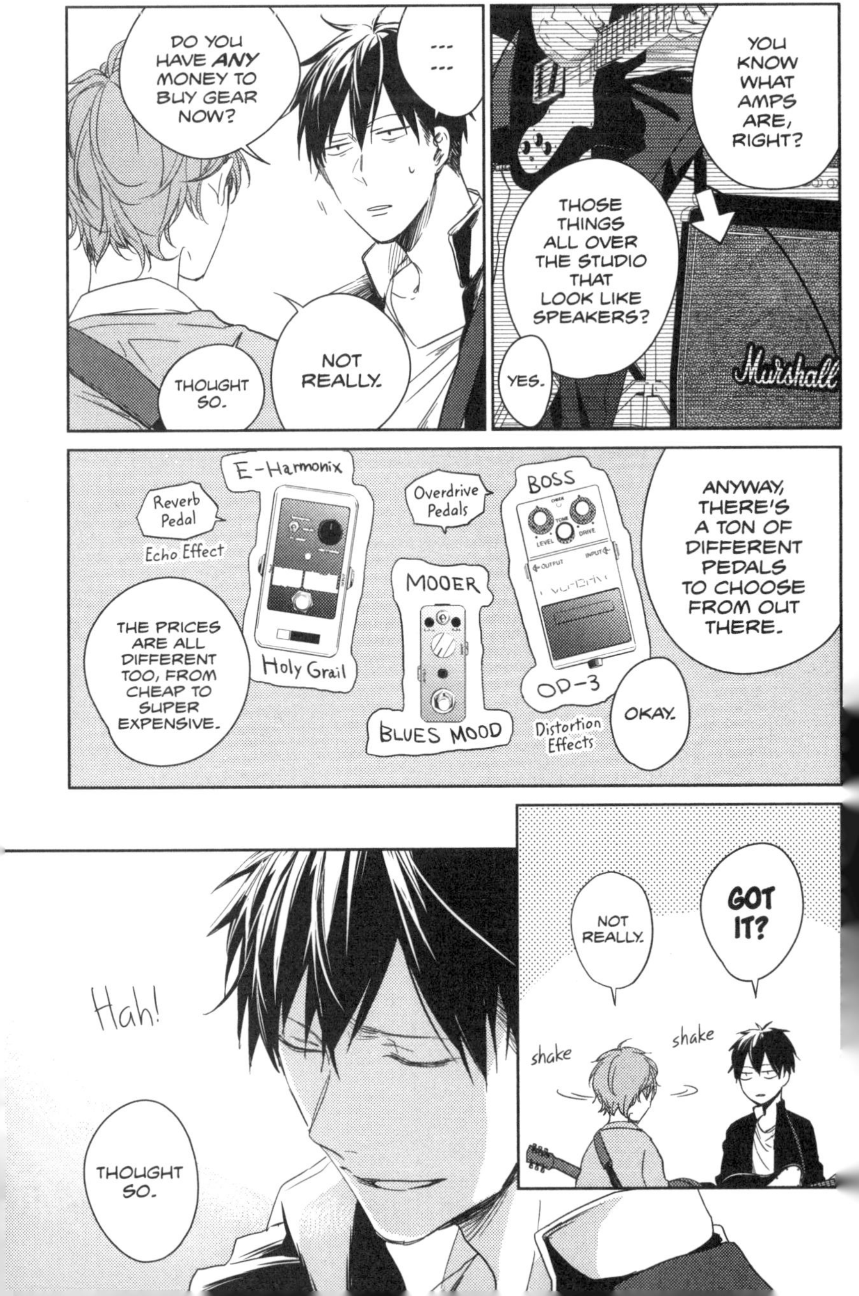
YOU KNOW WHAT AMPS ARE, RIGHT?
THOSE THINGS ALL OVER THE STUDIO THAT LOOK LIKE SPEAKERS?
YES.
Marshall
DO YOU HAVE ANY MONEY TO BUY GEAR NOW?
...
...
NOT REALLY.
THOUGHT SO.
ANYWAY, THERE'S A TON OF DIFFERENT PEDALS TO CHOOSE FROM OUT THERE.
BOSS
OD-3
Distortion Effects
OKAY.
Overdrive Pedals
MOOER
BLUES MOOD
E-Harmonix
Holy Grail
Reverb Pedal
Echo Effect
THE PRICES ARE ALL DIFFERENT TOO, FROM CHEAP TO SUPER EXPENSIVE.
GOT IT?
NOT REALLY.
shake
shake
Hah!
THOUGHT SO.

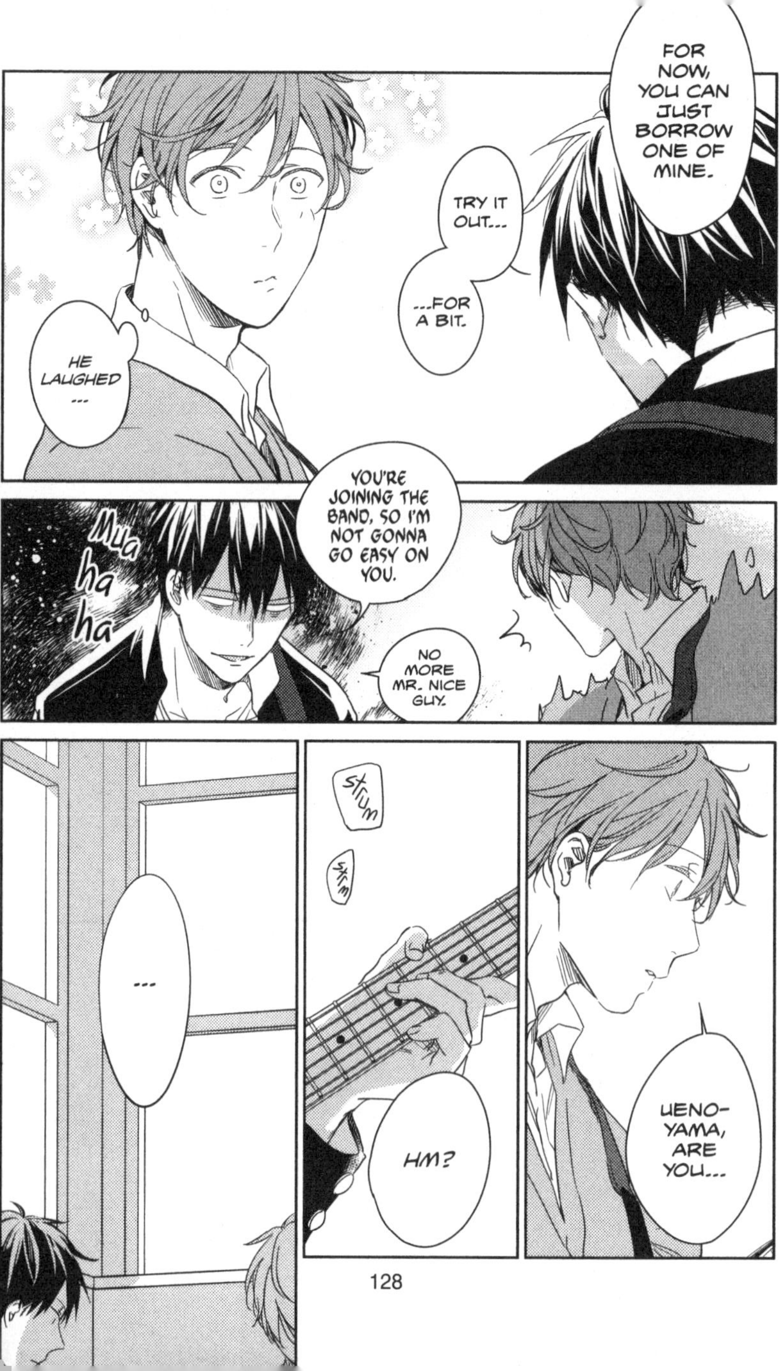
FOR NOW, YOU CAN JUST BORROW ONE OF MINE.
TRY IT OUT...
...FOR A BIT.
HE LAUGHED ...
YOU'RE JOINING THE BAND, SO I'M NOT GONNA GO EASY ON YOU.
NO MORE MR. NICE GUY.
Mua ha ha
UENO-YAMA, ARE YOU...
HM?
strum
...

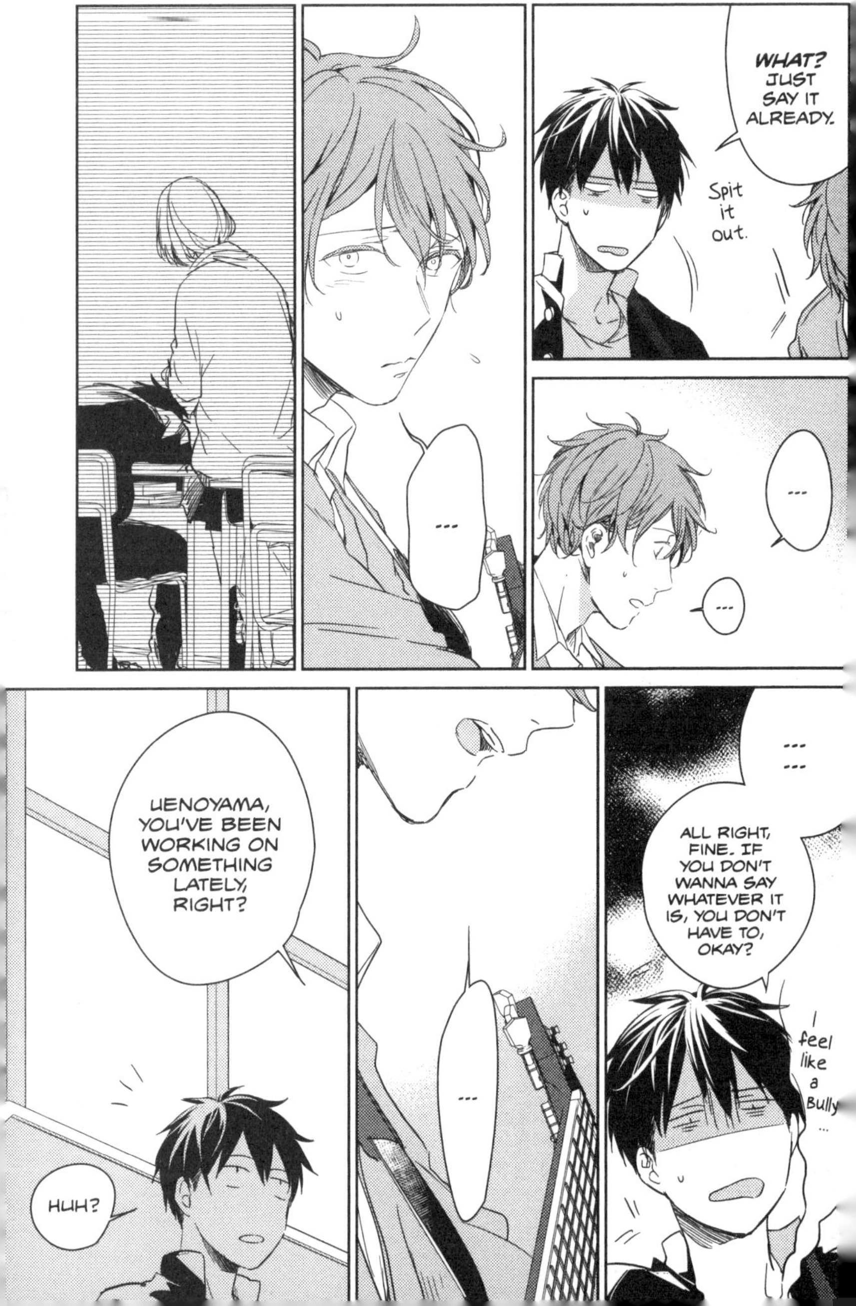
WHAT? JUST SAY IT ALREADY.
Spit it out.
...
...
...
ALL RIGHT, FINE. IF YOU DON'T WANNA SAY WHATEVER IT IS, YOU DON'T HAVE TO, OKAY?
......
I feel like a Bully...
...
UENOYAMA, YOU'VE BEEN WORKING ON SOMETHING LATELY, RIGHT?
HUH?

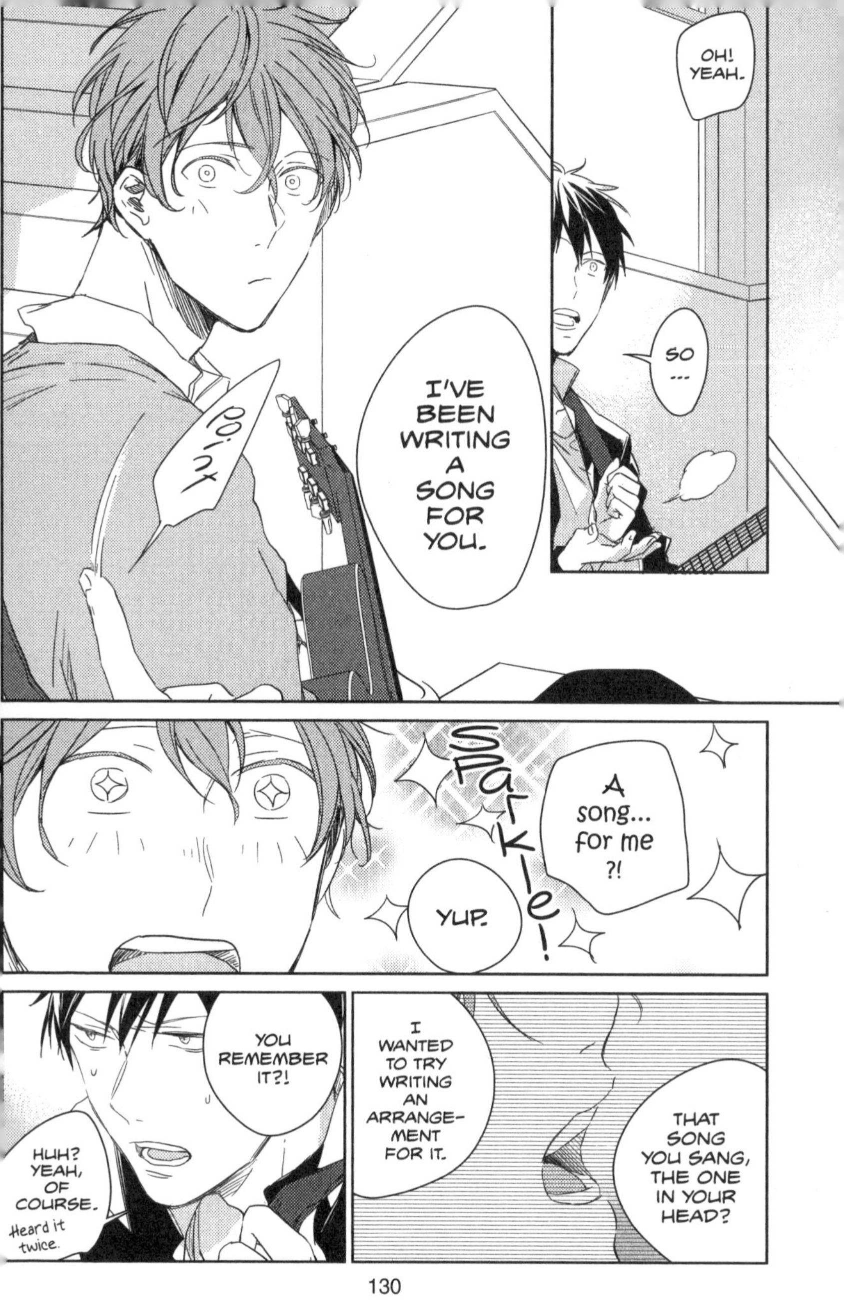
OH! YEAH.
SO ...
I'VE BEEN WRITING A SONG FOR YOU.
Point
A song... for me ?!
Sparkle!
YUP.
THAT SONG YOU SANG, THE ONE IN YOUR HEAD?
I WANTED TO TRY WRITING AN ARRANGE-MENT FOR IT.
YOU REMEMBER IT?!
HUH? YEAH, OF COURSE.
Heard it twice.

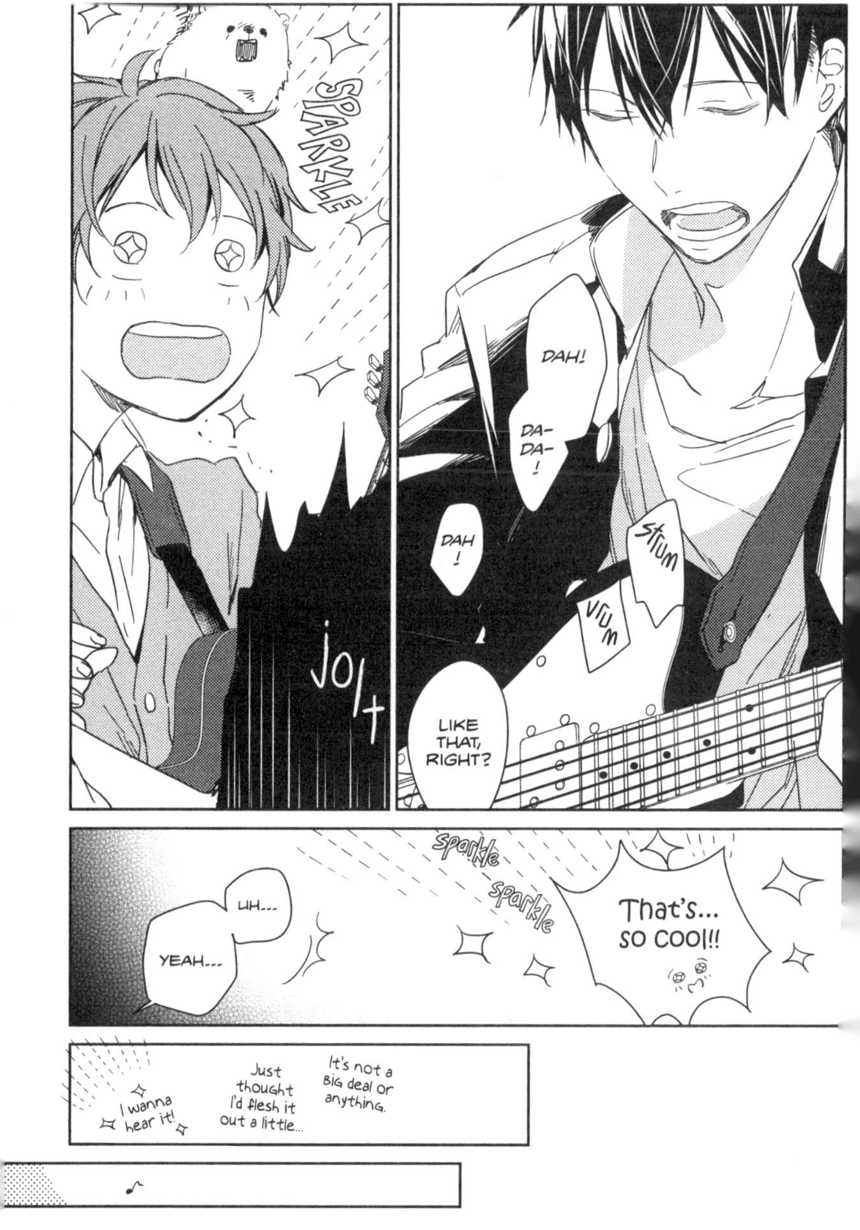
DAH!
DA-DA-!
DAH!
strum
vrum
LIKE THAT, RIGHT?
SPARKLE
jolt
That's... so cool!!
sparkle
sparkle
UH...
YEAH...
It's not a big deal or anything.
Just thought I'd flesh it out a little...
I wanna hear it!

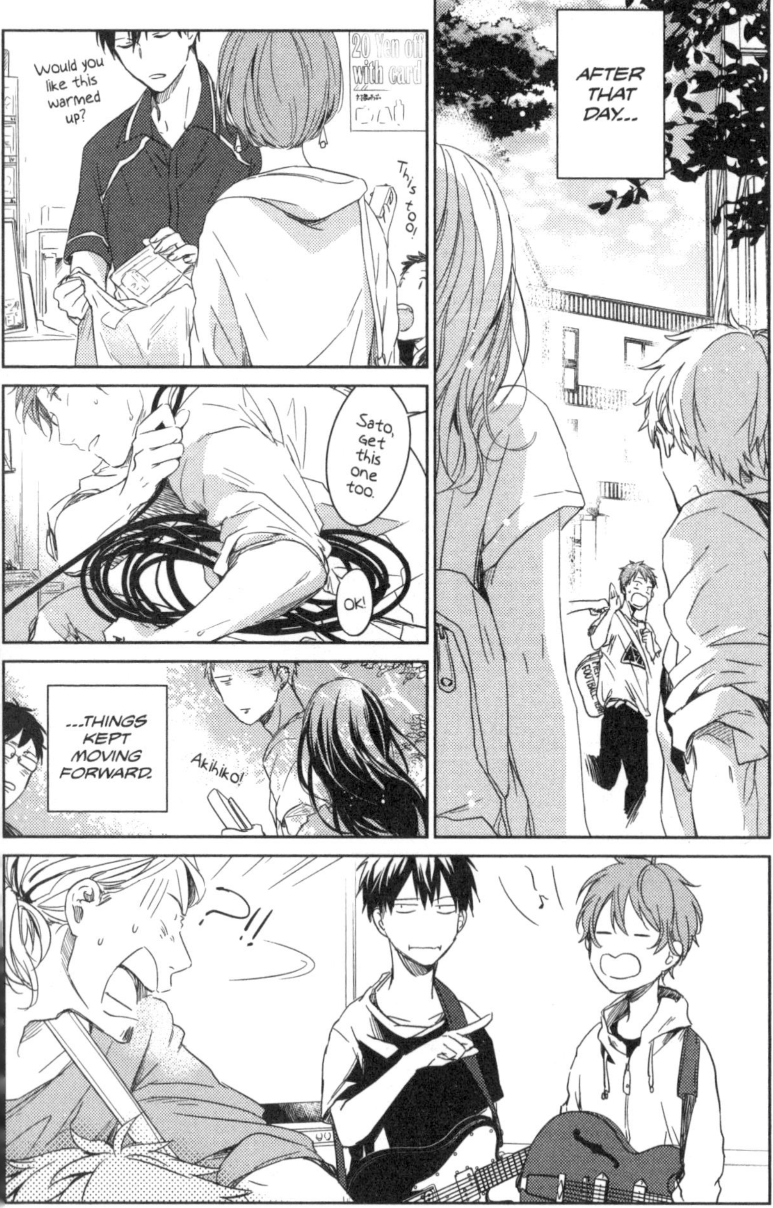
AFTER THAT DAY...
Would you like this warmed up?
This too!
20 Yen off with card
Sato, get this one too.
OK!
...THINGS KEPT MOVING FORWARD.
Akihiko!
!!

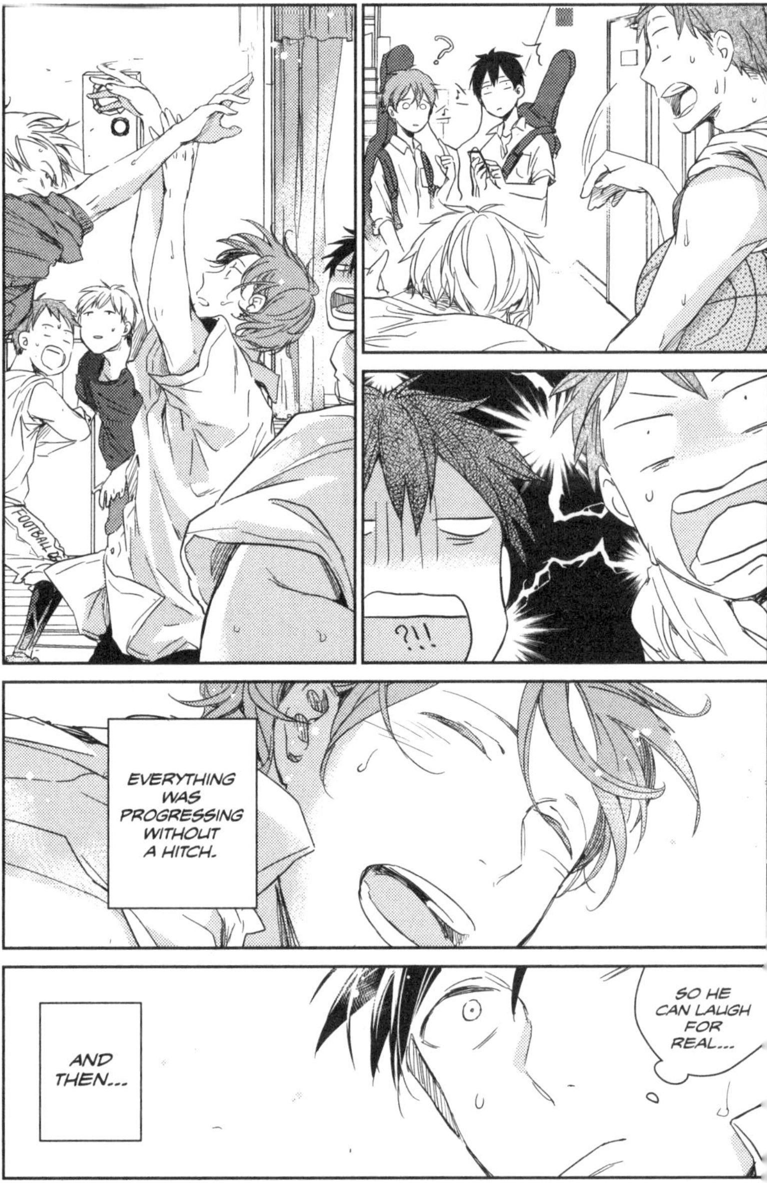
?
?!!
EVERYTHING WAS PROGRESSING WITHOUT A HITCH.
SO HE CAN LAUGH FOR REAL...
AND THEN...

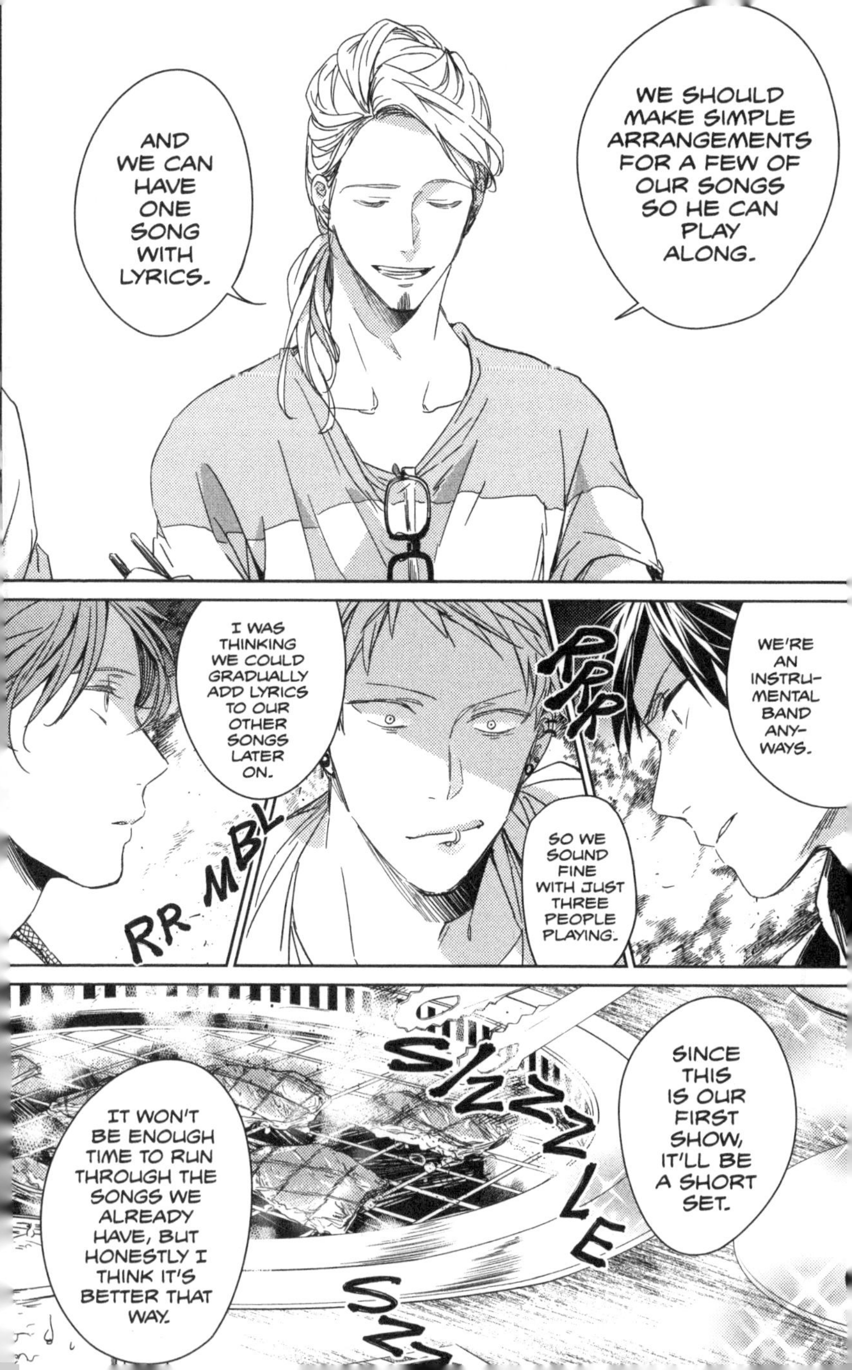
WE SHOULD MAKE SIMPLE ARRANGEMENTS FOR A FEW OF OUR SONGS SO HE CAN PLAY ALONG.
AND WE CAN HAVE ONE SONG WITH LYRICS.
WE'RE AN INSTRU-MENTAL BAND ANY-WAYS.
PRRR
SO WE SOUND FINE WITH JUST THREE PEOPLE PLAYING.
I WAS THINKING WE COULD GRADUALLY ADD LYRICS TO OUR OTHER SONGS LATER ON.
RR MBL
SINCE THIS IS OUR FIRST SHOW, IT'LL BE A SHORT SET.
SIZZZLE
IT WON'T BE ENOUGH TIME TO RUN THROUGH THE SONGS WE ALREADY HAVE, BUT HONESTLY I THINK IT'S BETTER THAT WAY.
SZZ

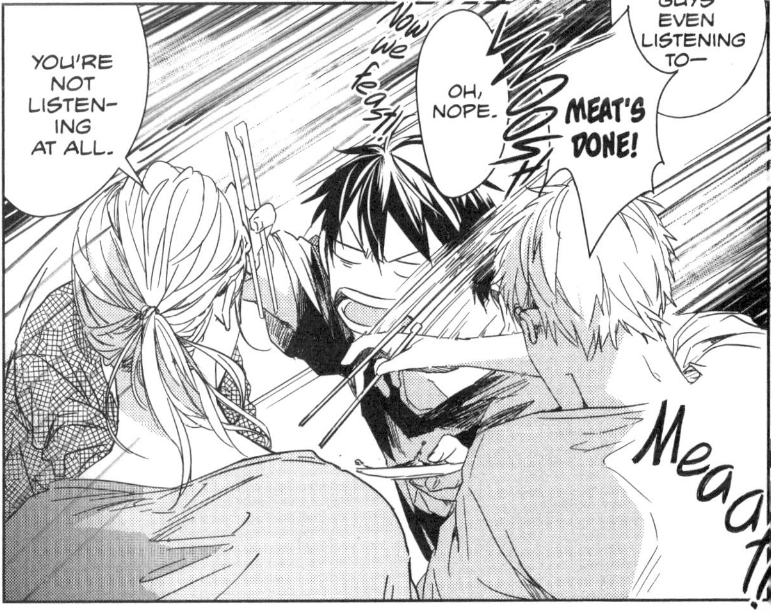
ARE YOU GUYS EVEN LISTENING TO—
MEAT'S DONE!
VWOOSH
OH, NOPE.
Now we feast!!
YOU'RE NOT LISTEN-ING AT ALL.
Meaat!!

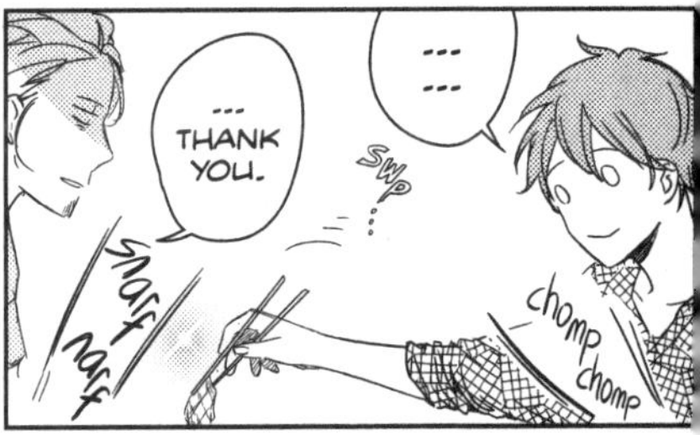
...
...
SWP...
...THANK YOU.
chomp chomp
snarf narf

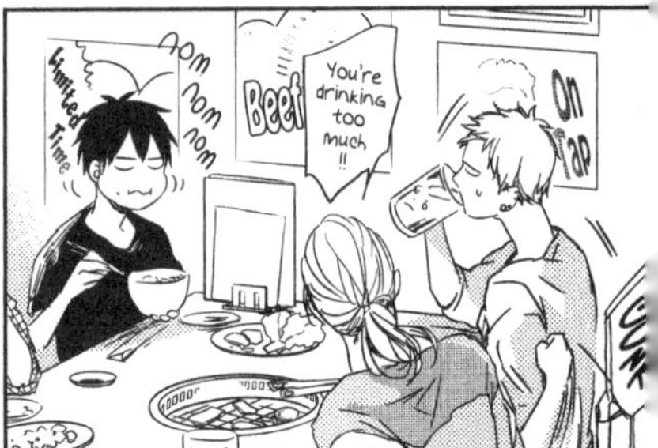
On Tap
You're drinking too much!!
Beef
nom nom nom nom
Limited Time

BEFORE WE KNEW IT...

...PLANS FOR OUR CONCERT WERE SET.

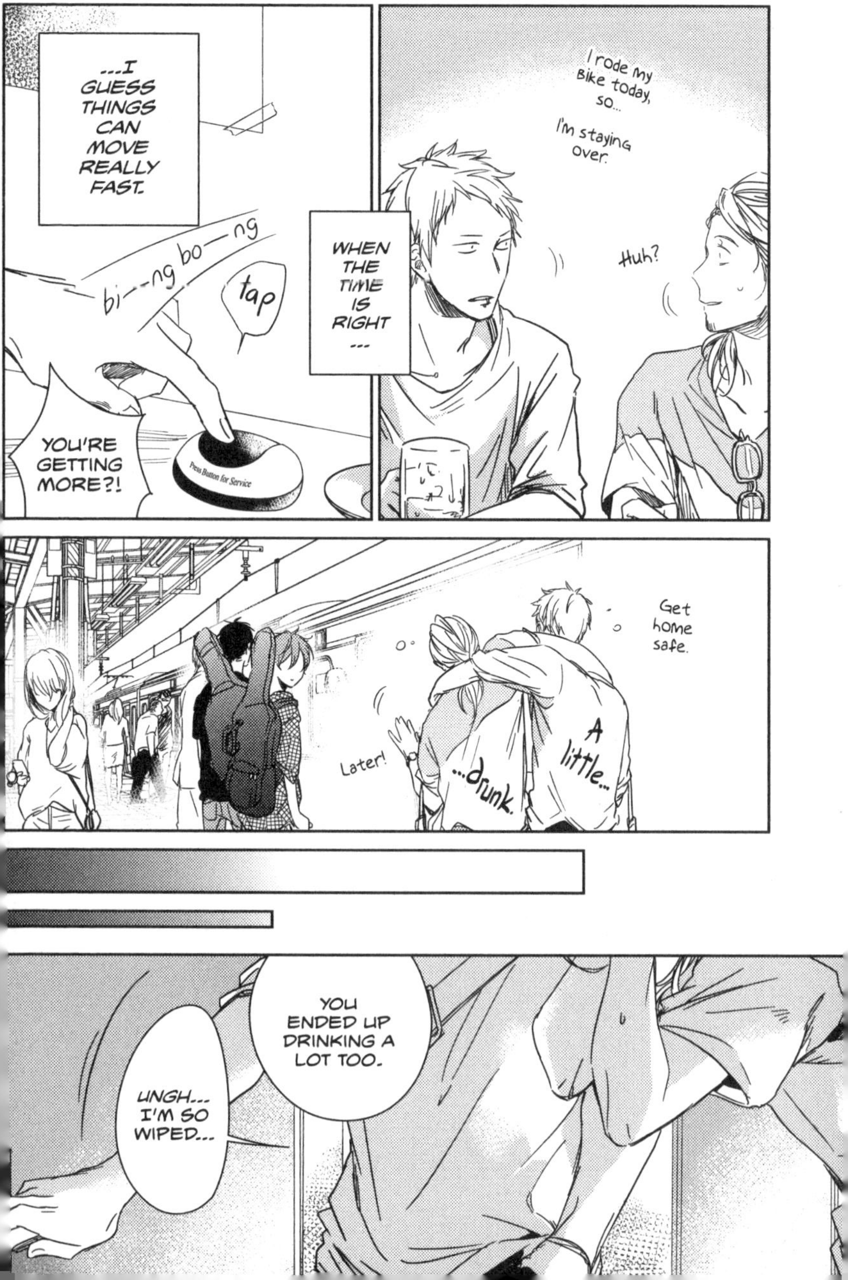
I rode my Bike today, so...
I'm staying over.
Huh?
WHEN THE TIME IS RIGHT ...
...I GUESS THINGS CAN MOVE REALLY FAST.
YOU'RE GETTING MORE?!
tap
bi--ng bo--ng
Get home safe.
A little...
...drunk.
Later!
YOU ENDED UP DRINKING A LOT TOO.
UNGH... I'M SO WIPED...
Press Button for Service

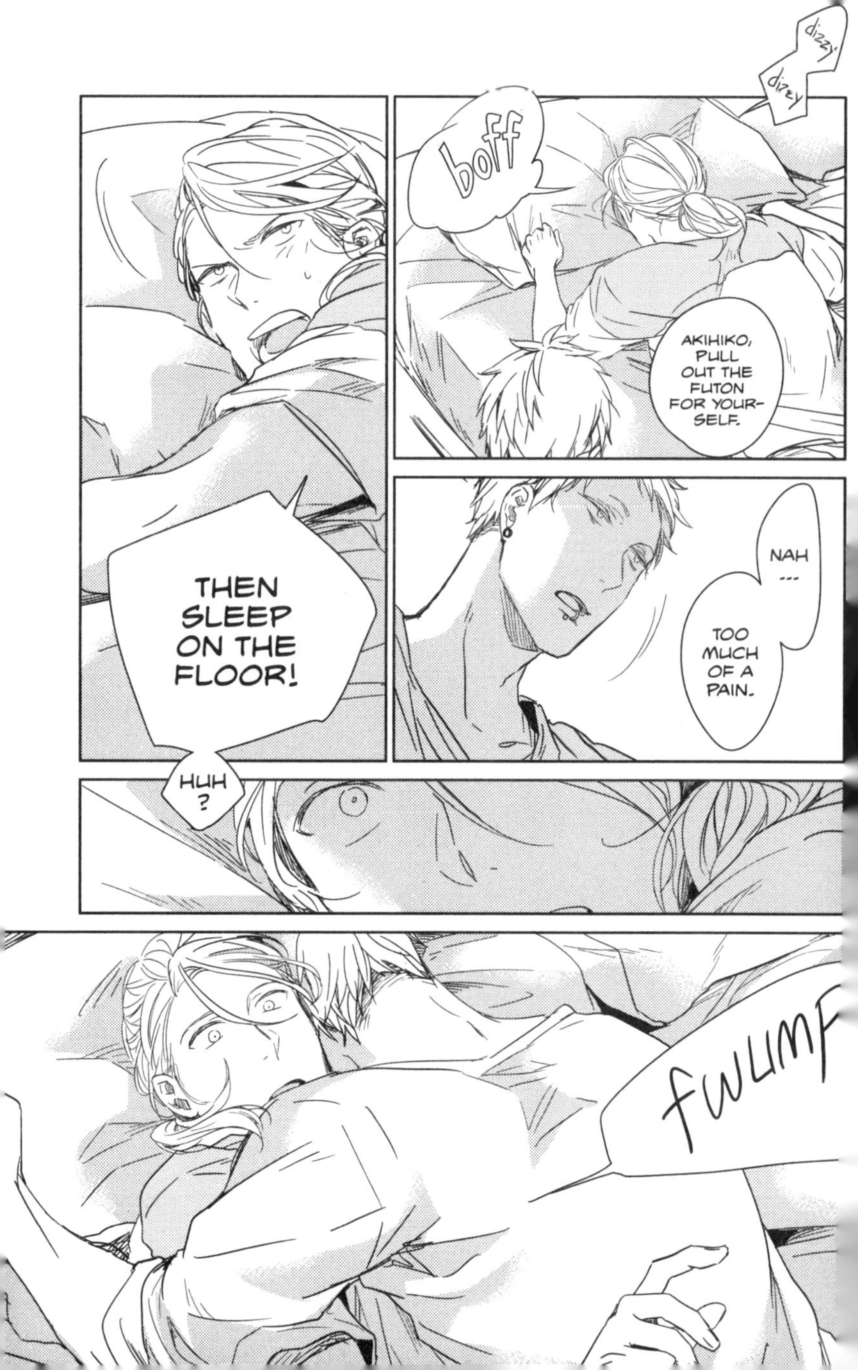
dizzy
dizzy
boff
AKIHIKO, PULL OUT THE FUTON FOR YOUR-SELF.
NAH ---
TOO MUCH OF A PAIN.
THEN SLEEP ON THE FLOOR!
HUH ?
fwumf

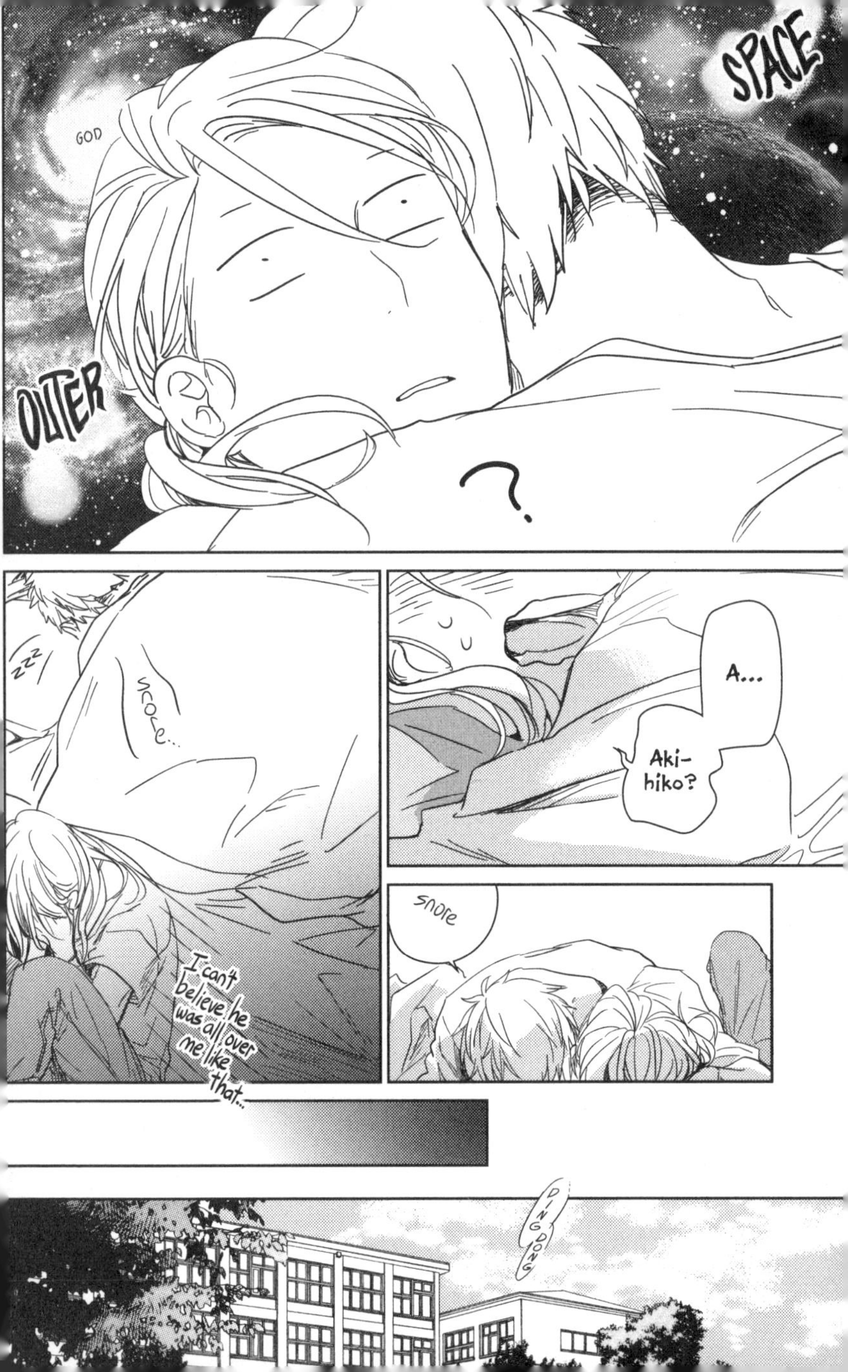
SPACE
GOD
OUTER
?
A...
Aki-
hiko?
snore...
zzz
I can't believe he was all over me like that...
snore
DING DONG

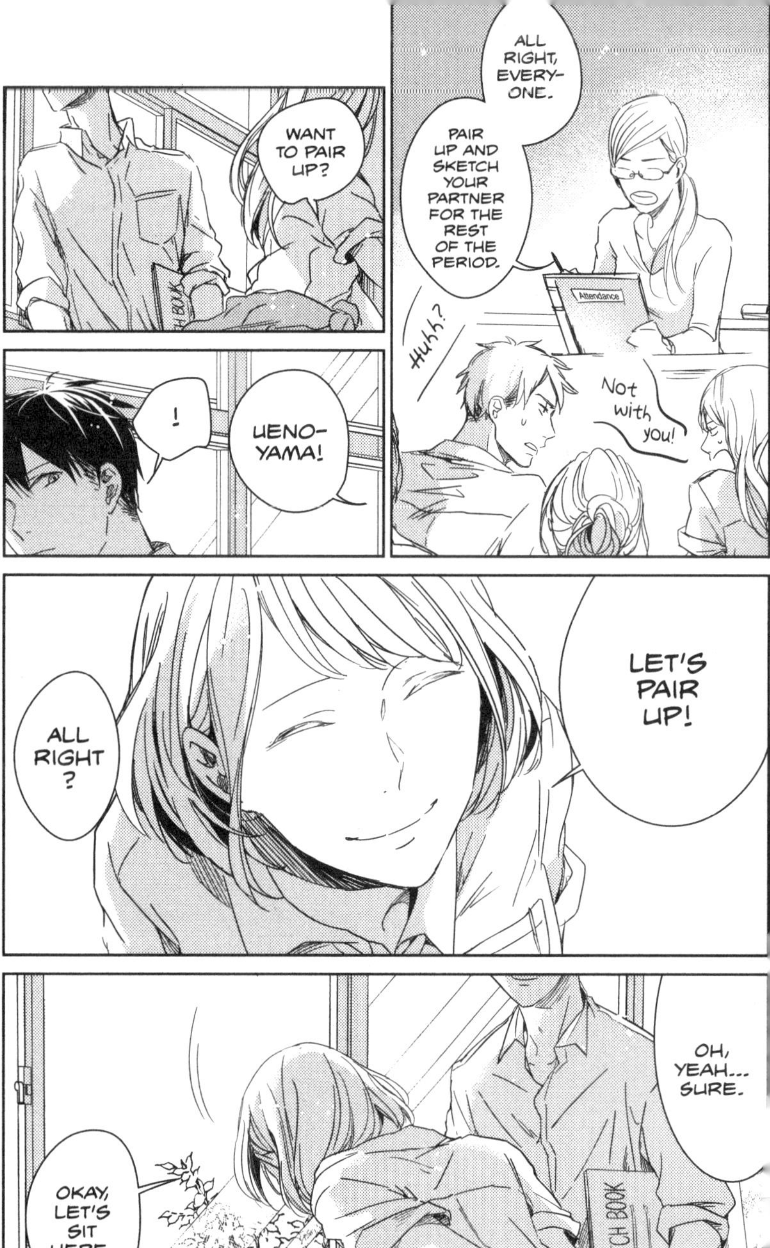
ALL RIGHT, EVERY-ONE.
PAIR UP AND SKETCH YOUR PARTNER FOR THE REST OF THE PERIOD.
Huhh?
Not with you!
WANT TO PAIR UP?
UENO-YAMA!
!
LET'S PAIR UP!
ALL RIGHT?
OH, YEAH... SURE.
OKAY, LET'S SIT HERE.

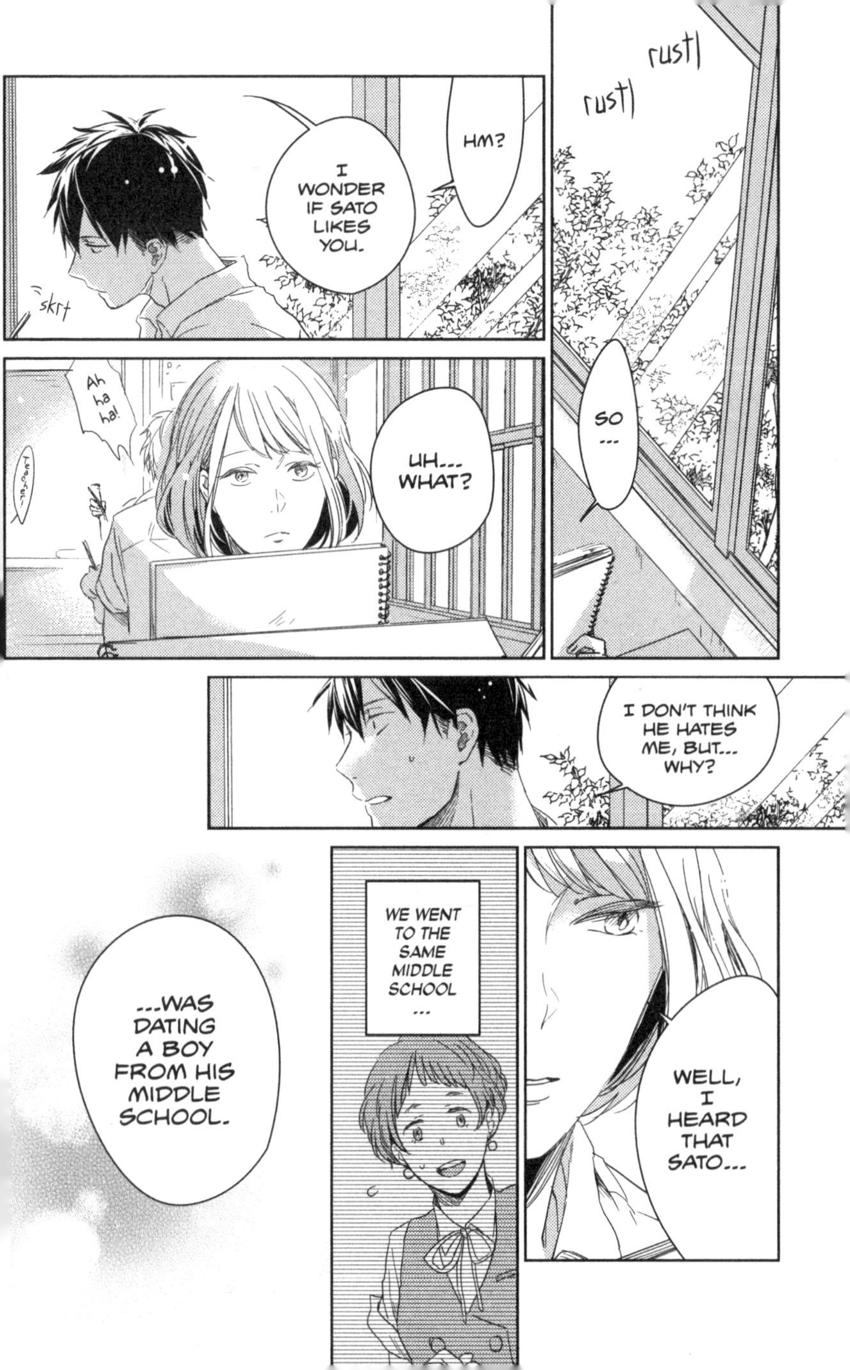
rustl
rustl
SO...
HM?
I WONDER IF SATO LIKES YOU.
skrt
UH... WHAT?
Ah ha ha!
Teacher!
I DON'T THINK HE HATES ME, BUT... WHY?
WELL, I HEARD THAT SATO...
WE WENT TO THE SAME MIDDLE SCHOOL...
...WAS DATING A BOY FROM HIS MIDDLE SCHOOL.

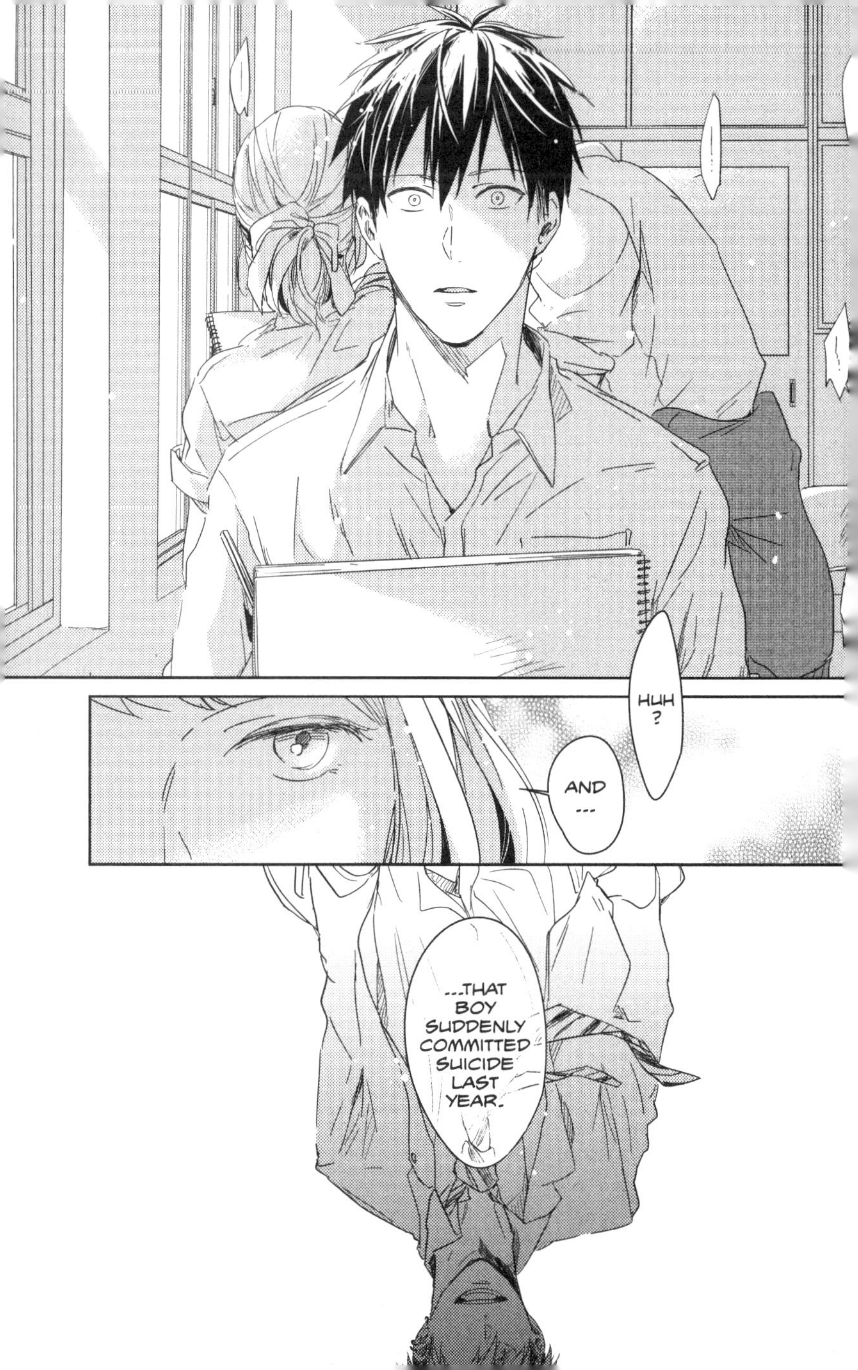

HUH ?
AND ...
...THAT BOY SUDDENLY COMMITTED SUICIDE LAST YEAR.

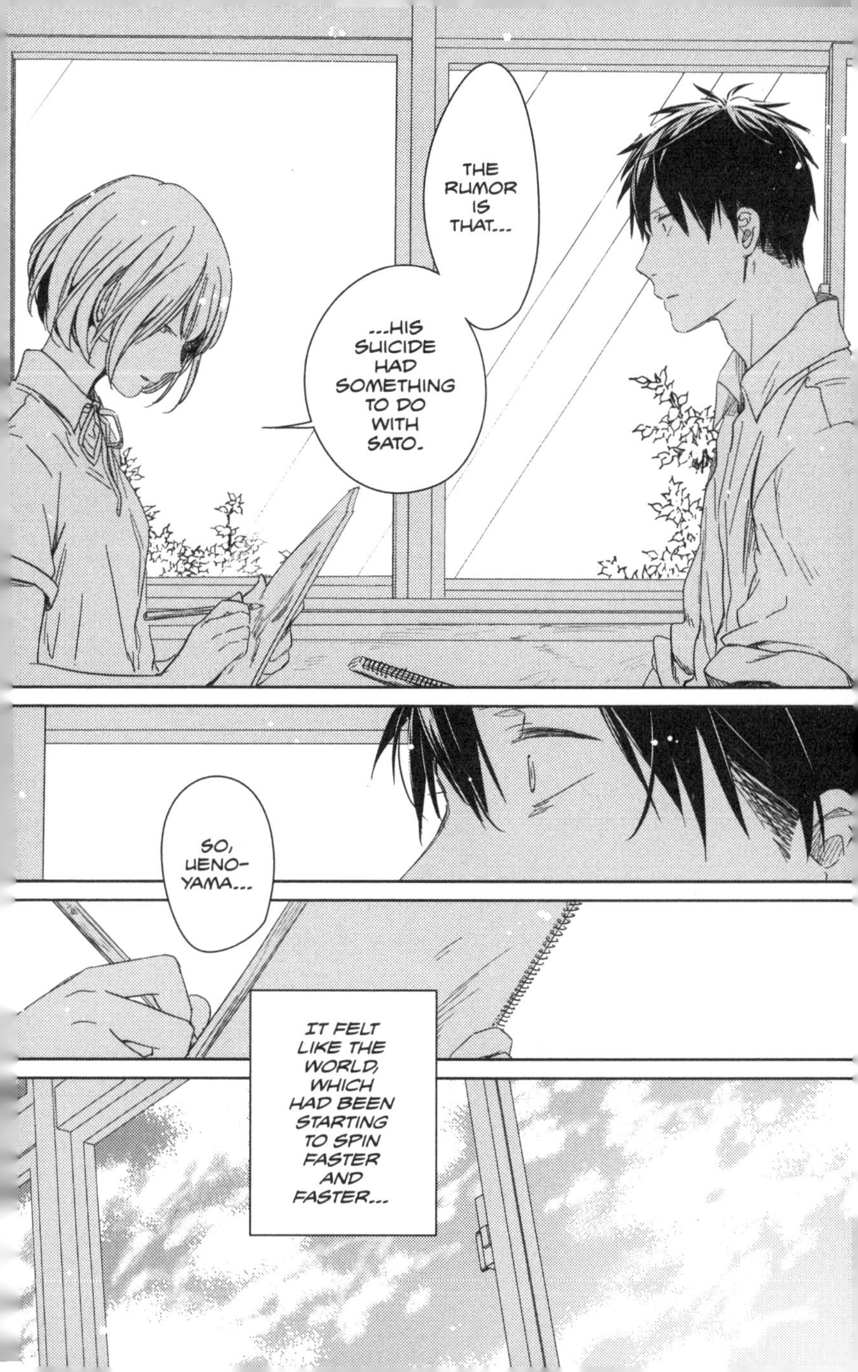
THE RUMOR IS THAT...
...HIS SUICIDE HAD SOMETHING TO DO WITH SATO.
SO, UENO-YAMA...
IT FELT LIKE THE WORLD, WHICH HAD BEEN STARTING TO SPIN FASTER AND FASTER...

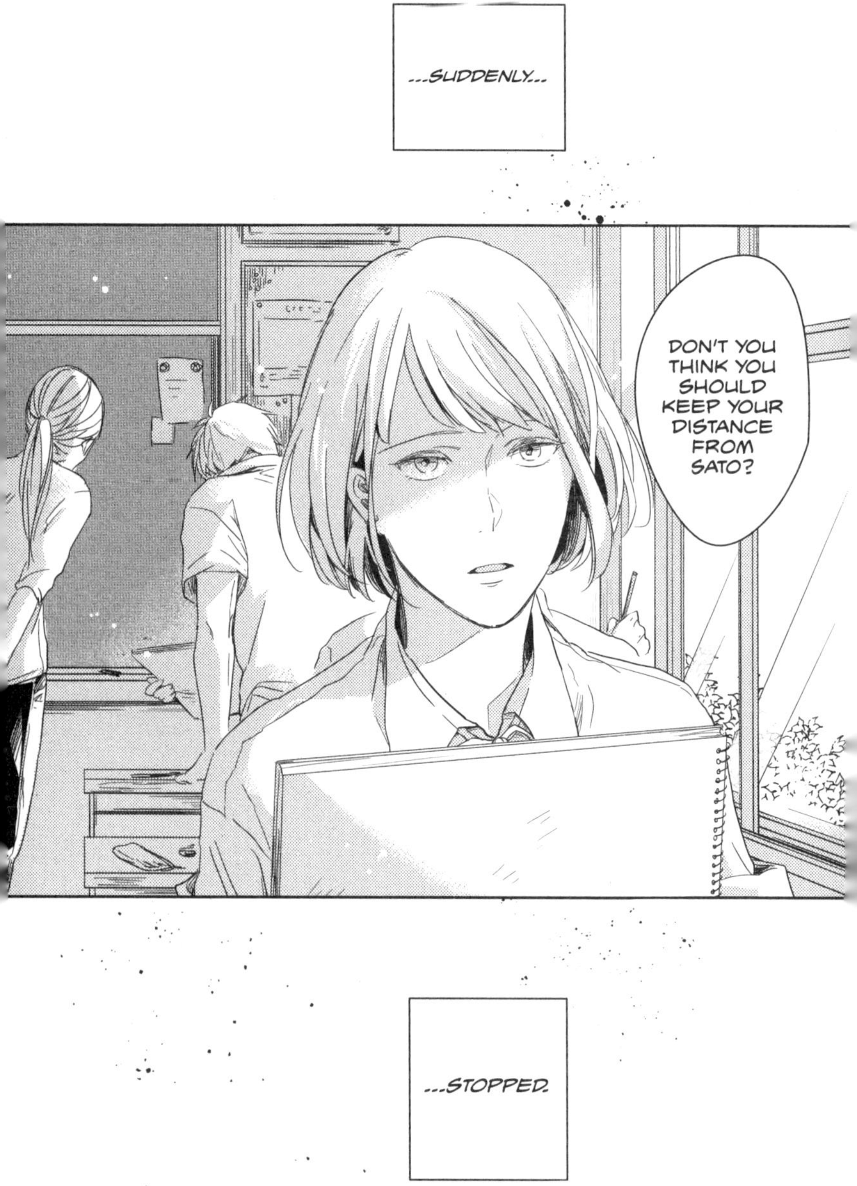
...SUDDENLY...
DON'T YOU THINK YOU SHOULD KEEP YOUR DISTANCE FROM SATO?
...STOPPED.

Haruki Nakayama (22)

178 cm

(Grad school student)

Birthday: 7/13 Sign: Cancer Blood Type: O

Bass → Fujigen
Neo Classic Series Jazz Bass
Woodgrain finish
Plays fingerstyle

Favorite Music: Prefers lighter music (compared to the other guys) and pop. Drawn to Japanese rock and light, slow-tempo dance. He's still diligent about listening to different genres.

Avoids music that's too mellow or too intense.

Film Major
Loves French New Wave films.

Family: Lives by himself.
(Moved from the country to the city.)

Dad, mom, and older sister are back home.

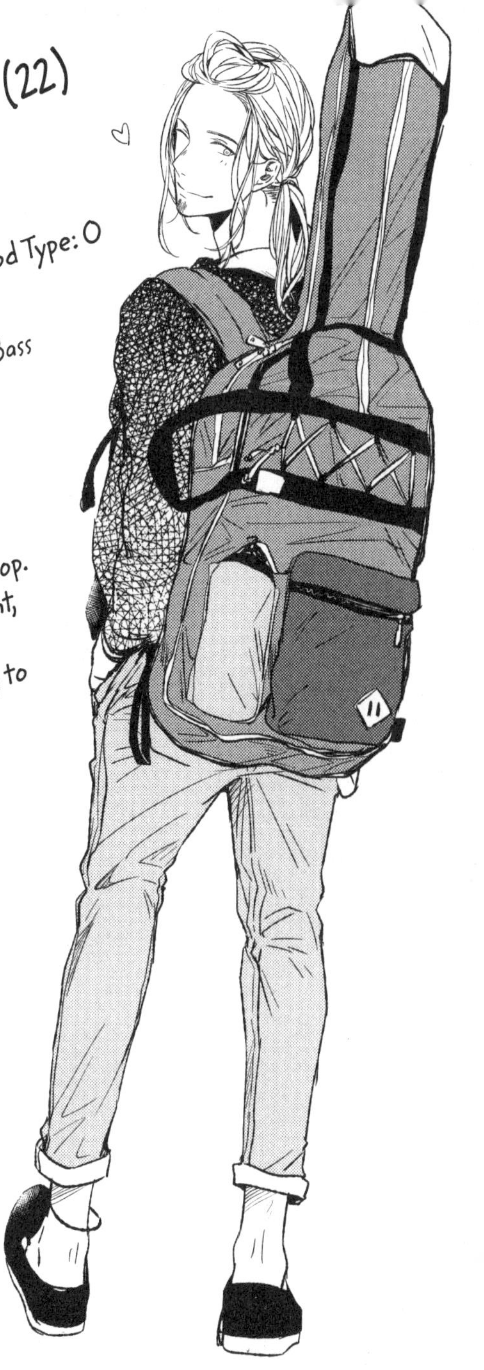

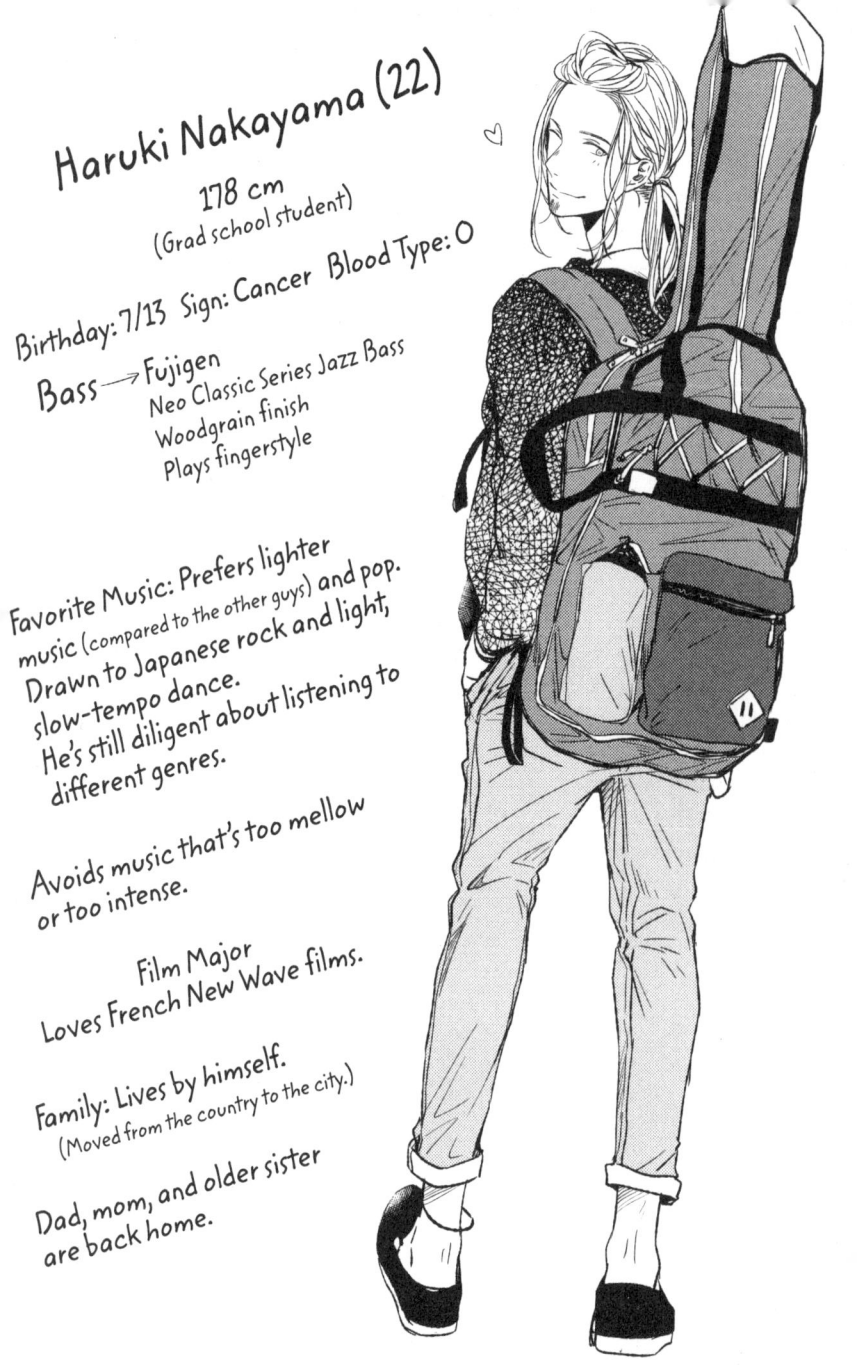